THE BIBLE IN MEDIEVAL TRADITION

GENERA

H. Lawre.

Philip D.

Thomas

The major intent of the series THE BIBLE IN MEDIEVAL TRADITION is to re-acquaint the Church with its rich history of biblical interpretation and with the contemporary applicability of this history, especially for academic study, spiritual formation, preaching, discussion groups, and individual reflection. Each volume focuses on a particular biblical book or set of books and provides documentary evidence of the most significant ways in which that work was treated in the course of medieval biblical interpretation.

The series takes its shape in dialogue both with the special traditions of medieval exegesis and with the interests of contemporary readers. Each volume in the series comprises fresh translations of several commentaries. The selections are lengthy and, in most cases, have never been available in English before.

Compared to patristic material, relatively little medieval exegesis has been translated. While medieval interpretations do resemble their patristic forebears, they do not simply replicate them. Indeed, they are produced at new times and in new situations. As a result, they lend insight into the changing culture and scholarship of the Middle Ages and comprise a store-house of the era's theological and spiritual riches that can enhance contemporary reading of the Bible. They, therefore, merit their own consideration, to which this series is meant to contribute.

The Letter to the
ROMANS

Translated and edited by

Ian Christopher Levy
Philip D. W. Krey
Thomas Ryan

WILLIAM B. EERDMANS PUBLISHING COMPANY
GRAND RAPIDS, MICHIGAN / CAMBRIDGE, U.K.

Published 2013 by
Wm. B. Eerdmans Publishing Co.
2140 Oak Industrial Drive N.E., Grand Rapids, Michigan 49505 /
P.O. Box 163, Cambridge CB3 9PU U.K.

Printed in the United States of America

19 18 17 16 15 14 13   7 6 5 4 3 2 1

Library of Congress Cataloging-in-Publication Data

The letter to the Romans / translated and edited by
Ian Christopher Levy, Philip D. W. Krey, Thomas Ryan.
pages   cm.   — (The Bible in medieval tradition)
Includes bibliographical references and index.
ISBN 978-0-8028-0976-6 (pbk.: alk. paper)
1. Bible. Romans — Criticism, interpretation, etc. —
History — Middle Ages, 600-1500 — Sources.
I. Levy, Ian Christopher.
II. Krey, Philip D., 1950-
III. Ryan, Thomas, 1961-

BS2665.52.L48   2013
227'.1060940902 — dc23
2013006752

www.eerdmans.com

Contents

CONTENTS

Editors' Preface

The medieval period witnessed an outpouring of biblical interpretation, which included commentaries written in Latin in a wide array of styles over the course of a millennium. These commentaries are significant as successors to patristic exegesis and predecessors to Reformation exegesis, but they are important in their own right.

This series, "The Bible in Medieval Tradition," seeks to place newly translated medieval scriptural commentary into the hands of contemporary readers. In doing so, the series reacquaints the Church with its rich tradition of biblical interpretation. It fosters academic study, spiritual formation, preaching, discussion groups, and individual reflection. It also enables the contemporary application of this tradition. Each volume focuses on the era's interpretation of one biblical book, or set of related books, and comprises substantial selections from representative exegetes and hermeneutical approaches. Similarly, each provides a fully documented introduction that locates the commentaries in their theological and historical contexts.

While interdisciplinary and cross-confessional interest in the Middle Ages has grown over the last century, it falls short if it does not at the same time recognize the centrality of the Bible to this period and its religious life. The Bible structured sermons, guided prayer, and inspired mystical visions. It was woven through liturgy, enacted in drama, and embodied in sculpture and other art forms. Less explicitly ecclesial works, such as Dante's *Divine Comedy,* were also steeped in its imagery and narrative. Because of the Bible's importance to the period, this series, therefore, opens a window not only to its religious practices but also to its culture more broadly.

Similarly, biblical interpretation played a vital role in the work of medieval theologians. Among the tasks of theological masters was to deliver ordinary lectures on the Bible. Their commentaries — often edited versions of their public lectures — were the means by which many worked out their most important theological insights. Thus the Bible was the primary text for theologians and the center of the curriculum for theology students. Some, such as the authors of *summae* and sentence commentaries, produced systematic treatises that, while not devoted to verse-by-verse explication, nevertheless often cited biblical evidence, addressed apparent contradictions in the scriptural witness, and responded under the guidance of nuanced theories of interpretation. They were biblical theologians.

Biblical commentaries provided the largest reservoir of medieval interpretation and hermeneutics, and they took a variety of forms. Monastic perspectives shaped some, scholastic perspectives still others. Some commentaries emphasized the spiritual senses, others the literal. Some relied more heavily on scholarly tools, such as dictionaries, histories, concordances, critical texts, knowledge of languages, and Jewish commentaries. Whatever the case, medieval commentaries were a privileged and substantial locus of interpretation, and they offer us fresh insight into the Bible and their own cultural contexts.

For readers and the Church today, critical engagement with medieval exegesis counteracts the twin dangers of amnesia and nostalgia. One temptation is to study the Bible as if its interpretation had no past. This series brings the past to the present and thereby supplies the resources and memories that can enrich current reading. Medieval exegesis also bears studying because it can exemplify how not to interpret the Bible. Despite nascent critical sensibilities in some of its practitioners, it often offered fanciful etymologies and was anachronistic in its conflation of past and present. It could also demonize others. Yet, with its playful attention to words and acceptance of a multiplicity of meanings and methods, it anticipated critical theory's turn to language today and the indeterminacy characteristic of its literary theory.

What this series sets out to accomplish requires that selections in each volume are lengthy. In most cases, these selections have never been available in English before. Compared to the amount of patristic material, comparatively little medieval exegesis has been translated. Yet, the medieval was not simply a repetition of the patristic. It differed enough in genre, content, and application to merit its own special focus, and it applied earlier church exegesis to new situations and times as well as reflected the changing culture and scholarship in the Middle Ages. The series, therefore, makes these re-sources more widely available, guides readers in entering into medieval exegetical texts, and enables a more informed and insightful study of the Church's biblical heritage.

*   *   *

Born in Tennessee and a participant in the 1960 Greensboro lunch-counter sit-ins, H. Lawrence Bond would go on to obtain both his B.D. and Ph.D. from Duke University. He was an ordained minister in the United Methodist Church and remained active in ministry up until the end of his life in 2009.

Larry had four desks in his library, a converted two-and-half-car ga-rage at his home in the hills around Deep Gap, North Carolina. Each desk, surrounded by books, represented one aspect of his life and career — teach-ing, writing, sermon preparation, and pastoral counseling. All four desks, and their corresponding commitments, were related to one another in Larry's multifaceted life as professor at Appalachian State University, preacher to a small community church in Linville Falls, scholar, and friend, and while some might wonder if so much activity prohibited further contri-butions to his specialty, the life and thought of Nicholas of Cusa, the fifteenth-century cardinal, reformer, theologian, philosopher, and writer on mysticism, Larry had no hesitation. For him it was the right balance.

In his last years, Larry set out on another adventure that built upon what he had learned from Nicholas and combined this with his own faith and the needs of preaching. It should come as no surprise that he was driven deep into the text of scripture and moved to reflect on the exegetical enter-prise as it was pursued in the Middle Ages. The Romans volume is a result of the turn in his life and learning, and a tribute to his willingness to envision an expanded horizon. Larry had been working diligently on translations for this volume, most notably on Peter Abelard's commentary, of which he had a profound understanding, and had all but completed at the time of his pass-ing. We, his fellow editors, then worked to bring Larry's translations into their final form, adding his work to our own translations. His scholarship, and indeed his spirit, permeates this present volume and even the whole se-ries itself.

Ian Christopher Levy
Philip D. W. Krey
Thomas Ryan

Abbreviations

AL	Aristoteles Latinus
CC	Cambridge Commentary *(Commentarius Cantabrigiensis)*
CCCM	*Corpus Christianorum: Continuatio Mediaevalis.* Turnhout: Brepols, 1971-
CCSL	*Corpus Christianorum: Series Latina.* Turnhout: Brepols, 1953-
CSEL	*Corpus Scriptorum Ecclesiasticorum Latinorum.* Vienna: Tempsky, 1866-
NPNF	Nicene and Post-Nicene Fathers, First Series
PG	*Patrologiae Cursus Completus: Series Graeca.* Ed. J. P. Migne. Paris, 1857-
PL	*Patrologiae Cursus Completus. Series Latina.* Ed. J. P. Migne. Paris, 1844-
ST	*Summa theologica.* Trans. Fathers of the English Dominican Province. Westminster, MD: Christian Classics, 1981

Introduction

Pre-Reformation Romans Interpretation

This introductory essay examines the Romans commentaries translated below, their immediate historical contexts, and their predecessors.[1] Although we translate only commentaries, they are by no means the only form of interpretation of the Pauline corpus, nor are they the most celebrated. Better known are Augustine of Hippo's and Martin Luther's conversions in response to Romans; each casts his encounter with Paul as the turning point in his life. In his *Confessions,* Saint Augustine recalls a voice that admonished him to "take and read." As a result, he opened a collection of Paul's writings by chance to Romans 13:13-14. After reading it, he felt "the light of confidence" in his heart, and the rest is history.[2] In 1545, the year before his death, Martin Luther penned the preface to his Latin writings. In doing so, he recalled the transformative effect of coming to a new understanding of Romans 1:17 some three decades earlier. As a result, he "felt altogether born again and [that I] had entered paradise itself. . . . And I extolled my sweetest word [the righteousness of God] with a love as great as the hatred with which I had before hated the word."[3]

1. For a list of Romans commentaries, see Joseph A. Fitzmyer, *Romans,* Anchor Bible (New York: Doubleday, 1993), 173-224; Werner Affeldt, "Verzeichnis der Römerbriefkommentare der lateinischen Kirche bis zu Nikolaus von Lyra," *Traditio* 13 (1957): 396-406.

2. Augustine, *Confessions,* 8.12, trans. R. S. Pine-Coffin (New York: Penguin, 1961), 177-78.

3. Martin Luther, "Preface to the Complete Edition of Luther's Latin Writings, 1545,"

1

To be sure, commentaries represent important reservoirs of Pauline interpretation, and they began to be composed early on. The oldest still extant is Origen's (d. ca. 254), although Clement of Alexandria (d. ca. 215) is said to have composed one even earlier.[4] Yet interpretation of Paul predates these commentaries. Already Colossians, a first-century deutero-Pauline letter, that is, one attributed to Paul but likely written by someone else after his death, is influenced by and aligns itself with the thought of Romans.[5] Likely written early in the second century, 2 Peter refers to Paul's letters in general, identifies them as scriptural, and warns of their misinterpretation; they contain "some things hard to understand, which the ignorant and unstable distort to their own destruction, just as they do the other scriptures" (2 Pet 3:16). Besides serving as an explicit warning, this text also serves, at least implicitly, as an invitation to correct interpretation.

In the middle of the second century, Marcion (d. ca. 160) advanced a distinctive interpretation of Paul that is reflected in his canon or list, the earliest extant and available only through the writings of others, of the Christian Bible. Besides excerpts from the Gospel of Luke followed by seven of the Pauline epistles, it contained nothing else. Most of the epistles appear in descending order of length. Thus the Corinthians correspondence (the two letters combined) precedes Romans, which is followed by the Thessalonians correspondence, Laodiceans (Marcion's name for Ephesians), Colossians, Philippians, and Philemon. The one exception to this organizational schema is Galatians, which Marcion located at the head of his list.[6]

The texts Marcion included and their order may well reflect his theology and represent an interpretation of Romans. He understood Christianity as a rejection of Judaism and of the creator God contained in its Bible, and he advanced Paul as the proponent of this position. He began the Pauline corpus with Galatians, perhaps because it was an early letter but perhaps also

---

in *Martin Luther: Selections from His Writings,* ed. John Dillenberger (New York: Anchor, 1961), 11.

4. C. E. B. Cranfield, *A Critical and Exegetical Commentary on the Epistle to the Romans,* International Biblical Commentary (Edinburgh: T&T Clark, 1975), 1:32. See Origen, *Commentary on the Epistle to the Romans,* trans. Thomas Scheck (Washington, DC: Catholic University of America Press, 2001-2), in two volumes.

5. Eduard Lohse, *Colossians and Philemon,* Hermeneia (Philadelphia: Fortress, 1971), 182.

6. For the account, discussed in this and the following two paragraphs, that emphasizes Marcion's role in the formation of the Christian biblical canon but cites and responds to other positions, see John W. Miller, *How the Bible Came to Be: Exploring the Narrative and Message* (New York: Paulist, 2004), especially chapters 6-8 and 12.

because it is the most polemical of Paul's epistles and contains the clearest critique of Judaism.

Marcion was likely one of the drivers behind the development of what came to be orthodox Christianity's biblical canon. Like Marcion's, it contained a significant amount of Paul, but it tempered him by including what would come to be called the Christian Old Testament so that the Pauline corpus would comprise a relatively smaller proportion of the entire Christian Bible. In what would eventually be called the Christian New Testament, it incorporated, among other things, letters attributed to the leaders of the more Jewish Jerusalem party, such as those by Peter and James. Its Pauline corpus would eventually begin with Romans, whose second verse highlights just what Marcion sought to sever, that is, the gospel's connection to and reliance on its Jewish forebears. Thus the early Church's Bible insisted that Paul be read within the context of Judaism's sacred scriptures and of a much larger collection of Christian writings. It thereby blunted precisely those characteristics that attracted Marcion.

And so it has gone through history. Paul seems to invite varieties of interpretation with his claim that he sought to be all things to all people (1 Cor 9:22),[7] and every period has responded, even our own, which has seen an entire series, entitled Romans through History and Culture, devoted to this biblical book.[8] Joseph Fitzmyer considers it "the most important of the Pauline writings, if not of the entire NT," and observes that "one can almost write the history of Christian theology by surveying the ways in which Romans has been interpreted."[9]

Thus Romans interpretation is crucial and occurs in a wide range of forms. As we have seen, it took place in Augustine's prayer and Luther's reflection. It happened in gestures to Romans in the deutero-Pauline biblical literature and quotes from Romans in early postbiblical literature. Marcion's choices about what to include in his scriptural canon were revelatory of his understanding of Romans. Even though much Romans interpretation exists in other genres, this volume is devoted to it as it appears on a much larger scale — in biblical commentaries. To be sure, biblical commentaries do not exist in isolation; they can serve as the basis for theological developments

---

7. On the "elasticity of the Pauline outlook," see Walter Bauer, *Orthodoxy and Heresy in Earliest Christianity,* ed. Robert A. Kraft and Gerhard Krodel (Philadelphia: Fortress, 1971), 233-35.

8. Seven volumes have been published in the Romans through History and Culture series, initially by Trinity Press International and now by T&T Clark.

9. Fitzmyer, *Romans,* xiii.

initiated by Romans reflection outside of commentaries. For example, as we will see, Thomas Aquinas penned an extensive commentary on the entire Pauline corpus from Romans through Hebrews in which he emphasized Paul's teaching on grace. The intense reflection occasioned by these commentaries influenced his work elsewhere on grace itself in the second part of the *Summa theologiae* and on Christ and the sacraments as the sources of grace in the *Summa's* third part. Thus study of commentaries on their own is beneficial, but it also bears fruit in understanding the contexts in which they were written. Because of the importance of patristic reflection on Romans for the subsequent history of theology and Romans exegesis, we devote the following overview to Romans interpretation in the early Church. It highlights the methods and themes that are so influential for the texts translated in this volume.

Patristic Commentaries

Christianity's first several centuries coincided with a major expansion of written textual interpretation, including the development of Rabbinic literature — the compilation of the oral Torah along with the interpretation of it and the written Torah. This period also witnessed increased production of commentaries on works by classical authors, such as Virgil, Homer, Plato, and Aristotle.[10] It was in precisely this period that Christians began to compile their own sacred scriptures, but they did not stop there. They also sought to interpret those scriptures. To do so, they turned to a genre that was becoming increasingly prevalent. The commentary would serve them well, and its use continues to our time.

As a result of the gradual closing by the first century B.C. of schools of Greek philosophy that emphasized dialogue and dispute in the spirit of the schools' founders, commentary on the founding texts of philosophical traditions became the preferred mode of education.[11] Indeed, to philosophize was

10. Peter Gorday, *Principles of Patristic Exegesis: Romans 9–11 in Origen, John Chrysostom, and Augustine* (New York: Edwin Mellen, 1983), 46; Francesco del Punta, "The Genre of Commentaries in the Middle Ages and Its Relation to the Nature and Originality of Medieval Thought," in *Miscellanea Mediaevalia*, vol. 26, ed. J. A. Aertsen and A. Speer (Berlin: Walter de Gruyter, 1998), 138-39.

11. Arnold I. Davidson, "Introduction: Pierre Hadot and the Spiritual Phenomenon of Ancient Philosophy," in Pierre Hadot, *Philosophy as a Way of Life,* trans. Michael Chase (Malden, MA: Blackwell, 1995), 5.

to comment. Yet commentary was not just the repetition of what famous predecessors had said, and it was not solely an intellectual exercise. Ancient philosophy, even in the commentary mode, was transformative; it was a "way of life." Furthermore, commentaries involved "creative mistakes" that resulted in new ideas and the development of doctrine.[12] For example, by the third and fourth century of the common era, neo-Platonists sought to defend philosophy against the increasing power of Christianity; one way of doing so was by downplaying differences within and between Aristotelian and Platonic systems.[13] That is, neo-Platonic commentators sought to present a united philosophical front by harmonizing Aristotelian and Platonic thought.

Similarly, Christianity moved from the oral teaching of Jesus to the early writers, such as Paul, who recorded it in New Testament texts. Once the biblical canon was closed, the commentary genre was ready at hand as a means by which to reconsider and extend biblical teaching in the service of transforming lives. The genre itself also offered Christian writers a way to frame Christianity as a new and superior philosophy.[14] Several Greek authors wrote commentaries on Romans. Many, including Theodore of Mopsuestia's, come down to us only in fragments. The most accessible early Greek work, available in volume 11 of the Nicene and Post-Nicene Fathers series, is John Chrysostom's thirty-two homilies on Romans delivered in Antioch before he became Archbishop of Constantinople in 397.[15] His homilies retain their oral texture, as do many commentaries, which often exist first in the form of homilies or lectures only later to be written down.

The Greek commentator who most influenced the west was Origen, early Christianity's prolific biblical scholar, who produced a wide range of material that addressed the Bible directly and indirectly.[16] Origen was not the first to write Pauline commentaries. That distinction likely goes, as we have

12. See the chapter entitled "Philosophy, Exegesis, and Creative Mistakes," in Pierre Hadot, *Philosophy as a Way of Life*, 71-77.

13. Richard Sorabji, "The Ancient Commentators on Aristotle," in *The Ancient Commentators and Their Influence*, ed. R. Sorabji (Ithaca: Cornell University Press, 1990), 3-5, 10-15.

14. Hadot, *Philosophy as a Way of Life*, 128-30.

15. John Chrysostom, "Homilies on Romans," in *A Select Library of the Christian Church*, Nicene and Post-Nicene Fathers, ser. 1, vol. 11. References to this volume appear parenthetically in the body of the introduction, and "thines" and "these" are changed to "yous." See also Gorday, *Principles of Patristic Exegesis*, 107.

16. See also *Early Patristic Readings of Romans*, ed. Kathy L. Gaca and L. L. Welborn (London: T&T Clark, 2005). For patristic exegesis more generally, see Charles Kannengieser's extensive *Handbook of Patristic Exegesis: The Bible in Ancient Christianity* (Leiden: Brill, 2006).

seen, to Clement of Alexandria, who had written short accounts of all the biblical books, including the Pauline letters.[17] These no longer exist. Similarly, Origen authored commentaries on numerous biblical books, including ones on each Pauline epistle. The original Greek for most of his Pauline commentaries, if it exists, does so only in fragments. Produced ca. 246, his work on Romans was as much for edification as for anything else.[18] It represents a bridge between east and west since it comes down to us primarily through an early-fifth-century (ca. 406) Latin translation by Rufinus of Aquileia.[19] Rufinus states that he reduced Origen's original by half, yet it remains a formidable work, Origen's second longest.[20] The scale of his work can be explained in part by his wide use of biblical quotation and by his willingness to entertain a range of interpretations of individual passages, a practice that could not continue in later Romans commentary. As Elizabeth Clark has noted, Christianity was "more open to varied expressions of the faith and required less in its affirmations of dogma than was the case one hundred and fifty years later. Considerable 'tightening' of what constituted orthodoxy occurred in the intervening period, so that some questions debatable [in the 230s and 240s] were deemed dangerous by the fifth century."[21]

Commentaries can allow authors to stake a claim of possession to the texts interpreted.[22] This certainly seems to be the case with Origen and his commentary on Romans. In his preface, he echoes 2 Peter 3:16 and acknowledges the difficulty of this epistle. It raises questions and contains language that "heretics" isolate and exploit for their own purposes. Indeed, early thinkers found Paul's epistles, as we have seen with Marcion, fertile ground for rejection of what came to be called the Christian Old Testament, the Law it contained, and the creator God it depicted. Others associated Paul's em-

---

17. Eusebius, *The History of the Church from Christ to Constantine*, 6.14.1, trans. G. A. Williamson (London: Penguin, 1989), 192. For an overview of this period, see chapter 1 of Maurice F. Wiles, *The Divine Apostle: The Interpretation of St. Paul's Epistles in the Early Church* (Cambridge: Cambridge University Press, 1967), 3-13.

18. "Epilogue of Rufinus," in Origen, *Commentary on the Epistle to the Romans*, 311.

19. Thomas P. Scheck, "Introduction to Origen," in *Commentary on the Epistle to the Romans: Books 1–5* (Washington, DC: Catholic University of America Press, 2001), 8, 12.

20. Thomas P. Scheck, *Origen and the History of Justification: The Legacy of Origen's Commentary on Romans* (Notre Dame: University of Notre Dame Press, 2008), 1.

21. Elizabeth A. Clark, *The Cultural Construction of an Early Christian Debate* (Princeton: Princeton University Press, 1992), 245.

22. Christina Shuttlesworth Kraus, "Introduction: Reading Commentaries/Commentaries as Reading," in *The Classical Commentary: Histories, Practices, Theory*, ed. Roy K. Gibson and Christina Shuttlesworth Kraus (Leiden: Brill, 2002), 2.

phasis on spirit over flesh with particular peoples, some by nature among the elect and some by nature not elect.[23] Still others read in Paul support for various determinisms. They believed humans are fated by their own fallen nature or by things external, such as the stars, and therefore lack free will, and this seems to be one of Origen's guiding concerns. "Heretics . . . are accustomed to add that the cause of each person's actions is not to be attributed to one's own purpose but to different kinds of natures. And, from a handful of words from this letter, they attempt to subvert the meaning of the whole of Scripture, which teaches that God has given man freedom of the will."[24]

Origen responds explicitly to each of these positions in the commentary. He sees Paul as a just "arbiter" who seeks to "offend" neither Jews nor gentiles, nor overly to encourage either.[25] Later he acknowledges that some "want there to be one God of the Jews and another God of the gentiles, that is to say, one God of the law and another God of the Gospels." Instead, Paul "says that not only is there only one God of the Jews and gentiles, but . . . the very same God justifies members of both peoples who believe, and this is based not upon the privilege of circumcision or uncircumcision but in consideration of faith alone."[26] Addressing theological anthropology, Origen opposes the schools of the Gnostic teachers Valentinus and Basilides, who "imagine that there is a nature of souls that would always be saved and never perish, and another that would always perish and never be saved." Instead, Origen takes Paul as highlighting human "liberty," "power of choice," and "freedom of will" to remain in unfaith or to be converted, by grace, to faith.[27] He holds for human freedom so strongly that he attributes to interpolation the discussion of God's hardening Pharaoh's heart.[28] Thus, by commenting on the Pauline corpus, including Romans — what Origen terms Paul's "more perfect" book — he challenges his opponents on their own field and thereby stakes a claim to Romans and its proper interpretation.[29]

Although Origen wrote in the third century, the Latin translation of his Pauline commentary does not appear until the very early fifth century.

---

23. Gorday, *Principles of Patristic Exegesis*, 44-45.

24. Origen, *Commentary on the Epistle to the Romans*, Book 2 (= Origen [2001]), preface, p. 53.

25. Origen (2001), 2.14.1-3, pp. 165-66.

26. Origen (2001), 3.10.1, p. 230.

27. Origen (2002), 8.11.1-7, pp. 175-78. For Origen on grace, see Origen (2001), 4.5.2, p. 259.

28. Origen (2002), 7.16.4, p. 114. See Origen (2002), p. 113, n. 371.

29. Origen (2001), preface, p. 53; Origen (2002), 10.14.3, p. 284.

Apart from scattered Greek fragments, the first extant Pauline commentaries are in Latin from the mid-360s by the Roman rhetorician and convert to Christianity, Marius Victorinus.[30] His was the first moment of the "astonishing rediscovery of Paul" in the fourth and fifth centuries.[31] Having translated Poryphry and Aristotle and commented on Cicero, he wrote Trinitarian treatises after his conversion as well as commentaries on Galatians, Philippians, and Ephesians that are extant; he likely wrote on Romans and the Corinthian correspondence as well.[32]

Although Victorinus's commentary on Romans no longer survives, a brief review of his work that does will be instructive for understanding his significance for subsequent Pauline commentary. Indeed, the circumstances surrounding his writing and his motives for doing so illuminate the reasons for the more general rediscovery of Paul. For one thing, he was a convert,[33] and his conversion points up the tensions between Christianity and traditional Roman religions.[34] It also exemplifies the growth within Christianity's ranks of the intelligentsia and, particularly, the wealthy who sought deeper engagement with its sacred texts.[35] It was also in Paul that he found "the proclamation of Jesus Christ" and "the foundational witness to Christian belief."[36] He also adapted the genre of commentary to his work on Paul. It allowed him to express his thoughts on Paul while, like other non-Christian commentators in antiquity, playing "down [his] own contributions through a filiopietistic approach to the authorities [he] revered and commented on."[37] He characterizes his scriptural work as a "plain commentary" (*commentatio simplex*), an unadorned work that would thus be capable of wider

30. Stephen Andrew Cooper, *Marius Victorinus' Commentary on Galatians: Introduction, Translation and Notes* (New York: Oxford University Press, 2005), 37.

31. Bernhard Lohse, "Beobachtungen zum Paulus-Kommentar des Marius Victorinus und zur Wiederentdeckung des Paulus in der lateinischen Theologie des vierten Jahrhunderts," in *Kerygma und Logos: Beiträge zu den geistesgeschichtlichen Beziehungen zwischen Antike und Christentum,* ed. Adolf Martin Ritter (Göttingen: Vandenhoeck & Ruprecht, 1979), 366.

32. Alexander Souter, *Earliest Latin Commentaries on the Epistles of St. Paul* (Oxford: Clarendon, 1927), 8-9. Cooper, *Marius Victorinus' Commentary,* 3.

33. Souter, *Earliest Latin Commentaries,* 8.

34. David G. Hunter, "Ambrosiaster," in *Dictionary of Major Biblical Interpreters,* ed. Donald K. McKim (Downers Grove, IL: InterVarsity Press, 2007), 123.

35. J. N. D. Kelly, *Jerome: His Life, Writings, and Controversies* (New York: Harper and Row, 1975), 94-95.

36. Lohse, "Beobachtungen," 365.

37. Cooper, *Marius Victorinus' Commentary,* 9.

acceptance.[38] His comments could be brief (especially compared to Origen's monumental work) and made little reference to other biblical texts.[39] He focused instead on the authorial intention and the literal sense of Paul. Victorinus also used Paul as a means of counteracting heresies, without naming them, particularly the Arianism that he opposed in his Trinitarian treatises.[40] Finally, he seems to have been disturbed by Judaizing, that is, Christian observances of Jewish faith and practices. As a result he emphasized terms like "justification" and "by faith alone" *(sola fide)* to such an extent that he was seen as a proto-Reformer, and Adolf von Harnack called him an "Augustine before Augustine."[41]

Alexander Souter claims that the main source of Victorinus's commentary "is no doubt the intelligence of the author himself."[42] There has been some dispute about his effect on subsequent commentators. He likely exercised little influence over Pelagius and the anonymous commentator on Paul (whom we will address below),[43] yet Ambrosiaster and Augustine drew specific themes and emphases from him. More generally, he exemplified a particular approach to biblical commentary that Ambrosiaster emulated and, thereby, disseminated to posterity.

Anyone who has spent time with Victorinus' Latin will appreciate the paradox that while his language can be terse to the point that one can barely grasp his meaning, his comments are at the same time expansive, prolix, and repetitive. One could consider Ambrosiaster the great "corrector" of Victorinus: abbreviate, soften the anti-Judaism, subtract the metaphysics of the soul which the Origenist Controversy made so theologically incorrect, name the heretics, and — perhaps above all — add cross-references to the Old Testament. The result was an exegetical work on the Pauline epistles fit to be copied copiously in several recensions until the arrival of the printing press. But Victorinus was the Latin who made the first step in adapting the various elements of late antique paideia for the purposes of a comprehensive commentary on the Pauline epistles.[44]

---

38. Souter, *Earliest Latin Commentaries*, 28.

39. Souter, *Earliest Latin Commentaries,* 22.

40. Lohse, "Beobachtungen," 365.

41. Cooper, *Marius Victorinus' Commentary*, 148-61. Harnack quote from Cooper, 149.

42. Souter, *Earliest Latin Commentaries*, 26.

43. Cooper, *Marius Victorinus' Commentary*, 188.

44. Cooper, *Marius Victorinus' Commentary,* 245-46.

Thus Victorinus does have an impact on subsequent exegesis, particularly through Ambrosiaster, to whom we now turn.

The first extant commentary on all thirteen of the Pauline letters was attributed by most ancients to Ambrose of Milan. Because of this attribution, it was disseminated broadly and had wide influence through the Middle Ages.[45] Only with Erasmus in the sixteenth century did this attribution begin to be questioned. By the seventeenth century, the author received the name of Ambrosiaster, or pseudo-Ambrose.[46] In part because of the commentary's pseudonymity and the pejorative name attached to it, it has received little scholarly attention until recently. Now it is seen as a "milestone in the history of the reception of Paul."[47] In fact, it is "generally acknowledged to be the most impressive literary and historical study of those writings prior to the Renaissance."[48]

The Ambrosiaster commentary (which actually comes down to us in three versions) was likely penned sometime in the 360s to 380s by an aristocratic Roman presbyter who could be characterized as traditional.[49] As such, his commentaries evince support for established political and ecclesiastical hierarchies.[50] He also claims that woman was not created in God's image (see the comment on Col 3:10) and that women are inferior (see the comment on 1 Tim 2:11-14).[51] Gerald Bray speaks of him as "philosemitic" because of his stress on Paul's Jewishness and his emphasis on the value of the Old Testament. His stress on justification by grace makes him a Luther

---

45. In the Standard Gloss or *Glossa Ordinaria* on Romans, almost 50 percent of the named references in the marginal gloss are to Augustine. The second most frequently cited is Ambrose (i.e., Ambrosiaster) at 25 percent. See Ambrosiaster, *Commentaries on Romans and 1-2 Corinthians,* trans. Gerald Bray (Downers Grove, IL: InterVarsity Press, 2009). For an overview of Ambrosiaster's commentary on Romans, see Gerald Bray, "Ambrosiaster," in *Reading Romans through the Centuries: From the Early Church to Karl Barth,* ed. Jeffery P. Greenman and Timothy Larsen (Grand Rapids: Brazos, 2005), 21-38.

46. Sophie Lunn-Rockliffe, *Ambrosiaster's Political Theology* (Oxford: Oxford University Press, 2007), 30-32.

47. Wihelm Geerlings, "Zur exegetischen Methode des Ambrosiasters," in *Stimuli: Exegese und ihre Hermeneutik in Antike und Christentum: Festschrift für Ernst Dassmann,* ed. Georg Schöllgen and Clemens Scholten (Münster: Aschendorff, 1996), 444.

48. Eugene TeSelle, *Augustine the Theologian* (New York: Herder, 1970), 157.

49. Hunter, "Ambrosiaster," 123-25.

50. David G. Hunter, "On the Sin of Adam and Eve: A Little-Known Defense of Marriage and Childbearing by Ambrosiaster," *Harvard Theological Review* 82 (1989): 286.

51. David G. Hunter, "The Paradise of Patriarchy: Ambrosiaster on Women as (Not) God's Image," *Journal of Theological Studies* 43 (1992): 447-69.

"avant la lettre" and provides evidence of "just how deeply rooted in patristic thought the German Reformer's theology was."[52]

In addition to the characteristics of Ambrosiaster's exegesis noted above, it is instructive to review his reading of Romans 5:12. Drawing a parallel between Adam's sin and Christ's salvific work, he writes, "[As] the one Adam [i.e., Eve, for she too is Adam] sinned and affected everyone, so the one Christ, the Son of God, has conquered sin in everyone." Later, Ambrosiaster returns to the end of Romans 5:12 and states, "Paul says that all have sinned in Adam, even though he really meant the woman, because he was not referring to the particular person but the universal human race. For it is clear that all have sinned in Adam as though in a lump [*massa*]."[53] For Ambrosiaster, Adam does not simply set a bad example. He is the one in whom *(in quo)* "all have sinned."[54] Adam in himself and in Eve confers, like a parent, his genetic heritage to subsequent generations. Later writers, including Augustine as we will see, will embellish Ambrosiaster's lump so that humans become a lump or mass of perdition.

Before turning to the major Romans commentators of the fifth century, Pelagius and Augustine, two predecessors deserve brief mention. The first, an anonymous commentary of the late fourth or early fifth century, illustrates how Pelagius continued to have an impact beyond late antiquity and through the Middle Ages. In the early 1970s, the German scholar Hermann Josef Frede produced an edition that includes the anonymous commentary along with two subsequent versions produced by later ancient editors who interpolated Pelagian themes into them. As late as the nineteenth century, the second interpolation was being attributed to Saint Jerome and was more strongly Pelagian than the first. Indeed, volume 30 of the *Patrologia Latina* contains this commentary under Jerome's name.[55]

---

52. Bray, "Ambrosiaster," 22-26.

53. Ambrosiaster, *Commentaries on Romans and 1-2 Corinthians*, 40.

54. By reading the *"in quo"* in the Latin version of Romans 5:12 as *in quo — id est, in Adam — omnes peccaverunt* ("in whom — i.e., in Adam — all have sinned"), he incorporates humanity in Adam and opens up the question, which Augustine and others would pursue in greater depth, of how it is that sin is passed on from one generation to the next. For the Latin, see Ambrosiaster, *In Epistulam ad Romanos*, ed. Henry Joseph Vogels, CSEL 81:1, pp. 162-65. For the English, see Ambrosiaster, *Commentaries on Romans and 1-2 Corinthians*, 40-41. Fitzmyer (pp. 413-17) identifies eleven possible meanings, including Ambrosiaster's, for the *eph' ho* that is translated into the Latin as *in quo*.

55. Hermann Josef Frede, *Ein neuer Paulustext und Kommentar*, 2 vols. (Freiburg: Herder, 1973-74), 1:185-205. See Theodore S. de Bruyn, "Constantius the Tractator, Author of an Anonymous Commentary on the Pauline Epistles," *Journal of Theological Studies* 43 (1991): 47.

Pelagius relied on the anonymous commentary to produce his work, but it did not on its own have a fully Pelagian account of sin and grace. Nonetheless, because of subsequent interpolations and its attribution to the great biblical scholar Jerome, it became one vector by which Pelagius continued to influence the Middle Ages.[56] Thus, on Romans 5:12, the anonymous commentator claims that "no one could fulfill the natural or biblical law because all had sinned by following Adam's example."[57] Yes, all sin, but it is not bred in our bones; instead, we are misled by the model Adam supplies. Pseudo-Jerome adds Pelagius's claim at this point and agrees that, historically, most did die spiritual deaths due to sin. Yet a few righteous people, such as Abraham, Isaac, and Jacob, did not. In advancing this claim, Pseudo-Jerome reflects Pelagius's optimism that there were some before Christ whose wills were not so deformed that they could not will the good.[58]

Surprising as it may sound, Origen is also a Latin commentator on Romans, the final one we consider before turning to Pelagius and Augustine. Even though Origen composed his commentary in Greek in the third century, it comes down to us, as noted above, via Rufinus of Aquileia's Latin translation from the first decade of the fifth century. It was likely aimed at wealthy Roman patrons who, having converted to Christianity, sought a deeper understanding of their faith's founding texts. Rufinus introduces Origen on Romans into the growing pool of Romans interpretation, and his translation turns out to be no disinterested effort, as he makes clear in prefaces to Origen's Romans commentary and other works.

Rufinus's preface to his translation of Origen's *On First Principles* is particularly revealing, not only about his polemical intentions but also his hermeneutical strategies. He uses the preface as an occasion to undermine critiques of Origen by revealing that Jerome — one of Origen's main critics and Rufinus's competitor for influence on wealthy patrons in Rome — had himself been a translator and even a plagiarist of Origen. He then asserts that Origen's *On First Principles* shows evidence of interpolation by heretics. "Wherever, therefore, I have found in his books anything contrary to the reverent statement made by him about the Trinity in other places, I have either omitted it as a corrupt and interpolated passage, or reproduced it in a form that agrees with the doctrine which I have found him affirming elsewhere."

---

56. de Bruyn, "Constantinus the Tractator," 47.

57. Frede, *Ein neuer Paulustext*, 2.38.

58. PL 30:668B. Theodore S. de Bruyn, *Pelagius's Commentary on St. Paul's Epistle to the Romans* (Oxford: Clarendon, 1993), 92-93.

Not content with simple excision of offending passages, Rufinus goes on to acknowledge, "If . . . he has occasionally expressed himself obscurely in the effort to be brief, I have, to make the passage clearer, added such remarks on the same subject as I have read in fuller form in his other books."[59]

In the epilogue to his translation of Origen's Romans commentary, Rufinus makes a similar claim and admits that he did "add some things and fill in what is missing and abbreviate what is too long." He distinguishes himself here from Jerome and levels an implicit charge of plagiarism against him by acknowledging the source of his material, namely, Origen. By composing commentaries thoroughly influenced by Origen without acknowledging that influence, Jerome stole "the title from [Origen], who laid the foundations of the work and supplied the material for the construction of the building."[60]

Origen's commentary on Romans, therefore, serves by way of Rufinus's translation as a critique of Jerome's newly found rejection of Origen. It also functions as a counterbalance to an increasingly deterministic reading of Paul as represented, as we will see, by Augustine. It also gets tangled up in the Pelagian controversy, to the namesake of which we now turn.

With his commentary on the thirteen Pauline epistles written sometime after 406 partly in response to Augustine's interpretation of Romans, Pelagius joined the cohort of fourth- and fifth-century Latin interpreters of Paul. His work provoked an extended dispute with Augustine that would occupy the later years of Augustine's life and induce Augustine to return repeatedly to Romans and refine his theology on grace and free will. Pelagius would also lend his name to a heresy, the charge of which continues to be leveled at theologians today.[61]

The outlines of Pelagius's life are not certain, but he likely grew up in fourth-century Britain under Roman rule, was likely from a family of means, and had an ascetic bent. Yet he was a layman, among the last to exercise such influence for centuries. From Romanized Britain with its emphasis on faith and good works,[62] he moved to Rome in the 380s. There he served as an ad-

59. Origen, *On First Principles,* trans. G. W. Butterworth (New York: Harper and Row, 1966), lxiii.

60. Origen (2002), "Epilogue of Rufinus," 312-13. In the preface to the commentary, Rufinus specified that he reduced the length of Origen's commentary by half (Origen [2001], preface, p. 52).

61. For example, W. Rush Otey, "The New Pelagians," in *Persons in Community: Theological Voices from the Pastorate,* ed. W. H. Lazareth (Grand Rapids: Eerdmans, 2004), 37-44.

62. M. Forthomme Nicholson, "Celtic Theology: Pelagius," in *Celtic Theology: An Introduction,* ed. James P. Mackey (Edinburgh: T&T Clark, 1989), 387.

visor to wealthy patrons who, often as recent converts, sought out his advice on the Christian life. Around 410, with the sack of Rome by Alaric, he and his followers were dispersed across North Africa. Their encounter with African Christianity was not a happy one. Celestius, one of his followers, drew out the implications of Pelagius's work for original sin and infant Baptism. These issues, and not the more basic claims about grace and free will, were initially the flash point in more conservative North Africa.[63] Pelagius's thought was condemned by emperor, council, and pope in 418, and he disappeared from history thereafter. Were it not for Alaric and the fall of Rome, Pelagianism might not have been a matter of concern, and Augustine might have turned his considerable energy and resources to other pressing matters.

Strikingly, for someone who would be remembered as a heretic, Pelagius puts his anti-heretical commitments on display from the outset, as in his comments on Romans 1:2 (p. 59).[64] His general practice in commenting on a verse is to articulate a short Pauline phrase and then explicate it briefly (a brevity and clarity that could well have facilitated its transmission to posterity).[65] For example, he talks about the gospel being anticipated by the prophets "'in the Holy Scripture'" (on Rom 1:2, p. 59). This leads him to emphasize, *pace* the Manichaeans, the holiness of the Old Testament and Jesus' Jewish ancestors. "Indeed," he says, "this entire passage contradicts the Manichaeans." Romans 9:5 allows him to extend his critique by emphasizing Jesus' Jewish roots, his humanity, and his divinity. This verse works "[a]gainst the Manichaean, Photinus and Arius, because he is from the Jews, and according to the flesh alone from them, and God blessed forever" (p. 115; p. 63). Elsewhere, "heretics" in general (on Rom 1:16, p. 63) and Marcionites (on Rom 7:12, p. 103) in particular come in for critique.

Pelagius is thoroughly grounded in Scripture, and he regularly quotes it — the New Testament more often than the Old. Moreover, he reads it critically and therefore claims that "it is uncertain whether [Paul] ever was in Spain," in contrast to what Romans 15:24 implies (p. 149).[66] Likewise, he seeks to downplay sweeping Pauline claims about human fallenness. Thus Pelagius tempers the remark that "death passed on to all people in that all

---

63. Peter Brown, *Augustine of Hippo: A Biography* (Berkeley: University of California Press, 1967), 344.

64. Page numbers in this and the following three paragraphs come from de Bruyn, *Pelagius's Commentary on St. Paul's Epistle to the Romans*.

65. Nicholson, "Celtic Theology: Pelagius," 410.

66. John Ferguson, *Pelagius: A Historical and Theological Study* (Cambridge: Heffer, 1956), 18-19.

sinned" (Rom. 5:12), commenting that "as long as they sin the same way, they likewise die" (p. 92). The implication is that if they do not sin as Adam did, they will not die. Indeed, some, such as Abraham, Isaac, and Jacob, did not die spiritually. Similarly, he rejects the position that Adam's sin is handed on to infants at birth. Instead, Adam sets a powerful "example or pattern" of sin.

While he emphasizes the priority of grace (see on Rom 5:1, p. 89), Pelagius's main commitment is against a Manicheistic determinism that held that humans are controlled by the fate of their physical nature. In contrast, he emphasized the human ability to choose and act on the good. "God is God of all by nature, but God of few in merit and will" (on Rom 1:8, p. 61). Thus God gives humans the means to act rightly; few, however, choose to do so. Humans are perfectible; Paul himself acts "to contradict those who attack the glory of perfection" (on Rom 15:25, p. 149). He agrees that the ungodly are saved "by faith alone" and, at the same time, emphasizes the importance of works for the baptized (see on Rom 3:27; 4:5, pp. 83, 85).

On the pericope on God's foreknowledge of Jacob and Esau, Pelagius attempts to preserve human freedom and at the same time God's prerogative. Citing Paul's quotation of Exodus 33:19 in Romans 9:15, "'I will have mercy on whom I have mercy,'" Pelagius offers several different interpretations of this and the subsequent verse. One reading that he wishes to exclude would hold that God's mercy bears no relation to human action; yet this derogates against God's justice. Instead, says Pelagius, Paul could be quoting an opponent whom he refutes elsewhere. Perhaps Paul really means to say, "This is correctly understood as follows: I will have mercy on him whom I have foreknown will be able to deserve compassion" (p. 117). That is, God anticipates meritorious human actions and responds to them with mercy — a position that the early Augustine also held.

Put simply, justice demands rewarding freely chosen right action and punishment of freely chosen wrong action. It would be unbecoming of God to condemn humans unable to choose the good. Thus Pelagius protects God by arguing that God created humans with the ability to choose to do the good, even though many freely choose not to.

Pelagius's commentary on Romans would continue to influence interpreters down to the Reformation because it endured anonymously and, in combination with interpolations by subsequent Pelagians, pseudonymously under the names of Jerome, Primasius, and others. His work would be associated with him only in the late nineteenth and early twentieth century. Similarly, the Vulgate prologues to the Pauline epistles, attributed to Jerome, have Pelagian origins.[67] As a result, Karlfried Froehlich would write, "It is outright dangerous that Pelagius' reading of Paul enjoyed such unquestioned authority under the safe name of orthodox writers. The vulnerability of the medieval reliance on 'tradition' in exegesis is obvious. But it was precisely the unmasking of the pervasive 'Pelagianism' of late medieval theology by the 'Augustinian' monk Martin Luther that led to the epochal Reform of the sixteenth century."[68] It is to Augustine that we now turn.

The figure who would have the most influence on subsequent Christianity and its reading of Paul was Augustine. Yet his work on Romans, which has elicited such prolific scholarship, is daunting to confine within the limits of an introduction. He is influential because subsequent readers of Paul through the Middle Ages, the Reformation, and beyond relied on or reacted to his insights in their own engagement with Romans. Indeed, Krister Stendahl bemoans this influence as misdirecting subsequent readers away from the Apostle Paul, who was an "extrovert with a robust conscience" — as compared to Augustine's sensitive and "introspective reading of Paul."[69] Augustine is also problematic in that he did not — as we will see and as opposed to the commentators translated for this volume — compose a complete commentary on Romans. Hence he does not benefit in writing from other, perhaps corrective, parts of Romans. This may explain his "tendency to construe the polarities and antitheses of Paul's terminology in terms of massive and sweeping dichotomies."[70] He took what were, for Paul, specific, historical issues and universalized them; local Pauline disputes became polemics with humanity-wide significance.[71]

Devoting such a short space to Augustine on Romans is also daunting because his written output was massive, and so much of it had to do with Paul. His first (*Against the Academics*, 2.1.1) and last (*Against the Second Response of Julian, Incomplete*, 6.41) scriptural citations are from Paul.[72] Augus-

---

67. Maurice Schild, "Leading Motifs in Some Western Bible Prologues," *Journal of Religious History* 12 (1972): 96-98.

68. Karlfried Froehlich, "Romans 8:1-11: Pauline Theology in Medieval Interpretation," in *Faith and History: Essays in Honor of Paul W. Meyer* (Atlanta: Scholars Press, 1990), 259-60.

69. Krister Stendahl, "A Last Word," in *Engaging Augustine on Romans: Self, Context, and Theology in Interpretation*, ed. Daniel Patte and Eugene TeSelle (Harrisburg, PA: Trinity Press International, 2002), 270.

70. Gorday, *Principles of Patristic Exegesis*, 146, 191.

71. Peter J. Gorday, "Jews and Gentiles, Galatians 2:11-14, and Reading Israel in Romans: The Patristic Debate," in *Engaging Augustine on Romans* (see n. 69), 224.

72. Thomas F. Martin, "Vox Pauli: Augustine and the Claims to Speak for Paul, An Exploration of Rhetoric at the Service of Exegesis," *Journal of Early Christian Studies* 8 (2000): 237-38.

tine's exegesis "was conditioned by his theological presuppositions,"[73] and so he revisited Romans throughout his pastoral career and in a range of genres to puzzle anew Paul's significance. His thoughts on this epistle are scattered through letters, sermons, treatises, and responses to questions spread over many years. Augustine often used Romans as a platform for his disputes with Manichaeans, Donatists, Pelagians, and others, but not always. His sermons on Romans 7 and 8, for example, do address Manichaean and Pelagian matters, but he also uses these texts to reveal facets of Paul's personality (Sermon 154) and to exhort his audience to hope (Sermon 157).[74] These themes seem appropriate for one engaged in pastoral care who must regularly respond to queries about spiritual matters, including about biblical interpretation.[75] Moreover, he repeatedly worked through particular passages in different settings over a long period of time. Much of his early Pauline interpretation was occasioned by his confrontation with Manichaeans, "the most radical and self-confident of Paul's expositors,"[76] and their reliance on Paul to ground their dualism and cosmic determinism. As a result, he carved out a role for human free will, a role that fades in the disputes that would occupy the last decades of his life — disputes occasioned by different readings of Paul.

The period from 388 to 396 was pivotal in his life and for Romans interpretation. His ordination as priest in 391 introduced the frustrations of this "arduous work" that "disquiet[ed] and crush[ed]" his spirit.[77] His installation as bishop in 395 burdened him with more pastoral responsibilities. Augustine composed four targeted forays into Romans during the period 394 through 396. These included questions 66-74 of *Miscellany of Eighty-Three Questions, Propositions from the Epistle to the Romans,* the *Unfinished Commentary on the Epistle to the Romans,* and the first book of his letter *To Simplician.* In the first three, he reserves some credit to human action.

---

73. Gerald Bonner, "Augustine, the Bible and the Pelagians," in *Augustine and the Bible,* ed. Pamela Bright (Notre Dame: University of Notre Dame Press, 1999), 237-38.

74. Augustine, *Sermons,* trans. Edmund Hill, The Works of Saint Augustine: A Translation for the Twenty-First Century 3.5 (New Rochelle: New City Press, 1992).

75. Pamela Bright, "Augustine," in *Reading Romans through the Centuries: From the Early Church to Karl Barth,* ed. Jeffery P. Greenman and Timothy Larsen (Grand Rapids: Brazos, 2005), 68.

76. Brown, *Augustine of Hippo,* 151.

77. Augustine, Letter 21.3, *Letters 1-99,* ed. Roland Teske, The Works of Saint Augustine: A Translation for the Twenty-First Century 2.1 (Hyde Park, NY: New City Press, 2001), 56.

Against moral determinism of various groups that held that humans were not free but controlled by the stars or some other cosmic means, Augustine sought to hold onto human freedom as a cause of graced action. "For by his free will, man has a means to believe in the Liberator and to receive grace so that, with the liberating assistance of him who gives it, he might cease to sin."[78] In his reading of Romans 9:15, Augustine leaves room for human initiative by maintaining that God foreknew that Jacob, rather than his brother Esau, would respond in faith and therefore merited.[79]

In 396, in answer to questions by Simplician, successor to Ambrose as Bishop of Milan, Augustine claims still to be mistaken about Romans and so returns to it yet again.[80] In later years, Augustine recounted that his letter *To Simplician* was the key to his response to Pelagianism, an insight that seems at odds with the historical record, since he would not even read Pelagius's commentary on Romans until 412 and therein recognize an opponent.[81] Yet, in a sense, *To Simplician* was part of the Pelagian controversy, inasmuch as it was within Pelagius's purview as he composed his commentary on Romans, which expressed positions that Augustine eventually rejected.[82] It is not Augustine's final word on grace since he would continue to write on the topic for over thirty more years; however, it could be seen as "Pelagius Anticipated."[83]

Augustine's change in *To Simplician* is subtle but dramatic. He had gradually restricted the significance of human freedom in salvation, but with the slight change he makes in this work, he "ruthlessly" shatters it.[84] Earlier, he held that God elects because God leaves some room for human freedom or foreknows human faith or rewards hidden merits. In *To Sim-*

---

78. *Propositions from the Epistle to the Romans,* 44, in Paula Fredriksen Landes, *Augustine on Romans, Propositions from the Epistle to the Romans and Unfinished Commentary on the Epistle to the Romans* (Chico, CA: Scholars Press, 1982), 16-17.

79. *Propositions from the Epistle to the Romans,* 6, pp. 30-33.

80. Augustine, Letter 37.3, *To Simplician,* in Augustine, *Responses to Miscellaneous Questions,* ed. Boniface Ramsey, The Works of Saint Augustine: A Translation for the Twenty-First Century 1.12 (Hyde Park, NY: New City Press, 2008), 174.

81. Augustine, *On the Predestination of the Saints,* 4.8, and *On the Gift of Perseverance,* 20.52, in Augustine, *Responses to Miscellaneous Questions,* 171-73.

82. de Bruyn, *Pelagius's Commentary on St. Paul's Epistle to the Romans,* 6, 26.

83. James Wetzel, "Pelagius Anticipated: Grace and Election in Augustine's *Ad Simplician,*" in *Augustine: From Rhetor to Theologian,* ed. Joanne McWilliam (Waterloo, Ont.: Wilfrid Laurier University Press, 1992), 121-32.

84. William S. Babcock, "Augustine's Interpretation of Romans (A.D. 394-396)," *Augustinian Studies* 10 (1979): 65.

plician, however, Augustine rejects these positions and argues at length that even faith is the result of God's grace.[85] Augustine also magnifies human fallenness, as he does in his later work, by interpreting the clay in Romans 9:21 as sinfulness. In *Eighty-Three Questions,* he makes the point twice that humans are a mass of sinfulness; he does not make it at all in *Propositions from the Epistle to the Romans;* he makes it regularly in *To Simplician.*[86] In sum, *To Simplician* is crucial for Augustine's interpretation of Romans; and Paul, especially in Romans, is crucial to Augustine's theology.

There is much more to the significance of Romans for Augustine. Within the Pelagian controversy, Romans interpretation had implications for the origin of the soul, predestination in conversion, original sin, and infant baptism. Augustine also preached on Romans and cited this text in other contexts, for example, in the *Confessions.* Yet he is best remembered for his work on grace and human freedom, and the conclusions that he draws from Romans about predestination and the extent of human perdition may strike modern ears as harsh.

Augustine saw God's offer of salvation, even if limited, as something to rejoice over; in justice, God is not bound to save anyone. On deeper inspection, Donatist and Pelagian positions seem just as difficult. They yoke humans with the "terrifying weight of complete freedom,"[87] and restrict salvation to heroes of righteousness. In response, Augustine holds out for a sort of "Christian mediocrity" that makes salvation much more widely available,[88] potentially, to any baptized believer. It would be accessible, Augustine claims with a hint of amazement, even for people who have intercourse "not merely for the sake of propagation, but also for the sake of pleasure, . . . [who] do not accept injuries with such patience, . . . [and who] own a family estate and give alms from it, but not as generously as the others"![89] For Augustine, it is not human effort, which he grows increasingly doubtful about in his years of ecclesial administration, that effects salvation. He holds out for a much surer

---

85. *To Simplician,* 2.4-12, in Augustine, *Responses to Miscellaneous Questions,* 188-94.

86. Augustine, *Miscellany of Eighty-Three Questions,* 68.3-4, and *To Simplician,* 2.16-22, in *Responses to Miscellaneous Questions,* 117-19, 198-207; *Propositions from the Epistle to the Romans,* 62, pp. 36-37.

87. Brown, *Augustine of Hippo,* 350.

88. Robert Markus, *The End of Ancient Christianity* (Cambridge: Cambridge University Press, 1990), 45-62.

89. *Answer to the Two Letters of the Pelagians,* 3.5.14, in *Answer to the Pelagians II,* trans. R. J. Teske, *The Works of Saint Augustine: A Translation for the Twenty-First Century* 1.24 (Hyde Park, NY: New City Press, 1998), 171. Cited in Brown, *Augustine of Hippo,* 348.

cause, namely, God's will, inscrutable though it is. This recognition is not meant to strike fear but hope in the faithful. We are to rejoice that God offers salvation because God need not.

The Standard Gloss

The next major resource we turn to is the twelfth-century's Standard Gloss *(Glossa Ordinaria),* which was largely a product of the Laon school. We skip to the twelfth century, not because of a lack of material in the intervening years. In fact, the late-sixth-century Cassiodorus composed two works on Romans. One appears in the *Patrologia Latina,* attributed to Primasius, a sixth-century African bishop (PL 68:415-506). Scholars at the beginning of the twentieth century determined that it was in fact Cassiodorus who edited Pelagius's Romans commentary, while his students completed the rest. This work is "an anti-Pelagian edition of Pelagius" that revises the original Pelagius "more on the doctrinal than on the linguistic side" in order, quoting Cassiodorus, "to remove . . . the error of heresy."[90] The Venerable Bede (d. ca. 735) — who is now known more as a historian because of his *Ecclesiastical History of the English People* — thought of himself as an exegete, as is evident in the few autobiographical details he provides at the end of this work. "I have . . . appl[ied] myself entirely to the study of the Scriptures."[91] Later medieval readers saw him in the same light, and selections from his exegesis figure in such works as the twelfth-century Gloss. He wrote on less commented works, such as on the Acts of the Apostles. He also collected patristic exegesis on works more frequently commented on, including the Pauline epistles. Yet there are only seven extant editions of his commentary on the epistles, with the result that it is not readily available to scholars today.[92]

Carolingian scholars devoted themselves to correcting versions of the biblical text. They also sought to meet growing interest in the meaning of this text and so turned to the Church Fathers for their interpretation. Indeed, the Carolingian period saw an explosion of biblical commentaries. They did so to such a degree that, in the ninth century, "most Carolingian

90. Alexander Souter, "The Commentary of Pelagius on the Epistles of St. Paul: The Problem of Its Restoration," *The Proceedings of the British Academy* 2 (1905-6): 420.

91. Bede, *Ecclesiastical History of the English People,* 5.24, ed. Bertram Colgrave and R. A. B. Mynors (Oxford: Clarendon, 1969), 567.

92. George Hardin Brown, *Bede the Venerable* (Boston: Twayne, 1987), 58.

scholarly work was essentially exegetical in orientation."[93] The end of the eighth century to the beginning of the tenth, in comparison to the previous 250 years, witnessed a fivefold increase in the number of biblical commentaries produced.[94] Leading Carolingian commentators included Rabanus Maurus, Florus of Lyons, Claude of Turin, Sedulius Scottus, and Haimo of Auxerre. They mined patristic texts to compile their own commentaries on the Pauline epistles, arranging material that would eventually be incorporated into the Gloss in a more compressed form. Haimo of Auxerre proved to be quite an influential exegete in his own right.[95]

The study of the Pauline letters in the second half of the eleventh century also helped pave the way for the Gloss. Berengar of Tours and Drogo of Paris wrote commentaries, but they survive only as fragments today. In contrast, the commentaries of Lanfranc of Bec and Bruno the Carthusian are extant and readily accessible in the *Patrologia Latina* (PL 150 and 153 respectively).[96] Working from a monastery in northern France, Lanfranc combined patristic excerpts from Augustine, Jerome, Ambrosiaster, Theodore of Mopsuestia, and John Chrysostom, along with his own original comments, to produce a text with both marginal and interlinear glosses.[97] More influential, however, was the work of Bruno the Carthusian, who produced commentaries on both the Psalter and the epistles while serving as master of the cathedral school at Reims before departing for the monastic life around 1077. Bruno's work and that of his students likely had a direct effect on biblical commentary at the Laon school.[98] Other biblical glosses,

---

93. Celia Martin Chazelle and Burton Van Name Edwards, "Introduction: The Study of the Bible and Carolingian Culture," in *The Study of the Bible in the Carolingian Era*, ed. Celia Martin Chazelle and Burton Van Name Edwards (Turnhout: Brepols, 2003), 5.

94. John J. Contreni, "Carolingian Biblical Culture," in *Iohannes Scotus Eriugena, The Bible and Hermeneutics*, ed. Gerd Riel and Carlos G. Steel (Leuven: Leuven University Press, 1996), 7.

95. For a complete translation of Haimo of Auxerre's Galatians commentary, see Ian Christopher Levy, *The Letter to the Galatians*, The Bible in Medieval Tradition (Grand Rapids: Eerdmans, 2011), 79-130. See also the introduction to Haimo in the same volume, 37-44.

96. For a complete translation of Bruno the Carthusian's Galatians commentary see Levy, *The Letter to the Galatians,* 131-83. See also the introduction to both Lanfranc and Bruno in the same volume, 44-49.

97. Margaret Gibson, "Lanfranc's 'Commentary on the Pauline Epistles,'" *Journal of Theological Studies* (n.s.) 22 (1971): 86-112.

98. Anselme Stoelen, "Les commentaires scripturaires attribués à Bruno le Chartreux," *Recherches de théologie ancienne et médiévale* 25 (1958): 177-247; and Anselme Stoelen, "Bruno

therefore, preceded (and followed) Laon's Standard Gloss. Indeed, other books, such as Gratian's canon law collection, the *Decretum,* were also glossed, including some in other languages such as Arabic.[99] Production of the Gloss continued with some variation for another hundred years. It enjoyed wide use after this period and through its early printed editions.[100]

At first glance, the Gloss likely strikes readers as overly busy at the expense of the Bible. "This little biblical text floating in its sea of gloss nearly drowns."[101] It consists of the biblical text printed in a larger hand and two glosses, or commentaries, in a smaller hand. The marginal gloss surrounds the biblical text and contains excerpts, some anonymous and some not, from earlier commentaries. The Gloss on the first chapter of Romans, for example, includes a strikingly large number of excerpts attributed by name to particular authors, including Ambrose (often Ambrosiaster), Augustine, Bede, Gregory the Great, Haimo of Auxerre, Hilary of Poitiers, Jerome, John of Damascus, and Origen. Most marginal glosses in the Romans commentary, indeed in the entire Gloss, remain anonymous. The other, the interlinear gloss, almost completely anonymous, appears between lines of the biblical text and briefly explains individual words and phrases.

The Gloss represents the culmination of centuries of exegesis and organization. It might appear derivative because it consists almost entirely of excerpts from earlier interpreters. Yet so much biblical interpretation is derivative in the sense that interpreters advance their analysis with the assistance of older resources and often in contrast to other interpreters with

---

le Chartreux, Jean Gratiadei et la 'Lettre de S. Anselme' sur l'eucharistie," *Recherches de théologie ancienne et médiévale* 34 (1967): 18-83. See also Artur Landgraf, "Probleme des Schriftums Brunos des Kartäusers," *Collectanea Franciscana* 8 (1938): 542-90.

99. Hermann Kantorowicz, "Note on the Development of the Gloss to the Justinian and the Canon Law," in Beryl Smalley, *The Study of the Bible in the Middle Ages* (Notre Dame: University of Notre Dame Press, 1964), 52-55.

100. The best available version of the Standard Gloss *(Glossa Ordinaria)* is Karlfried Froehlich and Margaret Gibson, *Biblia Latina cum Glossa Ordinaria,* Facsimile Reprint of the Editio Princeps Adolph Rusch of Strassborg 1480/81 (Turnhout: Brepols, 1992). The Gloss on Romans appears in vol. 4, pp. 273-306, and the Gloss on Romans 1 on pp. 273-77. For a discussion of different characteristics, including the complex layout of pages, in manuscripts of the Gloss as well as images of these manuscripts, see Christopher de Hamel, *Glossed Books of the Bible and the Origins of the Paris Book Trade* (Suffolk, Eng.: D. S. Brewer, 1984).

101. Stephen A. Barney, "Ordo paginis: The Gloss on Genesis 38," *South Atlantic Quarterly* 91 (1992): 940, cited in E. Ann Matter, "The Bible in the Center: The *Glossa Ordinaria,*" in *The Unbounded Community: Papers in Christian Ecumenism in Honor of Jaroslav Pelikan,* ed. William Caferro and Duncan G. Fisher (New York: Garland, 1996), 35.

whom they disagree. While not naming him, Saint Augustine, for example, drew on Origen (and many others) in developing his exegesis. The history of exegesis after Augustine through the Middle Ages and beyond involved the ongoing collection and refinement of resources from past eras. Scholars could then use these resources to read the Bible in light of new questions and so advance new interpretations.

Take, for example, the marginal gloss on a part of Romans 1:17, "the righteousness of God," that is identified as coming in part from Ambrose (in fact, Ambrosiaster). The Gloss edits out much of Ambrosiaster and so is about one third its predecessor's length. One thing it does not excise is Ambrosiaster's position that this verse contradicts Jews "who deny that Christ is the one whom God promised."[102] Including so little is an interpretive move; it places into stark relief this anti-Jewish claim. In another case, the Gloss turns to Ambrosiaster, without naming him, to make sense of Romans 9:15, "I will show mercy to whom I will, and I will have pity on whom I will." It does this even though Augustine is cited explicitly in the Romans Gloss as often as all other sources combined and even though Augustine importantly uses this verse to strike a blow at the human contribution to salvation. Ambrosiaster explains this verse, like the earlier Augustine, by saying that God foreknows conversion and persistence in the faith and therefore has mercy. Human action elicits God's proleptic mercy.[103] Thus authors of the Gloss select and, in so doing, interpret. It comes across as more anti-Jewish in Romans 1:17 and more optimistic about the human person in Romans 9:15.

The Gloss is also a paradigm of organization; its subsequent users owe a debt of gratitude to the generations of copyists who developed and perfected its arrangement. The "continuous commentary," which would grow increasingly important and is represented by the translations in this volume, did not include the biblical text and so did not need to arrange interpretation in proximity to the text interpreted; it could therefore be much more flexible. It could spill over from one page to the next and be easily updated. The Gloss, in contrast, needed just the right amount of biblical text so that the page could accommodate it along with its marginal and interlinear glosses; revisions were therefore much more difficult. "The *Glossa Ordinaria*

---

102. Ambrosiaster, *Commentaries on Romans and 1-2 Corinthians,* 9; *Biblia Latina cum Glossa Ordinaria,* 275.

103. Ambrosiaster, *Commentaries on Romans and 1-2 Corinthians,* 77; Augustine, *To Simplician,* 2.9-11, in *Responses to Miscellaneous Questions,* 192-94; *Biblia Latina cum Glossa Ordinaria,* 294.

. . . was static: the same indispensable work of reference in every good library. . . . [It] remained available and consulted, but essentially unchanged, until well into the fifteenth century."[104]

In response to the worry that the Gloss's interpretation would eclipse the biblical text, two responses are possible. First, it doesn't differ much from contemporary textual arrangements. Indeed, the Gloss resembles web pages that have central content surrounded by frames of links and advertisements. Or consider contemporary Bibles. Some Jewish Bibles include the biblical text nestled within interpretations by the likes of the medieval exegete Rashi. Even Christian Bibles include more than biblical text. In addition to it, they often include chapter and verse numbers, punctuation, word spacing, section divisions and titles, footnotes, and cross-references, none of which was available in original biblical manuscripts. As noted above, compared to other biblical commentaries that cite isolated words or phrases, the Gloss contains the entire biblical text; it practically lifts it up in celebration. It also functions as a foil. The marginal and interlinear glosses — collections of disjointed texts — do not themselves form a narrative but, in contrast, highlight and enhance the Bible's narrative.[105]

One might even say that the Gloss functions as an often hidden foundation for the commentaries translated in this volume. Citing it occasionally, the commentators rely on it even more than they are willing to admit, except for the latest commentator in this volume, Nicholas of Lyra, whose commentary would eventually be appended to the Gloss. At this point we can look at each of the commentators who have been selected for this volume, moving in chronological order, beginning in the ninth century and concluding in the fourteenth.[106]

The Anonymous Commentator of Mont Saint-Michel

In 1995 Gérard de Martel published a set of Pauline commentaries that originated in the Abbey of Mont Saint-Michel. Although the manuscript (Avranches 79) dates to the first part of the eleventh century, it seems that

104. Margaret Gibson, "The Place of the *Glossa Ordinaria* in Medieval Exegesis," in *Ad Litteram: Authoritative Texts and Their Medieval Readers,* ed. Mark D. Jordan and Kent Emery Jr. (Notre Dame: University of Notre Dame Press, 1992), 21.

105. Matter, "The Bible in the Center," 37.

106. Note that the commentaries themselves follow the order of the chapters in Romans and thus do not necessarily follow in chronological order.

the author was most likely an Irishman writing in the middle of the ninth century. As was typical of the Carolingian period, this author is heavily reliant upon patristic sources, which form the bulk of his commentary. Yet he tends to employ just a few in a given work, depending upon which sources he deems most useful to explicate the epistle. In the case of Romans, this commentator draws deeply on Origen, but also makes use of Augustine, Ambrosiaster, and Pelagius. Such reliance upon the Fathers does not thereby render his commentaries stolid and derivative repetitions. Despite specific reference to his own work as a "collection" in which he will gather the "little flowers of the fathers," he does not simply copy large passages verbatim in the manner of fellow Carolingian Rabanus Maurus. Rather, he fluidly weaves together his different sources, some of which he cites explicitly and some of which he has culled from earlier compilations (or *florilegia*, as they are known). With regard to his biblical text, it appears that he employs the Vulgate primarily, although he remains conscious of textual variants and frequently alerts the reader to alternative versions with phrases such as "or as other codices have it. . . ."[107]

The commentator does not offer a lengthy introduction to Paul the Apostle and his corpus of epistles, nor does he provide a substantial prologue to Romans itself. Yet we can learn something of his larger vision from his comments on the opening verses of this epistle. Here the commentator describes the gospel that had been promised beforehand in rather comprehensive terms. It comprises the incarnation, passion, resurrection, and ascension of Christ (CCCM 151:5). So, too, the righteousness of God (Rom 1:17) and the grace of faith that operates through love (cf. Gal 5:6) had been veiled in the Old Testament now to be revealed in the gospel of Christ (CCCM 151:11).

Romans 14 is principally concerned with the manner in which the gospel manifests itself in the day-to-day life of the community. Specifically, it addresses dietary regulations; some in the community were very strict in their observances, while others believed that they were free to eat what they liked. Amid the dissension, the Apostle counsels forbearance on both sides. The anonymous commentator, drawing upon his patristic sources, first outlines the historical situation for his audience. He notes that in the time of apostolic preaching many were already strong in their faith and ate foods indif-

---

107. For a full analysis see the introduction to *Expositiones Pauli Epistolarum ad Romanos, Galatas et Ephesios*, ed. Gérard de Martel, CCCM 151 (Turnhout: Brepols, 1995), v-xxix.

ferently with a sound conscience. The weaker ones among the community abstained from meat and wine, however, for fear that they might unknowingly consume meat that had been sacrificed to idols. The key issue for the commentator is that neither side should judge the other. Yet he seems especially concerned for the so-called "weak" members of the community who were scandalized by the practices of the "strong." The weak are to be welcomed and supported in their weakness. They must not be judged unfaithful according to human opinions (CCCM 151:131). Indeed, the weak should not be despised, precisely because "God has welcomed them" (Rom 14:3). God has called the weak as well as the strong. All, therefore, are welcomed by God as long as they are called according to God's grace (CCCM 151:132).

This is not to say that the Apostle forbids Christians to pass judgment in all matters whatsoever. For the commentator notes that Paul did indeed call for judgment in the case of the man who took his own father's wife (1 Cor 5:1-5). It is in uncertain matters, however, that the Apostle calls for restraint and for leaving judgment to God alone (CCCM 151:133). True righteousness — one in which we do not judge others but instead love them — will be manifested in patience. Hence there will be peace in which quarreling is eliminated so that the relationship of brothers and sisters may be preserved, and a spiritual joy in which the righteous delight in the benefits of the Holy Spirit (CCCM 151:139). Weaving together the material of the Fathers almost seamlessly, this commentator provides a clear, straightforward exposition of the text that should prove quite accessible to the modern reader. From the Carolingian era we can now move into the twelfth century, which — as already noted — was a creative and productive period not only for biblical commentary but for the theological enterprise as a whole.

William of St. Thierry

The first of the twelfth-century commentators translated for this volume exemplifies the flowering of the contemplative exegesis of the cloister. William of St. Thierry, originally a Benedictine abbot, entered the more austere and newly founded Cistercian monastic order in 1135. Like others in his day, William was doubtless attracted to the Cistercians on account of their most illustrious and charismatic member, the theologian and mystic Bernard of Clairvaux (d. 1153), with whom he would go on to collaborate in opposition to the work on Romans by another figure translated for this volume, Peter Abelard. William likely composed his commentary on Romans shortly after his entrance into the order, thus around 1135-38, at the abbey of Signy, the place where he later died in 1148.[108] With monastic humility, William begins his commentary by admitting how many difficult questions in Romans exceed his competence. Hence he will rely upon the writings of the holy Fathers, most notably Saint Augustine, whose comments he may have known through the Carolingian collection of Florus of Lyons. Indeed, William assures the reader that his own Romans commentary will be all the more acceptable, precisely because it is not based on novelty and vain presumption, but rather upon the solid authority and scholarship of the great doctors of the Church. Augustine is not the only source; he will also draw upon Origen among other ancients, and even some more recent commentators, who, William assures us, have not transgressed the boundaries of the Fathers. Modesty aside, however, William is a wonderful Latin stylist, a master rhetorician, and an insightful theologian in his own right, who does not simply reproduce the comments of previous generations. Yet like his confrere Bernard, he remained wary of scholastic novelties, which reflect human pride more than the humility required to hear God's Word aright. Biblical commentary for William the Cistercian monk begins with meditation and bears fruit both in deeper contemplation and in effective preaching. Thus he tells us that the joy of contemplating God's grace and glory and the need that these things be preached have compelled him to write this commentary. Indeed, it is grace above all that William extols in his preface to the commentary — the grace by which we were predestined prior to our existence, by which we are justified, that accomplishes the good in us, and that is the source of all human merit. For William, nothing happens for the good in the life of the believer that is not the result of divine grace. And William is confident that the whole Catholic tradition attests to that central truth (CCCM 86:3-5).

The second chapter of Romans affords William the opportunity to ex-

---

108. The Latin critical edition is *Expositio super Epistolam ad Romanos,* CCCM 86, ed. Paul Verdeyen (Turnhout: Brepols, 1989). For a complete translation with introduction see *William of St. Thierry: Exposition on the Epistle to the Romans,* ed. and trans. John Baptist Hasbrouck and John D. Anderson (Kalamazoo, MI: Cistercian Publications, 1980). For a full-length study of William see Jean Déchanet, *William of St. Thierry: The Man and His Work,* trans. Richard Strachan (Spencer, MA: Cistercian Publications, 1972). For more on the Cistercian order and its theologians see C. H. Lawrence, *Medieval Monasticism* (London: Pearson, 2001), 172-98; Jean Leclercq, *The Love of Learning and the Desire for God: A Study of Monastic Culture,* trans. Catherine Misrahi (New York: Fordham University Press, 1982), esp. 191-235.

amine the need for grace itself and the impossibility of attaining righteousness by one's own best efforts. Commenting on Romans 2:5 and the wrath
that is stored up for those who do not repent, William proves a keen ob-
server of human psychology. For he identifies two kinds of people who sin
obstinately. There are the overly confident who promise themselves God's
mercy and those who are driven to despair when they reflect upon the enormity of their own evil deeds. For those who presume upon divine mercy and
thus gamble with delays, God leaves the last day uncertain. For those in danger of lapsing into despair, however, God has made that day a haven of kindness (CCCM 86:29).

William does not mitigate the genuine possibility of condemnation;
indeed, it would cheapen grace if he did. The Cistercian monk threw himself
upon the grace of God, precisely because eternal judgment was a reality ever
present before his eyes. William assures his reader that on the day of judgment everyone will have to face whatever they had stored up for themselves.
Yet God is a discerning judge, aware of human frailty, and thus will take notice not so much of one's ability as one's will. We can only hope that venial
sins do not prevent an otherwise righteous person from attaining eternal
bliss, since this life is hardly ever free of such sins. God is merciful, but William cautions against the danger of human presumption. When the
wretched hear of eternal fire, they promise themselves purgatory, which they
imagine will be their salvation. "O the hope of those who are desperate!"
One may be saved by fire, William admits, but only insofar as one still values
Christ above all carnal delights (CCCM 86:29-30).

William's strict account of judgment day is rooted not in a bleak view
of the human person, but actually in a rather positive one. The human person, albeit by the grace of God, retains a certain level of dignity after the Fall.
Even when blinded by lust, says William, every rational soul can still reason.
Such truth as shines upon its reasoning should not be attributed to itself,
however, but to the divine light of truth by which the soul manages to find
the truth even in its weakened state. In fact, says William, there is no soul,
however perverse and yet able to reason, in whose conscience God does not
speak (CCCM 86:33).

Amid this talk of judgment and human sinfulness, we must not lose
sight of the fact that William wishes above all to extol God's grace. Hence he
reckons the Apostle Paul's discussion of the Law to be directed at the "enemies
of grace," whether Jew or gentile. William marks out four distinct levels of the
Law, and also progress in the Law, the point of which is to trace the movement
from sin to righteousness through the workings of God's grace and love. A

person at the lowest level lives according to the flesh in the deepest ignorance and with no resistance from reason. At the second level one is at least cognizant of sin through the Law. Yet apart from the assistance of the Holy Spirit, even as people wish to live according to the Law, they are overcome and sin knowingly. The third level brings hope, though, as God helps to fulfill what God commands. And even though we are not free from the prompting of the flesh, we have begun to be moved by God's Spirit with the more powerful strength of love. Something still fights against us even here, however, since all our infirmity has not yet been healed. Yet the righteous live by faith, and live righteously, as long as their delight in righteousness conquers and they do not submit to the evil of lust. If anyone prevails in these things with pious perseverance, then at the fourth and final level a peace remains that will be fulfilled after this life in the rest of the spirit and then in the resurrection of the flesh. In accord with Augustine, therefore, William will speak of these levels as prior to the Law, under the Law, under grace, and perfect peace (CCCM 86:35). From the monastic and contemplative world of William, we move now into the twelfth-century schools to introduce his adversary.

Peter Abelard

Peter Abelard (1079-1142) lived a rich life. He was a scholar associated with theology, philosophy, ethics, logic, and nominalism. He was a famed teacher whose lectures attracted crowds. He was a lover whose affair with Heloise produced a son, resulted in his castration, inspired letters, music, and poetry, and served as the basis for the autobiographical compilation of his calamities. He was a monk and abbot who would weather the attempts to have him condemned as a heretic. As Constant Mews writes, "For over eight hundred years, [Peter Abelard and Heloise] have functioned as mythic figures onto whom a variety of images and ideals have been projected relating to reason and authority, love and renunciation, wisdom and religion."[109] Thus posterity has celebrated and censured Abelard. He has been portrayed as reason's hero and a dangerous Pelagian. He (often along with Heloise) remains a popular culture reference today, having appeared in works by, among many others, Alexander Pope, Mark Twain, Helen Waddell, Cole Porter, Henry Miller, J. D. Salinger, Leonard Cohen, and Robertson Davies. He also wrote a commentary on Paul's Letter to the Romans.

---

109. Constant J. Mews, *Abelard and Heloise* (Oxford: Oxford University Press, 2005), 3.

As might be expected from such a rich background, Abelard wrote on a wide range of topics from scientific to theological to philosophical to musical to personal. Unlike most others in this volume, he published a limited number of biblical commentaries. He did not write on the entire Bible or even on the entire Pauline corpus. He left behind a commentary on the six days of creation in Genesis, penned in response to a request by Heloise, and a Romans commentary.

As if seeking to inoculate himself against the critique of Pelagianism that would be directed against him in response to his commentary on Romans, Abelard uses its prologue to highlight the significance of grace and diminish the role of works in salvation. It also offers a nuanced treatment of genre by contrasting the Gospels and the epistles. The former contain teachings. Though the latter also contain teachings, they primarily persuade readers to obey these evangelical teachings. Toward the end of the prologue he applies the dialectical method of juxtaposing different authorities initially to highlight apparently contradictory opinions and ultimately to resolve opinions about Paul's predecessors in Rome, a method that he will use throughout his commentary, that bears some resemblance to his method in *Sic et Non,* and that anticipates the scholastic method that would become more prevalent over the next century, especially with the publication of Peter Lombard's *Sentences.*

Likely written in the late 1130s, the commentary could be a compilation of Abelard's lectures on Romans. Modern editions rely on three manuscripts, two from the twelfth century and one from the fourteenth, and one main printed edition from the sixteenth century.[110] This work resembles other commentaries in that it treats the entire epistle verse by verse. It is attentive to grammar and the original language (272-73, 327). Throughout, it cites other books of the Bible and other biblical commentators. The most frequently cited author is Origen, but it recognizes that Origen's work comes down to us through his translator and intermediary Rufinus. Less frequently, it cites other Christian authors such as Gratian, and pre-Christian authors such as Plato and Aristotle.[111]

One of the most distinctive features of the commentary and one that

---

110. Steven R. Cartwright, "Introduction," in Peter Abelard, *Commentary on the Epistle to the Romans,* The Fathers of the Church Mediaeval Continuation 12 (Washington, DC: Catholic University of America Press, 2011), 6, 8, 14.

111. See Cartwright's indices to Abelard's *Commentary on the Epistle to the Romans,* 401-28.

figures significantly in Abelard's work on Romans 3 is the question, a form he holds in high esteem, as he indicates in the prologue to his *Sic et Non.*

> [C]onsistent or frequent questioning is defined as the first key to wisdom. Aristotle . . . urges us to grasp this wholeheartedly. . . . "[I]t will not be amiss to have doubts about individual points." For by doubting we come to enquiry, and by enquiry we perceive the truth. As the Truth Himself says: "Seek and you shall find, knock and it shall be opened to you" [Mt 7:7]. Christ gave us spiritual instructions by his own example when, at the age of about twelve, he sat and asked questions, and wanted to be found in the midst of the teachers, showing us the example of a pupil by his asking questions before he showed us that of a teacher by his preaching, even though God's wisdom is full and perfect.[112]

Abelard certainly puts this insight into practice throughout his *Commentary on Romans.* Already at the end of Romans 1, he pauses to ask three questions that take the biblical text as a starting point for in-depth theological reflection. Abelard does not answer these questions but enters into a dialogue with his other writings, to which he directs readers for more information. Many of the commentary's questions address God's justice. How could those not baptized be condemned? How loving is the withholding of saving grace from some? How just is predestination? He also wonders, should we love those already in hell and those condemned since "we want everyone to be saved and we [should] pray for everyone" (351)?

His use of the question form is particularly striking in the chapter translated for this volume and on the verse for which this commentary is most well known, Romans 3:26.[113] Actually, it is inaccurate to speak of one question. Abelard articulates twenty-three questions, one right after the

---

112. Peter Abelard, prologue to *Sic et Non,* in *Medieval Literary Theory and Criticism c. 1100-1375: The Commentary Tradition, Revised Edition,* ed. A. J. Minnis and A. B. Scott (Oxford: Clarendon, 1988), 99-100.

113. For a close reading of Abelard on the questions associated with Romans 3:26 by the initial translator of this chapter and co-editor of this series, see H. Lawrence Bond, "Another Look at Abelard's Commentary on Romans 3:26," in *Medieval Readings of Romans,* Romans through History and Culture, ed. William S. Campbell, Peter S. Hawkins, and Brenda Deen Schildgen (New York: T&T Clark, 2007), 11-32. For another recent treatment, see Thomas Williams, "Sin, Grace, and Redemption," in *The Cambridge Companion to Abelard,* ed. Jeffrey E. Brower and Kevin Guilfoy (Cambridge: Cambridge University Press, 2004), 258-78.

other, to try to understand why Christ had to die for us to be saved (to pay a ransom for humans whom the devil justly held in bondage?). To put it another way, what exactly did Christ's death accomplish? God could and, in fact, did save people in other ways — Jesus forgave several people's sins while he was still alive.

Unlike his initial questions in chapter 1, Abelard's questions here are given an answer, though brief. At the conclusion, he directs readers to his *Tropologia* (more likely *Anthropologia* — see the translation), which does not now exist, for a fuller response. The phrase in Abelard's response to his questions that has jumped out at readers through the ages is his claim that Christ redeemed us "by instructing us by word and example — *in ipsa nos tam verbo quam exemplo instituendo*" (21). If *instituendo* means simply teaching, then Abelard could be (and, indeed, has been) charged with exemplarism, that is, that Jesus was a person who set a good example and affected us subjectively but did not have an objective and transformative impact on humans. To make such a claim could diminish the greatness of Jesus' work. It could also diminish human need for grace to perform works worthy of salvation, thus opening Abelard up to the charge of Pelagianism.

Much else recommends this chapter. It discusses salvation for those who lived before Christ. So, what about the salvation of "Simeon, Anna, and the very mother of the Lord with her husband Joseph, as well as the father and mother of John the Baptist along with him"? It addresses the moral significance of intention, and it discusses love. We live in the "time of grace, in the time of love rather than of fear." "It is because of Christ himself that we are joined to him as closely as possible by an indissoluble bond of love." In fact, one of the results of Jesus' teaching (and reconstructing) us by word and example *(tam verbo quam exemplo)* is that we are "more fully bound . . . to God by love, such that we are so inflamed by such a great gift of divine grace."

As noted at the outset, Abelard lived a rich life. He wrote widely, taught many, and had friends in high places who would come in handy later in life. Yet he also angered people. These included Heloise's family who had him castrated, monks who eventually had him relieved of his duties as abbot, and theological opponents, including Bernard of Clairvaux and William of St. Thierry. Toward the end of his life, William wrote an extensive complaint against Abelard's positions that Bernard then abridged into his Letter 110, which contains nine lengthy sections. Among the concerns that Bernard expresses are the power the devil had over humans as a result of sin, God's justice versus God's mercy, the means Christ could have used and did use to redeem humans, and whether redemption was effected by Jesus' teaching by word and example, precisely the issues that Abelard addresses in his commentary on Romans 3.

As a result of the encounter between Bernard and Abelard in 1140 in Sens, France, Abelard was condemned. But because of the friendship of the Abbot of Cluny, Abelard was protected from this final humiliation and died in 1142.

Abelard continues to excite similar passions today. It is crucial, therefore, to understand what he says in his commentary on Romans 3 so that an accurate assessment can be made of his thought. Therefore, a careful reading of Abelard on Romans 3 will be well repaid.

Peter Lombard

Peter Lombard (d. 1160), the Parisian theologian best known for his great work of systematic theology, the *Sentences,* made a major contribution to the medieval exegetical tradition when he expanded upon the Psalter and epistles commentaries found in the Standard Gloss *(Glossa Ordinaria).* The Lombard's Great Gloss *(Magna Glossatura)* on the Pauline epistles, also known as the *Collectanea,* proved to be a mainstay for centuries to come and was frequently appealed to by the thirteenth- and fourteenth-century exegetes translated for this volume. Indeed, Thomas Aquinas, Peter of John Olivi, and Nicholas of Lyra were in continual dialogue with the Lombard, who belonged to the Abelardian school that produced such illustrious figures as Robert of Melun,[114] along with the anonymous Cambridge Commentator, whose work has been translated for this volume.

Translated for this volume is his rather substantial preface to the Pauline epistles. For more on the Lombard as a Pauline commentator, see the Galatians volume of this same series.[115] As noted there, Peter Lombard provides us with a fine example of the medieval *accessus ad auctorem,* that is to say, a contextual introduction to a biblical author. As the Lombard writes at the opening of his preface: "To understand things more fully, one should

114. For a complete translation of Robert of Melun's *Questions on Galatians,* see Levy, *The Letter to the Galatians,* 207-13. See also the introduction to Robert in the same volume, 56-57.

115. For a partial translation of Peter Lombard's Galatians commentary see Levy, *The Letter to the Galatians,* 185-206. See also the introduction to Peter Lombard in the same volume, 52-55.·

first seek their beginnings. For only then can one more easily give an account of the purpose of something having learned its origin" (PL 191:1297a). The Lombard therefore situates the Apostle's letters within both a literary and a historical milieu. The preface is not composed of entirely original material; some of it is drawn directly from Pelagius's own introduction to the epistles, and some depends on the Carolingian exegete Haimo of Auxerre. But sheer originality is not the Lombard's goal. Rather, he wants to offer the reader a concise overview that will render the texts more readily comprehensible. Therein lies his genius; he is able to arrange and classify his material in clear scholastic fashion. The Lombard will methodically explain what makes the Apostle Paul a unique author, why he wrote fourteen letters, and the rationale for their order in the biblical canon. Finally, the Lombard draws the preface to a close with an analysis of the internal structure of Romans that reveals Paul's purposes for writing to this fractious community.

The Cambridge Commentary

The Cambridge Commentary *(Commentarius Cantabrigiensis)* is an anonymous commentary on the Pauline epistles discovered by Artur Landgraf in a single manuscript belonging to Trinity College Cambridge (MS B I 39). Although the work cannot be dated precisely, it seems to have been written no later than 1152 and probably closer to 1141. Landgraf came to identify the author as a member of the twelfth-century school of Peter Abelard. For not only does it refer directly to Abelard himself, but its principal concerns and general theological tone closely resemble those of other members of that school, such as Peter Lombard and Robert of Melun.[116] This will be evident in the material translated for the present volume, and such correlations will be cited in the accompanying notes. If one mark of the Abelardian school stands out the most, it is the emphasis placed upon the internal disposition of the human person as the ultimate locus of righteousness before God.

The Cambridge Commentary begins with a prologue to Romans that attempts to fit the Pauline epistles as a whole into the larger plan of the biblical canon before offering more specific remarks about Romans itself. The prologue is quite similar in places to Robert of Melun's prologue to his own

---

116. *Commentarius Cantabrigiensis in Epistolas Pauli e Schola Petri Abaelardi*, vol. 1, ed. Artur Landgraf (Notre Dame, IN: University of Notre Dame Press, 1939), v-xlii. The text will be cited in parentheses as follows: CC.

"Questions" on the epistles. And, not surprisingly for the time, one also finds material drawn from Pelagius's Romans prologue, although cited — as was customary — under the name of Saint Jerome. The Cambridge prologue is worth looking at in some detail as a (among others) medieval introduction to a biblical book. This prologue begins with a broad view of biblical studies. Just as the entire universe was created to serve the human race, and human beings to serve God, so all the liberal arts are meant to assist in the grander study of Holy Scripture. Grammar, dialectic, and rhetoric (the trivium) chiefly, but also the arts that comprise the quadrivium, are attendants of the discipline of theology. It is along these lines, already mapped out in Saint Augustine's *De doctrina christiana,* that the Commentary extols the benefits to be gleaned from the ancient philosophical and poetical works. For no matter the original intention of their authors, the Holy Spirit had all along determined to direct them to the greater purpose of serving Scripture (CC 1).[117]

Delving into Scripture more specifically, the Commentary observes that both the Old and the New Testaments intend to teach, and to influence behavior, with the aid of rhetorical methods. It soon becomes clear that its treatment of the two Testaments has substantial bearing on the meaning of the Epistle to the Romans. The Old Testament can be divided into the Law, Prophets, and Histories. The principal function of the Law is to teach what must be done and to prohibit what must not be done. The Prophets and Histories, however, seek to influence human attitudes toward such obligations. They are additions to the Law designed to entice believers into a willing observance of what the Law commands. One could say that the Prophets and Histories were added to the Law to remedy what the Commentary takes to be a central deficiency in the Law itself. It could not lead people to perfection, for it contains nothing about loving one's enemy. This is not to say that the Law was wrong, but merely incomplete in its instruction. Hence one had to wait for Christ, who came not to destroy the Law but to fulfill it when he declared, "Love your enemy" (Mt 5:44) (CC 1-2).

The New Testament comprises the Gospels, epistles, Acts of the Apostles, and Apocalypse. The Gospels, whose function is to teach, take the place of the Law. Although it does move people by example on occasion, that is

---

117. See Robert of Melun, *Oeuvres de Robert de Melun,* vol. 2: *"Questiones Theologicae de Epistolis Pauli,"* ed. Raymond Martin (Louvain: Spicilegium Sacrum Louvaniense, 1938), 1-7. See also *Pelagius's Expositions of Thirteen Epistles of St. Paul,* vol. 2, ed. Alexander Souter (Cambridge: Cambridge University Press, 1926), 3-7.

not its primary purpose. The epistles and Apocalypse deal with promises concerning the final days, while Acts offers numerous examples of good conduct. The central goal of these latter three sets of books is to entice people into observing the evangelical precepts. Given the sufficiency of the Gospels, providing as they do all necessary instruction, one may wonder what need there is for the epistles. Drawing on the analogy of a city, the Commentary notes that the precepts laid down by Christ in the Gospels can be compared to fortifications that keep a city secure. They are essential; there is no salvation apart from obedience to these precepts. The epistles, on the other hand, provide ornamentation in the form of counsels, which inspire believers to fulfill the evangelical precepts. Helpful as they are, obedience to these counsels is not strictly necessary for salvation. An example of such counsels, therefore, would include Paul's teaching on marriage and virginity (1 Cor 7:12-31) (CC 2-3). While all the epistles are intended to influence behavior, each epistle has its own specific subject matter. In the case of Romans, it is the bitter dispute between Jewish and gentile believers in that city's church. In order to resolve this tense situation, therefore, the Apostle Paul sets out to undercut claims of human merit while extolling divine grace (CC 3-4).

At the very outset of chapter 1, when addressing Paul's greeting to the Romans, the Commentator displays his knowledge of classical rhetoric generally, and the art of letter writing *(ars dictaminis)* specifically. Such attention to style is indicative of the practice that had taken hold by the twelfth century of deliberately treating Paul as an author *(auctor)* and his epistles as precisely crafted literary productions. Hence the Commentator notes that it is the custom of letter writers to begin with a greeting where they show their affection for the recipients and thereby pave the way for an exhortation to good conduct. One begins an oration in this way, therefore, in order to render the audience at once attentive and well disposed to what will follow (CC 6). What is more, by demonstrating his affection for the Romans, Paul can draw them closer to himself on a personal level. Thus when he begins to rebuke them severely, they will see that he does so out of love. In this vein, Paul is also likened to the wise physician who first applies a soothing balm to the wound before gradually adding the more bitter medication (CC 14). All of this is consistent with Paul's overall apostolic commission, which consists in stirring the Romans to the obedience of faith (Rom 1:5) through his preaching so that they willingly submit themselves to what must be believed about God (CC 13).

Larger issues of Christology soon come to the fore when the Apostle states that Jesus Christ "was made . . . according to the flesh" (Rom 1:3). The

Commentator observes that, although one can say that the Son of God was "made" with regard to his human nature, and is therefore less than his Father in that regard, he is still fully equal to the Father with respect to his divine nature. To say he was made with regard to his human nature, therefore, is a way of saying that the Word united that human nature to his singular divine Person (CC 10). And so, when Paul speaks of Christ being "predestined . . . according to the spirit" (Rom 1:4), one attributes such predestination to the human nature rather than the divine Word (CC 11).

There was much discussion in the twelfth century regarding the precise language that could be employed concerning the filial relationship of the human nature to the divine nature. Given its complexity, we cannot enter into a full discussion of that topic.[118] Note, however, that the Commentator blithely employs the term "assumed human being" *(homo assumptus),* which loomed large in the Christological controversies of the day: "One might ask whether that assumed human being is the Son of God through nature, through adoption, or through grace." The Commentator ruled out the first option since that would presuppose the existence of some human being prior to his adoption by God. Nor, however, can he be the Son of God through nature since, with respect to his humanity, he is not of the same substance as the Father. Thus he must be Son of God through grace, since all that he had was acquired by grace (CC 12).

Such Christological questions — important as they surely are — remained at a more speculative level than more mundane concerns that the Commentator also addressed. Medieval society was held together to a great extent by the swearing of oaths in different contexts: feudal allegiances, judicial proceedings, and religious vows. Now the Apostle Paul had invoked God as his witness (Rom 1:9) when proclaiming his own fidelity. Thus it would seem that Paul is swearing an oath in this instance. But had not Christ himself forbidden the swearing of oaths (Mt 5:33-37)? Here one must ask whether the Apostle thereby contradicted the teaching of Christ. The answer to this question, however, is not merely an apparent scriptural conundrum to be solved. It is a matter of concern for people throughout twelfth-century Europe. Are they themselves permitted to swear oaths or not? The Commentator concludes that Christ never intended to forbid all oath swearing,

---

118. For analysis of these questions see Marcia Colish, *Peter Lombard,* 2 vols. (Leiden: Brill, 1994), 426-29. See also Philipp W. Rosemann, *Peter Lombard* (Oxford: Oxford University Press, 2004), 128-30; Richard Cross, *The Metaphysics of the Incarnation* (Oxford: Oxford University Press, 2002), 31-32, 240-41.

but only warned that one must not actively desire to swear an oath. The reason for this is that oath swearing is an inherently risky enterprise. There is the danger of perjuring oneself or somehow failing to accomplish what one had vowed. Hence the oath should be sworn only in matters of necessity when some greater good makes it worth such a risk (CC 15).

More specific to the immediate scholastic world of the Commentator is the legitimacy of applying logical analysis to biblical texts. The Commentator's teacher, Peter Abelard, had been attacked by the great Cistercian monks, Bernard of Clairvaux and William of St. Thierry, for supposedly subjecting the mysteries of faith to the tests of human reason. Thus when the Apostle Paul says that he is "not ashamed of the gospel" (Rom 1:16), the Commentator explains that some people are ashamed even today when they find themselves incapable of presenting good arguments on behalf of the Catholic faith. These people claim that the faith must not be examined, and in their own defense they invoke Saint Gregory the Great's remark that faith has no merit in matters that human reason can grasp through experience. In other words, some things just have to be taken on faith without any rational argumentation to support them. The Commentator finds that such an attitude runs contrary to the very example of Saint Paul himself. No one would have accepted Paul's proclamation of Christ's resurrection from the dead if he had been unable to offer a coherent and reasonable defense for it (CC 18).

Such confidence in human reason — at the service of faith and not at the expense of it — is also borne out in a discussion of what can be known about God apart from divine revelation. The Commentator contends that the ancient philosophers living prior to Christ could have recognized God not only in unity but even as a Trinity of Persons. It must be admitted, however, that they could not have reasoned their way to the incarnation of the Word. Much can be known of God through an examination of the great work of creation itself. As the greatest of all artisans, the invisible God was known by philosophers through that masterpiece that is the world. The philosophers, according to the Commentator, had discerned God's supreme craftsmanship in the world's great beauty and harmonious order. And seeing how God arranged all things so fittingly to human advantage, they came to recognize God as supremely kind. What is more, however, the Apostle implies that the philosophers not only understood the distinction of Trinitarian Persons, but even their procession, such that three different things could be shown to subsist in one reality (CC 21-23).

Yet for all that might have been known about God, Paul will still make the case that Jews and gentiles are altogether inexcusable. Neither people can reckon anything to their own merits, but instead must ascribe everything to divine grace. Both groups stand condemned, therefore, but on different charges. According to the Commentator, Jews are ungodly, whereas gentiles are unrighteous (Rom 1:18). To be ungodly, however, is more than being unrighteous. This distinction pertains to one's intentions. Properly speaking, the ungodly person is someone who knowingly acts against God. So defined, the Commentator concludes that Jews, with their superior knowledge of the divine will, were reckoned guilty under both the written Law of Moses and natural law. The gentiles, while not ungodly, were still unrighteous as they sinned only against natural law, which is common to all humankind (CC 21).

If both Jew and gentile stand condemned, it remains to be seen how anyone is saved. According to the Commentator, the gospel is the "power of God" (Rom 1:16) through which God justifies the human person. Here he plays on the Latin word *virtus,* which can mean both "power" and "virtue," which is itself a certain moral power that enables one to live uprightly. The gospel can be called "power" *(virtus)* because, just as virtues *(virtutes)* make one righteous, so the gospel instructs believers in all things necessary for salvation. Hence, in keeping with what he said in his prologue, the gospel constitutes a separate teaching apart from the Law as it has revealed to humankind the way to perfection. "The power of salvation," therefore, means justification for all who accept this gospel teaching and find comfort in it (CC 19).

According to the Commentator, "the righteousness of God" (Rom 1:17) refers to God's just recompense, whether for punishment or for glory. Yet the principles of God's remuneration are not based on someone's works, but on someone's will. This marks the crucial difference between Law and gospel. The criterion of righteousness before God is not based on exterior works, but on interior disposition (CC 19-20). The Commentator will have more to say about this in later chapters, where he again contends that the chief deficiency of the Old Law was its inability to lead anyone to moral perfection because it was wholly concerned with exterior actions. The Law simply commanded, "Do not kill," but the person living by the gospel knows that one must not even wish to kill. This, in turn, is what it means to live by faith, and therefore be justified by faith; it means conforming one's will — not just one's actions — to Christ. In genuine Abelardian fashion, the Commentator concludes that God will judge all people on the basis of their interior selves, what they intended in their hearts, no matter whether they actually refrained from murder or theft (CC 36-37). No doubt God is pleased by good works, but only those works that arise from a good will *(voluntas)* (CC 55-

56). One cannot draw a crude distinction between works and faith under this system. All Christians are called to do good deeds and live holy lives. It should be remembered that the moral law remains in force even as the ceremonial law has reached its conclusion. The real contrast, therefore, is between exterior works demanded by the Law, on the one hand, and, on the other, a deeper interior disposition constituted by faith in Christ. God's judgment will turn on whether one has replaced reliance upon exterior dictates of the old legal code with a renewed heart conformed to Christ in love. For to believe in Christ is to love Christ; and by loving Christ to direct one's life in his service, and so be incorporated into his body as a living member. Thus, for the Commentator, to be justified by grace is to be justified by the love of Christ infused into one's heart (CC 38-46).

Thomas Aquinas

The scholastic method that was pioneered in the twelfth century came to fruition by the middle of the thirteenth century with the rise of the university and the full assimilation of Aristotelian philosophy. The Dominican friar Thomas Aquinas (ca. 1225-74) was one of the leading schoolmen of his era. He is best known for his comprehensive works of theology — the *Summa theologiae* and *Summa contra Gentiles* — and for his philosophical commentaries, particularly on Aristotle. Yet he also wrote in other genres, such as prayers, sermons, letters, and biblical commentaries. Although these texts have received less scholarly attention than his theological and philosophical texts, they comprise an important share of his life's work. For example, he lectured and preached on Scripture until the end of his life. His commentary on Romans — the *Lectura super Epistolam ad Romanos* or *Ad Romanos* for short — falls into the latter category.[119] It represents one section within his larger project devoted to the entire Pauline corpus, which, for Thomas, begins with Romans and concludes with Hebrews.[120]

His commentaries on most of the Pauline letters come down to us as

119. Thomas Aquinas, *Super Epistolas S. Pauli Lectura,* ed. Raphael Cai (Turin: Marietti, 1953). References to this work will be by way of page numbers in this edition.

120. Thomas recognizes that questions about the authorship of Hebrews date back to antiquity. He concludes the preface to his commentary on Hebrews with a scholastic question that outlines two arguments or objections against its Pauline authorship. He continues with his general argument in favor — theologians of old, such as Pseudo-Dionysius and Jerome, both took these words to be Paul's. He concludes with replies to each of the two arguments.

secretarial records, known in Latin as *"reportationes,"* of his lectures on particular books. His work on the first eight chapters of Romans is classified as a *"correctio,"* which means that he returned and reworked the report of his lectures on Romans.[121] This, combined with the fact that the Romans commentary appears toward the end of Thomas's life, means that it lends important insights into his mature thought.

A comparison of his biblical commentaries with his more well-known theological works repays the attentive reader. The biblical commentaries share many of the structural features found in the *Summa theologiae,* such as careful organization. As in the *Summa,* the Pauline commentaries begin with a preface that sets out the direction of the entire work, which (as noted above) Thomas sees as a whole whose order is intentional and has meaning. In the preface to his Pauline commentaries, Thomas indicates that the theme of all the letters is grace. Subsequent epistles, and Thomas's treatment of them, examine different aspects of grace. Throughout his reading of Paul and, indeed, in all his biblical commentaries, Thomas uses textual division *(divisio textus),* a highly schematized approach to biblical interpretation, to organize his work based on the biblical text under study and to introduce the issues that he will address later on.[122]

Returning to the *Summa theologiae,* its preface indicates that it is directed by the "order of the [theological] subject matter" under consideration. This subject matter is then explicated, much as would have been done by the master *(magister)* in the classroom as he responded to a set of objections and offered a magisterial resolution of the issue. The biblical commentary, however, is largely driven by the biblical text itself. Having introduced in his preface to the epistles the general exegetical path he will take, and having gestured at the beginning of the Romans commentary toward the moves he will make there, he proceeds to work methodically through his plan chapter by chapter, verse by verse, and often word by word. Thomas does, however, draw on the article format so familiar to readers of the *Summa theologiae* to address questions that need development beyond the space normally allotted to a word or verse. For example, on Romans 12:14, which admonishes against cursing, Thomas points out the odd fact that curses are

---

121. For a brief catalogue of Thomas's biblical commentaries, see Jean Pierre Torrell, *Saint Thomas Aquinas: The Person and His Work,* trans. R. Royal (Washington, DC: Catholic University of America Press, 1996), 337-41.

122. For a discussion of Thomas's use of *divisio textus* in his commentary on the Psalms, see Thomas F. Ryan, *Thomas Aquinas as Reader of the Psalms* (Notre Dame: University of Notre Dame Press, 2000), 20-28.

found elsewhere in Scripture. "But on the other hand *(sed contra),* Scripture seems to contain many curses" (so why would Paul forbid them?) (185). As he often does in the *Summa,* he supplies an irenic response by drawing careful distinctions among different kinds of cursing and indicating that some are appropriate, some not.

The Pauline commentaries also embody a principle Thomas asserts in the *Summa's* first question, where he compares the value of the different kinds of authority that theology can draw upon. The most important authority is that of Holy Scripture since it consists of the "revelation made to the apostles and prophets" (ST I.1.8 ad 2). Many articles in the *Summa,* however, do not cite Scripture, but instead appeal to the least effective authority, that of the philosophers, which is "external and only probable." Some articles would lead one to believe that Thomas has forgotten this dictum or has little knowledge of or use for Scripture. This is not the case. For in his biblical commentaries, he comments on every verse of a given book and draws on passages from other biblical books in explicating the book under consideration. For example, he offers eight scriptural citations in his explanation of the passage from Romans 12:2 that reads, "Do not be conformed to this age, but be transformed in the renewal of your understanding" (cf. 179). This practice of scriptural citation shows that Thomas possesses a solid facility with Scripture.

It also suggests a belief that one passage in Scripture can illuminate another, since both are the Word of God. Some modern readers of the Bible could well characterize this as a naive canonical criticism. In other places, however, he displays what could be taken for more modern sensibilities. He does so where he makes historical claims about the demographics in the city of Rome when commenting on Romans 7:1 (95). He also recognizes the significance of languages for biblical interpretation when he notes the Hebrew, Greek, and Latin words for "father" in his reflections on Romans 8:15 (117). He reveals his grasp of matters grammatical in his reading of Romans 8:30 (127-28). In his interpretation of Romans 7:23 (106) and Romans 12:11 (183), he recognizes the importance of textual criticism in his acknowledgment that different Bibles offer different versions of the Letter to the Romans. Finally, in his remarks on Romans 7:8, Thomas articulates a basic hermeneutical principle; he prefers simpler to forced interpretations (99).

Besides offering insights into Thomas's approach to Scripture, the Romans commentary treats key theological issues from within a scriptural context. Thus, as Thomas indicates in his preface, the theme of the entire Pauline corpus is grace. The theme of Romans is grace in and of itself; other epistles address its different aspects. The question of grace raises the further question of human freedom that, Thomas acknowledges, sparked the Pelagian and other controversies (see his reading of Rom 7:18 in 104). On Romans 8:14-15, which speaks of the works of the Spirit, Thomas attempts to reconcile the necessity and priority of grace with an affirmation of human freedom (cf. 116-17). The word "led" in "led by the Spirit of God" (Rom 8:14) seems to imply a kind of servility and a denial of autonomy. To be sure, this verse applies to humans in terms of grace. Humans are led by the Spirit and do depend on grace. Yet Thomas depicts the Spirit's leadership as nuanced. It does not so much demand as persuade; it "illuminates us inwardly" and "moves hearts." Later he argues that the Spirit does incline humans to act, but as humans should, "by will and free choice." In this way, Thomas holds out for the necessity and priority of grace, which, at the same time, enables humans to act freely.

This same section occasions a lengthy reflection on fear, similar to what appears in *Summa theologiae* (II-II.19) on the gift of fear in which Romans 8:15 plays a confirmatory role. In the commentary this verse is the impetus that moves Thomas to distinguish different kinds of fear, most of which are instigated by aversion to punishment. One type, however, has love as its catalyst and relates to God in love and out of fear simply of separation from God. This is spiritual fear.

Elsewhere in the Romans commentary Thomas reveals a pastoral and affective side not always noticed in his better-known theological and philosophical works. For example, he acknowledges the human condition of suffering in his reading of Romans 8:22, which speaks of all creation as groaning and in labor. Humans suffer the delay of "anticipated glory." Thomas includes himself through his use of the first-person plural when he states that "not only the patriarchs who were before Christ but even we in the time of grace still suffer" (121-22). Yet we receive a foretaste of what is to come. "'The Spirit assists us in our frailty' (Rom 8:26), even if the Spirit does not remove it entirely" (123).

This last statement suggests a stance of hopeful anticipation. Indeed, the virtue of hope surfaces periodically in the comments translated in this volume. Thomas agrees with the Apostle Paul that "we are saved by hope" (Rom 8:24, 123). He addresses hope in his reading of Romans 12:11-12, which contains six exhortations that are interpreted as six different ways that love relates to God (183-84). The fourth way is through hope. "Hope causes a person to rejoice because of certitude, yet it afflicts because of delay. Proverbs 13:12, 'Hope deferred afflicts the soul'" (184).

The sixth way that love relates to God is through prayer, and Romans 12:12 elicits a lengthy and Scripture-laden reflection on prayer. We should persevere

> "in prayer," by which [Paul] means constancy in prayer. Luke 18:1, "We should pray always, and not grow weary." 1 Thessalonians 5:17, "Pray without ceasing." Through prayer, care is stirred up in us; fervor is enkindled; we are urged to serve God; the joy of hope is strengthened in us; and we are promised help in our tribulation. Psalm 119:1/120:1, "I called to the Lord in my tribulation, and the Lord heard me." (184)

Another passage, Romans 8:38-39, prompts an emotional, almost mystical reflection on the human relationship to the divine when Thomas characterizes at length Paul as Christ's lover.

> Paul's point, according to Chrysostom in his book *On the Heart's Compunction,* is not that angels could at some time try to separate him from Christ, but he held that even those things that are impossible would be more possible, so to speak, than that he could be separated from the love of Christ. By this he showed how great the power of divine charity was in him, and he revealed it for all to see. For it is the custom of lovers that they cannot conceal their love in silence but assert and proclaim it necessarily and loudly, and they cannot restrain its flames within their breast. They speak of it more frequently so that in the very persistence of telling of their love, they receive comfort and the cooling of this immense ardor. Hence this blessed and distinguished lover of Christ causes all the things that are and that will be, whatever can happen, and whatever can in no way happen, to be encompassed all together in one word. (131)

Though this excerpt speaks of Paul, it recalls a similar incident in Thomas's own life captured in the fifteenth-century Sienese Arte della Lana altarpiece by Sassetta for the annual celebration of the feast of Corpus Christi, whose liturgical office Thomas composed. The *Vision of Thomas Aquinas* depicts the crucified Christ informing a praying Thomas that he had written well of him and asking the saint what reward he would like in return. In response to Christ's request, Thomas answered, *"Nihil nisi te,"* the motto of the Blackfriars' edition of the *Summa theologiae,* "Nothing but you."

In conclusion, Thomas's biblical commentaries reflect his ongoing work as a biblical lecturer and preacher. They present his thinking on important theological topics grounded in biblical interpretation. They also reveal the deep spirituality of this important figure in the history of theology, a characteristic of this medieval saint that is often overlooked because of the attention directed to his more philosophical and speculative work. As we have seen, this side of him was important to him and to his early followers, and repays careful study today.

Peter of John Olivi

Mendicant theologians had come to dominate biblical exegesis by the latter part of the thirteenth century, teaching and writing for their orders at the universities and in the various study houses established throughout Europe. Peter of John Olivi (1247/48-98) joined the Franciscans around 1260 at a time when the order was experiencing significant turmoil within its ranks regarding the proper observation of evangelical poverty. His confrere, Saint Bonaventure, had been elected minister general of the order only a few years before in 1257, in the hopes that he might be able to stabilize an increasingly chaotic situation. Olivi became embroiled in these disputes over evangelical poverty, which were in turn connected to apocalyptic prophecies wherein a remnant of faithful adherents to the life and teachings of Saint Francis would be persecuted by powerful apostatizing forces within the order itself and the wider Church. As it was, Olivi found himself under suspicion throughout a good portion of his career owing to his views on issues ranging from philosophical questions to the mendicant life and biblical interpretation. Two of his most significant works of biblical exegesis, and indeed most controversial, were commentaries on the Gospel of Matthew and on the Apocalypse. In fact, his Apocalypse commentary, composed in 1298, was condemned at the Franciscan general chapter meeting of 1299 in Lyons and then later by Pope John XXII in 1326. For Olivi the Apocalypse revealed the decay in the Church, including corruption, heresy, and the use of Aristotle in the schools mediated by Islam. Above all, perhaps, this decay was marked by the Franciscan order's rejection of genuine poverty whereby the brothers would use material goods in only the most modest fashion — so-called "poor use" *(usus pauper)*. His time was also the time of antichrists. In fact, Olivi prophesied that the Church would produce a pseudo-pope who, with the secular authorities, would persecute those who wished to follow evangelical poverty.

He gave Saint Francis and poverty eschatological roles that rivaled the significance of the papacy, if not Christ himself.[123]

His commentaries on the Pauline epistles, however, did not seem to stir such controversy. Actually, the only extant works we have include fragments of a commentary on 1 Corinthians and a complete, albeit succinct, commentary on Romans. Olivi did compose an extensive prologue to the epistles, however, which will be discussed below. When precisely he wrote his Romans commentary is not certain, but it appears to be a product of his later career. Olivi relies throughout on Peter Lombard's Romans commentary *(Collectanea)*, which — as we noted earlier — is an expanded version of the Standard Gloss *(Glossa Ordinaria)*. Yet Olivi will also draw on Thomas Aquinas's more recent commentary on the epistle and sometimes provides a critique of the Dominican's position. That is hardly surprising given the intense debates between the Franciscans and Dominicans in the late thirteenth century not only on a range of philosophical issues, but also on the most perfect way to live the mendicant life. Olivi's Romans commentary often moves through the text quite rapidly as befits the scholastic style of the cursory gloss, wherein the biblical text is briefly explicated to clarify its literal meaning without further recourse to more detailed analysis of theological questions. At points, however, Olivi adopts a more magisterial style as he pauses to discuss the finer points of a complex issue. In fact, he sometimes runs through a series of verses in rapid succession and then doubles back to explore one or two in much greater detail. (Bear in mind that the Bible was divided into chapters but not verses by this time.) As for the actual biblical text that Olivi would have been commenting upon, it seems to be quite close to the so-called Paris Bible, although he does take note of alternative readings.[124]

In his general prologue to the Pauline epistles, Olivi contends that in order to contemplate their teaching on the highest level, one must have recourse to the Apostle's remark that "where the spirit of the Lord is, there is freedom" (2 Cor 3:17). It soon becomes clear, on this basis, that Olivi locates a Christological center within the Pauline epistles. For he then notes that the

123. For comprehensive studies of Olivi's career and his place within the larger Franciscan controversies, see David Burr, *The Spiritual Franciscans* (University Park, PA: Penn State Press, 2001); Burr, *Olivi and Franciscan Poverty* (Philadelphia: University of Pennsylvania Press, 1989); and Burr, *The Persecution of Peter Olivi* (Philadelphia: American Philosophical Society, 1976). See also Kevin Madigan, *Olivi and the Interpretation of Matthew in the High Middle Ages* (Notre Dame: University of Notre Dame Press, 2003).

124. See the introduction by Alain Boureau in *Petri Iohannis Olivi Lecturae super Pauli Epistolas*, CCCM 233 (Turnhout: Brepols, 2010), v-xxi.

authority, or efficient cause, of Paul's teaching is nothing other than the spirit of freedom, the very one for whom Paul was made a unique vehicle — namely, Jesus Christ. If one looks for the subject matter, goal, and form of Paul's teaching, one will always hit upon the spirit of freedom, which is the sevenfold spirit (Isa 11:2) that rests in Christ. Here, then, one will find the spirit of wisdom, understanding, counsel, fortitude, knowledge, piety, and fear. And it is this sevenfold spirit, itself the subject matter of the epistles, that results in a sevenfold freedom, a freedom of eternal truth. Hence one can truly say that "where the spirit of the Lord is, there is freedom," precisely because it is this spirit of Christ that leads to freedom (CCCM 233:3-4). More than this, however, the goal is to imprint, and to incorporate, this spirit within believers themselves (CCCM 233:6).

Olivi notes that the Church is divided between laity and clergy — or subjects and prelates, to use the medieval terminology — and so the Apostle Paul directs his letters to these two groups. Ten are directed to the laity, while four are intended for specific clerics: two for Timothy, one for Titus, and one for Philemon (Olivi admits that Philemon was not a cleric, strictly speaking, but he was the master of Onesimus). At all events, the purpose of the letters is to show that the community of the laity ought to be regulated by the obedience and fulfillment of the divine law contained in the Decalogue. As for the clergy to whom Paul writes, it is their job to govern the laity in accordance with the teaching and faith of the gospel which is contained in the Four Evangelists (CCCM 233:8-9). Nine of the ten letters written to the general communities correspond to the nine orders of angels in heaven. For just as this (Pseudo-Dionysian) celestial hierarchy reaches its pinnacle with Almighty God, so these nine letters are principally concerned with the effects of grace that descend from Christ the head to the members of his body. What sets the tenth letter, the Epistle to the Hebrews, apart from the other nine is that, whereas they are principally concerned with Christ's body the Church, Hebrews concerns itself with Christ the supreme head himself (CCCM 233:9).

Olivi believes that, in one form or another, each of the nine letters is concerned with grace within the life of the Christian community and its connection to Christ. As for the Epistle to the Romans, Olivi briefly notes in the general prologue that the Apostle wishes to show this community that both Jews and gentiles are equally in need of Christ's grace and can equally prosper by means of it. Although there is no space to go through it here, Olivi offers an elaborate rationale for the order of the first nine letters, and traces a rational progression of the Apostle's teaching on grace, beginning with its very necessity as seen in Romans and moving through its various manifestations and effects (CCCM 233:11-14). In the prologue to Romans itself, Olivi contends that this epistle is placed first owing to both its subject matter and its dignity. Olivi is indebted to Pelagius's prologue, which had noted the rivalry between the Jewish and gentile Christians at Rome. Hence Paul is writing to help bring an end to the contention with his emphasis on the universal need for grace. The Apostle adopts a style that sometimes humbles the community and sometimes exalts it, all for the purpose of leading it to harmonious relations and an understanding of the truth. And as with almost all his letters, says Olivi, the Apostle will mix instruction in the faith with the formation of good morals, both of which are essential for the Church. That is the broad characterization. Olivi further divides Romans into seven distinct parts: salutation; enticement through a show of goodwill; instruction in the faith; moral formation; removing any possible suspicions they may have; recommendations and salutations; and finally praise for God (CCCM 233:18).

Olivi begins Romans 4 by tracing the logic of Saint Paul's argument. The Apostle has already proven that the grace of Christ is necessary for all people. Now he is going to prove this point once again with regard to Abraham, the one to whom the righteousness of faith was uniquely commended and in whom the divine promises were uniquely confirmed. Hence the Apostle will first show that Abraham was not approved by God on the basis of a carnal observance of circumcision or the Law, but rather on account of the righteousness of faith. He will then demonstrate this point by showing that the promise made to Abraham cannot have been obtained through the Law, but rather through the righteousness of faith, when he says in Romans 4:13 that "the promise made to Abraham was not through the Law" (CCCM 233:90). To that end, Olivi finds that Paul proves *(probat)* that righteousness cannot come through the Law by formulating a deduction which leads to an unfitting or contradictory conclusion *(ad inconveniens seu ad contradictionem)* as follows: if righteousness were established in the Law only, then the faith of Abraham would be altogether annulled along with the promise that was also made to him. Of course, such a scenario is unacceptable. As it is, then, the Apostle will go on to conclude that justification is obtained by the merit of faith (CCCM 233:95-96).

The careful reconstruction of the Apostle's arguments had been a mainstay of the Pauline commentaries since the late eleventh century. Here in the late thirteenth century, with the scholastic adoption of Aristotelian methodology, much attention is paid to different levels of causality. The

Apostle says, "[Christ] was resurrected for our justification" (Rom 4:25). Olivi notes that some may ask how precisely Christ's resurrection from the dead can function as such a cause. This question elicits a threefold response. First, says Olivi, apart from faith in the event of Christ's resurrection we cannot be justified. Second, this event contains within itself the very life and power of Christ, as well as his own righteousness, through which we are justified. Finally, Christ's resurrection from the dead is a sort of pattern of our own spiritual resurrection, and thus our justification; in that sense it can be called the exemplary cause of our justification (CCCM 233:100). Elsewhere Christ is identified as the efficient cause of our access to grace (Rom 5:2), while our faith in Christ, together with charity, can be considered the formal cause of justification (CCCM 233:102).

Although Olivi, like most scholastic theologians, will speak of human merit within the soteriological process, his emphasis remains firmly planted in divine initiative. Good works are not discounted, but to be acceptable to God they must proceed from faith in the God who justifies by grace. God's love and grace remain the beginning and end of salvation. It is no accident, therefore, that the Church Father Olivi most consistently calls upon is the "Doctor of Grace" *(doctor gratiae),* Saint Augustine of Hippo. The Apostle Paul had written that "The grace [or free gift] of God is eternal life" (Rom 6:23). Commenting on that passage, Olivi opted to read the Latin *gratia* (grace) in the nominative case such that one can say — along with Saint Augustine — that it is not by our own merits, but by the mercy of God, that we are led to eternal life. Thus because our merits, by which eternal life is rendered, do not originate in ourselves, but are instead produced in us through grace, eternal life itself is rightly called grace. Olivi acknowledges that some people take the word *gratia* (grace) in the ablative case, but the central meaning remains the same. For it is by the grace of God alone that eternal life is given to us, although Olivi notes that this would not wholly exclude our own merits, which are themselves the product of grace (CCCM 233:115-16).

Divine initiative likewise reveals itself when human beings love one another and God. When Paul wrote that "The love of God has been poured into our hearts through the Holy Spirit" (Rom 5:5), Olivi — in tones reminiscent of Peter Lombard — contends that this love received from God is itself the very love by which we ourselves love God in return. What is more, according to Olivi, the Apostle implies here that love cannot be given to us by God unless God were to give himself to us along with his love, which is actually identical to God. Hence the very love that we have received, the love that is God (the Holy Spirit), is the same love by which we love God unto grace and eternal life. We remain active participants in these acts of love, but the impetus remains with God, for this gift of divine love produces love within us and even inflames us to love all the more (CCCM 233:103).[125] Peter of John Olivi died in 1298, but his work was deeply revered not only among a pocket of fellow Franciscans but also among some devout laypeople. Indeed, some in southern France seem to have revered him as a saint.

Nicholas of Lyra

Writing a few decades after Olivi's death, the last commentator that we will discuss, Nicholas of Lyra (1270-1349), was also a Franciscan and survived as an administrator in the order despite the tumultuous controversies in the order over the poor, or modest, use of material goods *(usus pauper)*. Contrary to Olivi, Nicholas chose a noncontroversial style in his commentaries and kept the affairs of the order separate from exegesis. He was most concerned with a Christological reading of the biblical text. In 1329, three years after Pope John XXII condemned Olivi's Apocalypse commentary, Nicholas of Lyra edited his cursory lectures on Romans. While Franciscan Provincial Minister in Burgundy, he continued his compilation of the *Literal Postill on the Whole Bible* (1322/23-31).[126] He edited these lectures, which he had given as a Bachelor of Theology at the University of Paris, in the first decade of the fourteenth century.[127] The commentary is not famous in the long tradition of Romans commentaries, but it is influential because of its encyclopedic nature and balance. It serves, moreover, as a model of the medieval biblical postill, likely a composite of two Latin words, *post* and *illa,* meaning "after" or "following" those (words). In a postill the text is followed immediately by brief explanatory comments, often not in complete sentences. Nicholas of

125. For an analysis of Peter Lombard's position and the subsequent scholastic reactions to it, see Rosemann, *Peter Lombard,* 85-90.

126. In the same period he edited his lectures on the other epistles of Paul, the Apocalypse (1329), and Daniel (1328) in his *Literal Postill.* He first lectured on Romans as a baccalaureate in Paris in the first decade of the fourteenth century. For a thorough introduction to Nicholas of Lyra's biblical commentary theory and method, see volume 1 of this series, *The Letter to the Galatians,* ed. and trans. Ian Christopher Levy, 69-77. He was elected Provincial Minister of Burgundy in 1324.

127. See Mark Zier, "Nicholas of Lyra on the Book of Daniel," in *Nicholas of Lyra: The Senses of Scripture,* ed. P. D. W. Krey and Lesley Smith, Studies in the History of Christian Thought (Leiden: Brill, 2000), 174.

Lyra's postill was cited both by Martin Luther and by Philipp Melanchthon during the Reformation.[128]

As this highly respected exegete of the Middle Ages compiled his greatest and most enduring work, *The Literal Postill on the Whole Bible,* he did not attempt an original work. Rather, Nicholas compiled and redacted the commentaries of earlier authorities and gave them his own flavor. He was a scholar's scholar who treated the work of his contemporaries and predecessors with great respect even as he questioned it in scholastic style and offered his own interpretation. The primary source of Chapters 9–11, 13, 15, and 16, selected from his Romans commentary for this volume, seems to be the *Summa theologiae* of Thomas Aquinas. Like Thomas, Nicholas of Lyra frequently employs the medieval scholastic method of asking questions and finding resolutions in his commentary. Although one cannot be sure whether Nicholas had the complete *Summa* on his writing desk, there is no doubt that he had portions of it at hand. In fact, his chief critic and reader, Paul of Burgos, regularly accused him of misreading Thomas in his *Additions to Nicholas of Lyra,* a set of exegetical responses that are regularly included in editions of the *Postill.*[129] Actually, one will notice in these selections that, in addition to Thomas, whom he employs but does not cite, Augustine proves to be the source that Nicholas cites the most.[130]

Nicholas is most famous for his development of the so-called double literal sense *(duplex sensus literalis)* in his commentaries. This will be evident in the selected chapters from Romans as the Apostle Paul cites Old Testament prophetic passages. In this exegetical method Nicholas draws two separate literal meanings from prophetic passages in particular: one meaning for the prophet's own time and another for the future that the prophet sees. Not all passages can be read in the same way. A text may refer literally only to the contemporary situation or only to that future thing of which it is a figure. On the one hand, this distinction between two historical persons or events is important to protect the historical integrity of the Old Testament context in its own right. But more importantly, it firmly grounds Christ and the New Testament itself in the unfolding events of salvation history. The

---

128. See Philip D. W. Krey, "'The Old Law Prohibits the Hand and Not the Spirit': The Law and the Jews in Nicholas of Lyra's Romans Commentary of 1329," in *Nicholas of Lyra: The Senses of Scripture,* 251-66.

129. See Krey, "'The Old Law Prohibits the Hand and Not the Spirit,'" p. 255, n. 15. In order to find Nicholas's citations from the *Summa,* it is always helpful to begin with Paul of Burgos's *Additiones,* where he will regularly indicate when Nicholas is using Thomas.

130. Especially the *Enchiridion.*

method provides Nicholas with a tool to deploy his Christocentric interpretation of the Old Testament and argue with Jewish exegesis of the Hebrew Bible. The second literal sense of an Old Testament prophetic passage that proclaims Christ is actually more literal than the first, which pertains to the prophet's own historical context. Nonetheless, both literal senses were valid in Nicholas's eyes, and he often emphasized that the sense was restricted to the historical context of the prophet. When Nicholas does employ this exegetical method, it will be noted in the text (as, e.g., with Rom 15:9).

The classic text for the double literal sense is 2 Samuel 7:14, where Solomon is declared to be God's son.[131] Nicholas's treatment of this passage shows how much the literal sense had developed in the late Middle Ages. What is more, it demonstrates his genuine respect for the history contained in both the Old and New Testaments. It also shows Nicholas's continuity with the conversation of biblical commentary that has its roots in the early Church and especially with Saint Augustine. John De Murro, a Franciscan master at Paris prior to Nicholas, paved the way for the double literal sense.[132] In fact, the outlines of this method are already intimated in Book 17 of Augustine's *City of God,* where the saint discusses how the promises made to David, which are not fulfilled in Solomon, are found to be more truly fulfilled in Christ.[133]

In the preface to his Romans commentary, Nicholas indicates that Paul composed this letter in Corinth. A scholastic theologian, he consistently divides the text *(divisio textus)* as an important part of his interpretation. Nicholas divides the epistle into the salutation (Rom 1:1-7), the narration (Rom 1:8–15:33), and the conclusion (16). The narration of the epistle begins at Romans 1:8, "First, I thank God for all of you." Here Paul announces the intention of the whole epistle: "Paul commends the grace through which

131. See also 1 Chronicles 22:7-10 and 17:13-14, Psalm 72, Daniel 8, and Hebrews 1:5.

132. Mark Zier, "Nicholas of Lyra on the Book of Daniel," 189-93.

133. See Book 17, chapters 1, 2, and 8. See, e.g., Book 17, 8: "Hence some things are written of Christ as if they were prophecies of Solomon, whereas Holy Scripture, which prophesies by events, also delineates in Solomon, in a certain sense, the figure of things to come. For besides the books of divine history in which his reign is chronicled, the name of Solomon is also written into the title of Psalm 72, in which a great many things are said which cannot all apply to him. Rather they apply to the Lord Christ; and so clearly do so that it is quite apparent that, in Solomon, the figure is contained after the fashion of a shadow, whereas, in Christ, the truth itself is presented to us." *De Civitate Dei,* CCSL 48:570-72. See also Augustine's discussion of twofold and threefold prophetic meanings in chapter 3 of *The City of God against the Pagans,* ed. R. W. Dyson, Cambridge Texts in the History of Political Thought (Cambridge: Cambridge University Press, 1998), 765-70. *De Civitate Dei,* CCSL 48:553-54.

some Jews and some gentiles at Rome were called to faith by showing that both need the grace of God for salvation, because acquired knowledge does not suffice for the gentiles for salvation, nor observation of the Law for the Jews." According to Nicholas, the Apostle Paul demonstrates this from chapters 1 to 11, and from chapter 12 he teaches them morals.

Nicholas struggles with Paul over whether the Jews were abandoned by God but concludes that, as a Jew himself, Paul argues with great pain in chapter 9 that their faithlessness is the cause of their suffering. In chapter 10 Nicholas argues that the Apostle prays for their conversion, and he admonishes the gentiles not to be arrogant in chapter 11. Even as Paul is a close reader of the Old Testament in his epistle, Nicholas is a close reader of Paul. Like Paul, he does not take an easy opportunity to attack the Jews, but carefully follows Paul's text and faithfully communicates the Apostle's ambivalence about, and hope for, his coreligionists. The problem for Nicholas, like Paul, is that without faith in Christ there is no salvation. The Jews, however, are God's elect and the promised chosen; and God does not revoke promises. In Paul's account of the situation, the Jews are the chosen ones, and yet that which they have been given to observe, namely, the good Law, is not enough to gain salvation. Those pious Jews in history, like Abraham, who lived in the faith of the promise, knew what faith in the Messiah was. Those Jews of Paul's day who emphasized the cultic Law of Moses did not have faith sufficient for salvation. The gentiles are not to boast or to be smug in relation to the Jews, according to Paul. It is through the Jews that the gentiles are saved, and the very existence of the Jews is a sign of God's faithfulness to historical promises. Like Paul, Nicholas had no doubt that the Jews would be saved. He follows Paul's logic, namely, that the resistance of the Jews has made it possible for the gentiles to come to faith, and after the sufficient number of the gentiles are saved, the Jews will be restored.

As is well known, Paul unravels the problem of the salvation of the gentiles through the Jews by his image of grafting a new olive branch onto an old one. He also relies upon an eschatology that renders the Jews and their rejection of Christ a means by which, in Paul's own mission work and in God's divine plan, the gentiles were able to hear the Word. As Paul experienced resistance from Jews he moved on to the gentiles, and thus salvation was made possible for the gentiles by the temporary resistance of the Jews. Nicholas preserves Thomas Aquinas's positions, and indeed also finds himself caught up in the profound ambiguity of Thomas's exegesis whereby Jews must serve as a source of comparison for Christian justification of the Messiah. Nicholas and Thomas need the Hebrew Scriptures both for their prophecies of Christ and for the rejection of the Jews for their denial of Christ.[134]

In relation to predestination and rejection, Nicholas again follows Thomas in the *Summa* even though it is important to note that he is writing biblical commentary rather than systematic theology. It is clear that, like Thomas and much of the medieval tradition, Nicholas affirms both predestination and free will. God causes predestination to salvation above human capacity, but rejection is not parallel to this. God saves the saved; the damned damn themselves.[135] Nicholas uses the same images as Thomas to reject predestination as God's foreknowledge of human merit, but he does acknowledge that God foresees sin and guilt in those who are rejected. Predestination and freedom of the will are not mutually exclusive — as Thomas had discussed at length in his own commentary.

As Nicholas's interpretation of Romans 13 demonstrates, he has high esteem for the role of temporal authority bestowed directly by God and thus its independence from spiritual authority. He distinguishes the roles of prelates in spiritual affairs and earthly princes in temporal affairs. Nicholas has a positive view of the role of temporal authority, as one discovers in his comments on Romans 13:3 — that it does not simply restrain evil but also promotes the good. Thus everyone, including clerics, should pay taxes to the prince since taxes provide for the common good for the whole country, as they are essential to the office of the temporal powers. Clerics should even forgo tithes where these are offensive because taxes are not essential to the office of the spiritual powers. Philippe Buc has argued that Nicholas was close to the Capetian and Valois royal families, and as a Provincial Minister wrote with a high degree of awareness of contemporary issues. As an administrator and friend of the court, he was exposed to royal claims of divinely granted sovereignty, which manifested themselves in the authority to tax for the common good, and especially to raise revenue for war.[136]

In chapter 13 Nicholas also distinguishes between the Old Law, which was based on fear, and the New Law, which is based on evangelical love. We are to do no harm to our neighbors since love is the fulfillment of the Law and its full observation. For all of the Ten Commandments are instituted for

---

134. John Y. B. Hood, *Aquinas and the Jews* (Philadelphia: University of Pennsylvania Press, 1995), 61, 111.

135. Peter Kreeft, *Summa of the Summa* (San Francisco: Ignatius Press, 1990), 176, n. 169.

136. See Philippe Buc, "The Book of Kings: Nicholas of Lyra's Mirror of Princes," in *Nicholas of Lyra: The Senses of Scripture*, 83-109. For taxes see especially 95-102.

the act of loving. The precepts of the first table are instituted to love of God, and those of the second table for the love of neighbor.[137]

In chapter 15 Nicholas focuses on how Paul encourages his readers to welcome one another by lovingly attending to the good of their neighbors even as Jesus Christ assumed a common humanity for the sake of both Jews and gentiles.[138] Christ, who is both human and divine — as the Council of Chalcedon determined in 451 — is the central theme of the Bible for Nicholas. Jesus Christ preached to procure salvation for the Jews in his own person and by way of promise. Salvation comes to the gentiles by way of mercy. Early in the commentary on chapter 15, Nicholas joins Paul in a brief tribute to those things concerning Christ in the Scriptures that serve our instruction (Rom 15:4): clarity of understanding, forbearance, internal happiness, and the security of obtaining glory so that we might have hope. Nicholas provides the scholastic definition of hope as "a certain expectation of future blessedness provided by grace and merits."[139] He spends a significant portion of the commentary on chapter 15 working with authoritative sources to clarify the historical circumstances and thus explain why the Apostle to the gentiles did not get to Spain nor had yet visited Rome as promised.

Finally, in chapter 16 Nicholas continues to demonstrate his historiographical and contextual interests, as well as his skill, when he comments on the catalogue of apostles and companions that Paul lists as examples to his readers. As he does throughout the massive literal postill, Nicholas surveys the Scriptures and the tradition to bring to life characters and contexts in

---

137. For the role of the Law and its distinctions see Krey, "The Old Law Prohibits the Hand and Not the Spirit." Nicholas distinguishes three kinds of old divine law: the ceremonial, which is determined by divine worship and concerns our relationship to God; the judicial, which is determined by justice to be maintained among people (i.e., human relations); and the moral, which is dictated by natural law. See the discussion of Nicholas's interpretation of Romans 7:12 on p. 256.

138. The incarnation and Christ's acceptance of a common humanity was an important doctrine for Nicholas. The role of the Cornelius story in the book of Acts was important to him as well as a strong Chalcedonian understanding of Christology. See P. D. W. Krey, "The Apocalypse Commentary of 1329: Problems in Church History," in *The Senses of Scripture,* 285-88. For a discussion of the use of the Cornelius story as a model for the salvation of the gentiles see also "The Old Law Prohibits the Hand and Not the Spirit," in the *Senses of Scripture,* 253-55.

139. In an early (1516/17) "Scholia on Psalm 5: On Hope," Martin Luther would challenge this scholastic definition of hope. He does not cite Nicholas but criticizes the scholastic definition that Nicholas employs. See "Scholia on Psalm 5: On Hope," in *Luther's Spirituality,* ed. Philip D. W. Krey and Peter D. Krey, Classics of Western Spirituality (New York: Paulist, 2007), 63.

Paul's missionary journeys. His ability to range over the biblical texts for allusions and to use the resources he had at hand are evidenced in his comments on Romans 16:16, "Greet one another." This was the manner of receiving the faithful in the first church as a sign of peace and love. And he says correctly, "with a holy kiss," thereby excluding the adulterous kiss by which Absalom kissed the people (2 Sam 15:5), the feigned kiss with which Joab kissed Amasa (2 Sam 20:9), the kiss of betrayal as Judas kissed the Lord (Mt 26:49), and the shameless kiss of the adulterous woman seizing and kissing the young man (Prov 7:13).

Nicholas concludes by reviewing what he reckons to be the hermeneutical key to Holy Scripture, namely, the Christocentric sense — that same sense by which Christ opened the Scriptures to the disciples on the road to Emmaus (Lk 24:27). This sacred secret of our redemption is now revealed in the time of the New Law so that all the gentiles might be obedient in faith. Paul's gospel is none other than the proclamation of that of which Christ is the author. The one who took on our common humanity is the mediator who leads us back into God; Christ in his human nature is given all power and gifts. By the grace of God in this human Christ, human beings are to love one another as they love themselves. To the human Christ is given honor before the saints and angels forever and ever.

Conclusion

In the spring of 1515 a young Augustinian friar began a series of lectures on the Epistle to the Romans in keeping with his duties as professor of Holy Scripture *(magister sacrae paginae)* at the University of Wittenberg. In doing so, Brother Martin Luther was taking his place within hundreds of years of medieval tradition. For not only was he a member of an order — the Hermits of Saint Augustine — that had been founded in the middle of the thirteenth century, but he was also taking up a text that placed him in direct dialogue with a commentary tradition that stretched back beyond the Carolingian Age, beyond Saint Augustine, beyond even Origen in the mid-third century. Layer upon layer of reflection had been accumulated and distilled, laid out on pages that were copied and re-copied, glossed and re-glossed.

Recounting myriad examples is beyond our scope here, but consider just one chain of tradition. The premier commentator of the ninth century, Haimo of Auxerre, was a major source of patristic material for the compilers of the Gloss at Laon in the early twelfth century. This Standard Gloss *(Glossa*

Ordinaria) on the Pauline epistles was then expanded into the Great Gloss *(Magna Glossatura)* of Peter Lombard a few decades later. When the Dominican friar Thomas Aquinas lectured on Romans in the middle of the thirteenth century, he would have had the Lombard's Gloss at his side. The Franciscan Nicholas of Lyra, composing his *Postill* on this epistle around 1329, had in turn Thomas's *Summa* open before him on his desk. Finally, almost two hundred years later in 1515, the Augustinian friar Luther would be in direct dialogue with his mendicant predecessor Nicholas.

Although one may doubt the wisdom of that old refrain — "Had Lyra not strummed his lyre, Luther would not have danced" *(Si Lyra non lyrasset, Lutherus non saltasset)* — the fact remains that Luther knew and respected the sober exegesis of his Franciscan predecessor. Of course, to say that Luther respected Nicholas is not to say that he always agreed with him. Indeed, one of the glories of the medieval exegetical enterprise was the learned discussions of the commentators, who offered retorts as though their interlocutors had not been dead for some decades, or even centuries, but were rather just down the next hallway.

One of the more famous, and perhaps definitive, instances of disagreement between Nicholas of Lyra and Martin Luther arises in the interpretation of Romans 1:17, "For in it [the gospel] the righteousness of God is revealed through faith for faith." This is, of course, an English rendering of the Greek text (according to the NRSV). Yet what is one to make of the Latin version, which reads: *Iustitia enim Dei in eo revelatur ex fide in fidem* (The righteousness of God is revealed in it [the gospel] from faith to faith)? What does this mean: "from faith to faith"? Nicholas, with typical conciseness, said it refers to someone "proceeding from an unformed faith to a formed faith" *(ex fide informi procedendo ad fidem formatam).* This comment would have been in keeping with the standard late medieval doctrine of "faith formed by love" *(fides caritate formata),* and Nicholas gives no indication that his reading might be at all controversial.

Commenting on this verse in his own Romans lectures (WA 56:172-73), Luther quotes Nicholas and promptly rejects his interpretation. A righteous person cannot live by such an unformed faith, says Luther, nor can anyone believe by means of it. Yet Luther is not solely reliant upon Nicholas. He also has recourse to the Lombard's Gloss (PL 191:1323c), where he reads that this phrase may refer to a movement from the faith of the Old Law to the faith of the New Law. Luther reckons this an acceptable interpretation, but insists that there is still only one faith by which people are justified, even as it may become clearer over time.

Here we see that Luther is leading his students through the most authoritative texts of the medieval exegetical tradition, presenting various interpretations and critiquing them as he goes. He moves back through the centuries, from the fourteenth to the twelfth century and even to the ninth, since the Lombard was actually conveying the comments of Haimo of Auxerre (PL 117:372d). Luther concludes that the Apostle is speaking less about the progression from one covenant to another and more about a personal development whereby the believer's own faith continues to grow. To support this reading, he appeals first of all to other scriptural passages, and then to the patristic authority of Saint Augustine (*On the Spirit and the Letter;* PL 44:211), whose text he may have been alerted to by a reference in the Gloss just a little earlier (PL 191:1323a). In sum, Luther has been in dialogue with a thousand years of Catholic tradition, which was indispensable to him as he attempted to present the text to his students in all of its cogency and depth of meaning.

We mentioned at the outset that the Epistle to the Romans played a major role in Luther's own spiritual journey, as it had for Saint Augustine, and here we catch a glimpse of the exegetical catena that inexorably bound the two men across the ages. We hope these translations will make available to a new generation the riches of Romans exegesis and its transformative theological and ministerial potential.[140]

---

140. For a discussion of principles guiding the translations in this series, please see Levy, *The Letter to the Galatians,* 9-15. In addition, both Septuagint/Vulgate and contemporary numbering is employed for Psalms citations.

PROLOGUE TO ROMANS

Peter Lombard

To understand things more fully, one should first seek their beginnings. For only then can one more easily give an account of the purpose of something, having first learned its origin. If, therefore, we show the manner of and reason for presenting the writing of the epistles after the Gospels, what we say seems true. We know, therefore, that in the Old Testament, after the instruction of the Mosaic Law, where the commands of divine worship used to be contained, prophetic doctrine was necessary. Such instruction, with the threat of punishment, restrained the renewed sins of the people and reminded them with guarantees of the good to obey and serve the God of the living. In the same way, in the New Testament after the Gospels, in which the arrangement of Christian religion and teaching of perfect holiness are handed on, the teaching of the epistles of Paul and others most usefully follows to strengthen the Church of God against heretical irregularities, to trim back fresh vices, and to prevent future questions. The rags that drew Jeremiah from the cistern were connected to ropes (Jer 38:11). Indeed, the sinner is led from the cistern *(lacus)* of ignorance and infidelity to the light *(lucem)* of grace and truth by the teaching of the epistles, as if bound by a threefold rope to the harmonious testimonies of the Law, the Prophets, and the Gospels. Among all the authors of the epistles, Paul excels perhaps in three or more ways, namely, in the depth of work, in the defense of faith, and in the praise of grace. He excels in terms of depth because this work is even more extensive and difficult to understand than the others. In defense of the faith because Paul, an expert in the Law and the Prophets, introduced testimonies in accordance with the authority of law and prophecy in defense of the Catholic faith so that he might be like the base underneath a column. In the praise of grace or the elevation of hope because he has fought bravely, prudently, and fiercely to praise the grace of God against the proud and arrogant and against those presuming in their own works. Without a doubt, this praise of grace was found more evidently and more clearly in him because, among other works, he persecuted the Church of God violently, for which he was deserving of the greatest punishment. Yet for cursing he received grace and for damnation he received mercy. In this very thing, our hope is greatly raised. For when we hear that David, a murderer and adulterer, regained the spirit of prophecy through penance, every despair of pardon is removed from us. In the same way, when we realize that Paul was initially a persecutor of the Church and afterward was made an apostle and preacher, our hope is not a little uplifted. Thus, in the Church the epistles of Paul are read more than other epistles, just as the Psalms of David are read more than the Prophets.

One should know that Paul wrote fourteen epistles — ten to churches, four to individuals — to suggest a kind of mystery and to show that his work contained the greatest things from each Testament. For the Old Testament is signified by the number ten and the New Testament by the number four. Therefore, he wrote fourteen to suggest that he was in agreement with each law and to scatter the accusation of rivals, namely of those misrepresenting him as the destroyer of the Law of God given by Moses, and of those ascribing to him hatred of the Jews. Wishing to reconcile these, he wrote ten epistles to the churches. Just as Moses handed over the teaching of the Ten Commandments to the Israelite people led forth from servitude to Pharaoh and the Egyptians, so also the Apostle of God by the teaching of the ten epistles informed the redeemed churches about the devil's power and the servitude of idolatry. Therefore, he wrote fourteen epistles to signify the concordance and fittingness of the two Testaments, which Moses also shows in the two stone tablets joined together on which the Ten Commandments were written. Our Moses also, that is, Christ, symbolized the same in celebrating Passover with his disciples at supper. For there the rejected stone that served as the cornerstone, presenting wonders to our eyes, joined the supercelestial bread with the type of the lamb, thus completing the Old Testament and beginning the New Testament. He symbolized the two Testaments with the lamb, which in the Old Testament was a ceremonial sacrifice, and with bread, which is the form of the sacrament of the new law. Joining these two, he declared the consonance of the two Testaments. For it is a wheel in the middle of a wheel, as Ezekiel saw (Ezek 1:15-21).

From what has been said, the most apparent reason for the mystery that Paul wrote fourteen epistles and clearly directed ten to churches and four to people is clear. As a result, the folly of those is repelled who say that the Epistle to the Hebrews was not Paul's but Barnabas's, Clement's, Tertullian's, or Luke's. This explanation has led them into error because his name is not inscribed in the title, and it has by far a more elegant and splendid style than other epistles he wrote. One can respond to them adequately in this way. If one ought not say it is Paul's because his name does not appear in the title, neither does that of Barnabas or any of the others, for it is written in the name of none of them. Nor ought it be supposed that it is not Paul's because it was more carefully written since naturally each is stronger in one's own language than in a foreign one. For he wrote this letter in Hebrew and the others in Greek. Indeed, he did not wish to make known his name because it was despised by the Hebrews, who considered him the destroyer of the Law. Therefore, about to handle the abolition of the Law and the ceremonies, he rightly left his name out lest hatred of the written name exclude usefulness of the subsequent text. And thus it, like the others, is Paul's epistle.

One should also inquire into the order of the epistles and why they are not arranged in the order in which they were produced by the Apostle, since the Epistle to the Romans is placed first but was not written before the others. He seems to have written the Epistle to the Corinthians before that to the Romans. This is evident from what he wrote about Corinth, "I commend to you Phoebe our sister, minister of the church at Cenchreae" (Rom 16:1). Cenchreae is located near Corinth, indeed, it is the port of Corinth. From this it appears written from Corinth. "Gaius, my host, greets you" (Rom 16:23). Writing to the Corinthians, he recalls Gaius, "I give thanks to my God that I baptized none of you except Crispus and Gaius" (1 Cor 1:14).

This epistle, in which the Apostle seems more perfect and ought to be understood as more difficult than the other ones, obtained primacy in the corpus of the epistles not because the Apostle wrote it first but because of the dignity of the Romans, who then ruled all peoples of the time. The Romans are interpreted as "noble" or "thunderous" because when the Apostle sent them this letter, they had dominion over all nations. They were therefore more noble than other peoples and thundered public and private commands. Their fame resounded in the mouth of all people. But Haimo says that the Apostle wrote from Athens to the Romans, "The Apostle wrote this epistle from Athens, city of the Greeks, to the Romans whom neither he, nor Peter, nor anyone of the twelve Apostles instructed first. Some of the believing Jews first evangelized the Romans. They received their faith in Christ from the Apostles in Jerusalem, and they came to Rome where the leader of the world was living, to whom they were subject." Consider carefully that Haimo says that the Apostle wrote from Athens; Origen, however, claims that he wrote from Corinth.[1] Again, consider that the same Haimo says that Peter preached first to the Romans since the *Ecclesiastical History* contains this, "The mercy of divine providence sent Peter to the Roman city in the time of Claudius. Coming first to the city of Rome, he opened the door to the Reign of Heaven with the keys of his Gospel."[2] Jerome also, discussing the passage in Romans where it is written, "So that I might share with you some spiritual gift" (Rom 1:11), states, "Paul says that he wished to confirm the Romans holding the faith by means of Peter's preaching, not that they had received less from Peter but that he was strengthening their faith attested to by the two apostles and learned people."[3]

Regarding the disagreement of these authorities, which seems divisive, we say that, among the apostles, Peter preached first to the Romans but not first with regard to all believers. Again, we assert that Paul wrote part of the epistle from Athens but completed it in Corinth and then sent it to the Romans. Or, rather, it is placed first because it destroyed the first level of error, namely pride, the root of all evils, as is written, "The beginning of all sin is pride" (Ecclus 10:14). Pride, which dwells in the minds of the lofty, hides from the people heavenly matters under cinder and hair shirt. It, therefore, overtook the Romans so that, fighting among themselves and preferring themselves to others, they created conflicts and schisms. For there were Romans converted to Christ from among Jews and gentiles. But the Jews despised the believing gentiles on account of the venerable ancestors from whom they thought themselves to have descended and on account of the Law that they alone among the other nations received. They said that they deserved to receive the grace of Christ and the faith of the gospel because of their observance of the Law, to which they were subject. They claimed that it was due to the merits of the works of the Law that they came to the gospel of our Lord Jesus Christ. But having been puffed up, they placed themselves above the gentiles, saying, "We are of the law of Abraham, to whom the promise was first made; we are the special people of God, who led us from

1. Haimo, in his *Commentary on the Epistle to the Romans* in PL 117:361, indicates that Paul wrote from Corinth. Origen, *Commentary on the Epistle to the Romans,* PG 14:835.

2. Eusebius, *Ecclesiastical History* 2.14, PG 20:140-41.

3. This material from Pelagius circulated under Jerome's name. See *Pelagius's Expositions of Thirteen Epistles of Paul,* vol. 3, ed. Alexander Souter (Cambridge: Cambridge University Press, 1926), 4.

Egypt with a mighty hand and wonderful signs, allowed us to cross the Red Sea on dry ground, fed us with manna in the desert, and produced water from the rock. With others abandoned in silence, we alone are worthy to receive the Law and to know God's will. The Son of God also came to us in particular, as he says in the Gospel, 'I was sent only to the lost sheep of the house of Israel'" (Mt 15:24).

But the gentiles claimed in contrast, "The more benefits you recall having been shown to you, the more you show yourselves to be inferior. Accordingly, with the same feet with which you crossed the sea, you danced later before the idol that you made with your own hands. And with that same mouth with which you gave praise to God a little before the drowning of Pharaoh and the Egyptians, you adored the idols. Moreover, you disdained the heavenly manna given in the desert, desiring to return to the fleshpots of Egypt. You also often drove the Lord to anger. Finally, you killed Christ, promised to you in the Law and the Prophets. Are we not worthier than you? Since we heard about Christ, we then believed in him. Thus the Lord says through the prophet, 'The people whom I had not known served me. As soon as they heard of me they obeyed me' (Ps 17:45/18:43-44). Thus, it happens that we have failed not from malice but from ignorance. For if we had the prophets or the apostles earlier, we would not have worshiped idols. But you boast of nobility of race; if there is any glory in that, then Ishmael and Esau can equally boast, since they were born of the same parents."

The Apostle has placed himself in the midst of these disputes, separating all their contentions there in this way and like a good preacher speaking to them with a clear voice. He has led them all to one accord, showing them that none are saved by their own merit (because all, Jews and gentiles, are mastered by sin) but by the grace of God. And thus he writes to the Romans about the above-mentioned dispute, refuting here the Jews, there the gentiles, and teaching them humility so that they might attribute all to the grace of God and showing that grace came freely to all due to faith in the gospel of Christ. He shows that this is named grace because it is not paid back like a debt of justice but freely given. For what is grace? It is freely given or bestowed, not paid back *(gratia/gratis)*. For if it were owed to you before you had grace, mercy would be paid back to you, not freely bestowed. This epistle is rightly placed first because it destroys the root of all evils, as noted above.

Having marked out the reasons for the work and the number and order of epistles, and having also explained whence and why the Apostle wrote to the Romans, there remains to discuss the subject matter, intention, and manner of proceeding. In general, the subject of all the epistles is the teaching of the gospel, the intention to warn readers to obey gospel teaching. But beyond these, we seek its own particular intentions and subject matter. And thus the first epistle has as its subject the vices of the Romans and the wonders of the grace of God to which the Apostle exhorts them. His intention is to rebuke them in their vices and to humble them to true peace and fraternal concord by the hand of grace. The manner of proceeding is as follows. In the custom of writing epistles, he begins with a greeting in which he commends himself, his task, and the author of the task, in all of which he suitably desires goodwill. After the greeting, he discloses the vices of each side. He shows the gentiles to have deviated by means of natural reason and the Jews by means of the Law. Then, in many ways, he shows justice and salvation to be equally for both, not through the Law but through faith in Jesus Christ, so that he takes them from the Law and establishes them in the faith of Christ alone. Concerning the goal of the epistle, it offers moral instruction and concludes in thanksgiving.

ROMANS 1

The Cambridge Commentator

Paul's Name

v. 1 Paul, etc. It is the custom of letter writers to begin with a greeting in which they show their affection for the recipients of their letter so as to exhort them to lead a good life. The reason for attaching such a greeting at the beginning of an oration is to render the audience at once attentive and well disposed to what will follow. This greeting prepares their attention for the one sent to preach the words of salvation and for the one sending that person. The Apostle demonstrates his goodwill when he shows the Romans that he wishes to come to them and that he desires to see them.

You ought to know that there is some disagreement about the name "Paul." Origen — or perhaps Rufinus — had composed twenty volumes on this epistle, which Rufinus then reduced to ten books, although they are still attributed to Origen. At any rate, Origen claims that the Apostle actually had two names prior to his conversion. From his parents he received the name "Saul," which is derivative in the way that "Julius" is taken from "Julus," inasmuch as he was from the progeny of Saul, who was the first king of Israel. Thus the name was given to him as a mark of glory. Hence the Apostle preferred to use this name to recommend himself.[1]

The Acts of the Apostles bears witness to the fact that he possessed this

---

1. Origen, *Commentary on the Epistle to the Romans*, PG 14:836-38. See Peter Abelard, *Commentary on the Epistle to the Romans*, CCCM 11:47. Rufinus of Aquiliae (340-410) was a translator of Origen's works from Greek into Latin.

name prior to his conversion when it states, "Saul, who is also Paul" (Acts 13:9). Yet, following his conversion, the Apostle no longer wished to be called by this name [Saul], which denoted pride and glory. Whereupon he would always begin his letters with the other name, Paul, which he previously had not been using. For by employing that name [Paul] at the outset of the epistle, he demonstrated the humility befitting an imitator of Jesus Christ.

On the other hand, some people claim that he took the name Paul on the basis of his first victory, calling himself "Paul" after he acquired the proconsul, Sergius Paulus, for the Lord (Acts 13:7), just as Scipio Africanus took his name from defeated Africa.[2] But Origen's theory seems more likely to us. For if we followed this second theory, that would mean that Paul placed his name at the beginning of the letters as a token of his own pride rather than as an indication of the humility of the one he was imitating.

Paul as Servant and Apostle

Servant. The Apostle calls himself a servant of God, which is to say that he devotes his time and energy to divine matters. Indeed, it is customary for a servant to be wholly concerned with the service of one's lord. But that would seem to run contrary to what the Lord himself says, "I will no longer call you servants but friends" (Jn 15:15), when he refers to himself as a servant. Yet he does not simply call himself a servant. For the title "servant," when simply posited, denotes a condition. Hence the Lord says, "I do not call you servants," in the sense of those who do not show esteem for someone out of love but rather out of fear. Now the servant of God is surely not a servant [in the sense of being a slave] but is instead a sovereign and free person for whom to serve is to reign. Thus if Paul were to designate himself a servant, which would be fitting, he would not be acting against what the Lord had said. In fact, he would be accomplishing what he should do either way. The lord is to provide for his servant; and the servant, insofar as he is able, is to show reverence to that lord.

It is not fitting for the Apostle to call himself by a name that would imply that he was named by the Lord for the sake of his [Paul's] own glory. Nor

2. Jerome, *Commentaries on the Epistles to Titus and Philemon*, CCSL 77c:83. See Abelard, *Commentary on the Epistle to the Romans*, CCCM 11:47-49. The Roman general Scipio (235-183 B.C.) defeated Hannibal in the Second Punic War and was thus known as Scipio Africanus.

is it fitting that everything whatsoever commanded by the Lord should actually be done. For God commands many things that should never be done since they are unsuitable. For instance, God commanded Abraham to sacrifice his son, although Abraham should never actually have done this. Rather, God gave him this command so that he might be proven worthy. Hence it is said, "Now I have come to know you" (Gen 22:12), which is to say, "I have made [your fear of the Lord] known."

Of Christ Jesus. With regard to these names, we should know that "Jesus" is the proper name by which he was called by the angel before he was conceived in his mother's womb (Lk 1:31). "Christ," however, is a title common to all those who are anointed as kings or priests. He was assigned the title "Christ," not because he had received bodily anointing, but because he was anointed spiritually in his conception. In fact, he received all those gifts together that are usually conferred on others one by one. We are referring here to the sevenfold grace [of the Holy Spirit]. Hence Christ is called the font or riverbed from whose fullness we all receive these things, while others are likened to small brooks upon whom such a gift is conferred. That is why Christ is called our very head. For just as all the senses are in the head by which the other members flourish, so all the gifts abide in him by means of which he brings life to his members.

Christ was anointed for the kingship that he might rule well over his own people. And he was anointed for the priesthood so that he might offer a sacrifice for their sake, just as he sacrificed himself upon the altar of the cross.

Note, however, that the Apostle may arrange the order of these names this way or that way in other texts. In this case, when he says **of Christ Jesus**, he is preserving the temporal sequence because "Christ" was first insofar as he was anointed with the aforementioned chrism. "Jesus" then came afterward insofar as he was the savior from the moment of his passion. Yet in other texts the Apostle reverses the order based on dignity, since "Jesus" was of greater benefit to us [as savior] than Christ [as anointed].

Called to be an apostle. Some come of their own accord, and others impose themselves in some manner, whether having bought their office or taken it by violence. Hence they have not been chosen in the manner of Aaron (Exod 28:1). Yet Paul was actually coerced by a certain measure of force when he was called, and then entered into his apostolate. For it was said to him after he had been struck down, "Saul, Saul, why do you persecute me?" (Acts 9:4).

Set apart. This is in keeping with what is recorded in the Acts of the

Apostles: "Set apart for me Paul and Barnabas" (Acts 13:2). Paul says this in opposition to those who were attempting to discredit him, claiming that Paul was not an apostle and had not been sent by the Lord. For, unlike the great apostles, he had not been present at the Last Supper, nor had he ever actually seen the Lord. On this basis, therefore, they said that he could not have been chosen. Paul defends himself against these people elsewhere when he shows that his own election is superior to that of the others. This is because the others had been chosen by a human being, namely, by Christ while he was still mortal, whereas Paul had been chosen by Christ after he had entered into his full divinity. Thus **set apart** means specially chosen, thereby referring to an election that took place apart from, and thus separate from, the others. It is along these lines that the Apostle says elsewhere, "He who set me apart from my mother's womb" (Gal 1:15), referring to the synagogue.

The Nature of the Gospel

For the Gospel. The term "Gospel" means "good news" because it is about events that have already taken place. Hence it differs from the Old Testament, which is about events that have not yet taken place. And although some event in the Old Testament may already have occurred, it is judged in its intention to be about what has not yet occurred. This is what is meant by the linen cord [of measurement] we read about in Ezekiel (Ezek 40:3; 47:3).

v. 2 Which beforehand. Here the Apostle notes the difference between the Old and the New Testament in keeping with what we said above, namely, that the Old is concerned with events that are yet to be fulfilled, while the New concerns those that have been fulfilled. Hence he refers to the gospel which **was promised beforehand through [his prophets]**. For we read in Jeremiah, "I will give them a new covenant [*testamentum*] in their understanding, and I will inscribe it upon their hearts."[3]

His [**prophets**]. This is to show that they are different from those [false prophets] through whom the demons speak. I tell you that he **promised** these things in the **Scriptures**, namely, the **Holy Scriptures**, as opposed to the works of Terence or Aristotle, which are not sacred writings. **In the Scriptures**, I say, **concerning his Son**, which refers to those things pertain-

---

3. This quotation does not appear exactly as such in Jeremiah, but is a conflation of Jeremiah 31:33 and Hebrews 8:10; 10:16.

ing to his **Son**. Or it can be read as though he were to say, "I was set apart for the gospel which was prophesied beforehand of me [Paul]; and this cannot be found just in any writings whatever, but in the **Holy [Scriptures]**. And then not just in any **Holy [Scriptures]**, but in those that pertain to his **Son**." Again, therefore, it is as if he were to say, "You will not be able to find me in the other Scriptures, but rather in those very Scriptures that speak of the Son of God." For it was in regard to Paul that the prophecy was specifically rendered, whereas nothing there pertained to another apostle. Hence it is said of the patriarchs, "Benjamin is a ravenous wolf, in the morning devouring the prey, and at evening dividing the spoil" (Gen 49:27). And again David says, "There is the young man Benjamin beyond consciousness" (Ps 67:28/ 68:27) because he was caught up into the third heaven in an ecstasy of mind (2 Cor 12:4). And in Job we read, "Who are you? Can you tie the rhinoceros to a plow so that it might harrow the ground?" (Job 39:10). For the Apostle was that rhinoceros who persecuted Christians by the horn on his nose when he received letters from the chief priests to drag those captured men of the Way to Jerusalem (Acts 9:2).

The Incarnate Word

v. 3 Who was made. Some say that in those same Scriptures one can find material concerning the Son of God. **Who**, namely, the Son, **was made according to the flesh** insofar as he is a human being. In fact, the human being is often designated by the term "flesh"; for instance, "All flesh will see the salvation of God" (Lk 3:6). The soul is often signified by the term "human being," just as a human being can be signified by "soul." For one can say, "Peter is in heaven," thereby referring to Peter's soul. Although sometimes one is only referring to the body when one says, "Peter is [buried] in Rome."[4]

 To him, that is, to his honor. Hence he says, "I do not seek my own glory, but his who sent me, [the glory] of the Father" (Jn 5:30; 8:50). Although one can say that the Son of God, that is, the Word, was made insofar as he is human, that does not mean that the Son himself was therefore made. Nor, when one says that the Son is less than his Father with respect to his human nature, does that mean that the Son himself is therefore less, since he is still fully equal to the Father [with respect to his divine nature]. Hence when one says that he was made insofar as he was human, this means that he united that

---

4. Abelard, *Explanation of the Apostles' Creed*, PL 178:625.

human being to his one person; and in the act of uniting it to himself he made it, that is to say, created [that human being]. So it is, then, that he is less than the Father with regard to his human nature, since he united to himself in the one person a lesser nature, which was inferior to the divine nature.

From the seed of David, that is, from Mary who is the seed of David. Commenting on this passage, Origen says that he should not be called "Son of David" unless he is said in some way to be the son of Joseph, who was his foster father.[5] Origen wants Mary alone to be of the priestly tribe and not of a royal tribe. Yet we cannot agree with Origen in this case. It is true that, at first, there could be no intermingling among the tribes, as Origen says, for God willed it lest discord arise on account of marriages in that land which was divided by estates. Later on, however, it was lawful for someone to accept a wife from another tribe, and thus Mary was from both tribes. Hence the Apostle says in the Epistle to the Hebrews, "It is evident that our Lord arose from Judah" (Heb 7:14). Notice, however, that the Lord is recounted indifferently within Holy Scripture as Son of David and Son of Abraham. In this passage he is specifically recounted as being from the seed of David as though from the seed of a sinner. For David sinned gravely through his adultery, which means that whatever God might have done for us cannot be ascribed to our own merits, but rather to God's grace. And it is on this basis that Jesus Christ is clearly also the Son of Abraham.

v. 4 Who was predestined. With regard to this passage, Origen says that "predestined" is not really suitable when used in reference to the Son of God. Rather, it ought to be "destined" because he was truly destined to us, that is to say, he was sent to us.[6] Yet Origen does not attend to the fact that **according to the flesh** ought to be taken up in this way: **Who was predestined Son of God [according to the flesh]**. And although we could speak in the same way of what came earlier, namely, the Word, nevertheless we attribute predestination to the human being and not to the Word. For instance, when we say "that human being was very wise," although we may be speaking of this body [taken as a whole], we are actually attributing the wisdom [specifically] to that person's soul. **In power**. This means so that he may be our power.

According to the spirit. Two statements made above may refer now to two items taken one by one. The Apostle had said that the Son of God was made **according to the flesh** he received from Mary, so it was as though he

---

5. Origen, *Commentary on the Epistle to the Romans,* PG 14:851.
6. Origen, *Commentary on the Epistle to the Romans,* PG 14:851.

had descended from an adulterous and sinful flesh that was wholly caught up in the act of adultery. Yet someone might ask how this could be possible. Hence the Apostle adds a qualifier here when he says, **according to the spirit of sanctification**. This refers to the one who sanctifies, namely, the one who cleansed the Virgin from every blemish of sin at the time of Christ's conception, since until that point all other acts of conception were fully immersed in sin. Hence David had said: "In my sins my mother conceived me" (Ps 50:7/51:5).[7]

Having established that, the Apostle says that he [Jesus Christ] was made our **power**, determining that he began to be our power from the time of his resurrection. For prior to the resurrection, the apostles were weak and feeble in their faith. Even Peter, who was stronger than the others, had still denied Christ during his passion. And in the midst of the resurrection itself, they still doubted and despaired of that very resurrection. After the resurrection, however, they were strengthened so that the very man [Peter] who grew anxious at the sound of the handmaiden's voice could later stand before Nero in all confidence. These words, therefore, **by the resurrection**, refer to the time of the resurrection. And lest Christ's resurrection appear merely putative or even fantastic, the Apostle adds, **of the dead of Jesus**. It is as if he were to say, "What was true in him [Jesus] has been fulfilled, or will be fulfilled, at some point in his members."

One may wonder whether that human being was assumed by the Son of God through nature, or through adoption, or through grace. We say that he is not the son of adoption, since every son who is adopted exists prior to his adoption and thus changes from being a non-son to being a son. Yet Christ was established as heir of all things from the first moment of his existence. Nor can he be called a son through nature since [in his humanity] he is not the same substance as the Father. Thus he must be a son through grace, because whatever he had, he had through grace. And while every son of adoption is a son through grace, not every son through grace is a son of adoption.[8]

---

7. The Latin *(in ipsa etiam conceptione)* is a little ambiguous with regard to whose conception the Commentator is referring to, whether it is Mary's or Christ's. The context better supports the reading given above, namely, that Mary was cleansed of all sin at the moment of Christ's conception in her womb. Cf. Abelard, *Commentary on the Epistle to the Romans*, CCCM 11:56.

8. The very terminology, "assumed human being" *(homo assumptus)*, raises difficult questions regarding the specifically filial aspect of Christ's human nature. Cf. Abelard, *Commentary on the Epistle to the Romans*, CCCM 11:57-58. See the Introduction, p. 37.

One may ask, since he is called the Son of God, or the Son of the Virgin, why he is not also called the Son of the Holy Spirit by whom it is said that he was conceived. For the Apostles' Creed states, "He was conceived of the Holy Spirit." And again we find that "the Holy Spirit will come upon you, and the power," etc. (Lk 1:35). In response to this question, we say that many things are born from something; these are not called sons. Saint Augustine remarks that hair, and even a louse, are said to be born of a human being, yet they are not called the sons of a human being.[9]

v. 5 Through whom. Here the Apostle commends the one sent, namely, himself, by way of the One who sent him. This phrase, **through whom**, refers to the Son of God. **Grace** refers to the gratuitous gift that is the remission of sins, which then inspired him to preach. **Apostleship** refers to the office of preaching to this end, namely, **the obedience of faith**. That is to say, so that we might so move people that they would wish to obey those things that must be believed about God. **For the sake of his name** refers to knowledge, because it is through Christ's name that every manner of thing is known.

v. 6 You who are called of Jesus Christ. Called by Christ, they have been marked by the glorious name of Christian. For there is no other people who have received their name from God apart from Christians. Thus the more careless we have been among the other nations, the more disgraceful we will appear before God. For it is said, "My name is blasphemed among the gentiles because of you" (Rom 2:24). The gentiles did not wish to be named after the handmaiden Hagar, but instead wished to be called "Saracens" from Sarah. And they are called "gentiles" because they are begotten *(geniti)* in such a way. For instance, pagans are called such from the word *pagus,* which means "farm." And so they are said to be like farmers at some distance from the city because they lived under no [civil] law. The city, on the other hand, is a gathering of people who come together so that they can live according to a system of justice.[10]

v. 7 Beloved of God. This refers to those to whom God displays love or those who say that they are God's beloved. **Called to be saints** means those who

---

9. Augustine, *Enchiridion,* 1.39, PL 40:251-52.

10. Medieval Christians often referred to Muslims as Saracens. It was generally believed that Jews descended from Sarah's son, Isaac, and Muslims from Hagar's son, Ishmael. The etymology in this instance is likely fanciful.

are called to sanctity or who already possess the title of saint, namely, the saints among the sanctified. **Grace**. Until this point the text is held in abeyance as though the Apostle were saying, "Paul, such and such a servant of the Lord, commands you to obey such things, as was said, so that there may be **grace**, etc., that is, so that the Holy Spirit might be given to you. **And peace** so that you might have peace and thus be reconciled both to God and to one another." Here the Apostle also briefly draws a distinction between the whole Trinity and the procession of the Holy Spirit from the Father and from the Son.[11]

Paul Exhorts His Audience

v. 8 First. Having set forth his greeting in which the Apostle grabbed their attention by recommending himself, the Lord, and his own apostolic office, he then connects those things that he has established with the salutation in the place of an exhortation. It is customary when writing a letter to wish good things to those to whom one is writing, lest they think that the writer has simply gone through the motions as a mere formality. That is why the Apostle demonstrates the affection he has for the Romans and thereby draws them closer to himself, so that when he begins to rebuke them severely, they will recognize that he is rebuking them out of love. He does this in the manner of a skilled orator who begins by flattering his audience, thereby enticing them so that they will listen to what he is going to say with an open mind. Or one could say that he proceeds like a wise physician who applies a soothing balm to the wound before gradually adding the more bitter medication.

Along these lines, therefore, I have wished good things for you, not merely in the customary fashion of letter writers, but rather out of my love for you. That is why it is **first**, or chiefly, that **I give thanks**. To give thanks is to praise or glorify someone for some favor freely conferred.

To my [God] for having done this **through Jesus Christ**, who reconciled me to God. Or one might say, **I give thanks [. . .] through Jesus Christ** himself. He adds that he also **gives thanks** because **your faith is proclaimed**, that is to say, it is set forth as an example for the whole world. For when the head [Rome] has been converted, the members will then be more easily con-

---

11. This affirms the Latin version of the Nicene Creed, which includes the *filioque* clause: "We believe . . . in the Holy Spirit . . . who proceeds from the Father and from the Son (*filioque*)."

verted. Hence Quintilian notes that what the superiors do seems like a command to their inferiors.[12]

Note that when it pleased the Lord to convert the world, the Lord proceeded by degrees. First of all, the Lord called the Jews to faith. For they had the Law and the Prophets, and it was from them that the Lord chose the apostles. Thereupon the Lord moved on to those taken over by the Apostle; these are the people who achieved preeminence in worldly learning, whom they call philosophers. This occurred so that through the philosophers the Lord might more easily convert those who had learned the arts from them. At last, having converted the leaders in matters of learning, the Lord moved on to those preeminent in matters of power, namely, the Romans. The Lord called them to faith so that, once the heads had been converted to the faith, the members could no longer resist.

v. 9 [God] is my witness. It is as if he were to say, "I say this truly from my affection for you, for **[God] is my witness** in the sense that I bear witness to God." The Apostle is speaking here by way of a mystery to convey that the Lord lives (cf. Gal 2:20).

One can ask what it would mean to swear by God. In response, we say that someone who swears by God asserts, "May God forsake me unless I hold to the oath that I have sworn." Or again, someone who swears by faith thereby asserts, "May my act of faith fail me unless I do what I have sworn to do." It is not a sin to swear an oath, but rather to desire to swear. Hence the Truth did not say that you may not swear an oath, but rather that you must not desire to swear an oath (Jas 5:12; Mt 5:33-37).[13]

Someone may also ask whether an oath should be sworn by a stone, and what it means to swear by a stone. In reply to this, we say that one who swears by a stone does not sin. For to swear by a stone is nothing other than what we already said above, namely, that the stone would fail me unless I hold to what I swear. Yet those people who were swearing by an idol, but not holding to what they swore, were indeed sinning. For they would have done so against their conscience.

---

12. Quintilian, *Declamatio*, 3.13. Abelard, *Commentary on the Epistle to the Romans*, CCCM 11:61-62.

13. Although the Latin is quite terse, the point is that, while swearing an oath is not evil in itself, one should not actively seek to swear since it can often be an occasion for evil. Thus oaths should be sworn only in matters of necessity to serve some greater good. See Robert of Melun, *Oeuvres de Robert de Melun*, vol. 2, pp. 18-20; and Peter Lombard, *Commentary on the Epistle to the Romans*, PL 191:1318.

One might object, furthermore, that one must not swear by created things, in keeping with the passage, "Do not swear either by heaven or by earth, but carry out the vows you have made to the Lord" (cf. Mt 5:33-34; Jas 5:12). That can be explained. Do not swear an oath means that you should not desire to swear an oath. And not only must you not desire it, but you must also [carry out the vows you have made] to the Lord. Be careful, therefore, that you do not swear to things that you should not carry out. For if you swear to what should not be sworn to, you are doubly guilty if you hold to it.

vv. 9-10 I serve God with my spirit, which is to say from his love, because the services of many are coerced. **The gospel of his Son** refers to the preaching of those things that have been fulfilled in his Son. **Without ceasing**. One renders prayer without ceasing who does not neglect to pray when one ought. It is as though the Apostle were to say, "So often I offer prayers for myself, and I pray also for you. And not only am I praying for you, but even **requesting** that **if by any means**, that is, in whichever way — whether through bad times or good, whether by land or by sea — **now at length [I may have a prosperous journey]**. Using two words here that both mean "at length" [*tandem aliquando*] is like using two to say "very many" [*plerique alii* rather than *plerique*]. Perhaps the Apostle was writing in his own language, and the conjunctions that fit well together in the one language proved to be superfluous in the other.

Prosperous, I say, not according to my will, which errs on many occasions, but **by God's will**, which cannot err. For the Apostle knew that the saints often erred in their petitions. The Apostle himself frequently prayed that the torment of Satan might be taken away from him, but his plea was not granted (2 Cor 12:7-9). Whereas the devil's plea was granted when he asked God to place Job in his power (Job 2:6).

v. 11 I desire. I ask for this that I might have it, and I do so based on my affection for you, since **I desire . . . to strengthen you**. This is not so that I might convert you, since you have already been converted, but so that you might be strengthened in what you have received.

v. 12 And at the same time be encouraged by you. For, as Boethius says, in a hypothetical syllogism, the one instructed in some doctrine is encouraged, as is the one who instructs the friend, because the former soon places great trust in that teaching received from the latter.[14] So it is with those whom the

---

14. Boethius, *On the Hypothetical Syllogism*, 1, PL 64:831.

Apostle says need to be strengthened, that they would find comfort in his strengthening, and that he himself, since he would feel all the more confident and secure about them, would then rejoice together with them.

By that which. The "which" here may refer to either the strengthening or the reciprocal encouragement. Thus he adds: **By that faith** about which they have had some doubts.

Yours and mine, since it is a common faith. In other words, it is catholic, which itself means universal or common. It is said to be common or universal because it would suffice for the salvation of all. This distinguishes it from the faith of heretics, whose faith is their very own and private. **Common to us both**. Hence this faith proves to be the connecting band of charity that binds and draws you to one another.

v. 13 I do not want. Here he speaks in response to those who might say, "Why, then, do you not come, since you have such a great desire to do this?" Hence the Apostle makes it clear by saying, **I do not want [you to be ignorant, brothers and sisters, that I have often proposed to come to you and have been prohibited to this point]**.

That I may have some fruit among you refers to what they have received, not what he brings.

v. 14 To barbarians. The Apostle calls the tribes in that region who had no doctrines "barbarians." He explains this when he says, **to the wise**, because of the Greeks, and **to the foolish**, because of the barbarians who were lacking doctrines, **[I am a debtor]**.

v. 15 So as much as is in me. Since some debtors are forced into debt and others go into debt freely, the Apostle clarifies that he is a debtor who is **eager**. That is, I am well disposed, not forced, but indeed willing **[to proclaim the gospel]** not only to others, but also **to you**.

The Power of the Gospel

v. 16 I am not ashamed. To digress for a moment, I am eager to proclaim the gospel because **I am not ashamed** of proclaiming Christ and even dying or being crucified. For although the gospel seems like foolishness to the gentiles and is a stumbling block to the Jews, it brings no shame upon me (cf. 1 Cor 1:23). Since on the one hand I will proclaim the gospel in its strength, and on the other in its weakness, I am ready to present a reasonable argument for each of these tenets of faith. Yet some people at the time were ashamed because they had not prepared any good arguments. There are even some people today who are not ready to present good arguments. They deceptively claim that the faith must not be examined, and they take solace in their ineptitude by invoking Gregory's remark that faith has no merit in matters that human reason can grasp through experience.[15]

Yet the Apostle clearly refutes such people in his Epistle to the Corinthians, where he says, "Those who speak in tongues and do not prophesy should be quiet in church" (cf. 1 Cor 14:4). For if we speak in tongues and do not prophesy, were some non-believer to enter the church, would that non-believer not say, "What sort of insanity is this?" Now who will supply an argument for the unlearned? Hence the Apostle says elsewhere, "So that you may know how you ought to answer everyone" (Col 4:6). And in this vein, Peter says, "You should be prepared to present an argument to anyone who asks" (1 Pet 3:15). Certainly, when the Apostle argues on behalf of such things as the Lord's passion and resurrection, or the resurrection of all the dead on the last day, he must have had good arguments for each one of these things, or else no one would have accepted him. Hence when he spoke of some great things of God, he then added, "Just as some of your own [poets] have said" (Acts 17:28). It would be ridiculous, as the speeches of Faustus make clear, were one to say that something could be mentioned and yet claim there is no need to supply rational arguments for its reality.

For it is the power. The following section of the text pertains to what the Apostle had been discussing earlier, namely, that **so much as it is in me, I am eager to proclaim the gospel to you**. That is to say, I am eager to instruct you in the evangelical teaching, which surpasses all other teachings because it is the **power of God**. For God justifies the human person through it. The Apostle compares the gospel to power *(virtus)* because, just as virtues *(virtutes)* make one righteous, so also does the gospel, which sufficiently teaches all things that are necessary for the human person and adds nothing superfluous. For in the gospel one receives a teaching separate from the Law, which led no one to perfection nor commanded us to love our enemy. Although the Law provided the initial elements of salvation, it did not bring the process to fulfillment. Hence God inspired the faithful with the things that were necessary, as with David who said, "If I have repaid my ally with harm or plundered my foe without cause, then let the enemy pursue and overtake me" (Ps 7:5-6/7:4-5).

15. Gregory the Great, *Homilies,* Book 2, Homily 26.1, PL 76:1197.

For salvation, that is, for justification. He demonstrates for whom it is **the power for salvation** when he says: **to everyone who believes**, namely, those who accept that teaching and find comfort in it. And this applies **to the Jew first** in keeping with the order of time, since Jews were first converted, and soon after **to the Greek** since Greeks were converted shortly thereafter. Or perhaps **first** refers to both Jews and Greeks, since they were converted before the other peoples. Or again, **first** could mean "chiefly" because in the time of the apostles as many from this group or that group had entered into the Church of God through faith.

v. 17 For the righteousness. This surely is **power**, for it is **in it**, which is to say that **the righteousness [of God]** is in the gospel. This means that the just recompense of God, whether for punishment or for glory, is revealed [**in it**], which is to say that it has been carefully explicated. The Apostle explains the principles of God's remuneration, and shows that God did not remunerate on account of works but rather on the basis of will, which the Law never did — in fact, just the opposite. In order to make this clear, the Apostle then adds, **from faith**, namely, the faith of punishments, **to faith**, referring to the faith of rewards. It is as though he were to say, "On the basis of our belief born of his instruction, we know what God remunerates to punishment and what to glory." Hence the justification of the human person rests in avoiding this and doing that, as we read, "Depart from evil and do good" (Ps 36:27/37:27). And insofar as the Apostle says, **from faith to faith**, he is also hinting at the order of nature because punishment preceded reward in God's remuneration. This is the case with the angels just as it will be at the last judgment.

Now the Apostle invokes the testimony of the prophet Habakkuk in order to prove the evangelical teaching that the human person is justified from the faith of punishments to the faith of rewards: **"the just person lives by faith"** (Hab 2:4). In other words, the just person lives by knowing that God is the remunerator of some things to punishment and some things to glory, and so the just person abides in righteousness by avoiding this and doing that. Surely, to live in righteousness can only mean to abide in righteousness, just as, conversely, to die is to recede from righteousness.

Human Guilt and Divine Wrath

v. 18 Revealed. To this point some things were attached to the greeting which — as we recall above — were presented by way of an exhortation to render the listeners attentive and well disposed to what they would hear. In his earlier remarks, the Apostle had intended to reprimand the Romans for their pride. He begins this section, however, by expanding upon the grace of God and human merits. He does this by exposing the weakness of arguments that Jews introduced and totally refuting the gentiles' attempt to excuse themselves on the basis of their own ignorance. The Apostle shows that they are altogether inexcusable, so that neither people might be able to reckon anything to their own merits, but instead ascribe everything to divine grace. To accomplish this he must, as we have said, repeatedly employ invectives now directed at this group, now at that, and sometimes directed at both at once. The Apostle begins by attacking both groups when he says, **The wrath of God is revealed from heaven**, etc. But when it comes to the recompense of God, which is twofold, the Apostle deals first with the recompense of punishment and then with the allotment of reward, thereby following the order of nature. For, as noted above, the recompense of punishment preceded the recompense of reward, just as it will at the end time.

The Apostle pursues this line of thought. **The righteousness of God is revealed in it**, because **the wrath** belongs to the just vengeance of God. The term "wrath" is employed by human beings who, from the wrath and disturbance of their souls, are accustomed to seek vengeance for their injuries. And so they use this term to describe divine revenge, even though there is no such turmoil whatsoever on God's part in the execution of divine revenge.[16]

From heaven denotes the difference from false gods. Or perhaps **from heaven** refers to the prelates of the Church through whom God exacts vengeance, since they can be likened to heavenly figures among human beings. Or again, **from heaven** may refer to the fall of the angels among whom God did not mete out punishment on the basis of works, but rather on their will alone, since they had no works to their name.

Over all ungodliness. To be ungodly is more than being unrighteous. The ungodly person, properly speaking, knowingly acts against God. At this point in the text **ungodliness** pertains to Jews who had been found guilty under both the written law and the natural law. The Apostle charges the gentiles with **unrighteousness**, however, because they had sinned only against the natural law. The reason he chooses the word **over** is that he wishes to

---

16. The Commentator's point is that, whereas human beings feel angry and are internally agitated when venting their wrath, God remains immune to such passions. This is because God is utterly simple, constant, and perfect. Anselm of Canterbury (*Proslogion,* 8) makes a similar point when attempting to reconcile divine impassibility with divine mercy.

demonstrate that God prevails over, and is superior to, those upon whom God wreaks vengeance. Many people wish to exact vengeance and yet cannot manage to accomplish what they wish. I say, **Over the unrighteousness of human beings**, but principally **of those who [suppress] the truth of God**. This refers to those who, despite the fact that they possess true knowledge of God, do not wish to obey God owing to their own wickedness.

Knowledge of God

v. 19 At this point someone might ask, "Did they really have knowledge of God?" Indeed, they did. For the Apostle will now address **what was known of God**. That is the knowledge which we now have of God, whether as unity or as Trinity, although there was no such knowledge of the incarnation. **It is manifest** not only, I say, to them, but even **in them**, such that it was known to others through them. It was surely **manifest** because **God revealed it to them**. God revealed this to them through God's own works. Good painters are known through their own works, even as they themselves are not seen. So it is, then, that the greatest painter of all, although invisible, was known by philosophers through God's own painting, which is the world. Hence Plato declared that intellect [*nous*] and mind were born of God and that soul permeated all things.[17] The philosophers discerned God's supreme craftsmanship in the great beauty of the world and even in the harmonious ordering of created things. And seeing how God arranged all things so fittingly to human advantage, the philosophers came to perceive that God is supremely beneficent.

v. 19 And this is **what was known of God**, namely, what we now know of God: how three things can be distinguished in God even as they all subsist in the same reality. **The invisible things** refers to the sevenfold grace. **From the creation of the world** does not mean through creation itself, but **through the things that were made** by us [the Trinity] in creation.

v. 20 The Apostle then comes to **the invisible things**. The title "invisible" refers here to the Holy Spirit, which is to say beneficence. And because this title indicates a spiritual nature, it is specifically assigned to the Holy Spirit. The fact that the Holy Spirit is spoken of here in the plural ["things"] is on account of the Spirit's effects. Hence the Spirit is often called "seven," and is

17. Plato, *Timaeus*, 34. Cf. Macrobius, *Dream of Scipio*, Book 2, chapter 2.

often said to be active and dashing about. For the Spirit is at once one and many, active, still, and dashing about. The Son, in turn, is designated with the title "power," that is, the wisdom of God. Hence the Apostle will elsewhere refer to Christ as the power and wisdom of God (1 Cor 1:24). With supreme expertise God creates all things, from whatever material, firm and stable in their own species. Hence all the individual works of God are praiseworthy. Now Boethius, in his *Categorical Syllogism,* says that we should extol the expertise of a builder who can construct a house from flimsy material.[18] Yet were the builder less careful than necessary, then even were the material sturdy, the house would itself be fragile and unstable. God the Father is designated by the term "divinity," for even as the other two Persons are indeed God, they have their being from the Father. Hence, as the holy doctors say, the title "divinity" is principally assigned to the Father.

The Apostle also seems to imply that the philosophers understood not only the distinction of the [Trinitarian] Persons, but even their procession, such that three different things could be shown to subsist in one reality. A suitable comparison drawn from human affairs would be the seal. For when a seal is impressed upon wax, three things are present: the copper material [from which the seal is made], the copper seal itself, and the impression [made by the seal]. These three are from the same copper substance. Yet they are distinct insofar as the seal is from the copper, and the impression is from both the seal and from the copper material.[19]

v. 21 They became vain, like smoke which, the higher it rises, the more it vanishes. And so, too, the greater their estimation of themselves, the less worthy they were in the sight of God.

v. 23 Glory is the honor they owed to their creator. [**They changed the glory**] **of the incorruptible** [**God**], who cannot be corrupted, **into the likeness of an image**. This should be taken intransitively [since they cannot actually change God].

v. 24 On account of which, namely, because they did not wish to glorify God, **God handed them over**. I do not say that God merely permitted them

18. Boethius, *On the Categorial Syllogism,* Book 2, PL 64:809b-c.

19. The point is that the three Trinitarian Persons are all of the same divine substance and yet can be distinguished on account of their unique relationship to one another. The Son is from the Father, but not vice versa; and the Spirit is from both the Father and the Son. Cf. Robert of Melun, *Oeuvres de Robert Melun,* vol. 2, p. 27; Abelard, *Theology,* PL 178:1068-69.

to go this route, but that God actually impeded them by placing a stumbling block before them, as was just. **To the desires** so that what they evilly willed they might then be able to carry out in their deeds. **So that they might impair**. This means so that they might afflict, for a certain power of nature is inferred in such persons, since the human members were not intended for such practices.

v. 25 [**They served**] **the creature**, namely, the devil in his idols.

v. 27 And the penalty refers to the punishment that followed upon their error, namely, the illicit impulses that disturbed and shook the interior mind.

v. 28 And just as, or because, **they had approved**, that is, they had praised and willed **lack of knowledge of God, God gave them up to their debased mind**, to a perverse judgment.

v. 29 Being filled up with all iniquity, that is, they were full of every form of iniquity. This refers to the individual vices, which the Apostle demonstrates by listing the various parts of iniquity (Rom 1:29-31).

v. 32 They did not understand, which means that they did not give heed. **But they also consented**. We say that people consent to something when they do not impede it, even as they could and should do so.

The Apostle had already rebuked the gentiles for their idolatry. But one may ask what exactly makes someone an idolater. In response, we say that an idolater is anyone who shows some reverence for images to the point of reckoning this crucifix better than that one, and thinks God will be more propitious in one place on account of its crucifix than in some other place on account of theirs. For it is in such crucifixes that the unlearned place their greatest trust. Hence the Greeks actually did a better job of it when they relied on pictures alone to preserve the memory of the Lord's passion. For just as texts are helpful to the literate, so can pictures assist the laity. Certainly, though, the form's distinctive characteristics are displayed more clearly in crucifixes than in pictures, and thus may be grasped more fully by the simple, who reckon there is some living presence in these crucifixes.

ROMANS 2

William of St. Thierry

God's Judgment upon Jews and Gentiles

v. 1 Therefore, O human, whoever you are, you have no excuse. The Apostle to the gentiles was an excellent teacher, who possessed marvelous wisdom in the gospel. He also knew how to be all things to all people and repeatedly made an effort to bring honor to his own ministry and to build it up. He brought down and humbled some of the gentiles from their previous condition. Afterward, in order to avoid increasing Jewish rebuke of the gentiles, he chastised the Jews so that both groups would be equally reprimanded and the consolation of Christ's peace would join them together more endearingly. He could have severely accused them of the same idolatrous filth and impurity as the gentiles. The books of the prophets, of course, are filled with such accusations. Yet he wisely refrained so that, should questions about the Law occur, which he knew would trouble them greatly, their patience would not then tire out and collapse under the weight of the questioning if it became too heavy. Moreover, after having turned from species to genus,[1] here he publicly corrects them all in a restrained way so that others might also profit from their correction and, as was stated, not wane in patience.

Since, as he says, all — those who judge and those who consent — are worthy of death, **Therefore, O human, . . . you have no excuse**. Those are without excuse to whom truth is not hidden and in whom iniquity perseveres. **O human**. O human, given a position of honor, you have the Law of

1. Thus from narrower to broader confines.

God and pass judgment according to the Law of God. And it is by means of the Law that every person is a sinner, either from original guilt or from adding one's own will to it, even if one is not aware of it. For, in addition, that very ignorance is undoubtedly a sin in those unwilling to understand, but it is punishment for sin in those unable to understand.[2] For this reason, **O human**, you who pass judgment on the basis of the Law are without excuse. But you too — everyone — who neither know the Law nor pass judgment based upon it, are nevertheless without excuse. For God knows that "God made the human being upright" (Eccl 7:30/7:29). God also gave the command of obedience and the witness of conscience in natural law, and therefore does not admit excuse. In neither sort of person, then, is there a just excuse but rather in each a just condemnation. For if those who could not understand "the invisible things of God from the creation of the world in the things that have been made" (Rom 1:20) are without excuse, how much more inexcusable are those who are instructed by God's Law and trust themselves to be guides to the blind and a light to those in darkness? It is to them, to be sure, that the Apostle specifically addresses this message: **O human**, you are certainly no spirit; you arrogantly attempt to excuse yourself, with a human understanding, rendering judgment by human standards. **When you pass judgment upon another, you condemn yourself. For you practice the things that you are judging**. The world is filled with people who judge others or even punish them for the very things that they themselves practice. Yet when they judge others, they pronounce sentence on themselves.

v. 2 For we know that the judgment of God, in accordance with truth, falls upon those who practice such things. Sometimes certain things that seem evil are done with good intent and what seems good with evil intent. There are still other things, whether done for good or evil, that accord with the doer's intent. True judgment, therefore, belongs only to one who knows how to judge the heart.

v. 3 Do you suppose, O human being, that when you judge those who do such things and yet do them yourself, you will escape the judgment of God? "Let those who hate God flee from before God's face" (Ps 67:2/68:1).

---

2. William is referring to the state of guilt (*culpa*) into which all human beings are born and thereby stand condemned under God's Law, and to actual sins which people commit of their own free will in the course of their lives. Note that ignorance of God's Law is no excuse since it belongs to the punishment (*poena*) that accompanies original sin.

For those who love God do not flee his judgments but desire them because they trust that they will be made righteous in them. On the other hand, those who flee cannot escape them.

v. 4 Or do you scorn the riches of God's goodness, patience, and long-suffering? Now that the Apostle has disturbed the one who scorns, he adds the reason for God's patience. **Do you not know that God's kindness leads you to repentance?** God's goodness is expressed in immeasurable riches. For just as God causes the sun to rise, so he does not fail to scatter good things on the good and the evil alike (cf. Mt 5:45). But God's patience is toward those who scorn, and his longsuffering toward those who fall short from weakness rather than intent. Indeed, although "some persevere in wickedness, God perseveres in patience, punishes very few sins in this life, lest we not believe in divine providence, and holds back many things for the last examination to impress upon us the future judgment."[3] "But the soul aware of itself in evil" is already completely given over to punishment although it "believes that God is not rendering judgment since the soul appears to suffer no punishment."[4] This is a condemned mind; this is a blindness and a hardness of heart; this is an interior darkness by which the sinner is shut off from God's inner light, although not entirely, as long as one dwells in this life. For there is also an outer darkness, which is understood to pertain more to the day of judgment, so that those who do not will to be corrected in this life are completely outside God. What does it mean to be completely outside God except to be at the peak of blindness? If, indeed, "God dwells in inaccessible light" (1 Tim 6:16) into which those enter to whom it is said, "Enter into the joy of your Lord" (Mt 25:21), **Do you not know that God's kindness brings you into repentance?** Are you willing to hear of the time of judgment?

v. 5 By your hardness and your unrepentant heart you are storing up wrath for yourself on the day of wrath and of the revelation of God's righteous judgment. Two kinds of people sin obstinately. Some promise themselves God's mercy, and others despair at the enormity of their own evil deeds. Because of those who, in their hope for mercy, gamble with delays, God has made the last day uncertain. And for those in danger of despairing, God has made it a haven of kindness. Unless they right themselves quickly,

---

3. Augustine, Letter 153, CSEL 44:5-9.
4. Augustine, *Sermons on the Psalms*, CCSL 38:69.

whether they are of one kind or the other, both are storing up wrath for themselves on the day of wrath. A treasure trove is where different kinds of riches are hidden away little by little so that they may be found together there in one pile. Three treasures are found in Scripture: earthly treasure, heavenly treasure, and that which is called the treasure of wrath. Those who with unrepentant hearts conceal their deeds in the treasure of wrath are said to be hard. Those who store up treasure on earth are called fools. "You fool, he says, this night they demand your soul from you" (Lk 12:20). The wise are also rich in regard to God, and whatever they do, they produce things worthy of the kingdom of heaven. The carnal store up [treasures] on earth; the brutish store them up in wrath; the spiritual store them up in heaven.[5]

The day of wrath is the day of judgment when everyone will be faithfully presented with the person, the object, or the place they had stored up for themselves. Then the judge will take notice not so much of their ability as of their will, which he will crown. You willed but perhaps were not able. Hence the judge will take notice of you as if you did what you willed. It is also said of you, "To each according to one's works" (Rom 2:6). Indeed, glory and punishment will differ there as greatly as merits vary here. Yet God forbid that some venial sins prevent a righteous person from eternal life. This life is hardly ever, or never, finished without them. Likewise, some good works will not benefit an impious person. It is very difficult to find a life even of the wickedest human being that is devoid of them. But when wretched human beings hear of eternal fire here, they promise themselves purgatory. Many, they say, will be saved there as though by fire. O the hope of the desperate! In the first place one should know that nothing can be imagined in this life harsher than that fire. Nevertheless, as the Apostle testifies, certainly those will be saved there by fire who do not build upon Christ as the foundation "with gold, silver, and precious jewels" but rather "with wood, hay, and stubble" (1 Cor 3:12). Yet they do not reject the foundation. In fact, they value it above all the carnal delights to which they are made captive or succumb when that critical moment arrives and they need to abandon either those things or Christ. If they do not value Christ, however, they do not have the foundation. Indeed, the foundation is valued above all the succeeding parts of the structure. What is more, no one's ignorance of Christ, or of the good here, thereby excuses them. They will not be exempt from burning in eternal fire except if they did not believe because they did not hear. If that is the case, perhaps they will burn less.

5. See Origen, *Commentary on the Epistle to the Romans*, PG 14:875b-76a.

vv. 6-7 These things in the interim are declared about the day of wrath on which **God will render to everyone according to one's works: eternal life to those who with perseverance in good works seek glory and honor and imperishability**. This is what the Apostle is saying, and here is the right order of the argument that follows. God will give eternal life for perseverance in good works to those who seek glory, honor, and imperishability. This is the case not only for Jews, to whom God's words are entrusted, but also for Greeks. For God's judgment is just, and he is God not only of Jews but also of gentiles. Yet to those who through the mind's contention and the soul's depravity do not believe the truth but follow after iniquity — wrath, indignation, tribulation, and anguish will be rendered not only to the gentile but also to the Jew. "For with God there is no respect of persons" (Rom 2:11).

This, to be sure, considers the literal meaning of the words. But now let us look for their inner sense. The Apostle says, **To those who with perseverance in good works**. For those who produce fruit in perseverance, there will be **glory and honor**. They will receive the glory of imperishability and immortality in the resurrection, and they will find a blessed happiness in both body and soul. But this will be the honor that humans possessed before having been "compared to senseless beasts" and having "become like them" (Ps 48:13/49:12), during that time when, abounding with the delights of God's paradise, humans continually enjoyed the vision and conversation of God. These things will be rendered in eternal life to those seeking eternal life. Of this the Apostle says, "This is eternal life: that they may know you, the only true God, and Jesus Christ, whom you have sent" (Jn 17:3). To those seeking God for God's own sake, therefore, he will be their eternal life, honor, and glory. God will be all in all.[6]

vv. 8-10 But to the contentious and those disobedient to the truth, and instead trust iniquity, wrath and indignation, etc. Understand, prudent reader, the things that are appointed to you, and notice that to those who do well it is said that God renders glory and honor, and eternal life; however, wrath and indignation, anguish and tribulation await the condemned. Yet such things are not rendered by God. For we receive the good things from God, whereas we inflict the evil upon ourselves.

The text reads: **to the contentious**. Contention causes heresies and ignites schisms and scandals. It causes disobedience to the truth and acceptance of iniquity. From the contentious, therefore, come wrath and indigna-

---

6. See Origen, *Commentary on the Epistle to the Romans*, PG 14:880a-b.

tion, anguish and tribulation. Wrath is torture of the soul inflicted by knowledge of sin. Indignation is understood as a sort of swelling of that very wrath, as if it were a wound and a disturbance spread through the body's parts. If, for example, we suppose wrath to be some very bad wound, its swelling and distention would be called the indignation of the wound. Tribulation results not in the breadth, of which it is said, "In my tribulation you have made room for me" (Ps 4:2/4:1). Rather, tribulation makes for a narrowing, which is contrary to this breadth, that is, contrary to doing good with a glad will through God's grace. The Apostle states, **To the Jew first**, who knew the Lord's will and yet did not act worthily. Hence he "will be struck with many blows" (Lk 12:47). Paul adds, **Then to the Greek**, who because of ignorance will perhaps "be struck with a few blows" (Lk 12:48). For it is one thing to know God and another to know God's will. A gentile, of course, could know of God from the creation of the world, but God's will is known from the Law and the Prophets.[7]

Written and Natural Law

vv. 11-12 For with God there is no respect of persons. Even blinded by lust, every rational soul thinks and reasons. Yet whatever truth shines forth to the soul in its reasoning should not be attributed to itself but to that light of truth by which the soul, even weakly illuminated, senses some truth through reasoning. There is no soul, however perverse and yet still able to reason, in whose conscience God does not speak. For the hand of our Creator wrote in our very hearts, what you do not want done to you, do not do to others, and whatever you wish that others do to you, you also do likewise to them (cf. Tob 4:16; Mt 7:12). Even before the Law was given, no one was allowed to be ignorant of this, so that there might be something by which even those who had not received the written law would be judged. But lest human beings protest that they missed out on anything, what they were compelled to see in their conscience was written and placed before their eyes. Only Jews received the written law, however, whereas both gentiles and Jews received the natural law.[8]

---

7. See Origen, *Commentary on the Epistle to the Romans*, PG 14:884-86.

8. It was generally understood that, whereas the Jews had received from God the written Law of Moses, the gentiles nevertheless had the natural law, which is accessible through the powers of human reason. These two sorts of law are not contradictory, however, even though the revealed written Law is more comprehensive than the natural law that is available to all human beings.

The works of the written law are divided into two parts. One treats the sacraments, and the other treats morals. Circumcision, the Sabbath, and other rites of this kind pertain to the sacraments. But "You shall not kill," "You shall not commit adultery," etc. (Exod 20:13-14) pertain to morals. If they are neither understood nor observed, they simply enslave. If they are both understood and observed, then they are beneficial, but in their own time, as when observed by Moses and the prophets. For this kind of servitude would still be beneficial if they [the Romans] were under the charge of a tutor and subject to fear. Nothing causes such pious fear in the soul as a sacrament that is not understood. But when it is understood, it produces joy; and if the time is appropriate, it is celebrated freely. Otherwise it is read and discussed merely with a spiritual sweetness. When understood, every sacrament is directed either to the contemplation of truth or to good morals. The contemplation of truth is based on the love of God alone, but good morals on the love of God and neighbor on which "all the law and the prophets depend" (Mt 22:40).[9]

With regard to morals, the written law and natural law are nearly the same and equally common to both Jews and gentiles, except that Jews have it written on tables and in their reason whereas gentiles possess it only in their reason. Obviously, this natural force is present in each, and it is by means of that force that the rational animal deems something to be legitimate and does it. Therefore, as stated here, **There is no respect of persons**. Yet **whoever has sinned under the law**, that is, whoever was appointed to observe the written law, **will be judged by the law**, which prohibits sins and assigns to individual sins their punishment. **Whoever has sinned without the** written **law** will be judged **without the law**. This means that those who did not receive the written law will not be judged by that law, since the natural law they did receive will be sufficient for their judgment.

v. 13 For it is not the hearers of the law, but the doers, of either the written or the natural law, **who will be made righteous before God**. What Paul means when he says that the doer of the Law alone will be made righteous before God needs to be rightly understood, lest it seem contrary to what he said elsewhere: "If it is from works, it is no longer from grace," and "[other-

9. Taken in part from Augustine, *Commentary on the Epistle to the Galatians*, CSEL 84:76. Medieval theologians generally believed that the moral law remained in force even after the advent of Jesus Christ, whereas the ceremonial precepts were then rendered obsolete. Jewish ceremonial law did serve a purpose in its own time, however, and also functioned as a symbol for the Christian sacraments that would later be instituted.

wise] grace is not grace" (Rom 11:6). God forbid that righteousness would come to someone keeping the Law by the works contained in the Law; instead, righteousness comes in order that one may keep the Law. In the very fact that one keeps the Law, one is made righteous by grace. For one is not first a doer of the Law as though one might be made righteous for having kept the Law. But just as humans are created so that they might live as humans, so those who keep the Law are made righteous so that they might live in a righteous way; or that they might appear to be what they are when keeping the Law, namely, righteous. Now we ought to understand that the Apostle is speaking here of Jews who have been converted to the Lord and fulfill the Law spiritually. The gentile converts do by nature what the Law requires, and by doing this are made righteous. Indeed, the spirit of grace renews in them the natural law that had been inscribed by nature on their heart by God, but was then erased by vice. Those converted to the Lord have God's Law written not on tablets, but on their hearts (cf. 2 Cor 3:3). Hence they have embraced the righteousness of the Law with the inmost affection of their heart, where "faith is working through love" (Gal 5:6).

vv. 14-16 For whenever the gentiles, who do not have the law, do by nature the things contained in the law, they, without having the law, are a law unto themselves. They show that the work contained in the law is written on their hearts, with their conscience bearing witness to them and their thoughts by turns accusing or else defending them on the day when, according to my gospel, God will judge human secrets. The Apostle wrote: "of thoughts accusing." The Latin translator appears to follow the Greek custom that employs the genitive case in place of the ablative, since the Greek language has no ablative.[10] But Paul says "of thoughts" because it is on the basis of thoughts that deeds are judged, and one is thereby reckoned innocent or guilty. When he said "of thoughts," he was not referring to those thoughts that existed then, but those that exist now. For even as all our deeds and thoughts may vanish from memory, they do not vanish from our conscience. They will all be brought forward into the light before God as judge. There will be a truly fearsome judgment where nothing is brought forward

---

10. The Latin translation of the Greek New Testament from which William is quoting reads *cogitationum accusantium* ("of accusing thoughts") in the genitive case instead of *cogitationibus accusantibus* ("with accusing thoughts") in the ablative, which is found in the Vulgate. On William's concern with grammar, scholarship, and theology, see Richard W. Southern, *Scholastic Humanism and the Unification of Europe* (Oxford: Blackwell, 1995), 79-89.

from the outside, but everything is produced from the conscience: the accuser, the witness, the judge, and the case.

Jews and the Written Law

v. 17 But if you are called a Jew and rest in the law. Here the Apostle undertakes a valid and necessary disputation about the Law. This is directed not only against Jews but also against enemies of grace and those Paul had reckoned contentious just a little earlier (Rom 2:8). In this regard, recalling the four distinct levels of the Law or progress in the Law will greatly help the reader's effort. A person at the first level lives according to the flesh in the deepest ignorance and with no resistance from reason. At the second level are those who have become cognizant of sin through the Law. Yet apart from the assistance of the Holy Spirit, even as they wish to live according to the Law, they are overcome and sin knowingly. With knowledge of the commandment urging it on, sin works every sort of disordered desire in the human being, and when a mass of transgression has been accumulated, the Scripture is fulfilled: "The law entered in, that sin might abound" (Rom 5:20).[11] Now the third level is one of good hope for human beings. God has so regarded human beings that we may believe that God helps fulfill what he commands. And even though flesh still provokes lust, we have begun to be moved by God's Spirit with the more powerful strength of love. There remains, however, something within that still fights against us. For all our infirmity has not yet been healed. Yet the righteous live by faith, and live righteously, as long as their delight in righteousness conquers and they do not submit to the evil of lust. If anyone prevails in these things with pious perseverance, then at the fourth and final level a peace remains that will be fulfilled after this life in the rest of the spirit and then in the resurrection of the flesh. Of these four different levels the first is prior to the Law, the second under the Law, the third under grace, and the fourth in full and perfect

---

11. Disordered desire *(concupiscentia)* is not actually sin itself but can lead to sin. Although the guilt *(culpa)* of original sin is removed through Baptism, the penalty *(poena)* remains, thereby subjecting all people to the power of disordered desire, which can be resisted only through the gift of grace. The Latin noun *concupiscentia* is translated as "disordered desire," except in Aquinas when it appears in tandem with the verb *concupisco*, meaning to desire in a disordered manner or to covet. For conciseness and to highlight the parallel between the noun and the verb, the singular noun is then translated as "covetousness." The plural *(concupiscentiae)* is translated as "disordered desires."

peace.[12] Nevertheless, grace was not previously lacking to those who should have received a share in it, although it was veiled and hidden at that time in keeping with the ordering of the epochs. The entire body of the Letter employs these four different levels, referring here to a person of God individually and there to the people of God generally.

If, the Apostle asks, **you are called a Jew**. The Apostle is a skilled physician of souls. He is treating two peoples who are sick [Jew and gentile]. His own stock appears to be the more dangerously ill, and he is weakened with the infirm. Yet he does not spare the gentiles, but actually rebukes them sternly. He notes the same crimes among the Jews and mildly reprimands them. For through the obedience of the gentiles, he hopes to spur the Jews to perseverance until, as physicians would, he alleviates the disease's cause, which is arrogance. As physicians are used to saying, once a symptom has been lessened, then one may administer a more secure remedy to what caused it. Thus he has not yet refuted [Jews] separately to relieve the illness, but has done so together with the others [the gentiles]. But now after a common admonition, he seeks for himself more unimpeded access to his ill patient. First, he uses the strong bonds of reason and sets about binding the one who is delirious. So by readily accepting gentiles as followers, he may adapt even the hardness of the Jews to grace. For both gentiles and Jews, in accord with the different levels mentioned above, are found to be under the Law, either written or natural.

vv. 17-20 But if you are called a Jew and rest in the law, and boast about God, and have known his will, and approve the more profitable things since you have been instructed by the law, you are confident that you yourself are a guide to the blind, a light to those in darkness, an instructor of the foolish, a teacher of infants, because you possess the form of knowledge and truth in the law. One should recognize that all the items presented here as though in praise of a false Jew ought to be taken ironically. Everything the Apostle says here resembles a medicinal plaster that causes pride to swell up in order to reduce its vanity and end its uselessness. For what is so inane as to boast about what one does not have, or to preach what one does not do? Indeed, that people was apathetic about the second level of the people of God, that is, with reference to the Law. Although they took so much pride in having received it, they failed to fulfill it even in a carnal way. Presumptuous about themselves, they approached grace more tardily. For if

---

12. See Augustine, *Commentary on the Epistle to the Romans*, CSEL 84:6.

they truly rested in the Law and gloried in God, they would not have done the very things that they preached must not be done.

He says, **If you are called a Jew**; yet you are not. To be sure, the Church is the true Judea, and the Lord God is clothed with the beauty of her confession (Ps 92:1/93:1).[13] You appear to take your name from the Fathers from whom you have actually departed. You used to have circumcision of the flesh as the sign of faith, but circumcision of the heart as that very faith itself. You were used to having kings from the tribe of Judah and for that reason were called Jews. But when you denied Christ as king of the tribe of Judah, you lost both the kingdom and the name together. **You rest in the law** while you condemn and ridicule the different errors of the gentiles; you rest in a carnal understanding of the Law and resolve that nothing further should be sought. And **you boast about God** as if you are the peculiar people of God and he is known only in Judea. **And you have known his will**. "For God has not done the same with every nation and has not revealed the divine judgments to them" (Ps 147:9/147:20). **And you approve the more profitable** among many profitable things. Because **you have been instructed by the law, you are confident** in presuming that **you yourself**, without the guidance of the Holy Spirit, **are a guide to the blind**; as a result, you "both will fall into the pit" (Mt 15:14). You are confident that **you are a light to those in darkness**, as if enlightening them, an **instructor** of the gentiles, **a teacher of the simple** who are **foolish** in the Law. It is as though they ought to learn from the Law to repeat the trifling verses of your fables because **you possess the form of knowledge and truth in the law**, that is, the formulated and true knowledge of the Law to which no one should dare add anything.

vv. 21-24 You then who teach another, will you not teach yourself? You who preach against stealing, do you steal? Jews robbed from each other. And what is worse, they also wanted to steal a sound understanding of the Law, grace from the Church, and Christ's coming from the world. By pursuing their own desires they also committed adultery in the flesh, although more so in the spirit. They followed after the idols of the gentiles, but even more the idols of their own hearts. They were sacrilegious in both, for they did not place the sacred in sacred places.

---

13. This is a classic allegorical reading whereby Old Testament references to Jerusalem or Israel and the like are understood to be spiritual references to the Church. To read this passage only on the literal-historical level, therefore, was regarded as a carnal, rather than a spiritual, interpretation.

They also **dishonored God by the transgression of the** very **law** about which they believed they were to boast. Indeed, they dishonored God, for they caused **"the name of God to be blasphemed among the gentiles"** (Ezek 36:20). The name Christian stems from Christ; therefore, when they blaspheme the name, they blaspheme the author of the name. Those Jews censured by the Apostle already share the Christian name, but since they foolishly boasted about their earlier status and put themselves ahead of the gentiles, the Apostle prudently humbles them from their earlier status. He proves that what they believed made them more striking and glorious, namely, the Law and circumcision, were now pointless and unnecessary. Both amounted to confusion for them rather than glory. After discussing the Law, the Apostle now turns to circumcision.

The Role of Circumcision

v. 25 Circumcision is of value if you obey the law, namely, the law of circumcision. For circumcision is cutting off evil from oneself. The law of circumcision is to persist in good works so that the following Scripture may be fulfilled, "Depart from evil and do good" (Ps 36:27/Ps 37:27). True circumcision is the circumcision of the heart, that is, a will unsoiled by any lust. This occurs not by the letter's teaching and threatening, but by the spirit's aiding and healing. **Circumcision**, therefore, **is of value if you obey the law. But if you violate the law**, so that instead you observe the circumcision of the flesh, **Your circumcision is made uncircumcision**, that is, it is reckoned as unfaithfulness.

vv. 26-27 If, then, a man who is uncircumcised keeps the precepts of the law, will not his uncircumcision be regarded as circumcision? And if he fulfills the law, will not the man who by nature is uncircumcision pass judgment on you, who by the letter and circumcision are a transgressor of the law? The Apostle says, **If a man is uncircumcised**, that is, he is one among those who have come from uncircumcision. The Apostle is writing of those who keep the precepts of the Law, and he compares them with Jews who transgress the Law by letter and circumcision of the flesh. He says that they should not be keeping that Law, namely, the law of works or sacraments. Instead, they should keep the precepts of the Law, that is, its moral discipline. In keeping the Law, an uncircumcised man is so greatly ahead of the circumcised who breaks the Law that the former will pass judgment on the latter. The Apostle rightly adds, **If he fulfills the law**. For whoever lives according to the letter observes the Law; whoever lives according to the spirit fulfills it. Yet perfection is found in the one who says, "I have not come to abolish the law but to fulfill it" (Mt 5:17).

vv. 28-29 Therefore, a person is not a Jew who is one outwardly; nor is circumcision something outward in the flesh, but someone is a Jew who is a Jew inwardly, and the circumcision is of the heart spiritually and not literally. This person's praise is not from human beings but from God. We should look carefully at the meaning of the Apostle's argument. For he is apparently addressing a variety of persons, some in one way and some in another. This might cause readers to misconstrue the direction of the Apostle's thought and become confused as if they had lost the way. As a result, readers would miss the end to which the arguer [Paul] intends to lead them. This end, stated briefly, is grace or the commendation of grace. To return to what was stated just above, Paul cherishes both Jews and gentiles with the love of a father. He embraces Jews in the flesh and in the spirit, but gentiles for the sake of the grace of the gospel and to the honor of his own ministry. He threatened the contentious, both Jews and gentiles, with anger and with its consequences, but he promised glory and honor to both Jews and gentiles who do good works. He humbles both Jews and gentiles and then elevates, or makes them equal by turns, and thus labors to temper and to guide them in everything so that neither group would receive more glory or envy.

At one time he says of the gentiles, "For whoever has sinned without the law will perish without the law." Then he immediately adds regarding circumcision, "Whoever has sinned under the law will be judged by the law" (Rom 2:12). Again, he lifts up the gentiles, "For when the gentiles, who do not have the law," etc. (Rom 2:14). Once more, he turns the discussion to the Jews when he says, "If you are called a Jew," etc. (Rom 2:17). But lest he appear too excessive in his rebuke of the Jews, he adds, "Circumcision has value if you observe the law." However, he immediately sets limits to boasting against the gentiles, "But if you violate the law, your circumcision is made uncircumcision" (Rom 2:25). He lifts up the gentiles somewhat when he says, "If, then, a man who is uncircumcised keeps the precepts of the law," etc. He goes on to raise their spirits still more: "If he fulfills the law, will not the man who by nature is uncircumcision pass judgment on you who by the letter and by circumcision are a transgressor of the law?" (Rom 2:26-27). Because there were, to be sure, many promises in the Law and the Prophets that seemed to treat circumcision, the Apostle also opened the way for gentiles to hope for these things. **Therefore, a person is not a Jew who is one out-wardly; nor is circumcision something outward in the flesh, but someone is a Jew who is one inwardly**, etc. Thereupon follows the text we now hold in our hands.

ROMANS 3

Peter Abelard

What Advantage Is There in Circumcision?

v. 1 Then what advantage? The contrary argument, which Jews could make against the reasoning stated above, the Apostle now raises for himself to re-solve. Indeed, Jews might say, "You have maintained that circumcision turns into uncircumcision, and uncircumcision into circumcision" (cf. Rom 2:25-29). **Then what advantage does a Jew have** over a gentile, that is, what greater benefit does circumcision confer on Jews than on gentiles, who were called "dogs" (Phil 3:2) and unclean? **Or what is the profit of circumcision** for the circumcised? This, to be sure, the Apostle adds as if an explanation of the preceding. It could well be that when he says **a Jew** we are to consider only those belonging to the tribe of Judah, for which reason they have been called Jews.[1] Also, the phrase **what advantage** could pertain to something good as well as to something bad, although perhaps more to something bad, since in the preceding passage he had chiefly rebuked the Jews. Now by "uncircumcision" the Apostle customarily means gentiles and by "circumcision" he means Jews.

v. 2 The Lord once granted **much**, that is, greater profit to Jews than to gen-tiles. And it is greater **in every way**, that is, in all ways, by instructing Jewish people through the Law, by strengthening them through countless miracles

---

1. In Latin this verbal correlation is immediately apparent: *Iudaei* (Jews); *ad tribum Iudae* (tribe of Judah).

and benefits, and by rousing them to the love of God. But among these gifts that God gave them, the Law was the **first**, that is, the greatest. Consequently, Jews were instructed not only by natural law, like the gentiles, but above all by the written law. This gift was **first**, which is to say, greatest because **the pronouncements of God were entrusted**, that is, committed, **to them** in the Law or even in the Prophets. Indeed, this gift can both teach them and keep them forever.

But notice that the Apostle does not actually say "committed," but rather **entrusted**, as if this teaching were adapted for them in time. Indeed, through the spiritual and right understanding of Jews and in their external rites, in which they greatly trusted, it was supposed to pass to us and come to a close. God, so to speak, is also called creditor of his own pronouncements; on their behalf God would require obedience from those to whom these things are entrusted. The Apostle calls these words the **pronouncements of God** as if they excelled other kinds of speech. **In every way**, that is, in the fruit of obedience and in teaching that brings salvation.

v. 3 Indeed, what? What do the divine pronouncements to this people matter, someone might ask, when because of their unbelief God has not fulfilled the good promised to them, whether the good of humankind's restoration through God's Son or that of any of God's promises? The Apostle refutes this in two ways: by showing that not all of them were unbelieving, so that the promises were not completely denied them, and that God, since "God is true" (Rom 3:4), cannot break promises. Read accordingly: I have stated correctly that the greatest among the divine pronouncements (Rom 3:2) is that through which God might win over his people. **Indeed, what** impedes the divine purpose? **If some have not believed** these pronouncements, that is, the ones promised or proclaimed to them there, has **their unbelief**, namely, the unbelief of those not believing, **cancelled out the faith of God**, by which they believed God, such that the belief of Moses himself, of Joshua, and of the other faithful would not have occurred?

v. 4 Not at all, since that would mean that their faith, which believed the promises foretold to them there, would be cancelled out and rendered useless. **God is true, however**. I have said **not at all**, not rashly but with forethought. This is because **God is true**, that is, steadfast or unwavering, in the things God promises or foretells. **But every human [is] a liar**, which is to say that humans are so changeable in purpose that they can easily change their plan or will.

Perhaps one may ask if the human in Christ, united with divinity, could lie or sin.[2] The God-human, however, seems to have been excluded since the first statement in the text, **God is true**, is immediately joined by **but every human is a liar**. Consequently, the statement that **every human is a liar** should be understood only of a plain human, and not of the human who is God. Without doubt, this human united with God, either after having been united or while united with God, could not sin at all. Similarly, the predestined, after having been predestined or while predestined, cannot be condemned.

But, to be sure, if one says unqualifiedly *(simpliciter)* that this human being, who is united with God, cannot sin in any way, then someone can doubt it. For if one cannot sin or do evil at all, what merit does anyone have in avoiding sin that one cannot commit anyway? Or how does one also say that one cannot incur sin in any way? Therefore, Boethius, in his *Against Eutyches and Nestorius,* writes of the human being whom God has assumed, "How can it happen that God assumed such a human being as Adam was before sin, when in Adam the will and the disposition were able to sin?"[3] Furthermore, we read in praise of a righteous person, "Who could have transgressed and did not transgress, and could have done evil and did not do it?" (Sir 31:10); and "That individual shall dwell on high," etc. (Isa 33:16). This certainly pertains to the free will of human beings; hence they have it in their power to do both good and evil. If Christ did not have this same power, he would seem to be deprived of free will, such that he avoided sin necessarily rather than voluntarily, and possessed free will from nature rather than from grace.

For what has been conveyed to someone by grace comes as a gift rather than from some special quality of the recipient's nature. What we receive as the gift of another rather than by ourselves should not be called natural, but instead freely given. Who would deny that this human being who is united to God in one Person, and consisting as he does of soul and flesh, can also subsist in his own nature just like other human beings? Otherwise it would seem that he is of lesser power, if he could not subsist in himself like the rest of humankind.[4] And it would also appear as though he possesses a nature

2. Note that Abelard does not speak of human nature *(natura),* but the human being *(homo)* that is united to the divine nature. As the discussion continues, this should be borne in mind, for what are the ramifications of saying that the divine Word united itself to a human being as opposed to a human nature?

3. Boethius, *Against Eutyches and Nestorius,* PL 64:1353.

4. Abelard is wading into a major point of theological debate in the twelfth century, one which actually got his student, Peter Lombard, into trouble: what precisely did the divine

that is composed more of accident than of substance.[5] Yet if he could also exist in and of himself, then why could he not also sin just like the rest of the human race?

It seems to us that in this case, as in other matters, we should pay careful attention to the force of the propositions. This means considering when the delimitation "possible" or "necessary" is included in some instances, and when a proposition is stated unqualifiedly, and so without added delimitation, in other instances.[6] It is certainly true, if stated unqualifiedly, that it is possible for someone who is predestined, and is to be saved, to be damned. This is because it is entirely possible that this same person might not have been predestined nor have been intended for salvation. Yet with the delimitation ["necessary"] it is not true to say that it is possible for someone to be damned who has been predestined or is to be saved. In this vein, it is possible for anyone maimed to have two feet, since every human being is a biped. And it is possible for someone blind to see. But it is not possible to have two feet, or to see, after one has been maimed or become blind. Otherwise it would be possible for there to be a regression from privation to possession, and that is completely false. Perhaps, then, it is not absurd for us to concede unqualifiedly that it is possible for the human being united with God to sin, although not after having been united with God or while united. It is surely impossible that Christ, who is simultaneously God and human being, would sin in any way at all, inasmuch as the very name "Christ" expresses the union of God and human being. And so it seems that the proposition that **every human being is a liar** is a true statement in every way.

As it is written, "That you may be justified." By the authority of a psalm (Ps 50:6/51:4), the Apostle shows how God is true in fulfilling promises and is steadfast in purpose. Indeed, God had promised David that Christ would spring from David's seed (2 Sam 7:8-16). After David's adultery this promise seemed completely annulled. What is more, it seemed utterly incongruous that God's Son should assume flesh from the seed of such a sinner. Consequently, since God had made this promise to David, it would have been necessary that God become a liar. But this could never happen.

Word unite itself to in the incarnation? This issue also arises in the selection translated for this volume from the Cambridge Commentator (also Abelard's student). See pp. 37, 71-72.

5. In keeping with Aristotle's *Categories* (1b-2b), substance refers to the nature or essence of something, while accidents are the accessory aspects, such as color and size, of a thing.

6. The following discussion is based on Aristotle's discussion of true and false statements in his *On Interpretation* (18b) and also *Categories* (13b).

Therefore, the same David, who had erred so severely, was aware of this when he said, "Against you alone have I sinned" (Ps 50:6/51:4), that is, against the honor of you alone — you who also direct iniquity for good and convert all things to your glory. He added, "And I have done evil in your sight" (Ps 50:6/51:4), with you knowing of it — you before whom nothing remains hidden. In this way it becomes obvious how righteous you are — you who, because you are just and true, cannot thwart your promise, although you know I have not deserved your keeping your promises to me. For if this sin were hidden to God, there would appear to be no reason why God should not fulfill the promise. But now, even as God knows that the sin has been committed and that the sinner has merited the contrary, God still preserves the immovable steadfastness of his own truth by fulfilling the promises. **"That you may be justified in your words."** By this David means **"that you may be justified"** by carrying out your words in the promises that you have made to me, which is to say that you appear just and truthful. **"And that you overcome"** human judgment **"when you are judged"** by human beings. This refers to your being accused of a lie as though, on account of my transgressions, you would be unable to fulfill your promise in the future.

v. 5 But if. The Apostle himself introduces opposition to the foregoing as if he might say, "It has been asserted that God is justified, that is, God appears just and truthful especially in light of such sins, since they could not obstruct his promise. Indeed, God even converts them to his own glory." **But if**, as stated above in the example of David, our sins point out the **justice of God**, that is, if they contribute to the praise and glory of God's truth, **what should we say?** In other words, what can be our response to the objection in the following question: **Is God unjust, who inflicts wrath?** This refers to vengeance on account of sins, which — as noted above — manifests God's justice. This is to say that they reveal God as exceedingly praiseworthy because of the unchangeable purpose of God's truth. The Apostle does not make this objection from his own person, as if it did not seem to him that in this God would act unjustly. Therefore, he adds, **I speak as a human being**, that is, according to sensual flesh, which does not understand the things that are of God (1 Cor 2:14-16). Hence he is not speaking here according to the spiritual human being who discerns all things, that is, who holds to the right judgment of reason in divine as well as human matters.

v. 6 And, therefore, **Not at all**. We may not assume that God acts unjustly by punishing sins, which also contribute to his glory. For although sins are not good in themselves, the fact that there are sins may actually be a good thing. Consequently, Augustine writes in the *Enchiridion:* "Nothing happens unless the Almighty wills it to happen. Either God permits it or God makes it happen. . . . We should not doubt that God works for the good even in permitting to happen whatever evil things may happen. For God permits it only on the basis of a just judgment, and surely all that is just is good." Likewise, "Indeed, unless it were good that evil things should exist, in no way would the Almighty permit them to exist."[7] **Otherwise**, that is, if it were different than we are saying, if God had worked unjustly in imposing vengeance for sins, **how** could God judge **the world?** How could God judge all people together, the good as well as the evil, inasmuch as God repays them for their merits with glory or with punishment?

v. 7 For if the truth. The Apostle returns once more to the objection noted above (Rom 3:5) as if commending it: by punishing sins, God rightly seems unjust if sins contribute to his justice. For they should no longer be credited as sins, but rather as good works that contribute to God's truth. This is saying, **For if, by my lying, the truth of God has abounded to his glory**, that is, if the immutability of God's truth is made more praiseworthy by the mutability and fickleness of my own professing — even as I may lie to God yet God cannot lie to me. **Why am I still being judged as a sinner** as long as what I do contributes to God's glory? Why should the things I do be reckoned as sins?

v. 8 And why not say instead, **"let us do evil that good may come,"** that is, let us sin so that God may be glorified by our sins? **As we are slandered** by certain people, and **as some assert that we are saying this**. [This is what they think] I and the rest of the spiritual ones are saying when we maintain that even evil things are so well ordered that they contribute to God's glory. Whence the doctor mentioned above also stated in Book 9 of his *On the City of God,* when discussing the goodness of God and the malice of the devil, "As God is the supremely good Creator of good natures, so God is the most just ruler of evil wills." Likewise in the same passage he writes regarding the devil: "When God created the devil, God was certainly not ignorant of the devil's future malevolence and foresaw the good that God would bring out of the devil's malice." Next, in the same place he writes, "For God would never have created anyone, not to speak of angels but of human be-

7. Augustine, *Enchiridion,* 95-96, PL 40:276.

ings, whose future wickedness God foreknew, unless God had equally known to what uses God could adapt them."[8] So too in Augustine's *Enchiridion:* "For the Almighty God, since God is supremely good, would never permit anything evil to exist among God's works, unless God were so omnipotent and good that he could bring good even out of evil."[9] **Of those** refers to those who slander us. That is, **of those** speaking not as much from their own judgment as from the effort to slander us. It is so manifest that evil has been ordered for good by God that the pagan philosopher Plato also clearly professed, "For indeed nothing happens whose origin is not preceded by a legitimate cause and reason."[10]

No One Is Righteous in God's Sight

v. 9 What then? I have said that it is just to condemn those who revile us. So it would seem that we have commended ourselves greatly, as though on account of our own merits we are the sorts of people in whom there is nothing to be slandered. **What then?** Can it be said that **we are superior** to those who ought justly to be condemned? Are we more worthy than they owing to our own merits and virtue? **In no way**. In fact, if we do possess what is good, it comes from God rather than from ourselves. Along these lines, the Apostle also writes, "It is not of the one who wills, nor of the one who runs, but of God who shows mercy" (Rom 9:16). God's mercy, rather than our strength, is sufficient for salvation, since of ourselves we are all simultaneously culpable. For, as we have shown above, both Jews and gentiles are without excuse. And the point is this: **For we have charged**. We have drawn up the case, as it were, in charging that both **Jews** and **Greeks** — who, it is agreed, are wiser — **are all under sin**. That is to say, they all stand accused and have earned punishment as transgressors. And here the Apostle returns to his attack as he gathers testimonies from the Scriptures by which to prove them all equally inexcusable defendants.

v. 10 As it is written, in Psalm 13/14, **"There is no one righteous,"** etc. This psalm, which contains the testimonies before us, conveys a general invective, so to speak, against all who, not recognizing the time of his visitation, con-

---

8. Augustine, *City of God,* 11.17, CCSL 48:336-37.
9. Augustine, *Enchiridion,* 3.11, CCSL 46:53.
10. Plato, *Timaeus,* 28a.

sidered it an abomination that God became incarnate and suffered for the sake of human redemption. Whence the same Apostle also says elsewhere, "But we preach Christ crucified, indeed a stumbling block to the Jews, and foolishness to the gentiles" (1 Cor 1:23). And so in the psalm, "The fool said, 'There is no God'" (Ps 13:1/14:1). This refers to "the natural person who does not perceive the things that come from the Spirit of God" (1 Cor 2:14). [He does not grasp] the mysterious wonder of our restoration. For when the fool looked at the human fragility taken on [by God], he said, "There is no God." Indeed, he has not said this merely with words, as Peter denied Jesus (Mt 26:69-75), but even in his heart because he believed such a thing.

"**There is no one righteous.**" This means that there are very few, as if none, who are just — who render to others what is their due. Yet far be it from us to believe that the Church will not persevere at least among some believers from the first elect to the last. The Church gathered up many believers before the time of the Law, and still more afterward. We see that here with the one who composed this psalm, and then later in the time of grace when she gathered countless others. Whence we read that also in the time of the advent of the Lord, after blindness had overtaken a very large portion of Israel, some survived. For example, there were Simeon, Anna, and the very mother of the Lord with her husband Joseph, as well as the father and mother of John the Baptist along with him. Yet often when it is said "all" or "none," this does not actually mean all, but rather a very large portion. It is like saying of a city in which only few people are good: "All are evil who live in it, or none in it are good." Hence Jerome's remark in *To Pope Damasus* concerning the prodigal son: "'My son, you are always with me, and all that is mine is yours' (Lk 15:31). This does not mean angels and thrones, does it? By 'all' you should understand the prophets and divine discourse. For along the lines that we have already explained, 'all' need not refer to the entirety but rather to the largest portion. For example: 'They have all turned aside' (Ps 13:3/14:3); 'All who came before me are thieves and robbers' (Jn 10:8); and 'To all people I have become all things, in order that I might gain all' (1 Cor 9:22); or 'All seek their own, not the things that are of Jesus Christ' (Phil 2:21)."[11]

v. 11 But as to why there is **no one righteous**, the Apostle adds that it is because **"There is none who understands God"** or **"seeks God."** No one bothers to heed God's promises or warnings, for "the natural person does not

---

11. Jerome, Letter 21, CSEL 54:136-37.

perceive the things that come from the Spirit of God" (1 Cor 2:14), but is instead "like the horse and the mule, in whom there is no understanding" (Ps 31:9/32:9). And since **"there is none who understands God,"** no one knows how to seek God through repentance, which has been lost through negligence.

v. 12 He links negligence to this when he says, **"all have turned aside."** After having forsaken God, they directed their zeal toward the world. For the sake of the temporal, they disdained the eternal and thus **"all"** alike, Jews as well as gentiles, **"have become useless"** to themselves. Indeed, none is so iniquitous so as to become useless in every way. For God, as we said, even makes the best use of evil, as with the wickedness of Judas or the devil. Indeed, in the same action God, both the Father and the Son, and Judas worked together. The Father handed over the Son, the Son handed over himself, and Judas handed over the Lord. And that handing over, which Judas also caused, led to the general redemption of all. Through the preaching of the Apostle Peter, some were converted and saved, but the Lord transformed the wickedness of Judas into the salvation of all. For our greater good, divine grace made use of Judas's bad deed as much as Peter's good deed. And who would doubt that the wickedness of the devil is always disposed for the good by God, since the devil does nothing without God's permission, whether by punishing the guilty, or by testing the righteous, or by doing anything whatever? Hence one's power can only be righteous, just as one's will can only be unrighteous, if one has the power from God and the will from oneself. "For there is no power," as the Apostle himself attests later on, "but from God" (Rom 13:1). Hence the Truth says to the unjust governor [Pilate], "You would have no power over me unless it was given to you from above" (Jn 19:11). Those who do evil, therefore, should be considered more as useless to themselves than useless altogether. For in the order of things, the divine arrangement, as we have shown, permits nothing to be done either uselessly or superfluously.

Explaining how they **"all have turned aside,"** or from what they **have turned aside**, namely, from good work, the Apostle adds, **"There is no one who does good."** There is no one who does rightly and who fulfills what ought to be done. Judas's act of handing over the Lord might appear to be good, since the Father and the Son did this at the same time. Yet Judas did not act in a good way, precisely because he acted from an evil intention, that is, from greed. For the Lord has taught that all works are to be judged by intention, "If your eye is pure," etc. (Mt 6:22; Lk 11:34). Otherwise Judas's work, in which the Father as well as the Son acted mercifully, should also be called good.

"There is not so much as one." The text repeats the earlier statement, **"There is no one who does good,"** so as to provide some delimitation, lest one suppose that this was said in general. Therefore, it is as if the psalmist had said, **"There is no one who does good"** until one ventures to believe and to join oneself through love to the one who truly is one and immutable by nature, and unique by preeminence, namely, God or Christ, who is "one God and one mediator of humans" (1 Tim 2:5). Through faith in this one, we will be saved without the works of the law, as indicated in what follows. The words, **"There is no one who does good, there is not so much as one,"** can also be understood as if the Apostle had said, "There is hardly anyone who does good, that is, there is almost no one. For where there remains only one, almost no one does."

vv. 10-19 "Their throat is an open grave." Those three subsequent verses, which we have in our Psalter, do not read continuously in the Hebrew, according to the witness of Origen or Jerome. For this reason in his commentary on Romans, Origen maintains:

> In some Latin manuscripts those verses that follow are found continuously in Psalm 13/14, but in almost all Greek manuscripts the text of Psalm 13/14 goes up only to the verse "there is no one who does good, there is not so much as one" (Ps 13:1 and 3; Ps 14:1 and 3). But that is what the Apostle says — **As it is written: "There is no one righteous. There is no one who understands, no one who seeks God"** — is not found in the psalm in the same words, but was written thus: "From heaven the Lord looked down upon the human children to see if there are any that understand and seek God." And his statement, **"There is no one righteous"** (Rom 3:10), I think, he has taken from: "There is no one who does good, there is not so much as one" (Ps 52:4/Ps 53:3). But the statement, **"Their throat is an open grave; with their tongues they have dealt deceitfully"** (Ps 5:10/Ps 5:9) will be found in Psalm 5. **"The venom of vipers is under their lips"** (Ps 139:4/Ps 140:3), I think, is taken from a psalm whose words were unchanged. **"Their mouth is full of cursing and bitterness"** clearly is taken from Psalm 9/10 (Ps 9:28/Ps 10:7). **"Their feet swift to shed blood"** you will find in Isaiah as well as Proverbs (Isa 59:7 and Prov 1:16). But as for the passage: **"Destruction and misery are in their paths; and the way of peace they have not known,"** I do not recall where it is written

entirely as it is here. Yet I suspect that it can be found in one of the prophets (Isa 59:7). However, in the Psalms it is written, "There is no fear of God before their eyes" (Ps 35:2a/Ps 36:1). But all these testimonies seem to have been collected so that the Apostle might show that when he charges that "Jews and Greeks are all under sin" (Rom 3:9) he is not expressing so much his own view as that of Scripture. That they "are all under sin" should be understood as a statement about those who are taught not to sin by either natural or written law.[12]

Jerome, in his preface to Book 16, *On Isaiah,* writes to Eustochius:

> You have posed a small question noting that the Apostle appropriated eight verses of Psalm 13/14 which are read in the churches and yet are not included in the Hebrew text: "An open grave," etc. (Rom 3:13). I have noticed that this testimony has been woven together from the Psalms and Isaiah. The opening lines, "an open grave," etc., are drawn from Psalm 5 (Ps 5:10/Ps 5:9). But what follows, "The venom of vipers is under their lips," is from Psalm 139/140 (Ps 139:4/Ps 140:3). Furthermore, the statement, "Their mouth is full of cursing and bitterness," is taken from Psalm 9/10. But the three verses which follow — "Their feet swift to shed blood"; "Destruction and misery are in their paths"; "And the way of peace they have not known" — are found in Isaiah (Isa 59:7-8). The eighth verse, "There is no fear of God before their eyes," is at the beginning of Psalm 35/36 (Ps 35:2/Ps 36:1).[13]

And Jerome adds:

> Finally, all the Greek authors, who through their erudition have left to us commentaries on the Psalms, note these versicles with a dart and move on. They frankly acknowledge that these verses are not found in the Hebrew, nor with the translators of the Septuagint, but rather in the common edition which in Greek is called "koine" [common], and is spread throughout the whole world.[14]

But now we will return to the text.

---

12. Origen, *Commentary on the Epistle to the Romans,* PG 14:929b.
13. Jerome, *Commentary on Isaiah,* CCSL 73A:641-42.
14. Jerome, *Commentary on Isaiah,* CCSL 73A:642-43.

v. 12 It was said, **"All have turned aside,"** and **"There is no one who does good."** And not only have they **turned aside**, but they also strive to make others turn aside and do much harm. As if it were not sufficient for them that they alone be damned, they seek out many allies as though for their own defense.

v. 13 "Throat." Since it is the instrument for forming or producing speech, **throat** signifies the spoken word that is emitted by the throat. Hence **"their"** spoken word, which persuades to evil, is like **"an open grave"** because of the evil conceived in the mind. It can be compared to the stench of a cadaver enclosed within, contaminating others and offending the noses of bystanders as it confuses and damages their natural judgment. **"Their tongues."** The Apostle offers a sort of explanation here of what he had previously expressed parabolically when he says that they speak deceitfully. For against their own conscience they recommend those things to which they persuade or disparage those from which they discourage.

Moses himself had called **"the venom of asps"** "incurable" (Deut 32:33), and thereby attests that it is worse than other poison. It is deadly, which is to say criminal. For it signifies sins that, as if through their persuasions, inject poison in others. But these sins to which they persuade are said to be **"under their lips,"** since they are so concealed in their cunning words that they cannot be detected by listeners. By the incurable **venom of asps** we can also understand that unpardonable sin against the Holy Spirit (cf. Mt 12:32; Lk 12:10). This involves, whether from envy or avarice, attributing to the devil some of the works that one knows full well come from God. Several of the Jews, in order to turn people away from Christ, disparaged his works as though diabolical (Mt 12:24, 27; Mk 3:22; Lk 11:15, 18). Nevertheless, they did not doubt that these things came about through the Spirit of God, that is, by divine grace. Hence they are said to have sinned against the Holy Spirit or against the gift of divine grace. They lied in opposition to their own conscience since they knowingly attributed these things to the devil when they ought to have been giving glory to God. Although that sin could have been wiped away by repentance, it was nevertheless forbidden irrevocably by divine judgment so that no one who had fallen into this sin might return upon recovering one's senses. That is why it is called unpardonable. Yet this sin still lurked under their lips. It did not appear on their lips because so long as they committed a crime against their own conscience they were holding something different in their heart than what they were revealing by their mouth.

v. 14 "Their mouth." For themselves, as well as for those who assented, they acquired condemnation and bitterness from the Lord. This is in keeping with what the prophet said, "The voice of the day of the Lord is bitter; the strong will meet with tribulation" (Zeph 1:14). Such a mouth is **"full of cursing and bitterness."** Such a curse may be deemed bitter indeed when it is uttered against the condemned in their damnation, "Depart, you accursed, into the everlasting fire" (Mt 25:41). Yet there is another sort of curse, one that might be considered mild and paternal, when we level the curse of "anathema" on someone for the sake of correction rather than damnation.

v. 15 "Their feet are swift to shed blood," that is, they have a disposition prone to homicide, even if they were not permitted to carry out the deed itself. For the foot with which we stride signifies the feeling, or the will, by which we are led to action.

v. 16 "Ruin and misery," that is, miserable ruin, is **"in their paths."** That is, deeds prepare one for eternal death. They also ruin others along with them, and by example corrupt others, so that they are scattered like dust blown by the wind from the surface of the earth. Such is the diabolical temptation that drives them hither and yon and casts them down from the stability of the earth of the living.

v. 17 "And the way of peace they have not known." For in their own ways, they are altogether obliterated by damnation since they have not known the way of God. This is to say that they have not known Christ through whom — as the mediator between God and human beings — we have been granted peace and are reconciled to God. For he is "our peace," as the same Apostle says, "and he has made both one" (Eph 2:14). Christ says also of himself, "I am the way" (Jn 14:6), and "I am the gate. Anyone who enters in through me will be saved" (Jn 10:9). This **"way of peace,"** namely, Christ, **"they have not known."** They regarded him with contempt owing to the weakness of his flesh, and they reckoned him a mere human being, thereby failing to honor him as God. Neither did they believe John [the Baptist], who threatened them when he said, "For now the axe is laid to the root of the trees. Every tree therefore that doth not yield good fruit," etc. (Mt 3:10).

v. 18 It is for this reason that he adds: **"There is no fear of God [before their eyes]."** This refers to their bodily eyes by which they gazed upon his fragility.

Hence they did not fear him as God since only his human fragility, and not the majesty of his divinity, was visible.

v. 19 Now we know. The Apostle now returns to his scolding of the Jews. For just as he took away their boasting of circumcision, so he also removes boasting in the Law or any sort of external observances. Otherwise he might seem to have commended the Law too greatly when he said, "For in the first place the Jews were entrusted with the pronouncements of God" (Rom 3:2). He first removes their boasting in the Law, therefore, by showing that they have actually been convicted by the Law rather than justified.

Next he introduces testimonies from the Law, namely, from the Old Testament, so as to establish that all are culprits, both Jews and gentiles. But we know that the Jews are greatly convicted by these testimonies, for the Law speaks to them alone, and not just about them. This is because the Law was given and prescribed to them only. This is what Paul says: **Now we know,** etc. It is as if he were saying: although we have collected from the Law testimonies presented against the gentiles also, we still know that the Law was not spoken to them, since it had not been given to them, even though it is about them. Rather, it was spoken to **these** alone **who are under the law,** referring to those who were bound by the declaration of the Law they received.

It should be noted that sometimes the word "Law" refers only to the five books of Moses, while at other times it pertains to the entire Old Testament, as it does in this passage. Therefore, according to Augustine in Book 15 of his *On the Trinity,* "By the word 'Law' sometimes all the words of the Old Testament are signified and other times only the Law that was given through Moses."[15]

So that every mouth may be shut, that is, every mouth is restrained and silenced from its own boasting and opened only for the glorification of God. For we have come to know that even the great glory of that special people of God, which they possessed from the Law, should be counted as nothing although they reckoned themselves justified by the works of that Law. And so [**the whole world**] **may be made subject,** that is, may humble itself **to God,** presuming nothing of its own glory, which has been removed even from those who seemed to be great before God.

v. 20 Because by the works of the law no flesh will be justified before [God], that is, it will not be justified in God's sight. The **works of the law**

---

15. Augustine, *On the Trinity,* 17.30, CCSL 50A:504.

here refer to the bodily observances to which this people of God gave very great attention, such as circumcision, sacrifices, keeping the Sabbath, and other symbolic injunctions of this kind. By the phrase **no flesh** the Apostle is referring to people who fulfill the works of the Law carnally rather than spiritually.[16] No such person will be counted as righteous in God's sight, though perhaps they may be in the eyes of human beings. For human judgment considers only external and visible things.

For through the law. The Apostle adds two more things to his previous remarks. To his statement "that every mouth may be shut and [all the world] made subject," he adds, **For through the law**. And to "Because from the works," etc., he adds, **But now apart from**, etc. In consequence, why should human beings be restrained from their self-congratulation regarding the Law? This is because through the Law they are deemed completely inexcusable from their sins. It is also because through the Law they came to recognize their sins more than they dismissed them, such that sins actually increased. Hence he will later go on to say, "In order that through the commandment sin might become sinning beyond measure" (Rom 7:13).

The Righteousness of God Comes through Faith

v. 21 But now. I have said that no one is justified in God's sight by the works that belong to the written law, namely, those formal precepts of which natural law knows nothing. **But now**, in the time of grace, **the righteousness of God has been disclosed**. This is what God approves, and that through which we are justified in God's sight. It is the love that **has been disclosed** by the teaching of the gospel **apart from the law**, irrespective therefore of those carnal and particular observances of the Law. I am saying that this is **the righteousness** to which **the Law and the Prophets attest** and what they also command.

v. 22 The Apostle immediately adds that this righteousness, **the righteousness of God**, depends on **the faith of Christ**, which we hold about Christ whether by believing him to exist, or by believing him, or by believing in

---

16. This is the classic medieval principle that the ceremonial rites prescribed by the Law of Moses should be understood spiritually *(spiritualiter)* and thus regarded as symbols pointing toward the greater reality of salvation in Christ and his Church. Failure to see their symbolic, and thus salvific, value was to understand them in a fleshly manner *(carnaliter)*.

him.[17] Therefore, when the Apostle also adds, **those who believe**, he does not mean only some who believe, for he intends this to pertain equally to them all. From the faith that we hold about Christ, love is propagated in us. For we maintain that God in Christ has united our nature to himself, and by suffering in this same nature God has shown us that highest love, of which Christ says, "No one has a greater love than this" (Jn 15:13). It is because of Christ himself that we are joined to him as closely as possible by an indissoluble bond of love. Hence in later passages the Apostle also wrote, "Who, therefore, will separate us from the love of God? Shall tribulation?" etc. (Rom 8:35). And again, "For I am certain that neither death," etc. (Rom 8:38). I tell you that this **righteousness** is held **over all** the faithful. That means that it is in the higher part of them, namely, in the soul where only love can exist, and not by the exhibition of exterior works.

For there is no [distinction]. I said correctly **over all** equally, gentiles as much as Jews. For there is no difference between them when it comes to this **righteousness of God through faith in Christ**, as once there was according to the works of the Law. Just as all have sinned, so they are justified without discrimination by this display of the highest grace of God toward us.

v. 23 For all have sinned and need the glory of God. They need, as if by obligation, to glorify God.

v. 24 Having been justified [by grace] as a free gift. For they have been justified, not by previous merits of their own, but instead **by the grace of the one**, God, who "first loved us" (1 Jn 4:10). In adding, **through** our **redemption** accomplished by Christ, the Apostle makes clear what grace really means: it is a free and spiritual gift of God.

---

17. When commenting on John 7:17, Augustine established what became a classic distinction regarding the different forms of belief. Resolving to do the will of God refers to believing: "This is the work of God, that you might believe in him *(credatis in eum)* whom he sent (Jn 6:29)." It is one thing to believe God *(credere ei)*, says Augustine, and another to believe in God *(credere in eum)*. Even the demons believe God, but they do not believe in God. Simply to believe God amounts to believing that what God says is true, while to believe in God means that by believing one loves God *(amare)*, cherishes God *(diligere)*, and enters into God so as to be incorporated into Christ's mystical body. And because Augustine says that this is what Paul means by belief in Romans 4:5, the definition finds its way into later commentaries on that epistle. See Augustine, *Commentary on the Gospel of John*, 29.6-7, CCSL 36:287.

v. 25 Whom God the Father has put forward to be the means of our expiation. That means that Christ is our reconciler **in his blood**, that is, by his death. This sacrifice is put forward, or established, by God not for all but only for those who believe. That is why the Apostle adds, **through faith**. This reconciliation pertains only to those who have believed and hoped for it. **For demonstrating God's righteousness** refers to God's love, which, as noted above, justifies us in his sight. This was done to manifest God's love toward us and to teach us how much we ought to love the One who for our sake "did not spare the Only Begotten" (Rom 8:32). **For the remission** means that through this righteousness, which is love, we may obtain the remission of sins. It is in this vein that the Truth himself speaks of the blessed woman who was a sinner, "Many sins are forgiven her because she has loved much" (Lk 7:47). I am saying that the remission has occurred, indeed, for sins of the past.

v. 26 Through the forbearance of God (Rom 3:25) refers to the patience of God who does not instantly punish the guilty and condemn sinners but waits a long time for them to return through penitence, to cease from sin, and thus to obtain forgiveness. At first the Apostle had said simply, **For demonstrating God's righteousness** (Rom 3:25). But now he adds, **In this present time**, that is, in the time of grace, in the time of love rather than of fear. Thus when he speaks of **God's righteousness**, of God's own righteousness, by adding the phrase **in this present time** of grace, he clearly intimates what he first understood this righteousness to be: a love that meets, as if particularly, the needs of human beings of our time, which is the time of grace.

It is possible to take **through the forbearance of God** with the statement that follows, **for demonstrating God's righteousness in this present time**. Consequently, it would mean that in times past God in forbearance delayed or postponed punishment, such that **in this present time** God might display the divine righteousness of which we have spoken, namely, his love. Thus he would show that, in willing, **God is just** and, in doing, God **justifies**. In other words, God wills to complete through Christ what God had promised concerning our redemption or justification. And just as God would have willed it, so then God would fulfill it in deed. **Whoever is of the faith of Jesus Christ** refers to one who believes God to be Jesus, that is, the Savior, through what Christ is — God and human being.

A Question concerning Redemption

It is at this point that a question of the utmost importance imposes itself.[18] How is it that we have been redeemed by means of Christ's death? In what way, according to the Apostle (Rom 3:25), are we justified by Christ's blood? We seem to be deserving of greater punishment, for as wicked servants we have committed the very thing for which our innocent Lord was slain.

First, we must ask, Why was it necessary for God to assume humanity and die in the flesh to redeem us? From whom has God redeemed us? Who holds us captive? By what justice has God liberated us from the power of whoever set the price to which God willingly submitted in order to set us free?

It is said that God has redeemed us from the power of the devil. Because of the transgression of the first human being, who subjugated himself to the devil by willful obedience, the devil was justly wielding complete power over him. And unless a deliverer came, the devil would always wield this power.[19] But if God has freed only the elect, how is it that, whether in this age or in the future, the devil did or will possess them more than now?

Was the devil also tormenting that beggar who rested in Abraham's bosom as he was the rich man who was condemned (Lk 16:19-31), although the devil may have tortured the beggar less? Was the devil holding dominion even over Abraham himself and the rest of the elect? In what way was that wicked tormentor holding dominion over this beggar, who is remembered as having been carried by the angels into Abraham's bosom? Abraham himself attests, "But now he is comforted here, and you are in agony" (Lk 16:25). And Abraham goes on to declare that "a great chasm has been fixed" (Lk 16:26) between the elect and the rejected so that the latter could never cross over to the former, let alone would the devil — who is more evil than all — hold dominion there where no wicked person has a place or an entry.

Also, what right could the devil have to possess humankind; unless it is

---

18. What follows is an excursus on the "Question" why Christ died, which might be considered Abelard's treatment of Anselm's famous topic in his *Why Did God Become a Human Being? (Cur Deus homo?)*. Abelard will conclude with his own brief "Resolution" to the question before returning to his verse-by-verse commentary on Romans 3.

19. The prevailing theory at the time — rejected by both Abelard and Anselm of Canterbury, although along different lines — was that the devil exercised rights over the fallen human race, rights which a just God would respect. This theory is given expression in the late eleventh-century commentaries on the Pauline epistles by Bruno the Carthusian (see, e.g., PL 153:64a; 70b; 146d).

perhaps with the Lord's permission, or even consignment, that the devil had received human beings in order to torture them? For if any bond servants wanted to abandon their lord and subjugate themselves to the power of another, would they be permitted to spend their life in such a way that their lord, if the lord wanted, might not lawfully seek them out and bring them back? Who really doubts that, if any lord's bond servant should seduce a fellow servant with incentives and cause this servant to depart from obedience to the proper lord, the servant's lord would reckon the seducer more guilty than the one seduced? How unjust would it be for the one who seduced the other to deserve thereby any privilege or authority over him? And even if this one had previously possessed some right over the other, would this one not deserve to lose that right because of the seduction? In fact, it is written, "Whoever abuses power that has been committed to him deserves to lose his privilege."[20] If one bond servant were about to be set over another of his fellow servants and to receive power over them, it would never be proper for the one more wicked — with absolutely no cause for privilege — to take charge over the other. But instead, more reasonably, it would be fitting that the one who was seduced should exercise a strict claim for reparation toward the one who had harmed the other by seduction. Furthermore, in return for human transgression, the devil could not grant immortality to them — a reward the devil had promised so as, by some right, to keep hold of the human race.

And so, for these reasons, it seems to have been proven that, by seducing a human being, the devil would not have acquired any right against the one he seduced. Although perhaps, as we noted, he has some right to the extent that it was permitted by the Lord, who handed the human being over for punishment as if to the Lord's jailer or torturer. For the human had sinned only against the human being's own Lord, whose obedience the human had abandoned. If, therefore, the Lord wanted to remit the sin, as was done for the Virgin Mary and as Christ also did for many before his passion — as reported of Mary Magdalene (Lk 8:2) and as it is written that the Lord said to the paralytic, "Be of good heart, my son, your sins are forgiven you" (Mt 9:2) — if the Lord was willing to forgive a sinful human being apart from the passion and say to the torturer, "Do not punish that one any further," of what could the torturer justly complain? For, as was shown, he had received no right of torment except by permission of the Lord. If, therefore, the Lord

---

20. C. 11 q. 3 c. 63 in *Corpus Iuris Canonicis*, ed. Emil Friedberg, 2 vols. (Graz: Akademische Druck–Universtät Verlagsanstalt, 1959), 1:660.

should cease to permit this, no right would be left to the torturer. And, what is more, if he were to complain or murmur against the Lord, it would be appropriate that the Lord instantly reply, "Is your eye wicked because I am good?" (Mt 20:15).

When, for the sake of the mass of sinful humanity, the Lord took upon himself a pure flesh and a human nature free from all sin, he inflicted no injustice on the devil. Indeed, as a human being, he did not by his merits obtain a guarantee that he should be conceived, be born, and persevere without sin. Rather, he received this through the grace of the Lord sustaining him. If, by the same grace, he wished to forgive sins to certain other human beings, was he not able to free them from punishment? Certainly, when the sins for which they were being punished have been forgiven, there appears to remain no reason why they should be punished for them any longer. He showed such grace to human beings that he united them to himself in his person. Was he not able, therefore, to render to them a lesser gift, namely, the remission of their sins?[21] So what was the necessity, or reason, or need, when by command alone the divine Mercy could free human beings from the devil? What, I ask, was the need that the Son of God in taking on flesh should have endured for our redemption such fastings, insults, scourging, and spitting, and at the last that most bitter and ignominious death upon the cross, so that he even endured the gibbet with the wicked?

In what way also, according to the Apostle (Rom 3:24), are we justified or reconciled to God through the death of the Son when God ought to have been the more angered against human beings? For humans committed a greater crime in crucifying God's Son than in transgressing the first command in paradise by tasting a single apple (Gen 3:16-19). The more human beings multiplied their sins, the more just God would have been in anger toward them. If that sin of Adam was so great that it could be expiated only by Christ's death, what expiation will suffice for the homicide committed against Christ? And what will suffice for the many huge crimes committed against him and against his own followers? Did the death of God's innocent Son so please God the Father that by means of that death God should then be reconciled to us who, by sinning, committed that act for which our innocent Lord was slain? For if this very great sin had not been committed, could God not have pardoned that much lighter sin [the first transgression]? If evil deeds had not been multiplied, could God not have done such a good thing?

In what way also has the death of God's Son made us more righteous

---

21. Cf. William of St. Thierry, *Disputation against Abelard*, 7, PL 180:270a.

than we were before, such that we ought to be freed from punishment? And to whom was the price of blood for our redemption paid except to the one in whose power we were, namely, God, who assigned us to the torturer? For it is not the torturers, but the lords of those held captive, who arrange or receive such ransoms. How also did God release the captives for this price if it were God who first exacted or set the price for their release? Indeed, how cruel and wicked it seems that anyone should require the blood of an innocent person as the price for anything, or that anyone should be pleased that an innocent person be slain. Still less, therefore, does it seem that God would consider the death of the divine Son so agreeable that by means of that death God should be reconciled to the whole world (2 Cor 5:19). These and similar matters appear to us to pose an extraordinary question concerning our redemption, or justification, through the death of our Lord Jesus Christ.

An Answer to the Question concerning Redemption

It seems to us that we have been justified by the blood of Christ and reconciled to God in the following way. It is by the unique grace manifested to us when God's Son took on our nature, and in that nature persisted in teaching [and reconstructing[22]] us by word and example even unto death. By this means God has more fully bound us to God by love, such that we are so inflamed by such a great gift of divine grace that true charity should no longer shrink from enduring anything for God. Indeed, we do not doubt that the ancient Fathers, waiting in faith for this gift, were also inflamed to a very great love of God, just as people in the time of grace. For it is written, "Both they who went before and they who followed cried: 'Hosanna to the Son of David!'" etc. (Mk 11:9). Moreover, each becomes more righteous, that is to say, becomes a greater lover of the Lord, after Christ's passion than that one was before, since a gift fulfilled inflames even greater love than one hoped for.

Our redemption, therefore, is that highest love existing in us through Christ's passion that not only frees us from the slavery of sin but also obtains for us the true liberty of children of God (Rom 8:21). Consequently, we do all things out of love, rather than fear, of him who has shown us such grace than which none greater can be found. For he himself attests, "No one has greater

---

22. H. Lawrence Bond, "Another Look at Abelard's Commentary on Romans 3:26," in *Medieval Readings of Romans,* ed. William S. Campbell, Peter S. Hawkins, and Brenda Deen Schildgen (New York: T&T Clark, 2007), 21.

love than this, to lay down one's life for one's friends" (Jn 15:13). Elsewhere the Lord says of this love, "I have come to cast fire on the earth, and what do I will but that it blaze forth?" (Lk 12:49). For this purpose he testifies that he came in order to spread the true liberty of love among humans. Closely examining this, the Apostle later declares, "Because the charity of God has been poured into our hearts by the Holy Spirit, who has been given to us. For why did Christ die?" (Rom 5:5-6). And again, "God commends his charity toward us in that when as yet we were sinners, Christ died for us" (Rom 5:8-9). But we will expound upon these things more fully in their proper place.[23] Now succinctly, as befits a brief exposition, this view of the manner of our redemption should suffice. But if our interpretations lack completeness, let us reserve further explanation for our treatise *Tropology*.[24]

v. 27 Where is your boasting? I have stated that the righteousness of God apart from the Law is now revealed through the faith of Christ to all alike who believe. So then, O Jew, **where is your boasting** any longer; where is that particular boasting that you once had about the Law and its bodily observances? Now **it is shut off**, that is, it has been taken away from you and annulled. **By what law has it been shut off? By the law of works**, namely, the law of some external deeds? **No, but rather by the law of faith** in "Jesus Christ" (Rom 3:26), that is, by the love arising from our saving faith through Christ.

Some people prior to their baptism already believe and love, like Abraham, about whom it is written, "Abraham believed God, and it was reckoned to him as righteousness" (Rom. 4:3). Consider too the example of Cornelius, whose alms before his baptism were accepted by God (Acts 10:4). And there are those who are truly penitent about past sins, as the publican who went down from the temple was justified (Lk 18:14). I do not hesitate to call such people righteous, or to say that when they render to others what is their due they really possess righteousness.[25] It is in this vein that we consider Jeremiah and John to have been sanctified from the womb (Jer 1:5; Lk 1:15), where they were especially enlightened. They already knew and loved God,

---

23. Abelard treats this matter later in his comments on Romans 5:5-8.

24. No such work has survived, and there is some question whether or not Abelard ever finished it. Constant Mews argues that Abelard intended here not *Tropologia* but *Anthropologia,* which he cites in comments on Romans 8:11, as an analogue to his *Theologia.* See Mews, *Abelard and Heloise,* 190.

25. Earlier in his commentary on Romans 3:10, Abelard describes someone as just or righteous *(iustus)* "who renders to others what is their due," thus in keeping with the classic definition of justice itself.

although it was still necessary for them to undergo the sacrament of circumcision, which at that time took the place of baptism.

Why, therefore, you will ask, was it necessary for people to be circumcised or baptized later, who were already justified beforehand by the faith and love that they possessed, and would necessarily have been saved if they then died? Indeed, no one can die as righteous, or as possessing charity, who would be damned. On the other hand, none can be saved without baptism or martyrdom, after the meaning and purpose of baptism has been taught to them. Yet some could die at the time when they possessed charity prior to baptism or martyrdom. If they should die at such a moment, you will say, they are necessarily both saved and damned. But we are saying that all who sincerely and purely love God for God's sake are already predestined to life. Hence they will never be overtaken by death until the Lord reveals to them, through preaching or the Spirit, what is necessary concerning the sacraments, and the Lord also gives them ability to understand this.

Some contend that those who were already righteous before baptism by believing and loving God, were they to die, then in that moment they should be both saved and damned. But indeed the same can also be argued with regard to anyone reprehensibly sinning who has been predestined to life, as with David when he was committing adultery. For just as anyone who was righteous ought to be saved, so should any righteous person who has been predestined. And just as anyone unbaptized would necessarily be damned, so should that adulterer.

So it was also the case with David, who at a certain time in his life, had he died, ought to have been both damned and saved. But in turn, as long as he had free choice, there was always a time in his life in which he could die in a good way and a time in which he could die in a bad way. Yet it was never necessary, in consequence, that anyone should die in both a good way and a bad way. On the contrary, there was neither a time in which any would have to die in a good way nor one in which any would have to die in a bad way. Rather, in those particular times in our lives in which any of us are able to die in a good way, we are also able to die in a bad way. Yet it is never true to say jointly that one can die in good and bad ways at the same time.

Now regarding those who possess charity before baptism and by this means are righteous, we grant that there would never be a time in which, if they died, they would necessarily be saved and damned simultaneously. For, in fact, those who possess charity before baptism could be without charity then [at death], and so die and be damned only. They could also die as baptized in that time in which they were not yet baptized, and thus be saved.

But if you should say that someone could die and at the same time both possess charity and be unbaptized, I no more accept this than if you had said that someone could die as an adulterer and at the same time be predestined. However, just as someone who is predestined must live well in order to be saved, so someone already righteous by trusting and loving must be baptized because of what the Lord had previously commanded about baptism (Jn 3:5), or even for the perseverance of that righteousness. For if those who possess charity before they are baptized should end their lives prior to their baptism, by no means would they persevere in that charity, since they would thoroughly despair of eternal blessedness and would have the foreboding that at their death they would immediately be damned forever.

But just as we maintain that before baptism one is already righteous by faith and love, although one's sins have not yet been remitted in baptism — that is, the penalty for them has not yet been entirely pardoned — so we also declare that after baptism infants and those unable to discern between good and evil — even if they have received remission of sins — are not yet righteous even as they are clean in God's sight. For they can neither be capable of charity or righteousness nor possess any merits. Nevertheless, if they die in this debility, when they begin to leave their body and see the glory prepared for them by the mercy of God, the love of God is born in them simultaneously with discernment. Lest Jews accuse us, or indeed accuse the Apostle, that we also are justified **by the law of works** — by such outward acts as baptism — let this suffice against the charge regarding our justification and that of all people. Justification consists in love even before the sacraments are received, whether ours or theirs. Reflecting on this, the prophet also used to say, "In whatever hour the sinner shall mourn for his sins, he will be saved" (cf. Ezek 33:12, 19).

v. 28 For we regard, that is we, whom the Lord has placed over his Church, deem or testify. "Hence," says Haimo, "we call witnesses 'judges or testifiers.'"[26] **For we regard** it as necessary that any **person**, a Jew as well as a gentile, be justified **by faith**. For "without faith it is impossible to please God" (Heb 11:6). **By faith** I mean without the works of the Law, namely, those external and bodily observances.

v. 29 Is God [the God] of Jews [only]? We regard, and correctly, that **by faith** the gentiles also obtain God's grace. Yet they do not observe the works

---

26. See Haimo of Auxerre, *Commentary on Romans*, PL 117:393d.

of the Law, as the gentile Job in times past and as those converted gentiles at present. The Apostle is pointing this out when he asks: **Is God [the God] of Jews [only]** by grace?

v. 30 For it is as if he were saying, "God is God of both peoples by grace." For **God justifies** both **through faith**, which leads to love. **God justifies the circumcision**, referring to the Jews, and **the uncircumcision**, referring to the gentiles. The Apostle's statement **from faith — through faith** is really a difference of expression rather than meaning. For this reason, in *On the Spirit and the Letter* Augustine maintains, "It was not said to make a distinction as if 'from faith' is one thing and 'through faith' another, but as a variety of expression."[27]

v. 31 [Do we nullify] then the law? Since we say that human beings are to be saved **through faith without the works of the law, do we nullify then the law through faith?** By commending faith, are we teaching that the law is invalid? **By no means! Rather, we uphold the law,** that is, we want the law to be fulfilled in all things. By attending not so much to the sound of the word as to the meaning and intention of the one who commands, those who are now truly fulfilling the figurative precepts are doing and believing what these precepts were meant to symbolize rather than actually be carried out. Finally, as the Apostle himself maintains, "Love is the fulfilling of the law" (Rom 13:10). In this regard the Lord says to the rich man after he recalled the law's command, "Do this, and you will live" (Lk 10:28).

---

27. Augustine, *On the Spirit and the Letter,* 29.50, CSEL 60:205.

ROMANS 4

Peter of John Olivi

The Example of Abraham

v. 1 What then are we to say? The Apostle has proven that the grace of Christ is necessary for all people with regard to the sins they have committed against God, who is the creator of all and renders justice to all. Here he proves this point once again with regard to the first father of the Jews, namely, Abraham, to whom the righteousness of faith was uniquely commended and in whom the divine promises were uniquely confirmed. In order to demonstrate this, the Apostle first shows that Abraham was not approved by God on the basis of a carnal observance of circumcision or the Law, but rather on account of the righteousness of faith. He will then demonstrate this point by showing that the promise made to Abraham cannot have been obtained through the Law, but rather through the righteousness of faith, when he says that "the promise made to Abraham was not through the law" (Rom 4:13).

v. 2 At the outset, though, the Apostle first asks what benefit Abraham found in his flesh, that is, in the carnal circumcision or the carnal condition. He introduces this question because he had said earlier that boasting in works of the Law was excluded (Rom 3:27). Therefore, he asks, **What then are we to say [If Abraham was justified by works, he has reason to boast, but not before God]?**

v. 3 Second, he demonstrates that he has nothing to boast of before God, for it is really based on the faith that Abraham had in God. The Apostle confirms this by appealing to Genesis 15:6 when he says, **"Abraham believed God, and it was reckoned to him as righteousness."**

vv. 4-5 Third, the Apostle confirms this point on the basis of reason: **To the one who works [wages are not reckoned as a gift . . .].**

vv. 6-8 Fourth, he confirms this through the saying of the psalm: **As David says, ["Blessed is the person to whom God reckons righteousness apart from works"].**

v. 9 Fifth, he proves this by examining the time of Abraham's justification, which occurred prior to circumcision: **Is this blessedness [conferred only on the circumcised?].**

v. 11 Sixth, he implies that circumcision was not the reason or cause of Abraham's justification, which he possessed already prior to his circumcision: **He received the sign [of circumcision].**

v. 11 (cont.) Seventh, on this basis he implies that it was through faith that Abraham was made the father of all believers, from among the gentiles as much as from the Jews: **so that he might be the father of all believers.**

In fact, in these last two instances, the Apostle presents the reason for Abraham's having received circumcision. It was a sign of the righteousness of faith which he had while as yet uncircumcised, as well as a sign that he had been established as the father of all who imitated his faith, whether among the circumcised or the uncircumcised.

v. 3 Hence he says, **"Abraham believed God,"** when God said to him, "your descendants will be as the stars of heaven" (Gen 22:17), and thus **"it was reckoned to him as righteousness."**[1] Yet one may wonder just how someone might be made righteous through this act of belief, since such belief does not concern articles of faith pertaining to God and to divine worship. The response to this question is twofold. First, it is because the promise made to Abraham was fulfilled in Christ's descendants and in the divine worship established and diffused in his descendants. This pertained to the principal ar-

---

1. Having commented on Romans 4:1-11 in a cursory fashion, Olivi now returns to Romans 4:3-5 in order to offer a more detailed examination of the deeper theological issues presented by the biblical text.

ticles of justifying faith. Second, the act of believing was thought to proceed from a perfect faith and to rely utterly on God rather than on the thing believed. For this reason I say that, although a superficial reading of the text speaks of a fleshly seed or offspring, and chiefly Abraham's act of circumcision, as though this were all a carnal matter, this was actually a sign of his great and deep faith.

v. 4 To one who works, performing works of the Law apart from grace, **wages**, or rewards, **are not reckoned according to grace, but according to a debt**. This means that such a person is not judged to be remunerated by grace, but rather on the basis of merit that is owed.

v. 5 Yet to one who does not work by carrying out the external works of the commands, **but believes in the one**, in God, **who justifies the impious**, which can be taken in the singular or plural, **faith is reckoned as righteousness**. This means that by faith alone taken up together with charity, a person is reckoned righteous before God.[2] The Apostle intends to prove here that the recompense to be granted is reckoned on the basis of grace alone, not as proceeding from a debt. The one who believes in God receives a reward on the basis of grace alone; whereas the one who works receives it because it is owed.[3] Hence that which was reckoned to Abraham because he believed, or to anyone else who similarly believes, is not to be imputed on the basis of works. It is true, therefore, that Abraham did not find glory before God by works. Note, however, that in this argument the Apostle expressly assumes that the believer had performed none of the works of the commandments and consequently is impious. For in the case of such a person it is made especially clear that one is not righteous on the strength of works, but rather by grace alone, through which one's sins are forgiven. By making his argument in this way, the Apostle implies that no one prior to faith has virtuous works, except by mere appearance or in such a manner that still does not exclude unrighteousness.

The question about how it can be true that the worker is repaid based on what is owed and not from grace can be understood in two ways. First, it could address human presumption, in which Jews abounded. In that case, to

---

2. Note that "by faith alone" *(sola fide)* means apart from works of the Law. Hence faith here is not separated from charity, which is also deemed essential for salvation.

3. Here, as in so many places throughout his commentary, Olivi is drawing upon Peter Lombard's *Commentary on the Epistle to the Romans,* which he will refer to as the Gloss *(in Glossa)*. Unless, however, Olivi specifically mentions it, we will not cite it in the notes.

the one who appears to fulfill the Law through external works, then by debt of justice such a person must be honored and remunerated at least in terms of temporal glory. Second, it can be understood conditionally. For example, if some reward should be paid to those who work by their own capacities, and as though from their own power, then it should be rendered as a debt rather than as proceeding from grace. We see this among those who, by their own deeds or talents, serve another human. Whence to a laborer in my vineyard I am bound as a matter of debt to pay a fitting wage, just as a king owes the soldier who fights on his behalf.

You might object that serving God does not compare to serving a human, since our entire nature, power, and action is from God. In response, if our action is worthy of remuneration, inasmuch as we did it without the assistance of God's grace, then it must be remunerated by debt. For then we would have made ourselves righteous and even better than God had made us; this point is more fully proven in the "Questions on Grace."[4] In that case God would surely have given us the natural power to perform righteous works and bestow righteousness upon ourselves. Yet God would not have given us that righteousness or its works unless either that power were essentially righteous, which is impossible, or one were first formed by God with the habit of righteousness. If so formed, then the reward of righteousness is given freely to that person by God, and thus is a result not of merit but of grace. Hence the Apostle so fittingly states that if we, apart from any righteousness granted us by God, perform righteous works that are worthy of reward, then the wages would be owed to us on the basis of merit rather than grace.

v. 5 Second, one may wonder how the Apostle can say, **To one who does not work, but believes in God, faith is reckoned as righteousness,** when it is said elsewhere that faith without works is dead and futile and that "Abraham was justified by works" when offering up his son (cf. Jas 2:17 and Rom 4:2). Here it should be said that the Apostle is speaking of works that do not proceed from faith, but are instead done prior to faith. James 2:22 refers to works done by faith, whence he adds there, "You see that faith was cooperating with those works," namely, those of Abraham, "and faith was brought to completion by works." We should remember that someone can possess the works of faith or grace in two ways. First, one may have such works in habit or intention. If in intention, all that remains is to carry it out, although it could be im-

---

4. This is a reference to Olivi's own "Questions on Grace," which are not known to be extant.

peded in some way. Taken in this sense, no one is justified apart from works. Second, one can, in addition to this, possess them in themselves. In this sense, the principle of righteousness abides in them more completely, but not the first form or principle, or the origin of righteousness. In the first sense, the Apostle correctly proposes that righteousness is from faith alone together with works. This may be evinced, moreover, in the justification of adults where there is always actual consent proceeding from the habit of grace, such that a person is righteous before performing a righteous work.[5]

When the Apostle says, "according to the purpose of God's grace" (cf. Rom 9:11),[6] he means according to this purpose, or on this basis, God freely (gratis) or by grace (ex gratia) determined to grant the grace of the God who justifies. It is as though he were saying, "The very faith that flows from the merciful intention of the God who predestines us, this faith has justified us."

v. 6 As David says, "Blessed is the person to whom God freely or acceptably **brings,"** that is, gives **righteousness without works** of the Law. For apart from whatever works of the Law people may do, they would also have had the contrary works, namely, sins. Or "without works of the Law" may mean not on account of preceding works, since this person did not have them.

v. 7 He states this when he says, **"Blessed are those [whose iniquities are forgiven]."** Thereupon the Apostle wants to prove that this blessedness — which is possessed now through grace that should be held in hope, and then finally through glory in actuality — is attainable for not only the circumcised but also the uncircumcised. For this reason he asks whether it exists only in the condition of circumcision or in the other condition as well.

v. 9 Thus in a second instance he states, **We say ["Faith was reckoned to Abraham as righteousness"]** in order to prove that justification is possible even for the uncircumcised. The Apostle assumes here that all the Jews would know about Abraham's righteousness of faith.

v. 10 In a third instance the Apostle asks, **How then [was it reckoned to him?].** Having been asked in which of the aforementioned conditions Abraham's faith had been **reckoned** to him, the Apostle responds that it was in

---

5. In order for an action to be truly righteous and thus acceptable to God as worthy of eternal life, it must proceed from a person who is already informed by the habit of grace (habitus gratiae), which is a gift from God.

6. This precise phrase is not found in Paul's epistles.

the condition of uncircumcision, which is made clear by the history recorded in Genesis.

A fourth instance is recorded in Genesis 15, which states that Abraham had a vision of God (Gen 15:1) and the promise was made regarding his seed (Gen 15:13).

v. 11 Chapter 17 (Gen 17:23) records a fifth instance. With Ishmael already born, Abraham was told to circumcise himself and every male in his household. This was **so that he might be**, and appear to be, **the father of all believers through uncircumcision**, that is, in the foreskin or in a state of uncircumcision. Here the word "through" is used in place of "in" or "with," as above in chapter 2 where he said, "You who through the letter [and circumcision]" (Rom 2:27). **So that it might be reckoned**, that is, so that it might appear that it is reckoned **to them as righteousness**.

v. 12 This means that their own faith is reckoned to them as righteousness just as Abraham's faith was to him, **and so that he might be**, that is, so that he might appear to be, **the father of the circumcision**, namely, of the spiritual sort of circumcision. **It was reckoned not only to the circumcised**, namely, of the carnal sort, **but also to those who follow in the footsteps of the faith of our father Abraham, who abided in uncircumcision**, thus referring to what was first entrusted to him while he was still in the condition of uncircumcision.

Yet one wonders why the Apostle invests Abraham with such fatherhood. For he does not seem to establish any greater claim to fatherhood in Abraham than there might be in any other person who believes perfectly and could thereby serve as an example of faith for others. In response, we can compare it to the situation of Peter, who, on account of his faith by which he declared, "You are the Christ," etc. (Mt 16:16-17), received primacy and foundational authority over the whole of Christ's Church, as Christ himself indicated when he said, "You are Peter," etc. (Mt 16:18-19). Similarly, then, Abraham received from God exemplary and foundational authority over all future faith, or over future believers, when God said to him, "You will not be called Abram, but will be called Abraham, for I have established you as the father of many nations" (Gen 17:5).

Christ indicates this primacy even with respect to the state of glory when he says in Matthew, "I say to you, many will come from the east and the west and will recline with Abraham, Isaac, and Jacob in the kingdom of heaven," etc. (Mt 8:11). He says this again in Luke 16 when Lazarus is borne

by the angels into the bosom of Abraham, and when the rich man cries out
to Abraham to send Lazarus to him and at length to the house of his father
so that he would see Abraham reigning with Lazarus (Lk 16:19-31). Moses often demonstrates that primacy by way of merit when he prays to God for the
people, as in Exodus 32, when the idol had been made, "Remember Abraham, Isaac," etc., and, "The Lord was appeased from doing the evil," etc.
(Exod 32:13-14). That primacy is also amply discussed within the books of
the *Celestial Hierarchy* and the *Ecclesiastical Hierarchy*. For, according to
[Pseudo-]Dionysius, in the state of reward the superior orders are like uni-
versals in comparison to the lower orders. By understanding such universal-
ity correctly here, and thus otherwise than we would in matters of logic, we
see that in the state of merit there are some who have a certain sort of uni-
versality of grace and merit with respect to others of a lower order.[7]

God's Promise Is Fulfilled through Faith

v. 13 Not through the law. Having demonstrated by means of Abraham's
faith that our justification comes not from the Law or by its works, but rather
by faith, the Apostle shows here that this is itself the result of the promise
made to Abraham and his seed. First, he proposes that the promise was not
made to him as though it could be obtained through the Law or through its
works, but rather through the merit of faith. Second, he proves this point
through a deduction that leads to an unfitting or contradictory conclusion.
For if righteousness were established in the Law only, and so too the hope in
obtaining the promised inheritance, then the faith of Abraham which alone
was commended to him would be altogether annulled along with the promise that was also made to him. For according to such a scenario, righteousness will not be based upon the merit of faith, nor come by virtue of the
grace of the promiser or the promise itself. And this is chiefly because the
Law apart from grace is the accidental cause of wrath or death, and also the
cause of a greater state of guilt. For law is the accidental cause of greater trespass if referring here simply to natural law, or the cause of greater criminality if referring to the written law.[8]

7. See Pseudo-Dionysius, *Celestial Hierarchy,* passim.

8. The Law is good in itself and thus cannot be the principal, or essential, cause of
wrath and death. Rather, it is the accidental, or secondary, cause *(per accidens causa)* inasmuch as wrath and death result from having transgressed the Law, but are not directly
caused by the Law itself.

vv. 16-23 Third, the Apostle concludes that justification is obtained from the merit of faith when he says, **Therefore it comes from faith**. Fourth, on this basis he adds that it is owed not only to those who belong to the condition of the Law but to all those who imitate the faith of Abraham when he says, **Not to the one who [lives] by the law**. And he confirms this through the text of Genesis 17 when he says, **As it is written** (Rom 4:17). Fifth, he commends Abraham's faith by showing that his faith merited his establishment as father of the future faithful and, in particular, his commendation of righteousness, and this where the Apostle says, **against hope** (Rom 4:18). Sixth, he shows that the commendation of his faith was not made on account of him alone, but also to commend the faith of future generations. For on this basis they could know that they were meant to be justified through faith as Abraham had been when he says, **It was not written [for him alone]**.

v. 13 Not through the law was the promise given **to Abraham**. Actually, one understands by promise the very thing that is promised, which was not to be given through the works of the Law, but by the merit of faith. **So that he would be heir of the world** means so that Abraham would be the possessor of those who come from the whole world, namely, of believers, since all believers are children of Abraham. His descendant Christ is the heir, that is, Lord of the world due to devotion and even through the merit of grace given to him. Christ did not have faith, properly speaking, but something superior in its place, and also in him was that which is more formally in that faith. Nevertheless, the Apostle understands by "seed" here those who believe in Christ, as becomes clear just a little later when he says, "so that the promise might be established for every seed" (Rom 4:16). So by "inheritance" he means both the inheritance of grace and that of glory.

v. 14 If they who are of the law, namely, these Jews, **are heirs** alone and by the sole power of the Law; if this is the case, then **faith is null**, without effect and annihilated, **and the promise abolished**, unfulfilled, and void.

v. 15 The Apostle proves this when he adds that it is because **the law [works] wrath**, referring to the condemnation it causes in an accidental manner. Thus it is clear that it does not make one an heir, but instead places one under a death sentence. The Apostle proves that the Law would cause death because **where there is no law, there is no trespass**. Here he supposes that where the Law exists apart from the power to fulfill it, there will necessarily be trespass, that is, transgression of the Law and consequently the death sentence. Note that if the law were taken generally to mean the whole law of nature, then the aforementioned proposition [**where there is no law, there is no trespass**] is true if taken simply. For if God were to command that no law be observed, there could not really be any guilt or criminality because nothing would have been done against God's command. If, however, one means the written law alone, then trespass refers to transgression of the Law given and imposed from the outside. This Law does indeed result in greater criminality and cause greater wrath, as Augustine indicates in the Gloss. There he notes that the text does not say, "Where there is no law, there is no wickedness" but "no trespass," since not every wicked person is a transgressor of the Law. Although those who have not received the Law can be called wicked, they cannot be called trespassers.[9]

v. 16 Therefore by faith they are, or were, heirs **so that, according to the grace** of faith and of the God who promises, **the promise would be made firm for every seed**. It is as though the Apostle were saying, "Otherwise the promise would not have been made firm for them because we cannot be made firm in the good except through grace, which chiefly establishes us in the good and infallibly leads us to eternal life." **But also to the one who is from the faith of Abraham**. The reason for this is clear in itself. For by this rationale the same right inheres in anyone who lives by faith on account of Abraham's initial paternity or causality. Here is a case where a form is more properly suited to those who participate in that form of faith through Abraham than to those who do not participate in that form of faith, even if they participate through Abraham in another form, namely, flesh. Hence if God made Abraham the father of many nations on account of his faith, this promise will apply more fittingly to those who imitate Abraham's faith than to those who can only claim his fleshly lineage.

v. 17 Before God, in whom he believed. This phrase is not actually found in Genesis 17. Yet the Apostle adds it here to show that paternity was given to him by the merit of faith and that this was the intention of God's words spoken to Abraham. For it was through these words that God demonstrated that Abraham was established father of the nations with respect to the worship and grace of God, and it was on this basis that he stood **before God**, or in the presence of the God, **who gives life to the dead**, etc. The Apostle adds this to

9. See Lombard, *Commentary on the Epistle to the Romans,* PL 191:1374b-c; and Augustine, *Sermons on the Psalms,* CCSL 38:946.

show that Abraham rightly believed in God, who was able to bring to life the bodies of Abraham and Sarah, which were otherwise as good as dead in their generative powers. And so it was that through this body God could call into being children who did not yet exist as though they were already alive. Indeed, it is through grace that God brings to life the gentiles who were dead in their sins and **calls** into the existence of grace those who **are not**, neither in reality nor in appearance, like the gentiles, just as God calls **those who are**, the Jews, who seemed to be something. Hence the meaning here is that God calls them to the existence of grace as if they already exist. For, according to Augustine in the Gloss, all future things have already come to pass in God's sight, as the saint says when commenting on Psalm 104.[10]

v. 18 He, Abraham, **against the hope** of nature, **believed in the hope** of the divine promise. It is as if the Apostle were saying, "Against the general course of nature and against common hope and judgment, Abraham believed and hoped in what God promised him." What he believed and hoped was **that he would become the father** [**of many nations**]. Now the term "that" *(ut)* can be read consecutively such that the sense would be that from his faith and hope it followed **that he would become the father**, etc., **according to what was said to him** by God in Genesis 15, "his seed will be as the stars of heaven" (Gen 15:5). Although it does not say there that his seed will be innumerable as the sands, either they both [stars and sands] are only found in chapter 22 and can both be read in that respect, or "stars" can refer to the good and "sands" to the evil (Gen 22:17), since both categories are innumerable to us.

v. 19 And he was not weakened in faith. This means that Abraham did not hesitate or vacillate, although when it came to his flesh he would have cause to vacillate. **Nor did he consider his body dead** even if the condition of his body might have dimmed his hope that the promise would be fulfilled and that he would produce children. For he said that his body was dead with respect to the act of generation.

v. 20 In the promising again of God. For according to Genesis 18, the promise was repeated to him that Sarah would have a son the following year in due season (Gen 18:14). **Giving glory to God** by believing firmly that God can do all things.

10. See Lombard, *Commentary on the Epistle to the Romans*, PL 191:1375d; and Augustine, *Sermons on the Psalms*, CCSL 38:1154.

v. 21 This is what he adds by explaining that **he fully knew that whatever [God promised God was able to do]**. For in this way the Apostle clearly shows that Abraham had the fullest faith and knowledge of faith concerning God.

Note that, according to Augustine in his book *On Correction and Grace,* the Apostle did not say, "whatever God foretold or foreknew," but "whatever God promised."[11] For God can foretell and foreknow many things that God could not do, namely, evil things. But God does do everything that God promises. Although human beings may do the good things that God promises, it is still God who brings these things to pass. For it is because God does these things that human beings may also do them. Yet they do not do them that God may do what God has promised. For otherwise the promises of God would be fulfilled not because they were in God's power but because they were within human power. This is Augustine's claim.

vv. 23-24 It was not written for his sake, to the praise of Abraham **only** [that **"it was credited to him"**], **but for our sake** to instruct **those who believe in him** [who raised our Lord Jesus from the dead] that our faith **will be reckoned**. Note that the Apostle expressly places the articles concerning Christ's death and resurrection together with the article concerning the Trinity, which he touches upon by positing the relationship of God the Father to the Son according to the resurrected flesh. He does this first because, in the act of justification, or of justifying faith, these things are more necessary; and second because our own resurrection from the death of guilt is signified and accomplished in the death and resurrection of Christ. For there we die to a sinful life, just as Christ died to the natural life of his flesh. Third, in the mortification of their bodies, Abraham and Sarah were finally revivified miraculously through God's grace. Due to their faith, both of the aforesaid realities are designated, and therefore one is fittingly adapted to the other.

v. 25 Who was handed over unto death **on account of our trespasses** so that they might be taken away, **and resurrected for our justification**, so that we might live righteously, which we were otherwise unable to do. Note that, according to the Gloss, both the death and resurrection of Christ take away our trespasses, and they both also justify us.[12] Yet Christ's death alone signifies the destruction of the old life, and his resurrection alone signifies the

---

11. Augustine, *On Correction and Grace,* 12.36, PL 44:938.

12. See Lombard, *Commentary on the Epistle to the Romans,* PL 191:1378a-b.

new life that begins with our justification and is perfected in the immortality of the future resurrection. Hence the Apostle aptly distinguished his words based on the difference of meaning. Note too that you will often find in the Scriptures distinct appropriations or correspondences of words of this sort.

Yet one wonders how the resurrection of Christ is the cause of our justification. In response, three things should be noted. First, it justifies through belief because without faith in this event we cannot be justified. Second, it does so insofar as this event contains within itself the life and power of Christ as well as his righteousness, through which we are justified. If Christ did not have within himself the life of glory that uniquely shines forth in his resurrection, and if he did not possess the righteousness on account of which he ought to have risen again, and the power through which he could also raise himself, then he would not have the power to justify us. For we can say here that God did not order his power for the justification of the world without first arranging for Christ's passion and resurrection to include in themselves the power to justify, so that they would be fully ordered to the act of justification. Third, Christ's resurrection possesses in itself the exemplarity of our spiritual resurrection, which is our justification itself, and on this account can be called the exemplary cause of that justification.

ROMANS 5

Peter of John Olivi

The Results of Justification

v. 1 Justified, therefore, by faith. Having demonstrated this proposition based on principles drawn from a look at the first father of the Jews, the Apostle then proves this very same point with regard to Christ, our redeemer, and his gift of grace. He does this through a comparison to the origin of our corruption and general sickness. In this part he proceeds in the following manner. First, from the aforementioned justification of faith, he infers an exhortation of all the faithful to have peace among themselves and with God. He does so by commending, together with this, the high state of Christian grace and its sublime and eternal hope.

v. 6 Second, he demonstrates the rationale for this sort of certitude by comparing the love of Christ by which he died for us even as we were still impious to the love that he has for us now that we are justified when he asks, **Why did Christ die [while we were still feeble]?**

v. 12 Third, he proves this by comparing Christ and his grace to the first human being and the general infection brought about through him when he says, **As on account of one human being [sin entered the world]**.

v. 15 Fourth, he shows that this comparison is not drawn between two equals, but rather between what is greater and lesser. He accomplishes this by demonstrating that the grace of Christ is far more copious and effective in its goodness than the sin of Adam was in its evil when he says, [**But the free gift**] **is not like the trespass**.

v. 20 Fifth, by pointing out that the grace of Christ so far exceeds Adam's sin, he shows that even the evil that had increased upon entering as an accidental result of the Law is overcome by grace. Thus however great that evil may have been, grace is all the greater and is present in more abundance. For he says, **But the law came in** [**with the result the trespass multiplied; but where sin increased, grace abounded all the more**].

(6:1) Sixth, he then rejects a certain erroneous opinion which can have been raised against what he said above. **What do we say?** [**Should we continue to sin so that grace may abound?**].

(6:15) Seventh, having taken a final opportunity to reject that error, he then moves on to reject a similar error when he says, **What then? Should we sin** [**because we are not under the law, but under grace?**].

v. 3 In the first place, the Apostle begins by commending the loftiness of grace insofar as it places us directly in God's presence and raises us up to eternal glory. Second, grace generally leads us to the suffering of tribulations where he says, **And not only that**. Third, he furnishes the reason why it leads us to suffer such things: it is for the greater consummation and certification of that grace and its hope. For he says, **Knowing** [**that suffering produces endurance**].

v. 5 Fourth, he shows how it draws forth in an essential or formal manner the infallible certitude of its hope when he says, **Hope, however, does not confound because the love** [**of God has been poured into our hearts**].

v. 2 Through whom we have access. Note that we have this access through Christ as if through an efficient and meriting cause, and through faith together with charity as if through a formal cause.[1] The Gloss, in a passage from Augustine's *Letter to Boniface*, asks, "If we are justified by faith, then

---

1. As efficient and meriting cause *(per causam efficientem et promerentem)*, Christ is the agent who makes access to grace possible through his own merits, which are deserving of reward. The virtue of faith informed, or actualized, by the virtue of charity (love) is the formal cause *(per causam formalem)* inasmuch as it determines the fundamental status of the person in the sight of God.

how is grace, which faith merits, not more fittingly paid as a reward than given as a gift?"[2] He responds that when faith obtains justification, it is not that human merit precedes God's grace, but rather that grace itself merits any increase, so that having been increased it might then merit and be perfected.

v. 1 So that we might have peace, which you Romans do not have, so long as you proudly contend with one another. For you imagine that you are justified by your own efforts and not by God's grace.

vv. 3-4 Tribulation produces patience in a material way, as the occasion arises, and by way of practice, but not by actually producing this effect.[3] **Patience . . . approbation**, that is, purification. For, according to Augustine, the more someone suffers for the sake of God the purer that person is rendered. Or **approbation** might refer here to a more certain experience and experiential confirmation of one's own virtue. For in the patient endurance of tribulations people can more fully test just how much, and what sort of, constancy and virtue they possess.[4] Either way one takes this, they both bring about a greater hope of glory.

v. 5 Hope does not confound. That is to say, it does not put us to shame because it is truly fulfilled. People are confounded when what they have placed their whole hope in does not come to pass, such that their hope is disappointed. Whereupon we are certain that this hope does not confound, but rather is fulfilled, as the Apostle shows when he adds, **Because the love of God [is poured into our hearts]**. He says "of God" here both because the love is from God and because through it we love God. **It is poured out** [*diffusa*] **through the Holy Spirit**, that is, shed [*effusa*] far and wide or infused [*infusa*] in a certain allotted amount. This action can be ascribed to the Holy Spirit, although it is in reality the work of the entire Trinity equally.

Which has been given to us. In saying this the Apostle implies that love cannot be given to us by God unless God were to give himself to us along with his love, which is actually identical to God. Here the love is as-

---

2. Lombard, Commentary on the Epistle to the Romans, PL 191:1378d. Augustine, Letter 130, CSEL 44:52.

3. Tribulation is the material cause *(materialiter)*, not the efficient cause *(effective)*, of patience. That is, it can give rise to patience inasmuch as it provides an occasion for it, but it is not the agent that actually produces it.

4. Augustine, *On Diverse Questions,* 82, CCSL 44A:246-47.

cribed to the Holy Spirit, although by another principle love is the Spirit's proper name. That love given to us, which is God, is the same love by which we love God unto grace and eternal life. It is on this basis that our own love that abides within is thereby caused to love instantaneously. These two gifts simultaneously taken up are a token and pledge making us certain in the hope of future glory.

Note that in the aforementioned gift, love, which is God, is united to us under a threefold relation. First, as by a loved object; it exists in respect to us as to something that is loved. Second, under a relation of cause to effect or with respect to the subject in which it operates; it exists in respect to us as a cause producing love within us, and by acting upon us, as it urges and enflames us to love. Third, it exists in respect to us as a gift or object rendered loveable by us through the love poured into us, possessed by us, and loved by us.

The Death of Christ

vv. 6-7 For why did Christ die at the appointed time, that is, only during the time of the Triduum? Perhaps the phrase "at the appointed time" can be read together with "feeble." For even though **we were feeble** with the sickness of sin within the realm of time, or temporally, in the eternal predestination of God, we were nevertheless healthy with regard to future time. I ask you, **Why did Christ die** if our hope was not to be fulfilled? It is as if he were to say, "In no way is this probable or even possible." And he proves this when he adds, **Scarcely**, that is, rarely or with difficulty, **does anyone die for the just** person, and yet Christ died willingly and readily **on behalf of** the unjust or **the impious**. I say "scarcely" because this can happen sometimes. **For perhaps someone might dare to die for the sake of a good person**, that is, for a just person. Yet Ambrose takes "just" to mean someone who is well practiced in the virtues and in the strict zeal for righteousness. "Good," on the other hand, refers to an innocent person whose cause, even if less good than just, is still quite pitiable, such that it would be easier for the most part for someone to risk death on behalf of such a person. Nevertheless, I think we should adopt the first reading because it better demonstrates both how serious and how remarkable it was to die for the impious. This is surely what the Apostle intends to prove in this passage. For in the same place he speaks of the impious themselves in various ways, namely, as sinners and as feeble, as he calls the just people righteous in one instance and good in another.

v. 8 Yet [God] commends his love, that is, God ardently magnifies and demonstrates the love that God has for us in order that we would be saved. This was accomplished, so the Apostle infers, because [Christ] died for us when we were still impious, which he proves when he adds, **While we were still sinners**.

vv. 9-11 Note that he repeats three times the same view or logical conclusion to achieve even greater confirmation. First, he does so by way of questioning or by expressing astonishment, second, by commending and demonstrating at the same time, and, third, by introducing a proof, namely, one that has been made, by reintroducing it when he says, **If when we were still enemies**. For it should be noted that the Apostle calls us feeble, impious, sinners, and enemies because of our sinful condition. In such a condition of sin, the Apostle implies that there is a natural destitution of power, loss of health, depravity of evil, and defect in our actions. Observe that he first says that **we will be saved from wrath**, and then that **we will be saved by his life**, because — at least in the order of nature — one is liberated from wrath and death before entering into eternal life. **But not only that**, not only will we be saved by his life, that is, through his life or abiding in that very life, but **even**, or also, **we boast in God**, now in the present. It is as if the Apostle were saying, "Not only do we hope to be saved in the future through Christ, but for this reason we also boast in God as though eternal life were already in our possession and attained by us through the grace of Christ. And so we even glory in God as though we were already existing in him."

Yet one wonders how God loved us on the basis of charity at a time when we were still impious and God's enemies. Although God loved the elect by the same charity when they were still impious and when later they were justified, nevertheless God loved them under a different aspect or principle. This is because God loved them when they were still impious for the very purpose of making them good, such that, having already made them, God loved them as though they were already good. The first love in us is called a desiring or deliberative love; the second a fervent love or one that seeks to please. In God the first is called an effective and imperative or voluntary love, since it is through that love that we might become good. The second is an intrinsic or enduring love. For God accepts our goodness that dwells within us and inhabits us, since we are now God's friends.

Adam and Christ

vv. 12-14 Therefore, just as through one [human being]. Here, based upon what has been said, the Apostle infers the comparison of Christ and his grace to Adam and the infection contracted from him. For it is on this basis that he intends to demonstrate and prove clearly his principal objective. First he sets up the comparison [between Christ and Adam], and yet the phrasing is faulty. For it would mean that just as through one human being sin was spread abroad **in this world**, among all human beings of this world, and by means of sin **death entered** into all, so then that through the one human being, Christ, justifying grace entered and then finally eternal life for all human beings. The Apostle implies this supplementation through what he adds at the end when he says, **He**, namely, Adam, **is the form**, that is, the image **of the future**. This form of the future refers to Christ, who, with respect to the time of Adam, was still to come. Christ is Adam's image or likeness if understood by way of opposition. For just as in Adam all die, so in Christ all are brought to life. Or it could be understood as a direct correlation, because just as Adam is the beginning of all by nature, so Christ is the beginning of all by grace. Nevertheless, in this instance the Apostle intended that it be taken more in the first sense.

Yet to avoid trampling over these words, the text can be read as follows. **Just as through one human being sin entered into this world**, namely, when Adam sinned and through his sin death entered into the world. This is when the necessity of dying was inflicted upon him, and the death sentence rendered as a condemnation. **So death also passed through into every human**, through that human or through that sin **in whom**, namely, in that human or by that sin, **all sinned**. For they contracted that sin through this cause. It is as if the Apostle were to say, "Just as Adam killed himself by means of his own sin, so through the diffusion of his sin into others it became the cause of temporal and eternal death for all." Yet he first sets forth the entrance of death into all before the entrance of sin. He does this to imply that from the entrance of death into all the diffusion of sin is thereby proven, as from a just punishment guilt is thereby proven. Or it can be read to mean that, just as by the very fact that sin entered into the world through the first human being, and through sin death, so based on the evidence of this fact we have proven that death passed into all through that one human being. This one human being is the one in whom all had sinned, a point that the Apostle adds in order to demonstrate that Adam's sin is the cause of death for all people. Note, however, that this was evident only to the faithful or to those who knew the Law.

Having set forth the first comparison between Christ and Adam, he then proceeds to remove a particular doubt, namely, how all had sinned in Adam, since prior to the time of the Law sin would not have been reckoned as though it were committed against the Law of God, and this would chiefly be so in the case of little children.

vv. 13-14 The Apostle rules this out when he adds, **Up until the law sin was in the world**, although at that time **it would not have been imputed**. Third, he proves this on the grounds that **death** at that time **reigned**. This means that death victoriously prevailed not only among adults who through their own consent had sinned like Adam, but even among others **who had not sinned** actually through their own consent like Adam, as is the case with infants. The Apostle supposes, however, that death would not have reigned among them unless some sin were in them.

v. 15 But not as the trespass. The Apostle demonstrates here that the aforementioned comparison is drawn from the lesser to the greater because the grace of Christ is greater and more efficacious in the good than the sin of Adam would be in the evil. And therefore he says that the **gift** of Christ's grace is not **just as the trespass** of Adam. The Apostle demonstrates that the grace of Christ exceeds the trespass of Adam in a twofold manner: first, when considered in its innate strength and copiousness; and second, in its expansiveness by expurgating not only Adam's trespass but even all other trespasses. Of the first he says, **If by the trespass of one**, Adam, **many died, how much more did the grace of God and the gift in grace**, given in grace and through the grace **of one human being, Jesus Christ, abound unto more**, or unto many. It **abounded**, that is, it was given abundantly. Note that the word "more" is taken here positively, not comparatively. For otherwise it would be false unless this were spoken also with respect to the angels in whom the grace of Christ also abounds in some manner. Yet the sin of Adam extends itself only to human beings. Or, again, unless the sense of "abounded unto more" means that — taken on its own — it could have abounded.

v. 16 As for the second, the Apostle says, **And not just as through one sin** of Adam, whereby human beings are infected and condemned, **thus through the gift**, as though they were equal, are human beings justified. For indeed this gift is more than that sin. The Apostle proves this when he adds, **For the judgment** of the divine sentence **from one** sin proceeds **unto the condemnation** of human beings. **Grace, however**, proceeds **from many trespasses**

unto justification. Through the grace of Christ not only is original sin blotted out, but all other sins as well.

v. 17 Thereupon the Apostle offers a persuasive conclusion to both of his earlier remarks when he says, **If by the vice of one**, etc. He actually proves here that just as Christ exceeds the guilt in his act of justification, so he exceeds the punishment owed the guilt in his acts of reward and prayer. Here he calls this grace by a threefold name — grace, gift, and righteousness — in order to show that it is given freely and that it justifies us.

v. 18 He then concludes the aforementioned comparison as though it has already been proven when he says, **Therefore, just as through the trespass of one** passing **into all human beings** as it proceeded **unto condemnation** of the impious, **so through one act of righteousness** diffused **among all human beings** who are justified, it went on, or proceeded, **unto the justification of life**, which is to say that it led to eternal life. Note that, according to Augustine, the fact that the Apostle says "all" does not mean that all those begotten through Adam would be regenerated through Christ. Rather, he means that, just as no one is carnally generated except through Adam, so no one is spiritually regenerated except through Christ.[5] Then, in order to bring greater clarity to the aforementioned conclusion and the inference posited above, he compares the merit of Christ's obedience to the demerit of Adam's disobedience. Specification of Christ's merit and Adam's demerit will do much to clarify the comparison.

vv. 19-20 Hence the Apostle adds, **Just as through the disobedience [of one human being]**. Thereupon, so that he might more fully demonstrate the excess of grace as well as the ineffectiveness of the Law, indeed even the burden accidentally introduced by the Law, he adds, **The law entered in**. It entered in secretly between the state of nature and the state of grace. Or perhaps **entered in** means that it entered subsequently after the entrance of the first sin into human beings **so that it might abound**. This can be read in two ways. In the first way it can be taken in a causal manner in the sense that "it was in order that trespass should abound." In that sense, therefore, the Law would become more abundantly burdensome, in order that trespass would be made manifest or made known and dreaded. In the second way, it can be read consecutively to mean "such that it abounded," that is, trespass

---

5. Peter Lombard, *Commentary on the Epistle to the Romans,* PL 191:1395a-b.

abounded following upon the entrance of the Law. From the Law there came, in an accidental manner, an increase of sin. This is because the same type of sin — all things being equal — carried greater guilt and accusation after the entrance of Law than before, and because disordered desire rushed in more forcefully once it was more expressly forbidden.

vv. 20-21 It seems more likely that the Apostle intends his remarks to be taken in this second sense, which becomes clear when he adds, **Where trespass abounded**, that is, where it was more abundant, **[grace] abounded all the more**, etc. **So that just as [sin] reigned** with much dominion **unto death** by introducing death, **so grace through righteousness** by which it justifies us **might reign**. That means so that grace might abundantly and forcefully lead us **into eternal life**, which it does **through Jesus [Christ our Lord]**.

Note that the grace of God is said here to abound all the more. This is not because a stronger grace will be given to the one who has greater sins, but because the effect of this liberation from sin and its fetters, and from the honor paid to the Law, was all the more abundant the more gravely one trespassed. Occasionally and even often in such cases, grace abounds or has abounded with greater strength owing to the greatness of the trespass. For in such cases, it often happens that a person becomes more humble with respect to the grace sought more ardently, more grateful with respect to Christ the giver of grace, and more cautious and firm with respect to the grace that must be preserved. One does this, moreover, if the phrase "where trespass super-abounded" is read according to the first explanation of the earlier phrase. For then the sense would be as follows. Where it abounded all the more, that is, where trespass was more abundantly known and considered as such, there [grace abounded all the more].

Note that in this chapter the Apostle proceeded by supposing what was a sort of principal conclusion, namely, that we are justified by the grace of Christ and that this is necessary and sufficient for all. Yet here he touches upon three principles that were known to those people to whom he was writing, and from which he was able to prove this point clearly. The first of these is that Christ died for the sake of reconciling us to God. The second is that through one human being death and even sin entered into all. And the third is that the merit and grace of Christ are more powerful for all those who have received this for the sake of their justification and salvation than was the sin of Adam taken together with all our own additional transgressions that lead to our depravity and condemnation.

The reason why the Apostle proceeds in this way is that he prefers here to show the excellence of grace and the superabundance of its efficacy rather than merely prove its existence. Now one may wonder, How is it that through the grace, righteousness, and obedience of Christ the human being we might be justified, brought to life, filled with the gifts of grace, and then at last be led through into eternal life? How can this be when the created grace of Christ could not be the efficient cause of our grace nor the form of our souls, since it would thereby formally vivify and fill us up? Nor could it be the instrumental agent of all our graces and chiefly of those graces that were in the fathers prior to the incarnation of Christ. Would it, therefore, suffice to say that only the meritorious cause of those graces existed after his incarnation? Questions that take up this issue must indeed be touched upon and dealt with. Yet at present we ought to be very cautious lest we either attribute less to him than he is due or attribute something to his created nature that is proper to the divinity alone. And if the words of Scripture are more carefully considered, especially those found in the letters of Paul, one will beware either way, because he himself attributes great things beyond measure to the grace and merit of Christ in his human nature, and nevertheless, in doing so, ascribes nothing of it to that which belongs to divine omnipotence.

ROMANS 6

Peter of John Olivi

Dying and Rising with Christ

v. 1 What then do we say? Here the Apostle removes a certain error that seems to have arisen from what he had said earlier: "Where trespass abounded, grace abounded all the more" (Rom 5:20).[1] For it seems to follow from this that one ought to sin and **continue in sin so that** later on **grace would abound all the more**. First, therefore, the Apostle poses this in the form of a question. Second, he rejects such a thing with abhorrence when he says, **By no means!** Third, he disproves it by constructing an argument that is based on the fact that Christ's grace is so much opposed to sin that it even killed and crucified us to sin. So great is this grace in itself that it has eternally, essentially, and irreversibly established us within the life of Christ, which is completely contrary to our old way of sin. His argument runs as follows. Having died to sin, we ought not to live in it, for we are dead to sin through grace. This is clear from the first sacrament of grace, namely, by means of Baptism, which sacramentally conforms us to the death of Christ and his burial, so that, having died to vices, we pass through into the new life of virtues and grace, assimilated in this way to the new life of the risen Christ.

---

1. Note that Olivi's rendition of Romans 5:20 is slightly different here than where he originally commented on the verse. Here sin did not merely "abound" *(abundavit)* but it "super-abounded" or "abounded all the more" *(superabundavit),* just as grace did.

vv. 2-3 The Apostle posits the major premise of this argument in the form of a surprising line of questioning when he says, **Those who have died [to sin]**. For this implies in some manner the minor premise, which he declares based upon the form of Baptism, **Do you not know, brothers and sisters?** Note where he says that we are baptized into the death of Christ as much by reason of the sign as by reason of the thing signified. By reason of the sign surely, because it is as though we are buried in the water when, through Baptism, we are submerged into it. The removal of the clothes and the cleansing of the filth accomplished by the water are signs of the removal of the previous life's garment and its filth. And by reason of the thing signified because it is the intention and virtue of Baptism that we might be incorporated into Christ the redeemer by participating in the merit of his death and consequently the grace of his life. For it is through this act that we might be rendered dead to our earlier sins and their sentence of guilt. The Apostle says that **we are baptized into Christ**. That means that we are baptized in the faith of Christ by professing his status and his name. Or perhaps to be baptized into Christ Jesus means that we are incorporated into him through a certain spiritual power of baptismal grace.

vv. 4-6 So that just as Christ was raised from the dead through the glory of God the Father, that is, through the glory given to Christ from God the Father or through the glorious power of God the Father. Then the Apostle says, **For if**, etc. For the sake of greater explication and confirmation, he leads us more fully through the likeness of Baptism to the death of Christ, and at last to his resurrection. Thus he notes that **our old self** is called this because it is subject to the corruption of vices, and chiefly to the original vice of the flesh. This self is called old because it came before the renewal of grace in time, just as the carnal Adam came before the new human Christ. It also clings to corruptible things, having neglected those eternal things that never grow old. Also, the wickedness by which the old self is designated is a sort of corruption of our virtue, just as old age is a corruption of youth and of virile strength and beauty.

The Apostle says, **[The old self] was crucified at the same time** with Christ, so that he might demonstrate how the efficacy or merit of Christ's passion exists with respect to the old self. In this regard one should know that the spark of disordered desire governing our flesh has a threefold power for evil.[2] First, it subjects people to a sentence of eternal death, and this is

---

2. In this sentence and elsewhere, "spark" translates the Latin word *fomes,* which liter-

called its state of guilt. Second, it controls humans' ability to assent and proves superior to their will. Third, it is powerfully and deeply rooted in the flesh or sensitive faculty, such that it is moved of necessity by its urges and law. Yet the grace of Christ's cross, in Baptism, crucifies and puts to death the senescence of sin. It accomplishes this first because it takes away, and in a sense kills, its sentence of guilt. Second, in the case of adults, it renders actual consent to [Christ's] dominion, such that we die to disordered desire with regard to the consent and the very sin within us. Third, its compulsion or tyranny, which of its very nature it exercised over the flesh, is restrained, beaten, and weakened through works of penance and the practice of virtues. To this extent the spark of disordered desire is crucified, although in itself it is not altogether dead.

The Apostle says that he was crucified **so that the body of sin might be destroyed**, insofar as it is of sin. On the one hand, the phrase **body of sin** can refer to the human being, insofar as one is subject to sin, and chiefly inasmuch as one is subject to it according to the flesh. For then it is destroyed to such an extent when sin itself is destroyed. Or **body of sin** could refer to the entire accumulation of original wickedness. For certainly, in keeping with our different powers, the body has different branches and different limbs; and with these one might understand the accumulation of actual sins that have been added onto original sin.

v. 7 Whoever has died to sin **has been justified [or absolved] from sin**. It is as though he were saying, "It is the same thing to die to sin as for sin to be remitted and the human being to be made righteous."

v. 8 We believe that we will also live with him by the life of grace and finally by the life of glory.

vv. 9-10 Thereupon the Apostle says, **Knowing that Christ**, etc. In order that he may more fully demonstrate on the basis of this likeness that we should not again return to sin, the Apostle shows that Christ **died once for all to sin**, that is, for the sake of sin. Now, according to some people, and according to Augustine, "sin" here refers to Christ's mortal flesh, which bore the likeness of sinful flesh.[3] For **rising [from the dead]**, he never again **dies**,

---

ally means tinder or kindling wood. In the moral sphere, it refers to the incitement to sin to which all humans are subject after the Fall.

3. Augustine, *Against Maximus*, 1.2, PL 42:744-45.

which is to say that he forever **lives to God**. He lives to the glory of God, or is conformed to God, or lives by the power of God. Or, perhaps, **to God** means that he is near to God or in the presence of God.

v. 11 On this basis the Apostle introduces his intention, **So you [must consider yourselves dead to sin but alive to God]**.

v. 12 And by this claim he first introduces what sort of people they must be in his estimation, and second what sort of works they should do when he says, **Let not sin, therefore, reign**. Just what he means by the term "reign" he explains when he adds **to obey**, etc. Note that we present our members to sin, to take up the arms of iniquity, at that time when we make them instruments of sin by corporeally committing evil acts with and through our members. Yet at this point someone could say, "We are not able to do what the Apostle commands because the power of the disordered desire of sin is so great that it rules over us, as though dragging us by necessity both to consent and to act."

v. 14 And so the Apostle counters this argument when he adds, **For sin will not have dominion over you**. Just what it means not to let it have dominion, he shows by adding, **since you are not under the law but under grace**. Note that to be "under the law" means for the Apostle that one is subject to it in servile fear and that one is ruled by the Law alone apart from grace. In this way, therefore, the condition of the Law may be distinguished from the condition of grace. He means that to be "under the law" is to be under its burdens, and consequently under its death-dealing obligation, which for those who do not have grace obligates them to eternal death. Existence under the Law is threefold. It means that sin has dominion over someone as much in consent as in the sentence of guilt. For apart from grace, and through consent, a human being is subject to it, or is placed under it; and through the sentence of guilt one is cast into condemnation.

Servants of Righteousness

v. 15 What then? Will we sin because we are not under the law but under grace? Here the Apostle moves on to another question that arises from the phrasing of what he has just said. For someone might believe that since we are freed from the fear and honor due the Law, and since we have Christ, who offered himself up as a sacrifice on our behalf, we could therefore safely sin. Yet he counts this out when he adds, **By no means!** He then proves his point based upon the opposition that abides between sin and grace. For sin first subjects the sinner to abominable uncleanness and the worst sort of servitude, and then finally to eternal death. On the other hand, grace cleanses and justifies; it sanctifies and renders one a servant to righteousness and holiness, and leads one at last into eternal life.

vv. 16-20 In this section the Apostle sets forth more fully the minor premise of his argument drawn from his above-mentioned opposition when he says, **Do you not know?** Second, he tries to entice them all the more toward his position by way of thanksgiving. He does this by showing them how, having rejected the servitude of sin through God's grace, they have sincerely obeyed the teaching and grace of Christ when he adds, **But thanks [be to God].** Third, so that he might lead them inexcusably to this point, he exhorts them along lines sufficiently proportionate to their human frailty. Let them give themselves to sanctifying righteousness at least as much as they had previously given themselves over to wicked and depraved uncleanness. Thus he adds, **I speak in human terms.** Fourth, so that he might convince them even more fully, he replies and explains the minor premise of the abovementioned argument as he adds, **When you were servants [of sin].**

With regard to the first point, note that here and above any sort of sin could generally be understood by the term "sin." Yet it properly refers to the vice of inherent disordered desire, which bears within itself the sentence of guilt, that is, before its sentence was remitted through the grace of Christ. Afterward, however, it is called sin for three reasons. First, according to Augustine, disordered desire came about by means of sin, just as we call the idioms and phrases of nations their tongue, since they come about through the tongue. Second, according to Augustine, disordered desire inclines one toward sin and even makes one a sinner if one consents to it, just as the cold is called sluggishness because it makes one sluggish. Third, in itself disordered desire is formally wicked, although on account of the grace of Christ it is not imputed to the regenerate as guilt.[4]

v. 16 Note that the will is moved by affections, and chiefly through those that govern its other affections. For the will consents to the affections that it follows as if to a rule and mistress of its own actions, indeed as though consent-

---

4. Augustine, *On Marriage and Concupiscence*, 1.23.25, CSEL 42:238.

ing to its highest good. That is why the Apostle says, **You were its servants** as if to a master, and on this basis **you must be obedient** to the master. This functions as the major proposition of his argument. Then, as if positing the minor premise for greater specificity he says, **Either** you would present yourselves as slaves **of sin** unto death as its reward **or** you would present yourselves as slaves of **obedience**, that is, slaves of a holy obedience **to righteousness**, namely, through this righteousness that one is to possess and acquire. Or perhaps, according to the Gloss, one ought to supply **of sin**, namely, of the sin that leads to death and **of obedience** that leads to righteousness.

v. 19 I speak in human terms means that I speak in ways that are sufficiently consonant with human instability and frailty. And I say this **on account of the weakness** or frailty **of our flesh**, referring to our sensual nature. Just what this would be, he demonstrates when he adds, **Just as you presented your members to serve**, by what you were doing, **uncleanness** with regard to carnal sins, **and iniquity** with regard to sins of unrighteousness, although uncleanness and iniquity could signify the same thing under different principles of sin. **Unto iniquity** means amassing iniquity unto ourselves, or perhaps [**to serve**] **iniquity** means to serve that which leads **unto iniquity**.

    So now, etc. Note that he says that this sort of reasoning is human or trivial because righteousness in itself ought to be more delightful, more lovely, and more fruitful than iniquity. It would be a great thing to endure toils, death, disgrace, and the loss of all things for the sake of righteousness. Yet apart from such trials, a person may delight in righteousness and, in keeping with it, might act in a delightful way. That, however, is not a great thing, because righteousness ought to be loved more now than iniquity was loved then. For according to Augustine, as recorded in the Gloss, the Apostle means to say, "If righteousness is not served more, let it be at least served to the extent that iniquity was served back then." For just as back then there was no fear compelling one to sin, but rather the desire and pleasure of sin led the way, so now to live justly, let not the dread of punishment urge one on. Instead, let the delight and love of righteousness lead one forward. "There are perhaps those who, as sometimes they had set the pleasure of sin before righteousness, so now place the delight in righteousness before the pleasures of the flesh. But they favor righteousness only because they dread suffering punishments and death."[5] This sort of reasoning is human and petty.

    5. Peter Lombard, *Commentary on the Epistle to the Romans*, PL 191:1410c; Augustine, Letter 145, CSEL 44:266-73.

vv. 20-21 When you were servants of sin, you were free from righteous-ness, that is, free from the yoke of righteousness. Yet such freedom is of the worst sort and very harmful. The Apostle demonstrates this when he adds: **What fruit did you have** in those sins **in which you are now ashamed?** It is as if he were to say, "You can report of no fruit except for opprobrium and confusion and finally eternal death." Hence he adds, **For the end [of them is death]**.

vv. 22-23 But now. Here he demonstrates the opposite with regard to the ser-vitude of God's grace. Thereupon he repeats them both together, adding, **The wages [of sin] is**, or "are," **death**. It is as though he were saying, "Eternal death is owed to sin, or to a sinner, just as a wage is owed to a soldier or la-borer." **But the grace of God is eternal life**, etc. The word "grace," according to the more accurate text, is in the nominative case here. Hence, according to Augustine, although one could say that the wage of righteousness is eternal life, he preferred to say that the grace of God is eternal life so that we might understand that it is not by our own merits, but by the mercy of God, that we are led through to eternal life. Hence because our merits, by which eternal life is rendered, are not from us, but are instead produced in us through grace; therefore, eternal life itself is rightly called grace. These comments are found in the Gloss, having been taken up from Augustine's letter to the pres-byter Sixtus and from his letter to Valentinus.[6] Yet some people read "grace" in the ablative case, such that the sense is that for the sake of the grace pos-sessed here, eternal life is given to us. Or it could mean that through grace, and from the grace of God alone, eternal life is given to us, although this would not exclude our own merits. Yet this still takes place **in Christ Jesus our Lord**, that is to say, through Christ Jesus.

---

6. Peter Lombard, *Commentary on the Epistle to the Romans*, PL 191:1412c-d; Augus-tine, Letter 194, CSEL 57:12.

ROMANS 7

Thomas Aquinas

LECTURE 1

v. 1 Above [on Rom 5:12], the Apostle shows that we are freed from sin through the grace of Christ; here he shows that through the same grace of Christ we are freed from servitude to the Law. In this matter he does two things. (1) He makes a claim. (2) He rules out an objection where he says, "What then will we say?" etc. (Rom 7:7). Regarding the claim, he shows that (1) we are liberated from servitude to the Law through the grace of Christ and (2) this liberation is useful, and he does the latter beginning with the words, "That we might bear fruit for God," etc. (Rom 7:4). Regarding the first, the liberation, he does three things. (1) He offers an example, from which he argues in support of his claim. (2) He articulates his claim, "For she who is under a husband," etc. (Rom 7:2). (3) He concludes with "Therefore, my brothers," etc. (Rom 7:4).

Freedom from Servitude to the Law

Now he offers his example as if already known. He says therefore, **Do you not know, brothers and sisters?**, as if to say that you ought not to be unaware of this. 1 Corinthians 14:38, "If any do not know, they will not be known." He gives the reason why they ought not to be unaware by adding, **I am speaking to those who know the law**.

But since the Roman gentiles were indeed ignorant of the Law of Moses, what is said here seems unfitting for them. Therefore, some take this to mean the natural law, of which the gentiles were not unaware, according to Romans 2:14, "For the gentiles, who do not possess the law, by nature do things that are of the law," etc. He adds, therefore, **For the law**, namely, the natural law, **has dominion over a person as long as** the person **lives**, namely, the law in the person. Indeed, it lives as long as reason effectively flourishes in a person. Yet in a person natural law is dead as long as natural reason succumbs to the passions. Isaiah 24:5, "They have broken the eternal covenant," namely, of the natural law.

This does not, however, seem to be the Apostle's intention. When he speaks absolutely and without qualification about the Law, he always speaks about the Law of Moses.

It should be said that the faithful in Rome included not only gentiles but also many Jews. Therefore, Acts 18:2 holds that Paul found in Corinth "a certain Jew by the name of Aquila, and his wife Priscilla, who had come recently from Italy because Claudius had commanded all Jews to leave Rome."

With reference to the Law of Moses [as opposed to natural law], **the law has dominion over people as long as** the people **live**. For the Law is given to direct a person along the way in this life. According to Psalm 24:12/ 25:12, God "has appointed a law for them on the way they have chosen." As a result, the Law's obligation is removed at death.

v. 2 Then with the words, "For she who is under a husband," etc., he clarifies what he said above by using marriage law as an example. (1) He furnishes the example; (2) he clarifies what he said symbolically, "Therefore, while he lives," etc. (Rom 7:3).

Regarding the first, he does two things. In the example, he shows how the obligation of the Law lasts as long as life lasts when he says, **For a woman who is under a husband**, that is, who is under the power of a husband. This is a matter of divine law; see Genesis 3:16, "You will be under your husband's power." **She is bound by the law**, which requires her to live with her husband. See Matthew 19:6: "Whom God has joined, let no one separate."

This indissolubility of marriage results especially from its being a sacrament of the indissoluble union of Christ and the Church or the Word and human nature in the person of Christ. Ephesians 5:32, "This is a great sacrament in Christ and the Church," etc.

When he says, **Now if he dies**, etc., he shows in the example how the obligation of the Law is removed after death. **Now if the husband**, namely, of the woman, **dies**, after her husband's death the woman **is released from the** nuptial **law**, that is, the law of marriage by which she is obligated to her husband.

For since, as Augustine states in his book *On Marriage and Concupiscence,* marriage is a mortal good, its obligation does not extend beyond this life.[1] Therefore, at the resurrection, in life immortal, "neither will they marry nor be married," as Matthew 22:30 states.

It is clear then that if anyone dies and rises, as happened with Lazarus, there will be no wife, as there had been, unless new arrangements are made.

Against this, some introduce Hebrews 11:35, "Women received back their dead through resurrection." However, it should be understood that women did not receive their spouses but their children, as happened to one woman through Elijah in 1 Kings 17 and another through Elisha in 2 Kings 4.

Otherwise, this text relates to sacraments that impress a character, a kind of consecration of the immortal soul. Every consecration remains as long as the thing consecrated remains, as is clear in the consecration of a church or an altar. Therefore, if any are baptized or confirmed or ordained and they die and then rise, they ought not receive the same sacrament again.

v. 3 Then with the words, **Therefore, while he lives**, he clarifies what he said symbolically.

First, regarding the obligation of marriage — which lasts for the woman **while her husband lives** — he describes her as an adulterer if she is with another man, that is, united sexually to him **while her husband lives**. Jeremiah 3:1, "If a man sends away his wife, and leaving him, she marries another man, is that woman not polluted and contaminated?"

Next, he says, **But if he is dead**, etc., he introduces a symbol regarding the dissolution of the obligation of the law of marriage after death. **If her husband**, namely, the woman's, **is dead**, the woman **is freed from the law of her husband**, by which she was obligated to her husband **so that she is not an adulterer if she is with another man** sexually, especially if she is joined with him in marriage. 1 Corinthians 7:39, "If her husband has died, she is free; let her marry whom she wishes."

From this it is clear that second or third or fourth marriages are permitted in themselves, not through some sort of dispensation as Chrysostom

---

1. Augustine, *On Marriage and Concupiscence*, 1.16.18, CSEL 42:231.

seems to say in his commentary on Matthew.[2] He says that just as Moses permitted a bill of divorce, so the Apostle permitted second marriages.

There is no reason, if marriage is dissolved by death, why the living spouse ought not to marry again. When the Apostle says in 1 Timothy 3:2 that "a bishop must be the husband of a single wife," he does not mean that second marriages are illicit, but [in comparison to first marriages], they are imperfect.[3] Thus a bishop should be the husband of a single wife in the same way that Christ is the spouse of the one Church.

v. 4 Then with the words, **Therefore, my brothers**, he concludes his primary claim, saying, **Therefore**, etc. That is, because you have been made members of the body of Christ and have died and been buried together with him, as noted above, you have died to the Law. That is, the Law's obligation ceases for you **so that now you may belong to another**, namely, to Christ, and be subjected to the law of him **who has risen from the dead**. You also, rising in him, have taken on a new life. Thus you are bound not by the law of a prior life but by the law of a new life.

However, there seems to be some divergence here. In the preceding example, when the husband died, the woman was freed from the law's requirements. But here the one who is released from obligation is the one who dies.

But if we consider correctly, each follows the same reasoning. Since marriage is between two people, there is a certain relation. So it does not make a difference; whichever dies, the marital law is lifted. So, whichever happens, it is clear that through the death, by which we die with Christ, obligation to the old Law ceases.

The Apostle then turns to a discussion of the usefulness of this liberation, saying, **That you might bear fruit**.

Concerning this he does three things. First, he asserts the usefulness, saying, **That you might bear fruit for God**. Through this we are made members of Christ. Remaining in Christ, we can produce the fruit of good work to God's honor. John 15:4, "As the branch cannot bear fruit on its own," etc.

v. 5 Second, where he says, **For when we were**, he shows that this fruit was hampered when we were under servitude to the Law, **when we were in the flesh**, that is, subject to the disordered desires of the flesh. See Romans 8:9,

---

2. Pseudo-Chrysostom, *Incomplete Commentary on Matthew*, 19.7, Homily 32.8 (PG 56:801).

3. See ST, Supplement 63.2 ad 2.

"You are not in the flesh but in the spirit." **Sinful passions** and affections, **which** indeed **resulted from the law**, either made known or occasionally increased as made clear above, **work in our members**. That is, they used to move our members. James 4:1, "What is the source of wars and strife; is it not disordered desires?" And **they bore fruit in death**; that is, they resulted in death. James 1:15, "When sin reaches maturity, it begets death."

v. 6 Third, with the words, **But now we are released**, he shows that those who are freed from servitude to the Law acquire the above-mentioned advantage. **But now we are released**, by the grace of Christ, **from the law of death**, that is, from servitude to the Law of Moses, which is called the law of death. This is so, too, because it killed physically without mercy. Hebrews 10:28, "Anyone violating the law of Moses dies without mercy." Or rather it is called the law of death because it killed at an opportune moment, according to 2 Corinthians 3:6, "The letter kills," etc.

We are released **from the law in which we were held**, like servants under the law. Galatians 3:23, "But before faith came, we were held in custody under the law." **Thus** we have been released **that we might serve in newness of spirit**, in a spirit renewed by the grace of Christ. Ezekiel 36:26, "I will give you a new heart, and I will place a new spirit within you." **Not under the aged letter**, that is, not according to the old Law. Or not under the aged sin, which the letter of the Law could not take away. Psalm 6:8/6:7, "I have grown old among all my enemies."

LECTURE 2

v. 7 After showing that we are freed by grace from servitude to the Law and that liberation is useful, the Apostle responds to an objection that arose as a result of the foregoing, namely, that the old Law is not good. Concerning this, he does two things. (1) He refutes the objection that the Law is not good. (2) He shows that the Law is good when he says, "For we know," etc. (Rom 7:14). Concerning the first [the refutation of the objections], he does two things. (1) He articulates the objection with regard to the Law itself. (2) He then dismisses it, saying, "Therefore the law is indeed holy," etc. (Rom 7:12).

The Law's Holiness

First, it has been said that sins' sufferings result from the Law, which is the law of death. **What then will we say?** follows from these things. Should we say that **the law is sin?**

This can be understood in two different ways. In one way, the Law teaches sin, as in Jeremiah 10:3, "The laws of the peoples are vain" because they teach vanity. In another way, law is called sin because the one who gave the law sinned by creating it. These two are related because if the Law teaches sin, then the legislator sins by creating it. Isaiah 10:1, "Woe to those who make wicked laws." So it seems that the Law teaches sin if sins' sufferings result from the Law, and if the Law leads to death.

Then when the Apostle says, "Indeed not," he refutes the objection. If the Law were in itself and directly causing sins' sufferings or death, it would follow that the Law is sin in one of the two ways, but not if the Law is the occasion of [or opportunity for] sins' sufferings and death. Concerning this, he does two things. (1) He shows what the Law does on its own. (2) He shows what results opportunely where he says, "But sin, seizing an opportunity," etc. (Rom 7:8).

Concerning the first, he does three things. First, he responds to the question, saying, the Law is **indeed not** sin. It does not teach sin, according to Psalm 18:8/19:7, "The law of the Lord is pure." Nor has the legislator sinned in creating an unjust law. Proverbs 8:15, "By me kings reign."

Second, he says, **But sin**, etc. Here he states what the Law itself does. It reveals sin; it does not take it away. He therefore says, **I did not know sin except through the law.** See Romans 3:20, "Knowledge of sin is through God's law." If this refers to natural law, then it means that people decide between good and evil based on natural law. Ecclesiasticus 17:6, "He filled their hearts with understanding and showed them good and evil." But the Apostle here seems to be speaking of the old Law, which he signified above, saying, "Not under the aged letter" (Rom 7:6).

The answer is therefore, without the Law, one could indeed know sin insofar as it is shameful and against reason but not insofar as it offends God. People recognize through divine law that their sins displease God because the Law prohibits them and requires their punishment.

Third, he says, **For covetousness**, etc. Here he proves what he said, **For I did not know covetousness except that the law said, "Do not covet."**

Consider that someone could take the claim that we cannot know sin except through the Law to mean the very act of sin that the Law both alerts us to and prohibits. This is true with regard to some sins. For Leviticus 18:23

says, "A woman shall not lie down with an animal." But this is clearly not what the Apostle means by Romans 7:7. For no one is ignorant of the act of covetousness since all experience it.

Therefore, one ought to understand, as is noted above, that sin is known through the Law only with regard to the guilt of punishment and offense against God. He proves this by way of covetousness since depraved covetousness is usually found in all sins. Therefore, the Gloss and Augustine say, "The Apostle has chosen a general sin, covetousness." The Law is therefore good because in prohibiting disordered desires, it prohibits all evil.[4]

Covetousness can be understood as a general sin if it is taken for covetousness of illicit things, which is of the essence of any sin. Yet Augustine called covetousness a general sin not in this way, but in the sense that some particular covetousness is the root and cause of every sin. The Gloss, therefore, speaks of covetousness as a general sin from which all evils come.[5]

The Apostle introduces a precept of the Law found in Exodus 20:17 that prohibits, in particular, the covetousness of avarice, "You shall not covet anything of your neighbor's." In 1 Timothy 6:10, he says, "The love of money is the root of all evils." This is so because "all things obey money," as Ecclesiastes 10:19 states. Therefore, the covetousness about which he speaks here is a general evil, not in sharing a class or species, but in sharing a cause.

Ecclesiasticus 10:15, "Pride is the beginning of all sin," does not contradict the Apostle. For pride is the beginning of sin with respect to aversion from God, while love of money is the beginning of sins with respect to conversion to a changeable good.

Now it can be said that the Apostle chooses covetousness in particular to make his case because he wants to show that without Law sin was not known inasmuch as it concerns offense against God. This is especially clear since God's Law prohibits covetousness, which is not prohibited by human law. For God alone considers someone liable because of covetousness of the heart. See 1 Samuel 16:7, "Humans see what is in the open, but God sees into the heart." Therefore, God's Law prohibited coveting of another's things, which are taken by theft, or of another's spouse, who is violated through adultery, more than the coveting involved in other sins. The former combine a certain kind of pleasure with the covetousness that other sins do not have.

---

4. Peter Lombard, *Commentary on the Epistle to the Romans*, PL 191:1416. Augustine, *On the Spirit and Letter*, 4.6, CSEL 60:157-59. Augustine, Sermon 155 1.1, PL 38:840-41.

5. Augustine, *On the Spirit and Letter*, 4.6, CSEL 60:157-59. Sermon 155, 1.1 (PL 38:840-41).

Then when he says, "But opportunity," etc., he shows what follows from the Law opportunely. (1) He introduces what he intends. (2) He articulates his claim, "Without the law," etc.

v. 8 He says first, therefore, that **sin, taking an opportunity through the commandment**, namely, of the Law prohibiting sin, **has produced in me every covetousness**.

By "sin," one can understand the devil in an extended sense because he himself is the cause of sin. In this regard, he produces every covetousness of sin in humans. 1 John 3:8, "Whoever sins is of the devil because the devil sins from the beginning."

However, because the Apostle did not mention the devil here, it can be said that any actual sin, as apprehended in thought, produces its own covetousness in a person. James 1:14-15, "People are tempted by their own covetousness . . . ; then covetousness gives birth to sin."

Yet it is better that we take Romans 7:8 to refer to sin, namely, to original sin, which (as noted above in Rom 5:12) entered this world through one person. Original sin, before Christ's grace, is in humans through guilt and punishment. However, with the arrival of grace, it changes into a condition of judgment and remains in act as a spark to sin, or it becomes a habit of covetousness, which produces all actual covetousness in humans. It may also refer to the disordered desires of various sins, such as the covetousness of theft, adultery, and so on. It may also refer to diverse degrees of covetousness as it consists in thought, delight, consent, and deed.

However, to produce this effect in a person, sin takes its opportunity from the Law, and thus he says, **Taking an opportunity**. With the advent of the commandment, there is now the matter of violation because "where there is no law, there is no violation," as Romans 4:15 states. Or the desire of forbidden sin increases, according to the reasons given above in the comment on Romans 5:20.

It should be noted that the Apostle does not say that the Law gave the opportunity to sin but that sin itself took the opportunity from the Law. For they who give an opportunity scandalize and therefore sin. This indeed happens when people do something improper that offends or scandalizes their neighbors, for example, by frequenting a dishonorable place, but with no evil intention. See Romans 14:13, "Rather, let us decide not to place an obstacle or scandal in the way of others." However, if people do something proper, such as give alms and, as a result, another is scandalized, they do not give an opportunity for scandal. They, therefore, neither scandalize nor sin, but another takes the opportunity to be scandalized and thereby sins. Thus the Law did something proper by forbidding sin; it did not, thereby, give an opportunity to sin. People, however, take the opportunity from the Law. It follows that the Law is not sin, but rather sin is from humans.

One should realize, then, that sins' sufferings, which pertain to the covetousness of sin, are not from the Law, as if the Law produced them. Rather, sin, taking the opportunity from the Law, produces them. For the same reason, the Law is called the law of death, not because the Law produces death but because sin produces death by taking the opportunity from the Law.

Read in the same sense, this text can be taken in another way so that it could be said that sin has produced every covetousness through the command of the Law and taken the opportunity to do so through that very command. However, the first interpretation is simpler and better.

Then when he states, "For without the law," he clarifies what he has said, and he does so through the experience of the effect. (1) He sets forth the effect and (2) repeats the cause, "For sin," etc. (Rom 7:11).

With regard to the first, he does three things. (1) He describes conditions before the Law. (2) He describes conditions under the Law, "But when it came," etc. (Rom 7:9). (3) Comparing the two, he deduces the effect of the Law, "It turned out to be death for me" (Rom 7:10).

First [with regard to conditions before the Law], he states earlier in this verse, "Sin, taking an opportunity through the commandment, produced in me every covetousness." From this it is apparent, **Without law sin was dead**. This does not mean that there was no sin because "through one person," who lived before the Law, "sin entered the world," as Romans 5:12 notes above. Sin was understood as dead either in terms of the knowledge of humans, who did not know that particular sins, such as covetousness, were forbidden by a certain law. Or it was dead as a cause of death, in comparison to what was to follow. For sin did not have as much power to lead people to death as it did later when it received the opportunity under the Law. What is weakened in power is considered dead. Colossians 3:5, "Mortify your earthly members." Such were conditions before the Law in terms of sin.

v. 9 How it was for humans before the Law he shows by adding, **But I once lived without the law**.

This can be understood in two ways. In one way, it concerns people who seemed to live by their own power while ignorant that sin was the cause of their death. Revelation 3:1, "You have the reputation of one living, but you are dead." Or the Apostle says this by way of a comparison to death, which results from the opportunity of the Law. For they are said to live who sin less in comparison to those who sin more.

Beginning with the words, **But when the commandment came**, etc., he describes conditions under the Law.

He does so first with regard to sin when he says, **But when the commandment**, given under the Law, **came, sin revived**. This can be understood in two ways, and first about humans who began to know the existence of sin in itself, which they had not known before. Jeremiah 31:19, "After you showed me, I struck my thigh; I am confused and ashamed." He said that **it revived** because, in paradise, humans had full knowledge of sin, not, however, through experience. Or **it revived** in the sense that the power of sin had the opportunity to grow when the Law was given. 1 Corinthians 15:56, "The power of sin is the law."

v. 10 Second, it can be understood about humans themselves under the Law, as he indicates with the words, **but I died**. This can also be taken in two ways. In one way, it means knowledge so that the sense of **I died** is that I know myself to be dead. In another, it is a comparison to an earlier condition so that the sense of **I died** is that I am bound to death more than before. Therefore, what was said to Moses and Aaron in Numbers 16:41, "You have killed the Lord's people," is in some measure true.

Third, when the Apostle says, **and was found**, he draws a conclusion about the effect of the Law by comparing conditions before and under the Law. **And**, according to what was stated above, **the commandment was for life**, both according to the intention of the one who gave the Law and with regard to the uprightness of the commandment and the devotion of the one who obeys it. Ezekiel 20:11, "I gave them good precepts and judgments; those who observe them will live in them." Due to human sin, the Law for me is an opportunity for death. Job 20:14, "The food in his stomach will be turned into the venom of asps within him," etc.

v. 11 Then with the words, **For sin**, etc., the Apostle restates the case as if to clarify the effect of the Law just mentioned, and so he writes that the aforementioned commandment, which was for life, is now found to be for death. **For sin, taking an opportunity through the commandment, seduced me**, that is, through the covetousness that it produced within me, as is noted in Daniel 13:56, "Beauty has deceived you, and covetousness has destroyed your heart." **And by it**, namely, by the commandment, sin taking an opportunity killed me. 2 Corinthians 3:6, "The letter kills."

v. 12 Then with the words, **Thus the law**, etc., the Apostle draws the intended conclusion. Not only is the Law not sin, but ultimately it is good because it both reveals sin and forbids it.

First, in his conclusion, he addresses the Law in its entirety when he says, As is clear from the foregoing, **the law** is **indeed holy**. Psalm 18:8/19:7, "The law of the Lord is pure." 1 Timothy 1:8, "We know that the law is good."

Second, he addresses a particular commandment of the Law, **and the commandment** of the Law **is holy** with regard to ceremonial precepts by which people are directed to the worship of God. Leviticus 20:7, "Be holy because I am holy." The law is also **just** with regard to the judicial precepts by which people are properly directed to their neighbor. Psalm 18:10/19:9, "The judgments of the Lord are true, justified," etc. The Law is also **good**, that is, upright with regard to moral precepts. Psalm 118:72/119:72, "The law of your mouth is good to me beyond heaps of silver and gold," etc. Since all precepts direct us to God, the Apostle calls the entire Law holy.

Law, Sin, and Death

v. 13 Then when he says, **Therefore, did the good**, etc., he poses a question about the Law's effect.

First the question, "Therefore, did the good," namely, the good in itself, **become death for me**; that is, was it in itself the cause of death? Indeed, someone could draw such a false conclusion from what was stated above that "the commandment, which was for life, proved to be death for me" (Rom 7:10).

Second, he dismisses the objection firmly, **Indeed not**. What in itself is good and life-giving cannot be the cause of evil and death, according to Matthew 7:18, "A good tree cannot bear evil fruits."

Third, beginning with the words **but sin**, etc., he harmonizes what he says now with what he stated above on Romans 7:8. The commandment proves to be for death not because it produced death but because sin, taking an opportunity through it, produces death.

Therefore, he says, **But sin, that it might be evident as sin**; that is, it is evident to be sin **through the good** of the Law, that is, through the commandment of the Law. It is good in itself because it causes the recognition of sin. This gives sin an opportunity insofar as it discloses sin.

Thus sin is not to be understood as producing death through the Law, as if without the Law there would have been no death. For the Apostle states above that "death reigned from Adam to Moses" (Rom 5:14), namely, when there was no Law. However, it is understood that sin produces death through the Law because the condemnation of death is increased with the coming of the Law.

The Apostle therefore adds, thus I say that sin produced death through the good **so that sin might become sinful**, that is, so that the commandment of the Law might opportunely cause sin, and this **beyond the measure** in which they were sinning before because, with the arrival of the Law's proscription, either the accusation of transgression appeared or the covetousness of sin grew, as was noted above on Romans 7:8.

As also noted on Romans 7:8, sin is understood here as either the devil or preferably the spark to sin.

LECTURE 3

v. 14 After the Apostle has ruled out those reasons why the Law seemed to be evil and of evil effect, he proves here that the Law is good.

In this regard, he does two things. (1) He proves the goodness of the Law from that very opposition to the good that is found in humans and that the Law cannot remove. (2) He shows what can remove the opposition to this sort of law [i.e., the law of sin], and he does so beginning with the word "Unhappy," etc. (Rom 7:24).

Concerning the first [the goodness of the Law], he does three things. (1) He proposes what he intends to argue. (2) He proves his proposal with the words, "For what I do," etc. (Rom 7:15). (3) He introduces the intended conclusion with the words, "I find therefore," etc. (Rom 7:21).

Concerning the first of these [the initial proposal], he does two things. (1) He proposes the goodness of the Law. (2) He then turns to the human condition where he says, "But I," etc. (Rom 7:14).

The Law's Goodness

First [regarding the goodness of the Law], it has been stated that the Law is holy, and so the Apostle says, **For we know**, we who are wise about divine matters, **that the law**, namely, the old Law, **is spiritual**; that is, it unites humans to spirit. Psalm 18:8/19:7, "The law of the Lord is pure." Or **the law is spiritual** could mean that it is given by the Holy Spirit, who is called the finger of God in Scripture. Luke 11:20, "If by the finger of God I cast out demons." Exodus 31:18, therefore, states, "The Lord gave Moses two stone tablets, written by the finger of God."

Yet the new law is called not only a spiritual law but also the law of the spirit, as is evident in Romans 8:2. This is the case not only because it is from the Holy Spirit but also because the Holy Spirit imprints it on the heart that the Spirit indwells.

Then when the Apostle states, **But I am carnal**, he presents the human condition.

This text can be explicated in two ways. In one, the Apostle speaks as someone in the state of sin. Augustine explains it this way in his book *Eighty-Three Questions.*[6] Later, in *Against Julian,* Augustine holds that the Apostle is understood as speaking in his own person, that is, as a human in the state of grace.[7] Let us continue by showing how these and subsequent words can be explained in both ways, although the second explanation seems better.

When he says, **But I**, the "I" should be understood as human reason, which is primary in the human. Thus humans seem to be their reason or intellect, just as mayors seem to be their cities; thus what they do, the city seems to do.

Humans are called **carnal** because their reason is carnal in two ways. In one way, reason is subject to the flesh; it consents to those things to which the flesh incites it, according to 1 Corinthians 3:3, "Since there is jealousy and contention among you, are you not carnal?" etc. These words are understood about the human not yet renewed by grace. In another way, reason is said to be carnal because it is assailed by the flesh, according to Galatians 5:17, "The flesh covets against the spirit." In this way, reason is understood as carnal even in a person established in grace. Each kind of carnality comes from sin; therefore, he adds, **sold under sin**.

Nevertheless, it should be noted that carnality, which causes rebellion of flesh against spirit [the second way noted above], comes from the sin of the first parent because this pertains to the spark whose corruption is derived from that first sin. The carnality that causes subjection to the flesh [the first way noted above] comes not only from original sin but also from actual sin, by which humans, obeying the disordered desires of the flesh, made themselves servants of the flesh. Therefore, he adds, **sold under sin**, either one's own sin or that of the first parent.

---

6. Augustine, *On Diverse Questions*, 83, CCSL 44A:150-63.

7. Augustine, *Against Julian the Pelagian*, 2.3.5-7, PL 44:675-78.

He says **sold** because sinners sell themselves into servitude of sin at the price of satisfying their own will. Isaiah 50:1, "Behold, you have been sold for your iniquities."

v. 15 Then when the Apostle says, "For what I do," etc., he reveals what he proposed. (1) The Law is spiritual. (2) The human is carnal, sold under sin: "Now it is no longer I," etc. (Rom 7:17). Concerning the first [that the Law is spiritual], he does two things. (1) He offers proof. (2) He introduces his conclusion with the words, "If I do what I do not want," etc. (Rom 7:16). The first [the proof] is taken from human frailty. (1) He proposes human frailty. (2) He presents the proof where he says, "But not I," etc. (Rom 7:15).

The Law as Spiritual

Human frailty is evident because it produces what one knows one ought not do. Therefore, the Apostle says, **For what I do, I do not understand**, namely, what should be done.

This statement can be understood in two ways; in one way about those who are subject to sin and who indeed understand in general that they should not sin. Nevertheless, overcome by the devil's promptings or by passion, inclination, or perverse habits, they sin. Therefore, against their conscience, they are said to do what they know they should not, as in Luke 12:47, "Servants who know their master's will and do not obey it will, deservedly, be beaten severely."

This statement can also be understood about those in a state of grace. Indeed, they do evil. They do not, however, follow through on an evil action or carry it out with mental consent. Instead, they do evil as a result of coveting in accord with a movement of the desire of the senses [*sensibilis appetitus*]. This covetousness is beyond reason and understanding because it precedes the judgment whose entrance impedes sin. Significantly, he does not say, I understand what should not be done, but instead **I do not understand**. The working of covetousness wells up before the intellect's deliberation and before comprehension. Galatians 5:17, "The flesh covets against the spirit, and the spirit against the flesh."

Then beginning with the words, **For not what I want**, etc., the Apostle proves what he said both by drawing a distinction and by noting an effect.

With regard to the distinction, he has already stated, **For what I do**, etc. There are two possibilities here, not to do the good and to do evil. They who do not do the good are said to sin through the sin of omission. When he says, **I do not understand**, he proves by noting an effect. The understanding moves the will; therefore, willing is the effect of understanding.

First, with regard to omission of the good, he states, **For I do not do the good I want**.

In one way, this can be understood about people in the state of sin. One ought to understand **I do** to refer to completed action that is carried out externally in work with the consent of reason. One ought to understand **I want** not about a completed act of the will, which commands work, but about a certain incomplete act of the will by which people in general want the good; just as in general they have right judgment about the good. Nevertheless, this judgment is subverted and distorted through perverse passion or habit. Such a will is distorted in particular so that it fails to do what in general it understands it ought to do and wants to do.

This text is also understood about people restored by grace. In such a case, it is fitting to understand **I want** as a complete act of the will enduring in the choice of a particular activity. **I do**, then, is understood about an incomplete action that consists in the desire of the senses alone that fails to attain the consent of reason. People in the state of grace want to preserve their spirit from deformed covetousness. They fail to do the good due to the disordered movements of covetousness welling up in the desire of the senses. This is similar to the statement in Galatians 5:17, "So that you do not do what you want."

Second, with regard to the commission of evil, the Apostle adds, **But I do the evil I hate**. If this text is about sinful humans, **I hate** is an imperfect hate by which every human naturally hates evil. **I do** means a perfect action in the performance of a work with the consent of reason. That hatred of evil in general is removed from a particular choice through the inclination of a habit or passion.

If, however, this text is understood about people in the state of grace, **I do**, in this case, means an imperfect action, which involves only the covetousness of the desire of the senses. **I hate**, then, is understood about a perfect hate by which someone perseveres in detesting evil until its final rejection. On this, see Psalm 138:22/139:22, "With a perfect hate have I hated them," namely, the evil ones insofar as they are sinners. 2 Maccabees 3:1, "When the laws were still strictly observed due to the devotion of Onias the high priest and to others' hatred of evil."

v. 16 Then when the Apostle says, **But what I do not want**, he concludes from his foregoing discussion of the human condition that the Law is good. No matter whether these words refer to people in a state of grace or sin, from the very fact that I do not want evil, **I consent to the law because it is good**. For it prohibits evil, which I naturally do not want.

It is clear that the reasonable human inclination to desire the good and flee evil is in accord with nature or grace, and each is good. So also the Law, which is consistent with this inclination in commanding good and prohibiting evil, is good for the same reason. Proverbs 4:2, "I will give you a good gift; do not forsake my law."

v. 17 Then when the Apostle says, "But now I," etc., he proves what he said about the human condition, namely, that it is "carnal, sold under sin" (Rom 7:14).

Concerning this, he does three things. (1) He proposes what he intends to argue. (2) He proves what he has proposed, "For I know," etc. (Rom 7:18). (3) He concludes, "But if what I do not want," etc. (Rom 7:20).

Because humans are "carnal, sold under sin," as if in some way servants of sin, it seems that it is not they who act, but they who are acted upon by sin. Those who are free act on their own and are not acted upon by another.

The Apostle therefore states, it has been said that "I consent to the law" (Rom 7:16) through intellect and will. **But now** when I act against the Law, **it is no longer I who** work against the Law, **but sin that dwells in me**. Thus it is clear that I am a servant of sin inasmuch as sin works in me as if it had lordship over me.

One can correctly and simply understand this to be about people in the state of grace. Because they covet evil in accord with the desire of their senses as it relates to the flesh, it does not proceed from the work of reason but from the inclination or of the spark. Humans are said to do what their reason does because by definition a human is that which is in accord with reason. Thus humans do not produce the movements of covetousness; they are caused not by reason but by a spark. This spark to sin is here called sin. James 4:1, "Where do the wars and controversies among you come from? Are they not from your disordered desires that wage war in your members?"

This passage cannot properly be understood about humans in the state of sin because their reason consents to sin, and therefore they themselves produce sin. Augustine states, as found in the Gloss, "Humans are much deceived who consent to the covetousness of their own flesh and decide to do what it desires. Having decided, they think they still should say, **It is not I who do it**."[8]

---

8. Augustine, *On Marriage and Concupiscence*, 1.28.31, CSEL 42:243; Peter Lombard, *Commentary on the Epistle to the Romans*, PL 191:1429.

Nevertheless, this text can, in a forced interpretation, also be expounded about the sinful human.

For action is attributed in the first place to a principal agent that moves on its own and not to an agent that moves or acts because of another by which it is moved. Yet it is clear that human reason, based on what is characteristic of it, is not inclined to evil but is moved to it by covetousness. Therefore, the work of evil, which reason does when overcome by covetousness, is not attributed principally to reason, which is here represented by the human, but rather to the very covetousness or habit by which reason is inclined to evil.

Yet sin is said to dwell in a person not as if sin is some thing, since it is a privation of the good, but as the permanence of this sort of absence in a person.

v. 18 Then when he says, "For I know," he proves that sin dwelling in a person produces the evil that the person does. (1) He posits the means of proving this claim. (2) He makes the means clear with the words, "For to will," etc.

Regarding the first, he proves that sin dwelling in people produces the evil that they do. This proof is indeed clear insofar as the words refer to a person in a state of grace who is freed from sin through the grace of Christ, as noted above in Romans 6:22. Therefore, they in whom the grace of Christ does not dwell are not yet freed from sin. Yet the grace of Christ does not dwell in the flesh but in the spirit. As the Apostle states in Romans 8:10, "The body is indeed dead due to sin, but the spirit lives due to righteousness." Therefore, the sin that the covetousness of flesh produces still rules in the flesh.

He understands the flesh here as including the sensitive powers. For thus the flesh is distinguished from the spirit and opposes it inasmuch as the desire of the senses [*appetitus sensitivus*] tends to oppose what reason longs for [*appetit*], according to Galatians 5:17, "The flesh covets against the spirit."

The Apostle therefore states, It has been asserted that sin works in me, even renewed by grace. One should understand "in me" here as the flesh together with the desire of the senses. **For I know**, through reason and experience, **that the good**, namely, of grace by which I have been transformed, **does not dwell in me** (Rom 7:18).

Lest **in me** be understood as reason, in the way proposed above, he explains, **that is, in my flesh**. For this good does dwell in me, that is, in my heart, according to Ephesians 3:17, "That Christ may dwell by faith in your hearts."

Therefore, it is clear that this text does not support the Manichaeans, who do not consider the flesh by nature to be good and so a good creation of God; even though 1 Timothy 4:4 states, "Every creature of God is good." The Apostle is not concerned here about a good of nature but about a good of grace, by which we are freed from sin.

If this text is taken to refer to people in the state of sin, it is superfluous to add, **that is, in my flesh**, because the good of grace dwells neither in the flesh nor in the mind [*mentem*] of the sinner. Yet someone may perhaps want to interpret this text in a forced way to mean that sin, which is a privation of grace, is in some way diverted from the flesh to the spirit.

Then when he says, "For to will," etc., he makes the means clear for proving that sin dwelling in a person produces the evil that the person does. (1) He does so with regard to human ability and (2) and with regard to the human action that demonstrates the ability, and this with the words, "For not what I want," etc. (Rom 7:19).

Human ability is first described with reference to the will, which seems to be under human power. Therefore, he states, **For to will is present to me**, that is, near to me, as if existing under my power. For there is nothing so established in the human will as the human will, as Augustine states.[9]

Second, he posits the ability, or rather the difficulty, of humans in carrying out the effect when he adds, **But I do not find the accomplishment of the good** within my power. Proverbs 16:1, "Humans prepare the soul"; and again in verse 9, "The human heart plans its way, but the Lord directs the steps."

This text seems to support the Pelagians, who claimed that the beginning of a good work is from us insofar as we desire the good. This seems to be what the Apostle says, **But I do not find the accomplishment of the good**.

However, the Apostle excludes this sense in Philippians 2:13, "God works in us to will and to accomplish."

Therefore, when he says, **For to will is present to me** already renewed by grace, it is due to the work of divine grace, by which not only do I will the good, but I also do some good. This is the case because I oppose covetousness, and, led by the Spirit, act against it. Yet, I do not find in myself the power to achieve that good so that I might completely reject covetousness. In this it is clear that the good of grace does not dwell in the flesh because, if it did, I would have the ability to achieve the good through grace dwelling in the flesh just as I have the ability to will the good through grace dwelling in the spirit.

---

9. Augustine, *On Free Will*, 3.3.6-8, CCSL 29:277-80. Augustine's text reads, "There is nothing so within human power as the human will itself."

If this text refers to humans in the state of sin, it could be interpreted so that **to will** is taken for the incomplete will, which from natural instinct in certain sinners is for the good. Yet that willing is **present** to people, that is, together with them as if they were ill unless grace gave to the will the ability to achieve the good.

v. 19 Then when he says, **For what I will**, etc., he makes clear what he had said about human action, which is a sign and effect of human ability. From this it appears that people do not find the accomplishment of the good in themselves because they do not do the good they wish but instead the evil that they do not wish, as was explained above on Romans 7:15.

v. 20 Then when he says, **But if I do what I do not want**, he concludes what he had proposed above, saying, **But if I do what I do not want, it is not I who work it but the sin that dwells in me**. This also was explained above.

One should note that with the same middle term, namely, **I do what I do not want**, the Apostle draws two conclusions, which he posited above, namely, the goodness of the Law in verse 16, "But if I do what I do not want, I consent to God's law because it is good." The other conclusion he posited above is the dominion of sin in humans, **But if I do what I do not want, it is not I who work it but the sin that dwells in me**. The first of these two conclusions pertains to the words, "The law is spiritual"; the second to the words, "But I am carnal, sold under sin" (Rom 7:14). He draws the first conclusion about the goodness of the Law from that middle term insofar as he says, **[I do what] I do not want**, because reason does not want what the Law prohibits; therefore, the Law is good. Yet insofar as he says, **I do [what I do not want]**, he speaks of the person ruled by sin, which opposes the rational will.

LECTURE 4

v. 21 Having shown that the Law is good because it accords with reason, the Apostle now draws two conclusions based on the two proofs he posited above. He introduces the second conclusion with the words, "But I see another law," etc. (Rom 7:23). Regarding the first conclusion, he does two things. (1) He introduces the conclusion based on what he said above. (2) He gives a sign for greater clarity beginning with the words, "For I am delighted," etc. (Rom 7:22).

Law as Delightful

As noted, he posited two proofs above. The first is that the Law is spiritual. Having already proved this, he concludes, **Therefore, I find** through experience that **the law of Moses** is consonant with **my wanting to do the good**, that is, with my reason through which I approve of the good and detest evil, since even the Law itself mandates the good and prohibits evil. Deuteronomy 30:14, "The word is very near to you, in your mouth and in your heart, that you might do it."

This was now necessary **because evil**, that is, sin or the spark to sin, **is present to me**, that is, is together with my reason as if inhabiting my flesh. Micah 7:5, "Guard the doors of your mouth from her who sleeps in your embrace," that is, from the flesh.

v. 22 Then when he says, **For I am delighted**, etc., he gives a sign that shows that the Law accords with reason.

For none are delighted except with something that is befitting to them. Humans are delighted, according to reason, in God's Law; therefore, God's Law is befitting to [or consistent with] reason. Thus, he says, **I am delighted in God's law according to the inward person**, that is, according to reason and mind, which are called the inward person. It is not that the soul is fashioned according to the form of the person, as Tertullian held.[10] Nor is it the case that it alone is the person, as Plato held, so that the human is a soul using a body. Rather, what is more fundamental in a person is called the person, as noted above on Romans 7:17.

Yet more fundamental in a person, at least based on appearance, is that which is exterior, namely, the body thus fashioned and called the exterior person. In truth, that which is called interior, namely, the mind or reason, is here called the interior person. Psalm 118:103/119:103, "How sweet are your words to my palate!" 1 Maccabees 12:9, "We have the solace of holy books in our hands."

v. 23 Then when he says, "But I see," etc., he offers another conclusion that responds to the proof made above, "But I am carnal" (Rom 7:14).

He states, **I see another law in my members**, which is the spark to sin, which can be called a law for two reasons. In one way, it has a similar effect because just as the Law leads to good, so the spark leads to sin. In another way, it has a similar cause.

---

10. Tertullian, *On the Soul*, 5, CCSL, 2.786-87.

If the spark is a kind of punishment of sin, it has a double cause. One cause is sin itself, which has received dominion in sinners and imposed the law, that is, the spark, on them, just as a lord imposed a law on conquered slaves. Another cause of the spark is God, who introduced this punishment for sinners since their inferior powers would not obey reason. In this regard, that very disobedience of the inferior powers, which is the spark, is called the law in that it was introduced through the Law of divine justice, like a just judge's sentence that coheres with the Law. 1 Samuel 30:25, "And from that day to this, he determined and established it as a law in Israel."

This law dwells originally in the desire of the senses, but it is found dispersed among all members that are subject to the covetousness [or desire] to sin. Romans 6:19, "As you have presented your members to serve uncleanness," etc. Therefore he adds, **In my members**.

This law has two effects in humans. First, it resists reason, and so the Apostle states, **fighting against the law of my mind**. That is, the Law of Moses is called the law of the mind in that it is harmonious with the mind or the natural law, which itself is called the law of the mind because it was placed into the mind naturally. Romans 2:15, "They who show the work of the law written in their hearts." Regarding this **fighting against**, Galatians 5:17 states, "The flesh covets against the spirit."

The second effect is that it reduces people to servitude, and so he adds, **and making me captive**, or leading me to captivity according to another text, **to the law of sin, which is in my members**, that is, in myself, according to the Hebraic manner of speaking, according to which nouns are used in place of pronouns.

The law of sin takes humans captive in two ways. In the case of sinners, it does so through consent and deed. With people in the state of grace, it does so through the movement of covetousness. Regarding this captivity, Psalm 125:1/126:1 states, "When the Lord turned back the captivity of Zion."

v. 24 Then when the Apostle says, "I, an unhappy man," etc., he addresses liberation from the law of sin, and he does three things in this regard. (1) He asks a question. (2) He offers a response where he says, "The grace of God," etc. (Rom 7:25). (3) He draws a conclusion with the words, "Therefore, I myself," etc. Regarding the first, he does two things.

First, he confesses his misery with the words, **I, an unhappy man**. This is due to the sin that dwells in a person, whether in the flesh alone, as in the righteous, or also in the mind, as in the sinner. Proverbs 14:34, "Sin makes the nations miserable." Psalm 37:7/38:6, "I am made miserable and deeply bowed down."

Second, he asks, **Who will free me from the body of this death?** This seems to be the question of one who desires, according to Psalm 141:8/142:7, "Lead my soul from prison."

Know that regarding the human body, one can consider the nature itself of the body. Because the body befits the soul, it does not wish to be separated from the soul. 2 Corinthians 5:4, "We do not wish to be unclothed but to be further clothed." One can also consider its deterioration [*corruptionem*], which weighs down the soul, according to Wisdom 9:15, "The body that is corrupted weighs down the soul," etc. Therefore, the Apostle expressly says, **From the body of this death**.

v. 25 Then when he says, **The grace of God**, etc., he responds to the question. People cannot be freed from the soul's or body's deterioration by their own powers, and this even though they consent with reason against sin.[11] Only through the grace of Christ are they freed, according to John 8:36, "If the Son frees you, you will be freed."

Therefore, it follows that the **grace of God** given **through Jesus Christ** will free me. John 1:17, "Grace and truth were brought forth through Jesus Christ."

Grace frees from the body of this death in two ways. It does so in one way so that the body's deterioration will not rule over the mind, drawing it to sin, and in another way so that the body's deterioration is removed entirely.

Regarding the first, it is appropriate to say to the sinner, **Grace** (Rom 7:25) has freed "me from the body of this death" (Rom 7:24). That is, it has freed me from sin to which the soul is led by the body's deterioration. Yet the righteous have already been freed in this regard. Thus, of them it is fitting to say regarding the second, the **grace of God** has freed "me from the body of this death" so that there is no deterioration of sin or death in my body, which will be the case at the resurrection.

Then when he says, **Therefore I myself**, he draws a conclusion based on someone in the state of sin and someone in the state of grace.

If the text is taken about the sinner, the conclusion to be drawn is as follows. It has been said that God's grace has freed me "from the body of this death" so that I will not be led to sin by it. Therefore, when I am freed, **I**

---

11. Deterioration here and elsewhere translates *corruptio* when it refers to the physical decay or deterioration that the body experiences due to sin.

[will] **serve the law of God with the mind** but, according to the flesh, [I serve] **the law of sin**, which remains in the flesh as a spark, by which the "flesh covets against the spirit" (Gal 5:17).

However, if these words are understood about the righteous person, the conclusion to be drawn is as follows. **The grace of God through Jesus Christ** has freed me "from the body of this death" (Rom 7:24) so that in me there is no longer the deterioration of sin and death. Therefore, **I myself,** the same as before being freed, **serve the law of God in my mind** in giving it my assent, **but I serve the law of sin in the flesh** insofar as my flesh, according to the law of the flesh, is moved to covet.

ROMANS 8

Thomas Aquinas

LECTURE 1

v. 1 Above, the Apostle showed that, by Christ's grace, we are freed from sin and the Law. Here he shows that by the same grace we are freed from condemnation. (1) He does so by noting that by Christ's grace we are freed from the condemnation of guilt. (2) By the same grace we are freed from the condemnation of punishment, and this where he says, "But if Christ," etc. (Rom 8:10). Concerning the first point [liberation from the condemnation of guilt], (1) he proposes what he intends to argue. (2) He proves what he has proposed, "For the law of the spirit of life," etc. (Rom 8:2).

Grace in the Faithful and Unfaithful

Concerning the first [his proposal about what he intends to argue], the Apostle does two things. First, based on an earlier discussion, he sets forth the benefit that grace confers. The grace of God through Jesus Christ has freed "me from the body of this death" (Rom 7:24), and our redemption exists in this. Therefore, now that we have been freed through grace, **no condemnation** remains because it is removed in regard to both guilt and punishment. Job 34:29, When God "grants peace, who can condemn?"

Second, the Apostle identifies those to whom this benefit is granted, and he sets forth two requisite conditions. He posits the first with the words, **To them who are in Christ Jesus**, that is, to them who are incorporated in him through faith, love, and the sacrament of faith [i.e., Baptism].[1] Galatians 3:27, "As many of you who have been baptized in Christ have put on Christ." John 15:4, "Just as the vine branch cannot bear fruit unless it remains on the vine, so neither can you unless you remain in me." They who are not in Christ Jesus are due condemnation. Therefore, "If any do not abide in me, they will be cast out and will wither, like the vine branch, and they will be gathered up, cast into the fire, and will burn" (Jn 15:6).

The Apostle posits the second condition with the words, **who walk not according to the flesh**, that is, who do not follow the covetousness of the flesh. 2 Corinthians 10:3, "Though we walk according to the flesh, we do not fight on its behalf."

Yet some wish to take these words to mean that even the first movements[2] in the unfaithful, that is, those who are not in Christ Jesus, are mortal sins apart from their consent, and this is to walk **according to the flesh**. For if **they do not walk according to the flesh** because they are in Christ Jesus, they are not worthy of condemnation when they serve the law of sin in the flesh according to the first movements of covetousness. It follows, in contrast, that the first movements are worthy of condemnation for those who are not in Christ Jesus.

They also introduce reason into this argument. They claim that for an act to be worthy of condemnation, it must proceed from the habit of a sin worthy of condemnation. Further, such is original sin in that it deprives people of eternal life. This is worthy of condemnation because the habit of original sin remains in the unfaithful whose original guilt has not been taken away. Whoever, therefore, has a movement of covetousness flowing from original sin has sin in them that is worthy of condemnation.

First, it is necessary to show this position to be false.

The first movement, though it remains in the unfaithful, is not mortal sin because it does not involve reason, which is what makes something sinful. Therefore, in the unfaithful the first movements cannot be mortal sins.

Moreover, with regard to the same kind of sin, the faithful sin more gravely than the unfaithful, according to Hebrews 10:29, "How much more do you think they deserve worse punishments," etc. If therefore the first movements were mortal sins in the unfaithful, how much more so in the faithful?

---

1. On Baptism as the "sacrament of faith," see ST III.49.5 co, 66.1 ad 1 *et passim*.

2. "First movements" here refer, in part, to the various ways in which original sin manifests itself venially in the unfaithful. First movements are sinful because of their basis in original sin yet not mortally so because they are not preceded by reasoned consent. Cf. ST I-II.89.5; II-II.36.3 and 37.1.

Second, it is necessary to respond to their arguments.

First, they do not get this from the Apostle's text. For he does not single out the first movements as incapable of condemning those who, though in Christ Jesus, observe the law of sin in the flesh. Nothing at all can condemn them. However, that one is not in Christ Jesus in itself makes one worthy of condemnation.

Moreover, if this refers to the first movements of those who are not in Christ Jesus, movements of this sort are worthy of condemnation based on the condemnation of original sin, which still remains in them and from which those who are in Christ Jesus have been set free. No new condemnation is imparted to them due to movements of this sort.

Regarding what they object to in the second place, their conclusion does not follow of necessity as they hold. For it is not true that any act proceeding from the habit of sin worthy of condemnation is also and itself worthy of condemnation. It can only do so when it is an act perfected by the consent of reason. For example, the habit of adultery — the movement of the covetousness of adultery, which is an incomplete act — is not a mortal sin, but only that completed movement involving the consent of reason. Moreover, the act proceeding from such a habit does not have another cause of condemnation apart from that habit, which accords with the meaning of habit. Therefore, because the first movements in the unfaithful proceed from original sin, they cause condemnation as a result not of mortal sin but only of original sin.

v. 2 Then when the Apostle says "law," etc., he proves what he stated. (1) He does so with regard to the initial condition about which he has just spoken, "There is no condemnation for those who are in Christ Jesus" (Rom 8:1); (2) and with regard to the second condition, "For them who do not walk according to the flesh" (Rom 8:1). He does this where he says, "In us who do not walk according to the flesh" (Rom 8:4), etc.

Concerning the initial condition, he does two things. (1) He sets forth the proof. (2) He elucidates what he claimed in terms of the cause of liberation, "For what was impossible for the law," etc. (Rom 8:3).

Regarding the proof, he offers the following account. The law of the spirit frees a person from sin and death. Now the law of the spirit is in Jesus Christ. Therefore, whoever is in Christ Jesus is freed from sin and death.

The Apostle proves that the law of the spirit frees from sin and death in the following way. The law of the spirit is the cause of life. Now life excludes sin and death, an effect of sin, since sin itself is the spiritual death of the soul. Therefore, the law of the spirit frees a person from sin and death. Since condemnation is only through sin and death, it does not exist for those who are in Christ Jesus.

Therefore, he says, **For the law [of the spirit of life in Christ Jesus has freed me from the law of sin and death]**.

Indeed, in one way the Law can be spoken of as the Holy Spirit so that **the law of the spirit** can be interpreted as the Law, which is the Spirit.

The Law is given to lead people to the good. As the Philosopher states in Book 2, Chapter 1, of the *Ethics,* the legislator's intention is to make citizens good. Human law does this only by indicating what ought to be done.[3] In contrast, the Holy Spirit, dwelling in the mind, not only teaches what ought to be done by illuminating the intellect about what to do, but also inclines the faculty of desire to act rightly. John 14:26, "The Paraclete, the Holy Spirit, whom the Father will send in my name, will teach you everything," that is, will teach what ought to be done, "and will remind you of everything I have told you," that is, will incline to right action.

In another way, the **law of the spirit** can properly be called the effect of the Holy Spirit, namely, faith working through love, since it also instructs interiorly about what to do. According to 1 John 2:27, His "anointing will teach you all things." It also inclines the faculty of desire to act, according to 2 Corinthians 5:14, "Christ's charity urges us on."

Indeed, this **law of the spirit** is called the new law, which is either the Holy Spirit itself or what the Holy Spirit produces in our hearts. Jeremiah 31:33, "I will place my law within them, and I will write it upon their heart." When the Apostle spoke about the old Law above [on Rom 7:14], he said only that it was spiritual, that is, given by the Holy Spirit.

In light of this discussion, we will find four laws introduced by the Apostle. First, the Law of Moses, "I delight in God's law within" (Rom 7:22); second, the law as a spark to sin, "I see another law in my members" (Rom 7:23); third, a kind of natural law, "the law of my members fighting against the law of my mind" (Rom 7:23). Fourth, he hands on a new law when he writes, **The law of the spirit**.

He also adds **of life** because as the natural spirit causes the life of nature so the divine Spirit causes the life of grace. John 6:63, "It is the spirit that gives life"; Ezekiel 1:20, "The spirit of life was in the wheels."

Now he adds **in Christ Jesus** because that Spirit is given only to those who are in Christ Jesus. For just as the natural spirit flows only to the member of the body connected to the head, so the Holy Spirit flows only to the

---

3. Aristotle, *Nicomachean Ethics,* 2.1, AL 26, fasc. 3, p. 164.

person joined to Christ the head. 1 John 3:24, "In this we know that God remains in us, because God has given us from the Spirit." Acts 5:32, "The Holy Spirit whom God gave to all those who obey God."

This Law, he says, **has freed me** because it is in Christ Jesus. John 8:36, "If the Son frees you, truly you are free." And this freedom is **from the law of sin**, that is, from the law as a spark, which inclines to sin. Or it is freedom **from the law of sin**, that is, from the consent and work of sin that holds a human bound by means of the Law. For by the Holy Spirit, sin is forgiven. John 20:22-23, "Receive the Holy Spirit. Those whose sins you forgive, they are forgiven them." **And** freedom **from the law of death**, not only spiritual but also bodily death, as will be proved below. It can liberate, therefore, because it is the spirit of life. Ezekiel 37:9, "Come, spirit, from the four winds, and blow over those slain, and let them live again."

v. 3 Then when the Apostle states, "For what was impossible," etc., he makes clear what he had stated, namely, that the law of life, which is in Christ Jesus, frees from sin. Below, he will prove that it frees from death. Here he bases his proof [about the law of life freeing from sin] on the cause, which is taken from the incarnation of Christ. In this regard, he posits three things. (1) The necessity of the incarnation; (2) the mode of the incarnation beginning with the words, "God sending God's Son"; (3) the fruit of the incarnation, "And concerning sin."

That the exposition might be clearer, let us take the first point second, the second point third, and the third first.

Effects of the Incarnation

I am right in stating that "the law of the spirit of life in Christ Jesus" (Rom 8:2) frees from sin. For **God**, the Father, sent **the Son**, that is, God's Son consubstantial and co-eternal with God. Psalm 2:7, "The Lord said to me, 'You are my son,'" etc. **Sending**, not creating or producing something anew, but God sent him as if he preexisted. Matthew 21:37, "Finally, the landowner sent his son to them," not that God might be where God was not because, as John 1:10 states, "He was in the world." Rather, God sent the Son in order to be in the world in a way in which God was not, that is, visibly through assumed flesh. Thus it follows in John 1:14, "The Word was made flesh, and we have seen the Word's glory." Baruch 3:38, "After this, God was seen on earth."

Therefore, the Apostle adds, **In the likeness of sinful flesh**. This does not mean that, instead of true flesh, the Son had the likeness of flesh as if it were imaginary, as the Manichaeans hold. As the Lord states in Luke 24:39, "A spirit does not have flesh and bones, as you see that I have." Therefore, the Apostle does not merely say, In the likeness of flesh but **in the likeness of sinful flesh**.

For the Son did not have sinful flesh. That is, he was not conceived in sin, for his flesh was conceived by the Holy Spirit, who takes sin away. Matthew 1:20, "For that which was begotten in her is of the Holy Spirit." Psalm 25:11/26:11, therefore, states, "I entered" into the world "in my innocence." Instead, he had the likeness of sinful flesh; that is, it was like sinful flesh in that it was capable of suffering. For human flesh, before sin, was not subject to suffering. Hebrews 2:17, "He had to become like his brothers and sisters in every respect so as to be a merciful and faithful high priest."

The Apostle speaks of the double effect of the incarnation. The first is the removal of sin, which he posits with the words, **For the sake of sin he condemned sin in the flesh.**

This text can be read as follows. God's Son was sent **for the sake of sin**, that is, because of the sin committed, at the instigation of the devil, against the flesh of Christ by his killers. **He condemned**, or destroyed, **sin** because when the devil attempted to hand over to death the innocent one, over whom he had no right, it was just that he should lose power. Therefore, Christ is said to have destroyed sin through his passion and death. Colossians 2:15, "Despoiling" on the cross "the principalities and powers."

But it is better to say that **he condemned sin in the flesh**, that is, he debilitated the spark in our flesh. That God's Son was sent **for the sake of sin** refers to the power of his suffering and death, which is called sin due to its likeness to sin, as was stated, or because by this he became a sacrifice for sin, which in Holy Scripture is called sin. Hosea 4:8, "They will consume the sins of my people." Therefore, the Apostle states in 2 Corinthians 5:21, "For us, God made sin," that is, a sacrifice for sin, "him who did not know sin." In satisfying for our sin, he took away the sins of the world. John 1:29, "Behold the Lamb of God. Behold him who takes away the sins of the world."

v. 4 The Apostle sets forth the second effect of the incarnation when he states **that the justification of the law**, that is, the righteousness that the Law promised and for which some were hoping from the Law, **might be fulfilled**, that is, perfected **in us**, that is, in those of us living in Christ Jesus. Romans 9:30, "The gentiles who did not pursue righteousness have attained the righteousness that is from faith." To 2 Corinthians 5:21, "For us, God made sin him who did not know sin," he adds, "so that in him we might become the righteousness of God."

This could not be accomplished other than through Christ. Therefore, the Apostle held that Christ can both condemn sin in the flesh and carry out justification. This **was impossible under the law** of Moses. Hebrews 7:19, "The law brought nothing to perfection."

Indeed, this was impossible for the Law, not because of a defect in it, but **in that**, or insofar as, **it was weakened through the flesh**, that is, due to the weakness of the flesh, which was in humans due to the corruption of the spark to sin. In consequence, it also happened that, when the Law was given, humans were conquered by covetousness. Matthew 26:41, "The spirit indeed is willing, but the flesh is weak." And above in Romans 6:19, "I speak in human terms due to the weakness of your flesh."

Thus it is clear that it was necessary that Christ become incarnate, as Galatians 2:21 also indicates, "If righteousness is through the law, Christ died in vain," that is, without cause. Christ needed to become incarnate because the Law could not justify.

Then with the words, "We who walk not according to the flesh," etc., the Apostle proves what he proposed with regard to the second condition, and he does so by showing that to avoid condemnation no one ought to walk according to the flesh.[4] In this regard, he does three things. (1) He proposes what he intends to argue. (2) He proves what he has proposed where he says, "They who are according to the flesh," etc. (Rom 8:5). (3) He discloses something he had assumed in the proof beginning with, "Because wisdom," etc. (Rom 8:7).

Flesh and Spirit

He indicates first that it has been asserted that the Law's righteousness is fulfilled in us **who** not only are in Christ Jesus but who also **walk not according to the flesh, but according to the spirit**. That is, it is fulfilled in us who follow not the disordered desires of the flesh but the urging of the Holy Spirit. Galatians 5:16, "Walk in the Spirit."

v. 5 He then proves what he had proposed with the words, **For they who are according to the flesh**, etc. To do so, he introduces two syllogisms. The first has to do with the flesh. They who follow the prudence of the flesh are led to

---

4. The two conditions are outlined above in the commentary on Romans 8:1.

death. Now they **who are according to the flesh** follow the prudence of the flesh.[5] Therefore, they **who are according to the flesh** are led to death.

He sets forth another syllogism regarding the spirit: They who follow the prudence of the spirit achieve life and peace. Now they **who are according to the spirit** follow the prudence of the spirit. Therefore, they **who are according to the spirit** achieve life and peace.

Thus it is clear that they who walk not **according to the flesh** but **according to the spirit** are freed from the law of sin and death.

First, he sets forth the minor premise of the first syllogism. **They who are according to the flesh**, that is, who are subordinate to the flesh as if subject to it. Romans 16:18, these "obey not" the Lord "but their own belly." They **savor** [*sapiunt*] **things of the flesh**. It is as if he were saying that they have the wisdom [*sapientiam*] of the flesh.

To savor [*sapere*] things of the flesh is to approve and to judge as good what is according to the flesh. Matthew 16:23, "You savor the things not of God but of humans." Jeremiah 4:22, "They savor doing evil."

Second, he sets forth the minor premise of the second syllogism. **They who are according to the spirit**, that is, who follow the Holy Spirit and who are led by it. Galatians 5:18, "If you are led by the spirit, you are not under the law." They **set their minds on** [*sentiunt*] **those things that are of the spirit**; that is, they have the right sense in spiritual matters. According to Wisdom 1:1, "Think of [*Sentite*] the Lord in goodness."

The reason is, as the Philosopher states in Book 3 of his *Ethics,* that what kind of person one is seems to be one's end.[6] Therefore, they whose souls are informed by a good or evil habit consider their end according to the force of their habit.

v. 6 Third, he sets forth the major premise of the first syllogism, **For the prudence of the flesh**, etc.

To understand this phrase, one should know that prudence is right reason about things to be done, as the Philosopher states in the *Ethics.*[7] Right reason about what is to be done [i.e., prudence] presupposes one thing and

---

5. Romans 8:6 provides Thomas with the terminology "prudence of the flesh" *(prudentia carnis)* that he uses elsewhere to distinguish among different kinds of prudence. In ST II-II.47.13, he cites Romans 8:6 to acknowledge that even sinners can have a kind of prudence that guides their actions toward an apparent good. For the treatise on prudence, the first of the four cardinal virtues, see ST II-II.47-56.

6. Aristotle, *Nicomachean Ethics*, 3.5, AL 26, fasc. 3, pp. 183-84.

7. Aristotle, *Nicomachean Ethics*, 6.4, AL 26, fasc. 4, pp. 481-83.

performs three tasks. Just as speculative reason presupposes the principles from which it builds proofs, so prudence presupposes an end, which is like the principle of actions. Right reason performs three tasks. First, it counsels rightly; second, it judges rightly about things counseled; and, third, it rightly and regularly commands what has been counseled.

Therefore, **prudence of the flesh** requires that someone presuppose as an end the delightfulness of the flesh and that one would counsel, judge, and command in terms of this end. Such prudence **is death**, that is, the cause of eternal death. Galatians 6:8, "They who sow in the flesh also reap corruption from the flesh."

Finally, he sets forth the major premise of the second syllogism when he says, **But the prudence of the spirit is life and peace**.

As stated above, prudence of the spirit is when someone, presupposing a spiritual good as an end, counsels, judges, and commands what is properly ordered to this end. Such prudence, therefore, is **life**, that is, the cause of the life of grace and glory. Galatians 6:8, "They who sow in the Spirit also reap eternal life from the Spirit." This is **peace**, or the cause of peace, for peace is caused by the Holy Spirit. Psalm 118:165/119:165, "Those who love your Law have abundant peace, O Lord." Galatians 5:22, "The fruit of the Spirit is charity, joy, and peace."

LECTURE 2

v. 7 Above, the Apostle proposed that prudence of the flesh is death. He now intends to prove this. (1) He proves the proposal. (2) He shows that the faithful to whom he writes are alien to such prudence where he states, "You, however," etc. (Rom 8:9).

Prudence of the Flesh

Concerning the first [the proof], he does two things. (1) He proves his proposal about prudence of the flesh in the abstract. (2) He adapts what he said in the abstract about prudence of the flesh to those who actually follow prudence of the flesh, and he does so where he says, "But they who are in the flesh" (Rom 8:8).

With regard to the first [prudence of the flesh in the abstract], he presents three intermediary proposals; each is proved by the one that follows.

With the first of the intermediate proposals, he proves what he set forth above [on Rom 8:6], namely, that prudence of the flesh is death, and he does so in this way. They who are hostile to God incur death. Luke 19:27, "As for those enemies who did not want me to rule over them, lead them here, and slay them before me." This is so because God is our life. Deuteronomy 30:20, "For God is your life." Therefore, they who are hostile to God incur death; furthermore, prudence **of the flesh is hostile to God**; therefore, prudence of the flesh is a cause of death.

It should be noted that what the Apostle above called prudence of the flesh he now calls **wisdom of the flesh**, not because wisdom and prudence are absolutely [*simpliciter*] the same but because in human affairs wisdom is prudence. Proverbs 10:23, "Wisdom is prudence to a human being."

To understand this, one should know one is called wise absolutely who knows the highest cause from which all things proceed. Now God is absolutely the supreme cause of all things. Therefore, wisdom is absolutely the understanding of divine affairs, as Augustine states in *On the Trinity*.[8] 1 Corinthians 2:6, "We speak wisdom among the perfect." Within any particular field, one is called wise who knows the highest cause of that field. Thus the architect is not called wise who knows how to hew rocks and stones but who conceives of and arranges a house in fitting form. The entire production proceeds from this, as the Apostle states in 1 Corinthians 3:10, "As a wise architect, I laid the foundation." Thus one is called wise in human affairs who, having a good understanding of the purpose of human life, orders all human life to this end, and this pertains to prudence.

Thus wisdom of the flesh is the same as prudence of the flesh. Of this wisdom, James 3:15 states, "It does not descend from above but is earthly, brutish, devilish."

This wisdom is said to be hostile to God because it inclines a person against God's Law. Job 15:26, "The wicked one opposes God with head erect and stiff neck."

To this proof he adds another intermediary proposal; the wisdom of the flesh **is not subject to the law of God**.

For someone cannot hate God as God since God is the very essence of goodness. However, according to this text, some sinners hate God in the sense that the command of the divine Law is contrary to their will. For example, adulterers hate God inasmuch as they hate this command, "Do not commit adultery" (Exod 20:14). Thus all sinners, inasmuch as they do not

---

8. Augustine, *On the Trinity*, 14.1.3, CCSL 50A: 423-24.

wish to be subject to God's Law, are enemies of God. 2 Chronicles 19:2, "You are joined in friendship to those who hate God."

Thus the Apostle fittingly proves that prudence or wisdom of the flesh is hostile to God because it is not subject to God's Law.

He proves this through a third intermediary proposal beginning with the words, **Nor can it be**.

As is evident from the above, prudence of the flesh is a kind of vice. Yet they who are subject to vice can be freed from it and become subject to God, according to Romans 6:18, "Freed from sin and made servants of God." Nevertheless, vice itself cannot be subject to God since it is a turning from God or God's Law, just as someone black can become white, but blackness itself can never become whiteness. In this regard, Matthew 7:18 states, "An evil tree cannot produce good fruit."

From this it is evident that the Manichaeans wrongly took these words as confirmation of their own error. They wished by these words to show that the nature of flesh is neither from God nor could it be subject to God, since it is hostile to God. This is not the case because the Apostle treats here of that flesh which is human vice, as was noted above [on Rom 8:3].

v. 8 Then with the words **But they who are in the flesh**, etc., the Apostle adapts what he said in the abstract about prudence of the flesh to people over whom prudence of the flesh actually rules. He states, **But they who are in the flesh**. That is, as long as they follow the disordered desires of the flesh through prudence of the flesh, they **cannot please God** because, as Psalm 146:11/147:11 states, "Those who fear God are pleasing to God."

Therefore, they who are not subject to God cannot please God as long as they remain that way. However, they can cease being in the flesh, as noted above, and then they will please God.

v. 9 Next, when the Apostle says, **But you**, etc., he shows those to whom he speaks that they are immune from prudence of the flesh.

In this regard, he does three things. First, he sets forth the state of the faithful, **But you are not in the flesh**. Here it is clear that he is not speaking about the nature of the flesh. For the Romans, to whom he was speaking, were mortals clothed in flesh. Instead, he takes flesh here as the vices of the flesh, as in 1 Corinthians 15:50, "Flesh and blood will not possess the reign of God." Therefore, he states, **You are not in the flesh**, that is, in the vices of the flesh, as if living according to the flesh — 2 Corinthians 10:3, "Living in the flesh, we do not fight according to the flesh." **But you are in the spirit**, that is, you follow the spirit. Revelation 1:10, "I was in the spirit on the Day of the Lord."

Second, he adds a condition, **If, nevertheless, the Spirit of God dwells in you**, namely, through charity. 1 Corinthians 3:16, "You are the temple of God, and the Spirit of God dwells in you."

He adds this condition because, although they received the Holy Spirit in Baptism, it could nevertheless happen that, due to sin's approach, they would lose the Holy Spirit. As Wisdom 1:5 states, "The Holy Spirit . . . is rebuffed at the approach of wickedness."

Third, he shows that this condition should exist in them when he says, **If they do not have the Spirit of Christ, they are not his**. For just as something is not a member of the body that is not given life by the body's spirit, so they are not a member of Christ who do not have Christ's Spirit. 1 John 4:13, "In this we know that he remains in us because he has given us of his Spirit."

It should be noted that the Spirit of Christ and the Spirit of God the Father are the same. It is called the Spirit of God the Father as it proceeds from the Father. It is called the Spirit of Christ inasmuch as it proceeds from the Son. Furthermore, the Lord everywhere attributed the Spirit simultaneously to both himself and the Father, as in John 14:26, "The Paraclete, the Holy Spirit, whom the Father will send in my name." And again in John 15:26, "When the Paraclete, whom I will send to you from the Father, comes," etc.

v. 10 Then when he says, "But if Christ," etc., he indicates that we are freed from punishment by the grace of Christ or by the Holy Spirit. (1) He shows that the Holy Spirit frees us in the future from bodily death. (2) He shows that, in the meantime, the Holy Spirit assists us against the frailties of the present life: "But likewise," etc. (Rom 8:26).

With regard to the first [our liberation from bodily death], he does three things. (1) He proposes what he intends to argue. (2) From this he infers a certain corollary: "Therefore, brothers and sisters, we are debtors," etc. (Rom 8:12). (3) He proves what he proposed where he says, "For whoever," etc. (Rom 8:14).

With regard to the first [what he intends to argue], one should consider what the Apostle said above about the Spirit of God and about the Spirit of Christ, although it is the same Spirit. (1) He shows what we obtain from the Spirit, inasmuch as it is Christ's. (2) He shows what we obtain from the Spirit inasmuch as it is God the Father's, "Because if the Spirit of the one who raised Jesus from the dead," etc. (Rom 8:11).

Christ's Spirit

He states, therefore, that they who do not have Christ's Spirit are not his. Thus, since you are Christ's, you have Christ's Spirit, indeed Christ himself dwelling within you through faith, according to Ephesians 3:17, "That Christ might dwell in your hearts by faith." **But if Christ** is thus **in you**, you must be conformed to Christ.

Now Christ came into the world that, with regard to the spirit, he was full of grace and truth. Yet, with regard to the body, he has the likeness of sinful flesh, as was noted above. This should also be the case for you because your **body, due to the sin** that still remains in your flesh, **is dead**. In other words, it is doomed to the necessity of death, as Genesis 2:17 says, "On whatever day you eat, you will die the death." This means that you will be doomed to the necessity of death. **But the spirit lives**, which has now been recalled from sin, according to Ephesians 4:23, "Be renewed in the spirit of your mind." It lives by the life of grace **because of the righteousness** by which it is justified by God. Galatians 2:20, "Insofar as I now live in the flesh, I live by faith in the Son of God." Above in Romans 1:17, "The one who is righteous lives by faith."

v. 11 Then when he says, **Because if the Spirit**, etc., the Apostle shows what we may obtain in the Holy Spirit, understood here as the Spirit of the Father. He says, **Because if the Spirit of the one**, namely, the Spirit of God the Father, **who raised Jesus Christ from the dead dwells in you**. Psalm 40:11/ 41:10, "But you, O Lord, have mercy on me, and raise me up." Acts 3:15, "God raised him from the dead," etc. Nevertheless, Christ himself rose by his own power because the power of the Father and Son is the same. It follows that, what God the Father did in Christ, God the Father would also do in us.

And so he adds, **The one who raised Jesus Christ from the dead will also give life to your mortal bodies**. He does not say dead but mortal because in the resurrection not only will death — that is, the necessity of death — be removed from your bodies but also mortality — that is, the potential to die — as Adam's body had before sin. For after the resurrection our bodies will be thoroughly immortal. Isaiah 26:19, "Your dead will live; my slain will rise again," etc. Hosea 6:2, "He will give us life after two days."

This is the case **because of God's Spirit indwelling** us, that is, in the power of the Holy Spirit dwelling in us. Ezekiel 37:5, "The Lord God says to these bones, 'Behold, I will send spirit into you, and you will live.'"

This is due to the **Spirit indwelling**, that is, due to the dignity our bodies have because they have been abodes of the Holy Spirit. 1 Corinthians 6:19, "Do you not know that your members are a temple of the Holy Spirit?" To be sure, they whose members have not been a temple of the Holy Spirit will rise again, but they will have bodies capable of suffering.

v. 12 Then when he says, "Therefore, we are debtors," etc., he deduces a corollary from what has been said. (1) He does so by stating its conclusion. (2) He assigns the reason where he says, "For if," etc. (Rom 8:13).

First, by way of conclusion, the Apostle states, It has been said that many good things come to us through the Holy Spirit and that death results from prudence of the flesh. **Therefore, we are debtors** to the Holy Spirit due to the benefits received from the Spirit. As a result, we should live according to the Spirit and not according to the flesh. Galatians 5:25, "If we live in the Spirit, let us also walk in the Spirit."

v. 13 Then when he says, **For if according to the flesh**, he assigns the reason for the foregoing conclusion.

He does so first with regard to the flesh. **For if you live according to the flesh**, namely, by following the disordered desires of the flesh, **you will die** by the death of guilt in the present and by the death of condemnation in the future. 1 Timothy 5:6, the widow "who lives for pleasure is dead."

Second, he assigns a reason with regard to the Spirit. **But if by the Spirit**, that is, through the Spirit, **you mortify the deeds of the flesh**, that is, the works which come from the covetousness of the flesh, **you will live** by the life of grace in the present and by the life of glory in the future. Colossians 3:5, "Mortify your earthly members." Galatians 5:24, "They who are Christ's have crucified their flesh with its vices and disordered desires."

LECTURE 3

v. 14 After proposing that the Holy Spirit will bestow on us the life of glory that will remove all mortality from our bodies, the Apostle here introduces the proof. (1) He shows that the Holy Spirit bestows such a life of glory. (2) Beginning with, "If only we suffer," etc. (Rom 8:17), he explains why it is delayed.[9]

---

9. Thomas here cites Romans 8:17 as "If only . . ." *(si tamen)*; below he cites it in the more commonly accepted way as "But if" *(si autem)*. "If only" is closer to the Greek.

The Holy Spirit

With regard to the first matter [the role of the Holy Spirit], he offers the following argument. All who are children of God obtain the eternity of the life of glory. Furthermore, all whom the Holy Spirit rules are children of God. Therefore, all whom the Holy Spirit rules obtain as their inheritance the life of glory.

(1) The Apostle presents this argument's minor premise. (2) He presents the major premise beginning with "But if," etc. (Rom 8:17). Concerning the minor premise, he does two things. (1) He proposes what he intends to argue. (2) He proves what he has proposed where he says, "For you have not received," etc. (Rom 8:15).

Regarding the first [the proposal about the minor premise], there are two points to consider, the first of which is how people are led by the Spirit of God. The statement, **All who are led by the Spirit of God**, can be understood as referring to those who are ruled as by a leader and director. The Spirit does so in us by illuminating us inwardly about what we ought to do. Psalm 142:10/143:10, "Your good spirit will lead me," etc.

Yet they who are led do not work by themselves. Therefore, not only does the Holy Spirit instruct those who are spiritual about what they should do, but the Holy Spirit also moves their hearts. Therefore, the statement, **All who are led by the Spirit of God**, is better understood in the following way.

Those things are said to be acted upon that are moved by a higher impulse. Therefore, we say about animals that they do not lead but are led because they are moved by nature to carry out their actions and not from their own movement. Similarly, those who are spiritual are principally inclined to some action not by movement of their own will but by the impulse of the Holy Spirit. According to Isaiah 59:19, "He will arrive like a violent river that the spirit of God drives on." See also Luke 4:1, which depicts Christ in the desert being led by the Spirit.

This does not, however, exclude the fact that spiritual people work by will and free choice. It does mean that the Holy Spirit causes that very movement of the will and free choice in them, for, according to Philippians 2:13, "It is God who works in us, both to will and to accomplish."

[Regarding the proposal in the minor premise], the second point to consider is how **those led by the Spirit of God are children of God**.

This is evident from the likeness to fleshly children who are generated through fleshly seed and thus proceed from a father. The Holy Spirit is spiritual seed proceeding from the Father. Therefore, some are generated into God's children by this seed. 1 John 3:9, "None born of God sin because the seed of God remains in them."

v. 15 Then when he says, "For you have not received," etc., he proves what he proposed in the minor premise, namely, that those who receive the Holy Spirit are children of God, and he does this in three ways. (1) He does so by the distinction of the gifts of the Holy Spirit, (2) by our confession, "By which we cry," etc. (Rom 8:15), and (3) by the Spirit's testimony, "For the Spirit itself" (Rom 8:16).

With regard to [the distinction of the gifts of the Holy Spirit], consider that the Holy Spirit produces two effects in us. One is fear; see Isaiah 11:3, "The spirit of the fear of the Lord will fill him." The other is love; see above in Romans 5:5, "God's charity has been poured in our hearts by the Holy Spirit who has been given to us." Fear produces servants; love does not.

The Gift of Fear

For evidence of this, consider that fear has two objects. The first is evil that some avoid out of fear. The second is that which seems to make this evil present. For it is said that a person can fear both the killing and the king who can kill. Yet, from time to time, it happens that the evil that one avoids is opposed to a bodily or temporal good that one perhaps loves inordinately, and therefore one avoids the temporal suffering caused by another. This is human or worldly fear and not of the Holy Spirit. The Lord prohibits this. Matthew 10:28, "Do not fear those who kill the body."

Now there is another fear that avoids evil contrary to created nature, namely, the evil of punishment. Nevertheless, it avoids suffering this for a spiritual reason, because of God, and it is praiseworthy at least inasmuch as it fears God. Deuteronomy 5:29, "Who would give them such a mind as to fear me and to keep all my commandments?" This second fear is from the Holy Spirit.

Yet, to the extent that such a fear does not avoid an evil such as sin, which is opposed to spiritual good, but avoids only the punishment, it is not praiseworthy. It has this defect not from the Holy Spirit but from human fault, just as unformed faith, inasmuch as it is faith, comes from the Holy Spirit but not the fact that it is unformed. Similarly, if people, through this second kind of fear, do good, they do not do it well because they do not do it willingly but are compelled by the dread of punishment, and this is characteristic of servants. This fear, therefore, is properly called servile because it causes people to act as servants.[10]

There is yet a third fear that avoids evil because it is opposed to spiritual good, such evil as sins or separation from God that one fears to incur due to God's just vengeance. With respect to each object, this third kind of fear is attentive to the spiritual yet keeps an eye on punishment.

This fear is said to be initial because it should be in people at the beginning of their conversion. They fear punishment due to past sins, and, due to grace infused in love, they fear separation from God through sin. As Psalm 110:10/111:10 states, "The fear of the Lord is the beginning of wisdom."

Now there is a fourth kind of fear, which with respect to each object keeps an eye only on the spiritual because it fears only separation from God. This fear "that remains for eternity" is holy, as is noted in Psalm 18:10/19:9. Just as initial fear is caused by imperfect charity, so this fear is caused by perfect charity. 1 John 4:18, "Perfect charity drives out fear." Therefore, initial fear and chaste fear do not differ in terms of charitable love, which is the cause of each, but only in terms of the fear of punishment. Just as the former fear causes servitude, so charitable love brings about the freedom of God's children. It causes a person to act freely for God's honor, and this is proper to God's children.

Therefore, the old Law was given in fear, and this was signified by the thunder and the like that occurred in the giving of the old Law; see Exodus 19:16 and following. As Hebrews 12:21 states, "What was seen was so terrible." Therefore, prompting observance of God's commands through the infliction of punishments, the old Law was given in the spirit of servitude. As Galatians 4:24 states, "The one [covenant] from Mt. Sinai bore children into servitude."

God's Heirs

Therefore, the Apostle states the following. It is correct to say that **those who are led by the Spirit of God are children of God. You have not again**, in the new law as was the case with the old Law, **received a spirit of servitude in**

---

10. Thomas speaks of formed and unformed faith in ST II-II.4-5. He notes, e.g., that demons can have faith because God's mighty works can compel their intellects to acknowledge the truth about God, but love does not move or form this faith, which cannot, therefore, lead to salvation (ST II-II.5.2; see II-II.4.3-4).

fear of punishments (Rom 8:14-15), a fear the Holy Spirit caused. **But you have received the spirit**, namely, of charity, which is **the spirit of the adoption of children**, that is, that through which we are adopted as God's children. Galatians 4:5, "So that we might receive the adoption of children."

Yet this does not mean that there are different spirits. For it is the same Spirit who in some causes servile, or imperfect, fear and in others produces love, a kind of perfect fear.[11]

Then when the Apostle states, **By which we cry**, etc., he discloses the same — that is, that those who receive the Holy Spirit are children of God — through our confession.

For, instructed by the Lord, we profess ourselves to have a Father God when we pray, "Our Father who art in heaven" (Mt 6:9). It is fitting not only for Jews but also for gentiles to say this. He, therefore, includes two words with the same meaning, namely, "Abba," which is Hebrew, and "Father," which is Latin or Greek. He does so to show that this prayer pertains to both people. For the same reason, the Lord says in Mark 14:36, "Abba, Father, all things are possible for you." Jeremiah 3:19, "You will call me Father."

We say this not so much with the sound of the voice as with the intention of the heart, which, due to its magnitude, is called a cry. So it was with the silent Moses in Exodus 14:15, "Why do you cry out to me" with the intention of your heart? This magnitude of intention proceeds from the affect of filial love, which the Spirit produces in us. Therefore, the Apostle says, **By which**, namely, by the Holy Spirit, **we cry out, "Abba, Father."** Thus, in Isaiah 6:3 the seraphim, who are understood as aflame with the fire of the Holy Spirit, "cry out one to another."

v. 16 Then when the Apostle says, **For the Spirit itself**, etc., he demonstrates the same based on the testimony of the Holy Spirit, lest some perhaps claim that we are deceived in our confession. He states, Therefore, I say that by the Holy Spirit "we cry out, 'Abba, Father,'" **for the Spirit itself gives testimony that we are children of God** (Rom 8:15-16). However, the Spirit gives testimony not with an outward voice for human ears, as the Father bore witness to the Son in Matthew 3:17, but through the effect of the filial love that the Spirit causes in us. Therefore, **the Spirit gives testimony**, not to our ears, **but to our spirit**, etc. Acts 3:15, "We are witnesses of these words."

---

11. See ST II-II.19 for a discussion of the different kinds of fear, including the gift of fear.

v. 17 Then beginning with the words, **But if we are children**, etc., the Apostle posits the major premise.

First, he shows that an inheritance is owed to children. If some are children, namely, by the Spirit, it follows also that they are heirs because an inheritance is owed not only to natural but also to adopted children. 1 Peter 1:3-4, "He remade us into a living hope . . . into an inheritance," etc. Psalm 15:6/16:6, "Splendid to me is my inheritance."

Second, he shows what this inheritance is by describing it, first, in relation to God the Father, **heirs indeed of God**. They are said to be someone's heirs who receive or secure the main part of the possessions, not just some small favors. See Genesis 25:5-6, in which Abraham gave all he possessed to Isaac but bestowed gifts on his concubines' children. The main good by which God is rich is in and through God and not through some other thing. God is not in need of extrinsic goods, as Psalm 15:2/16:2 states. Therefore, the children of God secure God as their inheritance. Thus Psalm 15:5/16:5, "The Lord is the portion of my inheritance." Lamentations 3:24, "'The Lord is my portion,' said my soul."

Yet, since a child does not secure an inheritance unless the parent is dead, it seems that a person could not be an heir of God, who never dies.

The answer is that this position holds for temporal goods that many people cannot own at the same time; therefore, one must die for another to be a successor. Yet many can possess spiritual goods at the same time. In this case, the parent need not die for the children to be heirs.

Nevertheless, one can say that God dies to us inasmuch as God is in us through faith, yet God will be our inheritance inasmuch as we will see God face to face.

Second, the Apostle describes this inheritance in relation to Christ with the words **but coheirs with Christ**. For since he is God's principal offspring through whom we become God's children, so also is he the principal heir to whom we are joined in inheritance. Matthew 21:38, "This is the heir," etc. Micah 1:15, "Still, I will give you an heir."

Then when the Apostle states, "Yet if we suffer," etc., he reveals the reason for the delay of this life of glory. (1) He addresses suffering and (2) the excellence of future glory in comparison with present sufferings, "For I consider," etc. (Rom 8:18).

With regard to the first, it should be noted that Christ, the principal heir, achieved the inheritance of glory through his sufferings. Luke 24:26, "Did not Christ have to suffer and so enter into his glory?" We ought not secure our inheritance more easily. Therefore, we should also achieve our inheritance through sufferings. Acts 14:21 (22), "We must undergo many trials to enter into the reign of God." So that we can suffer together with Christ, we do not immediately receive an immortal and impassible body.

Therefore, the Apostle says, **Yet if we suffer**, that is, if we together with Christ patiently put up with this world's trials, we do so **that we may also be glorified** with Christ. 2 Timothy 2:11, "If we have died with him, so also will we rule with him."

LECTURE 4

v. 18 After having demonstrated and stated that we are freed through the grace of Christ, the Apostle now assigns the reason for the delay of immortal life, which is the inheritance of the children of God. It is necessary for us to suffer with Christ to reach the fellowship of his glory. Because someone could characterize this kind of inheritance as onerous — one can arrive at it only by enduring suffering — the Apostle here compares the excellence of future glory to the sufferings of the present time.

(1) He sets forth what he intends to prove. (2) He proves his proposal where he states, "For the eager longing [*expectatio*]," etc. (Rom 8:19).

Present Suffering and Future Glory

First, it has been stated that it is necessary for us to suffer so that we may also be glorified, lest we should avoid suffering to gain glory. **For I**, who have experienced both, **consider**. Sirach 34:9, "A man experienced in many things will ponder many things." The Apostle experienced suffering abundantly, according to 2 Corinthians 11:23, "In labors and prisons more abundantly." He also contemplated future glory, according to 2 Corinthians 12:4, "He was caught up into paradise and heard secret words," etc. Thus, **I consider that the sufferings of the present are not** sufferings **comparable to the future glory that will be revealed in us**.

Then the Apostle makes four points to show the excellence of this glory. First, he designates its eternity when he says, **to the future**, namely, after this time, and nothing is after this time except eternity. That glory exceeds the sufferings of this time as the eternal surpasses the temporal. 2 Corinthians 4:17, "Our present trial is momentary and light and produces in us an eternal weight of glory beyond all measure."

Second, he designates its dignity when he says, **glory**, and this implies a certain radiance of dignity. Psalm 149:5, "The saints will rejoice in glory."

Third, he designates its manifestation when he says, **that will be revealed**. Now the saints have glory, but one hidden in their conscience. 2 Corinthians 1:12, "This is our glory, the testimony of our conscience." However, then that glory will be revealed in the sight of all, in the sight of both the good and the evil, about whom it is said in Wisdom 5:2, "They will be amazed at the suddenness of the unexpected salvation."

Fourth, he designates its truth when he says, **in us**. For the glory of this world is empty because it is in those things outside a person such as in wealth's splendor and in human opinion. Psalm 48:7/49:6, "They glory in the greatness of their wealth." However, the glory about which the Apostle speaks concerns that which is within a person, according to Luke 17:21, "The reign of God is within you."

Therefore, **the sufferings of the present**, if they are considered in themselves, lack much in comparison to the magnitude of this glory. Isaiah 54:7, "For now I have briefly forsaken you, but I will gather you with great mercies." However, if suffering of this sort is considered as what a person, due to the charity produced in us by the Spirit, voluntarily endures for God's sake, that person deservedly merits eternal life through it. For the Holy Spirit is the fountain whose waters, or effects, well up to eternal life, as John 4:14 states.

Then when the Apostle says, "For the eager longing of the creature," etc. (Rom 8:19), he clarifies his proposal through the excellence of this glory. (1) He does so based on the creature's eager longing and (2) on the Apostle's eager longing where he says, "But not only," etc. (Rom 8:23). Concerning the first [the creature's eager longing], he does two things. (1) He posits it. (2) He makes it evident when he says, "To vanity," etc. (Rom 8:20).

Creation's Eager Longing

v. 19 First, it has been held that future glory exceeds present sufferings, and this is manifest in the following text. **For the eager longing of the creature**, that is, the creature itself eagerly longing, **eagerly longs for the revelation of the children of God** because, as 1 John 3:2 states, "We are now children of God; what we will be is not yet apparent." For outward sufferings hide the dignity of divine filiation in the saints. Later that dignity will be revealed when they receive immortal and glorious life. Thus, in Wisdom 5:5

an impious person says, "Behold how they are counted among the children of God."

The Apostle states, **The eager longing [of the creature] . . . eagerly longs**.[12] This duplication signifies an intensification of eager longing as in Psalm 39:2/40:1, "Eagerly longing, I eagerly longed for the Lord."[13]

One should know that the term **creature** here can be taken in three ways.

In one way, it can refer to the righteous, who in particular are called creatures of God, whether because they remain in the good in which they were created or due to excellence because every creature serves them in some way. James 1:18, "God willingly gave birth to us by the word of truth so that we might be a kind of first fruits of God's creatures."

This creature, that is, the righteous person, **eagerly longs for the revelation of the glory of the children of God** as a reward promised to them. Titus 2:13, "Eagerly longing for the blessed hope and the coming of the glory of our great God."

Second, **creature** can mean human nature itself, which is dependent on the goods of grace. Human nature is indeed in unrighteous people, but in them it is not yet justified but is as if unformed by grace.

Human nature in people already justified is partly formed by grace. Nevertheless, it is still unformed with respect to the form it will receive by glorification.

Thus the creature itself, that is, we ourselves, insofar as we are considered among the goods of nature, **eagerly long for the revelation of the glory of the children of God**. This eager longing belongs to us through grace, as if we were to say that matter eagerly longs for form, or colors eagerly long for the completion of the image, as the Gloss mentions.[14] Job 14:14, "All the days that I now fight, I eagerly long for my relief to come."

In a third way, this term can be understood about sensible creatures, as elements of this world. According to Wisdom 13:5, "Through the greatness and beauty of the creature, its creator can be seen and so known."

A creature of this sort **eagerly longs** for something in two ways. For the eager longing of the sensible creature, insofar as it is from God, is ordered to some end, and this comes to pass in two ways.

In one way, God impresses some form and natural power on such a

---

12. The text in Latin is, *Expectatio creaturae . . . expectat.*

13. The text in Latin is, *Expectans expectavi Dominum.*

14. Peter Lombard, *Commentary on the Epistle to the Romans,* PL 191:1442.

creature, and it is thereby inclined to some natural end. For example, we might say that a tree eagerly longs for the production of fruit, and fire eagerly longs for [or aims at] a point above.

In another way, God orders the sensible creature to some end that transcends its natural form. As the human body will be clothed in a certain form of supernatural glory, so every sensible creature, in that glory of the children of God, will obtain a certain newness of glory, according to Revelation 21:1, "I saw a new heaven and a new earth." In this way, the sensible creature **eagerly longs for the revelation of the glory of the children of God**.

v. 20 Then when the Apostle says, "To vanity," etc., he clarifies the eager longing noted above. He posits three things: (1) The necessity of eager longing, (2) the goal of eager longing, where he says, "Because the creature itself," etc. (Rom 8:21), and (3) the sign of eager longing, where he says, "For we know that every creature," etc. (Rom 8:22).

The necessity of eager longing results from the defect to which the creature is subject. For that which lacks nothing has no need to long eagerly for anything. The Apostle reveals the defect of the creature when he says, **For the creature was made subject to vanity**.

If by **creature** here is understood the righteous, they are **made subject to vanity**, that is, to those bodily conditions that are mutable and fallen. Therefore, the Apostle speaks of vanities as Ecclesiastes 1:2 does, "Vanity of vanities, all things are vanity."

Yet they are subject to vanities because of the necessities of the present life. They must deal with them, yet **not willingly**. They do not love such temporal things as do those against whom Psalm 4:3/4:2 speaks, "Why do you love vanity and seek falsehood?" Nevertheless, such a **creature** is subject to vanity of this kind **on account of God**, that is, by God's ordination, **who made it**, that is, the righteous person, **subject** to sensible creatures of this sort. Nevertheless, this is done **in hope**, so that one day the person would be freed from such dealings "in the resurrection," namely, when they "neither marry nor are given in marriage, but will be like angels in heaven" (Mt 22:30).

If **creature** is understood with regard to human nature itself, the second meaning suggested above, **it was made subject to vanity**, that is, to possibility, as Psalm 38:6/39:5 states, "Truly, all things are vanity, every person living." It is **not** subject **willingly** because such vanity is inflicted as punishment on human nature. Punishment is involuntary as guilt is voluntary. Nevertheless, human nature is **made subject** to sufferings of this sort **on account of God**, that is, by God's judgment **who made it**, namely, human nature, **subject** to defects but, nevertheless, **in hope** of one day avoiding such sufferings. Isaiah 28:28, "The thresher will not thresh forever."

If **creature** is understood with regard to the sensible creature [the third meaning suggested above], **it was made subject to vanity**, that is, to mutability, **unwillingly**. For defects that cause mutability — such as disease, old age, and the like — run counter to the particular nature of this or that thing whose desire is for self-preservation. However, they are in accord with universal nature. Nevertheless, the sensible creature is made subject **to vanity** of this sort **on account of God**, that is, on account of God's ordination, **who made it subject in hope**, that is, in eager longing for glorious renewal, as was noted above.

v. 21 Then with the words, **Because even the creature itself**, etc., he shows the goal of this eager longing.

The creature's eager longing or hope is not in vain **because the creature itself will be freed from the servitude to deterioration for the freedom of the glory of the children of God**.

If **creature** here is understood as the righteous person, **servitude to corruption** means worry about the search for food and clothes and other things by which one is in bondage to our mortality. This is a kind of servitude from which the saints, striving for **the freedom of glory of the children of God**, will be freed. Although they may now have the freedom of righteousness, which is from servitude to sin, they do not yet have the **freedom of glory**, which is from servitude to misery. Job 39:5, "Who has set the wild ass free?"

If **creature** here is understood as human nature, it **will be freed from the servitude to deterioration**, that is, literally from deterioration [*corruptione*] and the ability to suffer, and it will aim for **the freedom of the glory of the children of God**, a freedom not only from guilt but also from death, according to 1 Corinthians 15:54, "'Death is swallowed up in victory.'"

If **creature** is understood as the sensible creature, it **will be freed from the servitude to deterioration** or of mutability because in every change there is some deterioration, as Augustine and the Philosopher state.[15] This freedom from deterioration also corresponds to the **freedom of the glory of the children of God** so that as sensible creatures themselves are renewed, so is their dwelling. Isaiah 65:17, "I am creating new heavens and a new earth, and the former things," that is, the creature's earlier mutability, "will be forgotten."

---

15. Augustine, *Against Maximinus*, 2.12.2, PL 42:768. Aristotle, *Physics*, 8.1, AL 7.1, fasc. 2, pp. 281-82.

Yet the Apostle says, **even the creature itself**. If he were referring to the first sense, he would mean not only us apostles but also other righteous people. But in the second sense, he means not only the righteous but also human nature itself, which in some has not yet been renewed by grace. However, in the third sense, it means not only people but other creatures as well.

v. 22 Then when the Apostle says, **For we know**, etc., he sets forth the sign of this eager longing. **For we know**, we apostles instructed by the Holy Spirit and by experience, **that every creature groans and is in labor until now**.

It would be difficult to take this phrase to mean sensible creatures in the first place because the Apostle says, **groans and is in labor**; this seems appropriate only for the rational creature. Yet it can be so explained that when he says **groans**, it is the same for him as saying "does not desire." For we groan about that which is repugnant to our will. Hence, inasmuch as the defects of a sensible creature oppose the natural desire of a particular nature, that sensible creature is said to groan. When he says, **is in labor**, it is the same to him as the "eager longing" the Apostle spoke of above. For being in labor is the way of producing offspring.

The second difficulty is that he says, **every creature**; these words would also seem to include celestial bodies. Hence, even the Gloss holds that the sun and the moon occupy their assigned place not without struggle.[16]

Yet it ought to be interpreted so that struggle is understood as motion, just as sometimes rest is understood as a break from work. So in Genesis 2:3 God is said to have rested on the seventh day. In this way, groaning can be understood as a mutability [*corruptione*] that is involved with local motion; for example, something ceases to be in one place and begins to be in another. Now then, being in labor is understood as the destiny of celestial bodies to be renewed.

If, however, this text is interpreted with regard to people, **every creature** is said of human nature because it has things in common with every creature. With the spiritual it shares intellect, with the animal bodily movement and the corporal body. Therefore, this creature, that is, the human, **groans** in part because of the evils it suffers and in part because of hoped-for goods that are deferred. Lamentations 1:22, "Many are my groans." Human nature is **in labor** because it suffers the delay of anticipated glory with a certain affliction of the soul. Proverbs 13:12, "Hope deferred afflicts the soul."

16. Peter Lombard, *Commentary on the Epistle to the Romans*, PL 191:1445.

John 16:21, "The woman in labor experiences anguish." Psalm 47:7/48:6, "Pains as of one in labor."

The Apostle says, **Until now** because the groaning is not taken away by our justification but remains **until now**, that is, until death. Or **until now** because even if some are already freed who are in glory, still we remain. Or **until now** because not only the patriarchs who were before Christ but even we in the time of grace still suffer the same things. As 2 Peter 3:4 states in the voice of the impious, "Where is the promise of his coming now? From the time when the fathers slept, all things thus continue as from the beginning of creation."

It should be noted that one can speak of anything under God as being a creature of God.

Some, therefore, have wanted to interpret these words as about any creature, even about holy angels, but it is quite unsuitable to say that they have been made subject to vanity or that they groan or are in labor since they have already attained that glory whose likeness we long for eagerly. According to Matthew 22:30, "They will be like angels of God in the heavens," and therefore these words are more suitably expounded as was stated above.

LECTURE 5

v. 23 Above, the Apostle presents the excellence of future glory based on a creature's eager longing; now he shows the same based on the apostles' eager longing. What great people long for so anxiously cannot be small. Concerning this he does two things. (1) He proposes what he intends to argue. (2) He proves his proposal where he says, "For in hope," etc. (Rom 8:24).

Concerning the first of these, he does three things.

Humanity's Eager Longing

First, he proposes the dignity of those longing eagerly when he says, It is **not only it**, namely, the creature, that longs eagerly for the glory of God's children,[17] **but even we ourselves**, namely, the apostles, **have the first fruits of the Holy Spirit** because the apostles had the Holy Spirit at an even earlier time and more abundantly than others. Just as with the fruits of the earth,

---

17. Above, *expecto* has been translated as "eager longing." In this lecture, the English word "awaits" and its cognates are also used to translate *expecto*, which has the dual sense of waiting and expectation.

those that reach maturity first are richer and more pleasing. Jeremiah 2:3, "Israel is holy to the Lord, the first fruits of the Lord's crops." Hebrews 12:22-23, "You have approached . . . the assembly of the firstborn who have been enrolled in the heavens."

From this it is evident that the apostles are to be preferred above all other saints and, having the Holy Spirit more abundantly, outshine by whatever measure — whether that of virginity, teaching, or martyrdom.

Yet some can say that, on account of Christ, other saints suffered greater torments and put up with greater austerities than did the apostles.

Yet one should know that the magnitude of merit, principally and with respect to the essential reward, depends on charity. The essential reward consists in the joy that one has from God. Now it is manifest that they who love more will rejoice more in God. Therefore, in John 14:21, the Lord promises that beatific vision to his beloved: "If any love me, they will be loved by my Father, and I will love them, and I will show myself to them." In contrast, a person merits an accidental reward based on the quantity of works because there is joy in such works. Therefore, the charity with which the apostles performed their works was greater, and, as a result, they possessed the heart to do many greater works, as the opportunity arose.

If someone should say, One can truly attempt to have charity equal to the apostles', one should answer that human charity is not from oneself but from God's grace, which is given to each "according to the measure of Christ's gift," as Ephesians 4:7 states.

God gives grace to people in proportion to the role to which they are elected. So, for example, to the human Christ was given the most excellent grace because he was elected in order that his nature might be assumed into union with the divine person. After him blessed Mary, who was elected to be Christ's mother, had the greatest fullness of grace. Among the rest, the apostles were elected for greater dignity so that they might hand on to others what they immediately received from Christ himself that pertains to salvation. Thus, in a sense, the Church is founded on them, as stated in Revelation 21:14, "The wall had twelve columns, and the names of the apostles were written on them." And 1 Corinthians 12:28, "God placed the apostles first in the Church." Therefore, God bestowed grace more abundantly on them than on others.

Second, the Apostle posits the anxiety of eager longing when he says, **And we ourselves groan inwardly**. Groaning designates the affliction suffered due to the delay of something awaited with great desire. According to Proverbs 13:12, "Hope deferred afflicts the soul." Psalm 6:7/6:6, "I have labored in my groaning."

This groaning is more internal than external not only because it proceeds internally from the affect of the heart but also because it involves interior goods. This is why the Apostle uses the word **inwardly**. Lamentations 1:22, "My many groans."

Third, he posits the thing eagerly longed for, **Eagerly longing for the adoption of God's children**, that is, the completion of this adoption. For adoption of this sort by the Holy Spirit, justifying the soul is a beginning. Above (Rom 8:15), "You have received the spirit of the adoption of children." It will be completed in the glorification of the body itself. Therefore, the Apostle states in Romans 5:2, "We glory in the hope of the glory of God's children." He then adds in this verse, **the redemption of our body**, so that just as our spirit has been redeemed from sin, so our body might be redeemed from deterioration and death. Hosea 13:14, "I will redeem them from death." Philippians 3:21, "[Christ] will reform our lowly body."

v. 24 Then with the words, **For in hope**, etc., he proves what he said with the following argument. Hope is about those things that are not now seen but are eagerly longed for in the future. We are saved by hope; therefore, we eagerly long for the fullness of salvation in the future.

In the argument, he first posits the minor premise. For we, apostles and other faithful, **have been saved by hope** because we are hopeful about our salvation. 1 Peter 1:3, "God has regenerated us in living hope." Psalm 61:9/62:8, "Hope in God, you the entire assembly of God's people."

Second, he sets forth the major premise, **But hope**, that is, the thing hoped for, **which is seen**, as if now possessed, **is not hope**, that is, not a thing hoped for but something possessed. For hope is eager longing [*expectatio*] for something future. Zephaniah 3:8, "Wait [*Expecta*] for me, says the Lord, on the day of my coming resurrection."

Third, he offers proof of the major premise, **What**, that is, why **does one hope for what one sees?** It is as if he said that hope implies a movement of the soul toward something that one does not possess. Since, if one already owns it, one need not be moved to it.

Because hope arises in some way from faith, the Apostle assigns that work of hope, which is a matter of faith, to things not seen. On this see Hebrews 11:1, "Faith is conviction about things not seen."

v. 25 Fourth, he posits the conclusion to his argument: **But if we hope for what we do not see**, it follows that **we wait** [*expectamus*] **in patience**.

For this reason patience properly produces endurance, with a certain serenity, of tribulations. Romans 12:12, "They are patient in tribulation." Because the delay of a good thing involves a kind of evil, the unwavering awaiting of absent goods with tranquility of soul is attributed to patience but pertains above all to long-suffering, as in James 5:7, "Be patient, brothers and sisters, until the coming of the Lord." Patience is here taken in both ways because the apostles were serenely awaiting glory in the face of both delay and tribulation.

v. 26 Then when he says, "But similarly," etc., he shows how the Holy Spirit assists us with the failings of the present life. The Spirit does so with regard to (1) the satisfaction of desires and (2) the direction of external events where the Apostle says, "But we know," etc. (Rom 8:28).

Concerning the first [the satisfaction of desires], he does two things: (1) he proposes what he intends to argue; and (2) he clarifies his proposal where he says, "What we ought to pray for," etc.

Therefore, he first states, it has been said that our mortal bodies will be brought to life by the Holy Spirit when our frailty is removed from us, **but similarly**, and in the state of this life in which we are still subject to frailty, **the Spirit assists with our frailty**, even if the Spirit does not remove it entirely. Ezekiel 3:14, "The spirit also lifted me and took me up, and I left bitter in indignation of spirit," as if frailty had not yet ceased entirely, "for the hand of the Lord was with me comforting me." And in this way the Spirit took me up. Matthew 26:41, "The spirit is indeed willing, but the flesh is weak."

Then when he says, "What we ought to pray for," etc., he clarifies his proposal. (1) He shows the necessity of the Holy Spirit's assistance with regard to the frailty of the present life. (2) He shows the manner of this assistance where he says, "But that very Spirit," etc. (3) He shows the effectiveness of this assistance where he says, "The one who searches" (Rom 8:27).

The Apostle states first, rightly I say, that "the Spirit assists with our frailty." **For** we suffer frailty in that **we do not know what we ought to pray for as we should**, like "a man whose way is hidden, and whom God has surrounded in shadows" (Job 3:23).

One should consider that the Apostle says that there are two things we do not know, what to ask for in prayer and how to ask. However, both seem false.

We do know what to pray for because the Lord taught us this in Matthew 6:9, "Hallowed be thy name," etc.

The answer is that in general we can know what it is appropriate to pray for, but we cannot know this in particular.

First, if we desire to perform some work of virtue, which is to fulfill

God's will "in heaven as on earth," it is possible for that work of virtue not to be fitting for this or that person. For example, for someone who can make effective progress in action, the quiet of contemplation is not fitting. The reverse holds as well, as Gregory states in his *Moralia* on Job 5:26, "Entering the grave in fullness."[18] Thus Proverbs 14:12 states, "There is a way that seems right to a person but that finally leads to death."

Second, some desire a temporal good for the sustenance of life; this is to seek "our daily bread." But this can lead to mortal danger for many have perished on account of wealth. Ecclesiastes 5:12, "Wealth kept to the detriment of its owner."

Third, some desire to be freed from any trouble of temptation, which, nevertheless, serves them in the maintenance of humility. In the same way, Paul sought to have the thorn removed from him. However, it was given to him "lest the extent of the revelations [he received]" aggrandize him, as is noted in 2 Corinthians 12:7.

Similarly, it seems that we would know how to pray; according to James 1:6, "Let them ask in faith without hesitation."

In this regard also it ought to be said that we can know in general, but in particular we cannot altogether discern by the movement of our heart whether, for example, we seek something out of anger or from the zeal of justice. So in Matthew 20:20-23, the petition of the sons of Zebedee is rejected because although they seemed to ask for participation in divine glory, nevertheless their petition stemmed from a kind of vainglory or self-exaltation.

Then when the Apostle says, "But the Spirit," etc., he sets forth the manner of the Holy Spirit's assistance, **It is the Spirit who pleads for us with inexpressible groanings**. This statement seems to support the error of Arius and Macedonius, who held that, since pleading is the role of one who is lesser, the Holy Spirit is a creature and less than the Father and Son. But if, from the Apostle's claim that the Spirit intercedes, we understand the Spirit to be a passible creature and less than the Father, it also follows that when the Apostle says that the Spirit intercedes with groanings, we should understand the Spirit to be a passible creature deprived of beatitude. This is something no heretic ever claimed. For groaning is from anguish, which pertains to misery.

And so this ought to be explained as **the Spirit pleads**; that is, the

18. Gregory the Great, *Morals on the Book of Job,* 6.37, CCSL 143:327-28. In this text Gregory the Great uses Job 5:26, "Entering the grave in fullness," as an opportunity to compare the active and contemplative lives in which he interprets "grave" as symbolic of the contemplative life.

Spirit makes us pleaders, as in Genesis 22:12, "Now I know that you fear the Lord"; that is, I have caused the knowledge.

The Holy Spirit causes us to plead inasmuch as the Spirit causes right desires in us. For pleading is a kind of unfolding of desires, and right desires proceed from charitable love, which the Spirit causes in us.[19] Romans 5:5, "God's charity has been poured into our hearts by the Holy Spirit who has been given to us."

With the Holy Spirit directing and moving our hearts, our desires can be nothing but profitable for us. Isaiah 48:17, "I am the Lord who teaches you profitable things." Therefore, the Apostle adds, **for us**.

But because we desire much of God and plead eagerly, we suffer delay with sorrow and groans. Therefore, he adds, **with groans**, which the Spirit causes in our hearts inasmuch as the Spirit causes us to desire heavenly things that are delayed for the soul. It is the mourning of the dove that the Holy Spirit causes in us. Nahum 2:8/2:7, "They are led away mourning like doves."[20]

The Apostle speaks of **inexpressible** groanings either because they concern something inexpressible, such as heavenly glory (2 Cor. 12:4, "He heard secret words that may be spoken to no one"), or because they cannot adequately tell of the movements of the heart insofar as they proceed from the Holy Spirit. Job 38:37, "Who will tell of the order of the heavens?"

v. 27 Then when the Apostle says, **But the one who searches**, etc., he shows the effectiveness of the help by which the Holy Spirit assists us. **But the one who searches hearts**, that is, God, to whom it belongs to search hearts. Psalm 7:10/7:9, "God, the searcher of hearts and kidneys."

Now God is said to search hearts not because through a process of inquiry God knows the secrets of the heart but because God knows clearly those things that lie hidden in the heart. Zephaniah 1:12, "I will search Jerusalem with lamps."

God, I say, searching hearts **knows**, that is, approves (according to 2 Tim 2:19, "The Lord knows who are the Lord's") **what the Spirit desires**, that is, what the Spirit causes us to desire. Psalm 37:10/38:9, "O Lord, before you is my every desire."

Therefore, the desires of the Spirit that the Holy Spirit causes in the

---

19. Aquinas sees prayer as the interpreter of desires (*desiderii interpres;* see ST II-II.83.1 ad 1 and 9 ad 2). On "charitable love" or "the love of charity," see ST I-II.66; II-II.18.2 ad 3; II-II.19.4 ad 3.

20. "Groans" and "mourning" in this paragraph both translate variations of the same Latin word, *gemitus.*

saints are acceptable to God because the Spirit **intercedes for the saints**, that is, causes them to request in accordance with God, that is, what fits with divine pleasure. Proverbs 11:23, "The desire of the righteous is all good." As an example, the Lord spoke to the Father, Matthew 26:39, "Not as I will but as you will."

LECTURE 6

v. 28 Above in Romans 8:26, the Apostle shows that, with regard to fulfilling our desires, the Holy Spirit assists us with the frailties of the present life. Here he shows how the Spirit helps us with external events by directing us to our good.

(1) He proposes what he intends to argue. (2) He proves his proposal where he says, "For they whom God foreknew," etc. (Rom 8:29). (3) He draws the conclusion, "Who therefore will separate us," etc. (Rom 8:35).

Concerning the first, two things are to be considered.

The first is the magnitude of the favor the Holy Spirit confers on us so that all things work together for the good.

God's Love of the Saints

For evidence of this, one should consider that whatever occurs in the world, even if evil, happens for the good of the universe. As Augustine states in *Enchiridion* (cf. 3.11), "God is so good as to permit no evil to exist, except that God is so powerful as to be able to draw something good from any evil."[21]

Yet evil does not always result in good for the individual in whom it exists. For example, one animal's deterioration results in the good of the universe, insofar as through the deterioration of one, another is generated. Nevertheless, the deterioration does not result in good for that individual. This is so because the good of the universe in itself is willed by God, and all parts of the universe are ordered to that good.

The same reasoning seems to hold concerning the ordering of the noblest parts to others because the defect of the other parts is ordered to the good of the noblest.[22] But whatever happens to the noblest is ordered to

---

21. Augustine, *Enchiridion*, 3.11, CCSL 46:53.

22. "Defect" in this sentence translates *malus*, which in the previous paragraph was translated as "evil." Thomas here seems to be alluding to 1 Corinthians 12:12-31 and its analogy of the higher and lower parts of the body to the higher and lower parts of the universe.

their good alone because God cares for them for their sake, and for the others for the sake of the noblest. In the same way, the doctor cares for a foot injury as a way of caring for the head.

Of all parts of the universe, God's saints are preeminent, and Matthew 25:23 pertains to them, "He will place him in charge of all his affairs." Therefore, whatever happens, whether affecting them or other things, results in their good entirely. This is verified in Proverbs 11:29, "The fool will serve the wise" because even sinners' evils result in good for the just. Therefore, God is said to have special concern for the righteous, according to Psalm 33:16/34:15, "The eyes of the Lord are on the righteous." This is the case in that God cares for them by permitting nothing evil to happen to them that cannot be converted to their good.

This is clear even regarding the evils of punishment that they suffer. As the Gloss states, "They exercise humility in their weakness, patience in affliction, wisdom in contradiction, benevolence in hatred."[23] Thus 1 Peter 3:14 holds, "Blessed are you if you suffer anything for the sake of righteousness."

But do sins in the righteous also work together for the good?

Some say that these words, **All things**, do include sins because, according to Augustine, "Sin is nothing, and people become nothing when they sin."

On the contrary, the Gloss states, "God works all things for the good in them so that if any err or go astray, even this causes them to progress in the good."[24] Also in Psalm 36:24/37:24, "When the righteous fall, they will not be hurt because the Lord supports them by the hand."

Yet, according to this account, it seems that the righteous always rise again in greater charity because human good consists in charity. If the Apostle did not have charity himself, he realizes that he would be nothing (see 1 Cor 13:2).

The answer is that human good consists not only in the amount of charity but especially perseverance in it unto death. Accordingly, Matthew 24:13 reads, "The one who perseveres unto the end will be saved." Thus, when the righteous fall, they arise more cautious and humble. Therefore, after the Gloss notes that their error causes them to progress in the good, it adds that this is so because "they return more humble and wise." For they learn that they ought to lift themselves up with trembling, not presuming for themselves some enduring assurance gained through their own power.

23. Peter Lombard, *Commentary on the Epistle to the Romans*, PL 191:1448.

24. Augustine, *Commentary on the Gospel of John*, 1.13, CCSL 36:7; Peter Lombard, *Commentary on the Epistle to the Romans*, PL 191:1448.

Second, it is necessary to consider to whom this benefit applies.

The Apostle attends to this first from the human side when he says, **To those who love God** (Rom 8:28).

For love of God is in us through the indwelling spirit, as a habit, as is noted above on Romans 8:2, and it is the Holy Spirit who directs us along the right path, as is stated in Psalm 26:11/27:11. 1 Peter 3:13 states, "Who would harm you if you were zealous for the good?" And Psalm 118:165/119:165, "Those who love your law are much at peace, and for them it is not a stumbling block."

And this is reasonable because, as Proverbs 8:17 notes, "I love those who love me." To love is to desire good for the beloved. However, for God to desire is to produce. "Whatever God has desired, God has done," as Psalm 134:6/135:6 states. And, therefore, God converts all things to the good for those who love God.

Predestination and Glory

Next, the Apostle attends to this from the side of God. First, God predestined the faithful from eternity; second, God calls them in time; and third, God sanctifies them. The Apostle touches on all three when he says, **To those who have been called saints according to God's decree**, that is, predestined, called, and sanctified. Here **decree** refers to predestination, which, according to Augustine (*On the Predestination of the Saints,* 17), is a decree of mercy, as in Ephesians 1:11, "Predestined according to God's decree." **Called** pertains to vocation. Isaiah 41:2, "The Lord called them to follow." **Saints** refers to sanctification, as in Leviticus 21:8, "I the Lord who sanctify." The Apostle, in the person of the saints, claims he knows this when he says, **We know**. Wisdom 10:10, "Wisdom gave the just one knowledge of holy things." This knowledge comes from experience as well as contemplation of love's effectiveness (Song of Songs 8:6, "Love is as strong as death") and of eternal predestination (Isa 46:10, "My entire will shall be fulfilled, and my every plan will be accomplished").

v. 29 Then when the Apostle says, "For they whom God foreknew," etc., he offers proof with the following argument.

None can harm those whom God promotes, and it is the predestined who love God that God favors; therefore, nothing can harm them, but all things benefit them as good.

(1) He proves the minor premise, namely, that God promotes them. (2) He proves the major premise, namely, that since they have been promoted by God nothing can be harmful to them, and he does this where he says, "What then will we say?" etc. (Rom 8:31).

Concerning the minor premise, that God favors those who love God, he does two things. (1) He proposes those things that pertain to the saints' favor from eternity and (2) those things that are in time where he says, "They whom God predestined," etc. (Rom 8:30).

He posits two terms relating to God's promotion from eternity, namely, foreknowledge and predestination, when he says, **For God also predestined those whom God foreknew**.

Some say that predestination here means the preparation that takes place in time by which God prepares the saints for grace. They say this to distinguish foreknowledge from predestination.

Considered correctly, both are eternal; where they differ is logically. For, as was noted above concerning the words "he who was predestined" (Rom 1:4), predestination implies a certain preordination in the soul about things one is about to do. From eternity God has predestined the benefits that were to be given to the saints. Therefore, predestination is eternal. It differs from foreknowledge logically because foreknowledge implies only knowledge of future things. However, predestination implies a certain causality with respect to the future. Indeed, God has foreknowledge also about sins, but predestination is about salvific goods. Therefore, the Apostle says in Ephesians 1:5-6, "We are predestined according to God's decree to the praise of the glory of God's grace," etc.

Concerning the order of foreknowledge and predestination, some say that foreknowledge of meritorious good and of evil is the reason for predestination and reprobation. Therefore, God is understood to predestine some because God foreknows that they will do the good and believe in Christ. And according to this, the text is read, **Those whom God foreknew to be conformed to the image of the Son, God predestined**.

And this indeed might be reasonable if predestination involved only eternal life that is given for merits, but under predestination falls every salvific benefit that is divinely prepared for humans from eternity. Therefore, for the same reason, all the benefits that God confers on us in time have been prepared for us from eternity. To claim that some merit is presupposed on our part, the foreknowledge of which is the reason for the predestination, is nothing other than to claim that grace is given for our merits, and that we are the source of our good works, whose consummation is from God.

Therefore, the text should more fittingly read, **Those whom God foreknew, God also predestined to be conformed to the image of the Son**. Conformity here is not the cause of the predestination but its goal or effect. For the Apostle says in Ephesians 1:5, "God has predestined us to the adoption of the children of God."

The adoption of children is nothing other than conformity. For the one who is adopted as a child of God is truly conformed to God's Son.

This is the case first by right of sharing in Christ's inheritance, as was noted in Romans 8:17, "If children, heirs also; heirs indeed of God, but co-heirs with Christ." Second, this is due to sharing his splendor. For he is born of the Father as the splendor of the Father's glory; see Hebrews 1:3. Therefore, God conforms the saints to God by illuminating them with the light of wisdom and grace. As Psalm 109:3/110:3 states, "In saintly splendor from the womb before the morning star, I begot you," that is, pouring forth every saintly brilliance.

Now the phrase, **to the image of the Son**, can be understood in two ways. In one way the construction is appositive so that this would be the sense: Conformed to the image of God's Son, who is image. Colossians 1:15, "He is the image of the invisible God." The construction can also be understood as transitive so that the sense would be, God predestined us to be conformed to God's Son that we might bear his image. 1 Corinthians 15:49, "Just as we have borne the image of the earthly, so let us also bear the image of the heavenly."

Now the Apostle says, **God also predestined those whom God foreknew**, not because God predestined all those foreknown but because God could not predestine unless God foreknew. Jeremiah 1:5, "Before I formed you in the womb, I knew you."

What follows from this predestination he adds, **That he would be firstborn of many siblings**.

For just as God wished to communicate God's natural goodness to others by sharing with them the likeness of this goodness so that not only is God good but also the author of goods, so also the Son of God wished to communicate the conformity of his sonship to others because not only is he himself Son, but he is also the firstborn of children. Thus he, who through eternal generation is only-begotten according to John 1:18, "The only-begotten who is in the bosom of the Father," **is**, through conferral of grace, **firstborn of many siblings**. Revelation 1:5, "He is firstborn of the dead and prince of the kings of the earth."

Therefore, Christ has us as siblings. This is the case not only because he has communicated to us the likeness of sonship, as the Apostle states here, but also because he assumed the likeness of our nature, according to Hebrews 2:17, "He had to be made like his siblings in every way."

v. 30 Then when he says, **Those whom God predestined**, etc., he sets forth what the saints receive from God.

First, he sets forth calling [*vocationem*]: **God has also called those whom God predestined**. One's predestination cannot be in vain, according to Isaiah 14:24-25, "The Lord of hosts has sworn, 'Indeed, as I have thought, so will it be, and as I have proposed, so will it happen.'"

Predestination first begins to be carried out in a person's calling, which has two parts, one of which is external and comes by way of a preacher's mouth. Proverbs 9:3, "She sent her handmaids to call to the city." In this way, God called Peter and Andrew, as Matthew 4:18 states. The other calling is internal, none other than a kind of mental inspiration by which the human heart is moved by God to assent to matters of faith and virtue. Isaiah 41:2, "Who has raised the righteous from the east and called them to follow?"

This calling is necessary because our heart does not convert itself to God unless God draws us. John 6:44, "None can come to me unless the Father who sent me draws them." Lamentations 5:21, "Convert us, Lord, to you, and we will be converted." This calling is effective for the predestined because they assent to this calling. John 6:45, "Each who has heard from my Father and has learned comes to me."

Therefore, second, the Apostle posits justification: **Those whom God has called, God has also justified** through an infusion of grace. Romans 3:24, "Justified freely by God's grace."

But even if this justification can be frustrated in some because they do not persevere to the end, yet in the predestined justification is never frustrated.

Third, he posits glorification, **They whom God justified, these also has God glorified**, and this in two ways, through the progress of power and grace and through the exaltation of glory. Wisdom 19:22, "In all things, Lord, you have glorified and honored your people."

This text uses the perfect tense, "has glorified," instead of the future tense, "will glorify," to refer to increase in glory, or due to future certitude, or because what in some is future is complete in others.

v. 31 Then when the Apostle says, "What then will we say?", he reveals the major premise, namely, that no one can destroy God's promises. (1) He shows that the predestined cannot suffer harm as a result of the evil of punishment. (2) Neither can they suffer harm as a result of the evil of guilt, and he does this where he says, "Who will accuse?" etc. (Rom 8:33).

The evil of punishment is twofold. It consists in the imposition of evils and in the removal of good things.

First, those promoted by God do not suffer harm from the efforts of persecutors. Thus, the Apostle states, **What then will we say?** As if to say, "When God offers so many good things to the elect, what can be said against them that these benefits might be annulled?" The answer is, "Nothing." Proverbs 21:30, "There is no wisdom; there is no prudence, and there is no counsel against the Lord." Or, **What will we say?** Those who see these things are astonished. According to another version of Habakkuk 3:2, "I considered your works and trembled." Or, **What will we say about these things?** That is, what could we suitably render to God for so many benefits? Psalm 115:12/116:12, "What will I render to the Lord for all the things the Lord has done for me?"

The Apostle adds, **If God is for us**, namely, by predestining, calling, justifying, and glorifying, **who is against us**, that is, who could be against us successfully? Isaiah 50:8, "Let us stand together; who is my adversary?" Job 17:3, "Place me next to you, and let any hand strike me."

v. 32 Second, he shows that God's saints cannot suffer harm due to removal of what is good, saying, **Who did not even spare God's own Son**, etc.

Above, the Apostle spoke of many children, saying, "You received the spirit of adoption of children" (Rom 8:15). He now separates this child from all others, saying, **God's own Son**, not an adopted son as heretics hold, but natural and coeternal. 1 John 5:20, "God has given us understanding that we might be in his true Son," Jesus Christ, about whom the Father says in Matthew 3:17, "This is my beloved Son."

But when he says, God **did not spare**, it ought to be understood that God did not exempt him from punishment. For he had no fault from which God could have spared him. Proverbs 13:24, "The one who spares the rod hates the child."

Nevertheless, God the Father did not spare the Son, as if to add something to him who is perfect God in all things. God subjected him to suffering for our good. Therefore, the Apostle adds, **But God handed him over for us all**. That is, God exposed him to suffering for the expiation of our sins. Romans 4:25, "He was handed over for our sins." Isaiah 53:6, "The Lord placed on him all our iniquity."

God the Father handed him over to death by making him incarnate and able to suffer and by breathing into his human will such love by which he underwent suffering willingly. Thus it is said in Ephesians 5:2 that he handed himself over, "He handed himself over for us." Judas and the Jews also handed him over outwardly, as was indicated above on Romans 4:5.

It is to be noted that when the Apostle says, **Who are God's own**, etc., he means that God exposed to tribulation not only other saints for human salvation (and this according to Hos 6:5, "For this reason, I struck them among the prophets," and 2 Cor 1:6, "When we suffer, it is for your encouragement and salvation") but even his own Son.

All things exist in the Son of God himself, as in a primordial and preoperative cause. Colossians 1:17, "He is before all things," etc. Therefore, since he was handed over for us, all things have been given to us. Therefore, the Apostle adds, **How has God also with him**, who was given for us, **not given us all things** so that all things might happen for our good, to enjoy the highest things, namely, the divine persons, to live together with rational spirits, to use all lower things — not only what is favorable but what is hostile? 1 Corinthians 3:22-23, "All things are yours, but you are Christ's, and Christ is God's." Whence it is clear that, as Psalm 33:10/34:9 states, "Those who fear God lack nothing."

LECTURE 7

v. 33 After showing that the saints, whom God promotes, can suffer no harm from the evil of punishment, the Apostle here shows that they can suffer no harm from the evil of guilt.

(1) He advances a proposal. (2) He excludes an objection where he says, "Christ Jesus," etc. (Rom 8:34).

With regard to the proposal, one should consider that guilt afflicts a person in two ways — first, through accusation and, second, through condemning judgment.

None Can Accuse the Saints

First, he shows that no accusation can harm God's saints, and this is due to divine election. Whoever elects someone thereby seems to approve of that one, and the saints are elected by God. Ephesians 1:4, God "elected us in him before the foundation of the world to be saints." Whoever accuses rejects the one accused, but a person's accusation is of no avail in comparison to God's approval. And therefore the Apostle says, **Who will** effectively **accuse the elect**, that is, those whom God has chosen to be saints? Therefore, Revelation 12:10 states, "The accuser of our brothers and sisters is cast out."

Second, the Apostle shows that no accusation can be harmful to saints.

He does so based on another of God's benefits, namely, that by which God justifies us. The Apostle presents this benefit when he says, it is **God who justifies**, according to what he said above in Romans 8:30, "God has also justified those whom God has called." 1 Corinthians 6:11, "But you have been justified."

v. 34 Indeed, condemnation against the unrighteous has a place. However, **who is it**, then, **who will condemn** those justified by God? Job 34:29, "When God grants peace, who will condemn?"

Then when he says, **Christ Jesus**, he excludes the objection. Some might fear that Christ Jesus would accuse and condemn them as a transgressor of his commands, just as the Lord says about Moses in John 5:45, "Moses, in whom you hope, accuses you." Some fear that Christ himself would condemn because "he was made by God the judge of the living and the dead," as Acts 10:42 states. He is also immune from sin, or, as 1 Peter 2:22 puts it, "He who did not sin." Therefore, he seems able to accuse and condemn on the basis of John 8:7, "The one among you who is without sin, let that one throw the first stone."

In response, the Apostle writes, **Christ Jesus**, as if to say, Will Christ Jesus accuse or even condemn the elect of God? And he indicates that the answer is "No" because Christ Jesus confers great benefits on the saints through his humanity as well as through his divinity.

The Apostle enumerates four benefits of his humanity.

The first is death. He **who died**, namely, for our salvation. 1 Peter 3:18, "Christ died once for our sins."

The second is resurrection, by which he gives us life, spiritual life now and bodily life in the end. Therefore, he adds, **Who has also risen from the dead**, as above in Romans 4:25: "He rose for our justification." He adds, **Nay more**, because it is better to remember him now from the power of the resurrection than from the frailty of the passion. 2 Corinthians 13:4, "For although he was crucified due to our frailty, he lives by the power of God."

The third is the confession of the Father when he says, **Who is at the right hand of God**, that is, equal to God the Father in divine nature and in the more excellent goods in his human nature. This also is for our glory because, as Ephesians 2:6 states, we are "seated with God in the heavens in Christ Jesus." For inasmuch as we are members of Christ, we are seated in him with God the Father. Revelation 3:21, "I will give to the victor the right to sit with me on my throne, just as I also was victorious and sat with my Father on his throne."

The fourth is his intercession when he says, **Who also intercedes for us**, as if being our advocate. 1 John 2:1, "We have an advocate with the Father — Jesus Christ." It belongs to the office of advocate not to accuse or condemn but to repel the accuser and prevent condemnation.

He is said to intercede for us in two ways.

He does so in one way by praying for us, according to John 17:20, "I pray not only for them," namely, the apostles, "but also for them who will believe in me through their word." His intercession for us now is his desire for our salvation. John 17:24, "I will that where I am they may also be with me."

In another way, he intercedes for us by presenting in God's sight a humanity assumed for us and mysteries celebrated in it. Hebrews 9:24, "He entered into heaven itself that he might now appear in the presence of God for us."

v. 35 Then when he says, "Who therefore will separate us," etc., he draws a conclusion based on what he has already stated. Because this conclusion seems almost incredible to the inexperienced, he proposes it in the manner of a question. In all, he does three things.

(1) He poses the question. (2) He shows the necessity of the question where he says, "Just as it was written," etc. (Rom 8:36). (3) He sets forth an answer where he says, "In all these things," etc. (Rom 8:37).

This question can be deduced in two ways from the foregoing.

Saints as Inseparable from God's Love

In one way, so many benefits have been divinely conferred on us and so effectively that no one could be against them. The purpose of all these benefits is that we might be "rooted and founded in charity" (Eph 3:17). **Who therefore will separate us from the charity of Christ** (Rom 8:35) by which we love Christ and neighbor as he commanded in John 13:34, "I give you a new command," etc.?

Otherwise, God confers great benefits on the saints. When we consider them, the charity of Christ so burns in our hearts that nothing can quench it. Song of Songs 8:7, "Many waters could not quench charity."

He then proposes the evil things through the suffering of which someone could be tempted to abandon the charity of Christ. He sets forth (1) what pertains to life and (2) what pertains to death.

Concerning what threatens the preservation of this life, he lists (1) present evils and (2) future evils.

Concerning present evils, he posits (1) what pertains to the endurance of what is evil and (2) what pertains to the lack of what is good.

The endurance of evil things can be considered in two ways. Indeed, they affect the one suffering in two ways, and, first of all, externally in the body. And to this pertains **tribulation**. This word comes from "thistles" [*tribulis*], which are pungent herbs. Genesis 3:18, "Thorns and thistles will it bring forth for you." Therefore, some are said to suffer tribulation when they are pricked externally. But the righteous are not overcome by this. Psalm 33:20/34:19, "Many are the tribulations of the righteous, but the Lord will free them from them all." Evils also afflict a person in the heart's interior anxiety as long as one does not see how to turn from or avoid them. And in this regard, the Apostle adds, **Or distress**? Daniel 13:22, "I encounter distress on every side," and "what I will choose, I do not know" (Phil 1:22).

In another way, evils of this sort can be considered in terms of the one inflicting them, and so the Apostle adds, **Or persecution**? Persecution seems to pertain properly to someone who pursues another into flight, as in Matthew 10:23, "If they persecute you in one city, flee to another." Nevertheless, persecution is often understood as infliction of harm on another. Psalm 118:157/119:157, "Many are they who persecute me and cause me to suffer."

Next he sets forth the evils involving the withdrawal of the goods necessary for life, namely, food and clothing. See 1 Timothy 6:8, "We have food and clothes; with these we are content." Hunger pertains to the withdrawal of food; the Apostle therefore adds, **Or hunger**? Nakedness pertains to the withdrawal of clothing. He therefore adds, **Or nakedness**? 1 Corinthians 4:11, "Even until now, we hunger, thirst, and are naked."

Concerning future evils, he adds, **Or danger** threatening in the future? 2 Corinthians 11:26, "Dangers of floods and dangers of robbers." Concerning death, he adds, **Or the sword**? Hebrews 11:37, "They died by the sword."

v. 36 Then when he says, **As it is written**, etc., he shows the necessity of this question when he states that, because of Christ's love, the saints endured everything threatening them.

He then introduces the psalmist's words (Ps 43:22/44:22), as if stated by a martyr, in which he first locates the cause of suffering. As Augustine states [in numerous places], "The punishment does not make the martyr; the cause does."[25] The psalmist therefore says, **"For your sake,"** etc. Matthew 10:39, "They who would lose their soul," that is, their life, "for my sake, will find it." 1 Peter 4:15-16, "Let none of you suffer as a thief or murderer. . . . But if you suffer as a Christian, do not be ashamed." They suffer for Christ's sake not only who suffer for the sake of faith in Christ but also who suffer for any righteous work done on behalf of the love of Christ. Matthew 5:10, "Blessed are they who suffer persecution for the sake of righteousness."

Second, he posits the severity of the suffering, **"We are put to death,"** that is, we are handed over to death. Esther 7:4, "I and my people have been handed over to be destroyed and murdered."

Third, he posits the duration of persecution when he says, **"All the day,"** that is, throughout life. 2 Corinthians 4:11, "We who live are always handed over to death for the sake of Jesus."

Fourth, he posits the readiness of those who intend to kill when he says, **"We are counted as sheep for slaughter,"** that is, destined to be killed in the market, that is, killed with zeal. So also the saints were killed intentionally and with zeal. John 16:2, "The hour is coming when all who kill you will think they do so out of obedience to God." Zechariah 11:4-5, "Feed the flock to be slaughtered. They who came to possess it slayed it with impunity."

v. 37 Then when the Apostle says, **But in all these things**, he answers the question.

First, he proposes an answer, saying, **But in all these things**, namely, in the evils that I have placed on you, **we overcome**, since in all things we maintain undiminished charity. Wisdom 10:12, "She gave the righteous a difficult contest, that they might win and know that wisdom is mightier than all."

This victory is not due to our strength but comes through Christ's assistance. The Apostle therefore adds, **Because of him who loved us**, that is, because of his assistance or because of the love that we have for him, not as though we loved him first, but because "he loved us first," as 1 John 4:19 states, and 1 Corinthians 15:57, "Thanks be to God, who gave us victory through Christ Jesus."

v. 38 Second, having proposed an answer, he clarifies it when he says, "I am certain." He shows thereby that the saints' charity is inseparable from God's love.

---

25. See, e.g., Augustine's Sermon on Psalm 34:23, CCSL 38:320.

(1) He shows that God's love cannot be separated from creatures that exist. (2) Nor can it be separated from creatures that are not but could be where he says, "Nor any other creature" (Rom 8:39).

Concerning the first claim, that God's love cannot be separated from creatures that exist, he makes two points. First, he sets forth those things internal to the human, saying, **For I am certain that neither death**, which is especially dreadful, **nor life**, which is especially desirable, **can separate us from the love of God** (Rom 8:38-39). Romans 14:8: "If we live, we live for the Lord; if we die, we die for the Lord."

In these two, that is, in life and death, are included all that he discussed above on Romans 8:35. For the first six pertain to life, and one, namely, the sword, pertains to death, as was noted above.

Then he sets forth those things external to the human. He first mentions spiritual creatures, saying, **Neither angels**, namely, those of a lower status who are responsible for the care of individual humans. Psalm 90:11/91:11, God "has given angels charge over you." He next says, **Nor principalities**, namely, those that are responsible for care of the nations. Daniel 10:20-21, "Now I return to fight the prince of the Persians. When I went forth, the prince of the Greeks appeared, and there was no one to help me except Michael, our prince." He then adds, **Nor powers**, the highest order of ministering angels. Luke 21:26, "The powers of heaven will be moved."

Now this can be understood in two ways, first, about the evil angels who battle against the saints. Ephesians 6:12, "Our wrestling is not against flesh and blood but against the principalities and powers." In another sense, it can be understood about good angels. Paul's point, according to Chrysostom in his book *On the Heart's Compunction,* is not that angels could at some time try to separate him from Christ, but he held that even those things that are impossible would be more possible, so to speak, than that he could be separated from the love of Christ. By this he showed how great the power of divine charity was in him, and he revealed it for all to see. For it is the custom of lovers that they cannot conceal their love in silence but assert and proclaim it necessarily and loudly, and they cannot restrain its flames within their breast. They speak of it more frequently so that in the very persistence of telling of their love, they receive comfort and the cooling of this immense ardor. Thus this blessed and distinguished lover of Christ causes all the things that are and that will be, whatever can happen, and whatever can in no way happen, to be encompassed all together in one word. Likewise, Galatians 1:8 states, "But if we or an angel from heaven preach to you beyond what I have preached to you, let that one be cursed."

The Apostle then sets forth sensible creatures, of which he identifies two kinds.

First, from the perspective of time, creatures can be differentiated into those of the present and those of the future. Thus, he says, **Neither existing**, that is, present **things**, whether they bring sadness or delight. 2 Corinthians 4:18, "We do not contemplate those things which are seen." Then he adds, **Nor future things**, the fear nor the desire of which can separate us from Christ. Thus he said in Acts 21:13, "I am ready not only to be bound but also to die in Jerusalem for the name of the Lord Jesus."

Then he sets forth the diversity of sensible creatures in terms of their extent. He first touches on the extent of power when he says, **Nor strength**, that is, no creature, no matter how strong, can separate me from Christ, not even strong fire or water because, as Song of Songs 8:6 says, "Love is as strong as death."

Next he sets forth the magnitude of love and describes it with terms, such as height and depth, that are more appropriate to the body.

v. 39 Thus, **Neither height**, from which someone might threaten to cast me off as in Luke 4:29, "They led Jesus to the top of the hill that they might cast him off it." **Nor depth**, in which someone might threaten drowning. Psalm 68:3/69:2, "I am sunk in the mire of the deep."

These three terms can also refer to human affairs. For people could turn others from God in three ways, and in one way by compelling them with power. However, 1 Samuel 2:2 states, "None is as strong as our God." Second, they could also do so by overwhelming with the height of authority, to which Psalm 82:19/83:18 provides a response, "You alone are the Most High over all the earth." Third, they could do so by seducing with profound wisdom; however, Job 11:8 states, "[The perfection of the Almighty] is deeper than the netherworld; what can you know?"

Height and **depth** can also refer to what is favorable and what is hostile, according to 2 Corinthians 6:7, "By the armor of righteousness on the right and on the left." Or according to Chrysostom, who, in his book *On the Heart's Compunction,* states, "'Height' and 'depth' seem to me to point to nothing other than the reign of heaven and hell."[26] It is as if the Apostle meant, I would not fear if it were necessary to fall from heaven or even if I were drawn into hell for Christ.

Regarding those things that do not exist but can, he adds, **Nor** other

---

26. John Chrysostom, *To Demetrius on Compunction,* 1.8, PG 47:406.

creatures. According to Chrysostom, the Apostle speaks of those things that do not exist as if to say that those things that do exist do not suffice.[27] In a certain way, he challenges even those things that do not exist to battle.

None of these **could separate us from the charity of God**. 1 Corinthians 13:8, "Charity never passes away." The charity of God **in Christ Jesus our Lord** was given to us through Christ insofar as he gave it to us through the Holy Spirit. Luke 12:49, "I came to cast fire on the earth, and what do I want except that it be kindled?"

But in light of Ecclesiastes 9:1-2, "People do not know whether they are worthy of love or hate; all things are kept uncertain until the future," does the Apostle mean that he is certain that nothing can separate him from charity?

In response, one can say that he does not speak singularly about himself but speaks in the place of all the predestined. Because of the certitude of predestination, he proclaims that nothing can separate them from charity. This certitude can also be caused by the virtue of charity, which, insofar as it is in them, cannot be separated from them since they love God above all things. But because some at times withdraw from charity, it is not due to a defect in charity but to a defect in free will.

However, if Paul is speaking about himself, he could not be certain about this, except perhaps through a revelation in which he heard, "My grace is sufficient for you," 2 Corinthians 12:9. For in regard to the possibility of free will, he says elsewhere, 1 Corinthians 9:27, "Lest by chance, having preached to others, I myself might be disqualified."

27. John Chrysostom, *To Demetrius on Compunction*, 1.8, PG 47:406.

ROMANS 9

Nicholas of Lyra

The Problem of Israel's Unbelief

v. 1 I am speaking the truth. After the Apostle shows that Christ accomplished the end of the Law, which had to be followed totally, lest it seem that the Jews have been abandoned as if hated, here he shows his feeling toward them in three ways: first, by his suffering because of their stubbornness; second, by praying for their conversion in the following chapter; third, by restraining the gentiles from their arrogance in chapter eleven. He divides the first into two parts. First, he shows his love. Second, he removes the question that has arisen, where he says, **It is not as though the word of God had failed** (Rom 9:6). Concerning the first he says, **I am speaking the truth in Christ**. By speaking of himself he shows that to judge by the powers of reason is not sin. The Apostle makes this proposition because the Jews did not believe him readily. **My conscience** is well ordered.

v. 2 I have great sorrow, as to the mind, **and unceasing anguish**, moving from the spirit to the flesh. One must add, because of the faithlessness of the Jews. As he says,

v. 3 For I could wish that I myself were accursed, that is, cut off from him. This can be understood in two ways. In one way it refers to the time in which he persecuted Christ in his members,[1] and this because of his zeal for the Law

---

1. That is, the Church.

of the Jews (Phil 3:6). Thus he wished to be **cut off from Christ**. In another way, it refers to the time after his conversion in which he preached the Catholic faith. Then at one time he sought to be cut off from Christ by delaying his time of glory[2] so that it might be extended to the time of the conversion of the Jews to faith in Christ, as he says to the Philippians, "I do not know which I prefer, . . . to be with Christ" permanently [or] "to remain in the flesh, which is more necessary for you" (Phil 1:22-24). The second he would do **for the sake of my own people**, for their conversion. **My kindred according to the flesh**: the Apostle was Jewish by birth, from the tribe of Benjamin, as he himself says (Phil 3:5).[3] He speaks of adoption of children because that people is specifically called the child of God, "Israel, my firstborn" (Exod 4:22).

v. 4 [Theirs is] **the glory** because they were created in the divine image. **The covenants**, namely, the commands of God given to the people through Moses. **The giving of the law**, that is, precepts of the Decalogue given by God to the people. **The deference**, the worship of God. **And the promises**, of the prophets concerning Christ.

v. 5 To them belong the patriarchs, and from them, as is clear in Matthew, **comes the Messiah according to the flesh**. This is said to show not only the human nature in Christ according to which he descends from the fathers of the Old Testament, but also the divine, according to which he proceeds from the Father. Therefore he adds, **God, who is over all, be blessed**, by which he makes clear the error of Arius, who said that Christ is pure creature.

God's Promise to Israel Has Not Failed

v. 6 It is not as though. Here concerning the above he resolves the question. Since the promises concerning Christ were made for the Jews, who nevertheless did not receive him, someone could believe that the divine promise was in vain. Therefore he resolves this question about the divine promise through two examples. The second begins with the words, **Nor is that all** (Rom 9:10). Concerning the first he says, **It is not as though**; one should add, **The word of God had failed** to be fulfilled due to the infidelity of the Jews. For some of them as apostles and many others accepted the faith of

---

2. Paul's own death.
3. Cf. Romans 11:1.

Christ in whom the promise of God was fulfilled. **For not all Israelites**, that is, from Jacob, called Israel by another name, are descendants. One should add, **Truly belong to Israel**, through the imitation of his faith. For he declares that not all of Abraham's children are his true descendants, but only those who are descended through Isaac, and this is what he says:

v. 7 Not all of Abraham's children are his true descendants, according to the witness of Scripture. **Not all are**, because the children of Abraham from Hagar and from Keturah are not called his descendants, which he shows through Scripture, **"It is through Isaac that descendants shall be named for you."** Moreover, concerning the other children the Apostle adds,

vv. 8-9 It is not the children of the flesh, by virtue of natural birth, such as Ishmael and the children of Keturah, **who are the children of God**, that is, according to the worship of his elect. **But the children of the promise**, that is, of the divine promise, **are counted as descendants**, namely, of Abraham. These are the ones in Scripture he means when he says, **The word of promise**, and adds, **"I will return to you** about this time," that is, in one year, **"and Sarah shall have a son."** This the author and others allege, following the translation of the Septuagint, which at the time of the apostles was considered more authentic.[4] It is said here that Isaac is the son of promise because he was born by divine power against nature. His father was a hundred, and his mother was ninety and sterile. The promise made to Abraham there that his descendants would be as the stars even before he had a son did not fail, although this promise was not fulfilled in all his children but only in Isaac. Thus neither did the promise through the prophets concerning Christ fail, although not all the Jews received him through faith, but only the elect.

v. 10 Nor is that all. Here he introduces the second example according to the proposition, and it is divided into two parts. First he provides the example, and second he resolves the question, at the place, **What then are we to say?** (Rom 9:14). Moreover, he uses the son, Isaac, as an example. Although Isaac was the son of the promise, as was noted, and through him God's promise to the descendants of Abraham was to be fulfilled, nevertheless, it was not fulfilled in his two sons, Esau and Jacob, but only firmly and truly in Jacob. By the same reason the promise concerning Christ was not fulfilled in all of the

---

4. Nicholas is keenly aware of the difference between the text of the Bible used by the Apostle and the texts in use at his time.

Jews but in some, according to the special election. Therefore he says, **Nor is that all**. It is clear that Sarah had a son by the help of grace. **Something similar happened to Rebecca**, according to Genesis, "Isaac prayed to the Lord for his wife, because she was barren; and the Lord granted his prayer, and his wife Rebecca conceived" (Gen 25:21). **She had conceived children by one husband**, and had twins. The matter about the twins is not in the text but must be understood, on account of which it was placed through glossing, and afterward scribes inserted it into the text.[5]

v. 11 [Rebecca was told] **even before they**, that is, Esau and Jacob, **had been born so that God's purpose of election**, that is, the free predestination of God, **might continue**, that is, the promise of God might be firm and fulfilled.

v. 12 [God's promise was fulfilled] **not by works**, because they were not yet born, **but by his call**, that is, from God, whose election precedes all things. **She**, that is, Rebecca, **was told, "The elder,"** that is, Esau, **"shall serve the younger."** This was fulfilled at the time of David, who was Jacob's descendant, because he made the Edomites pay tribute to him (2 Sam 8:14). And because that rejection of Esau and the election of Jacob were signs of rejection and election to glory, the Apostle adds,

v. 13 As it is written, in Malachi 1:2, **"Jacob I loved."** Concerning this text what is meant here is that the love came **before they had done anything good or bad**, and this abrogates Origen's error, who said that preceding merits earned in a previous life are the cause of divine predestination and rejection, because Esau and Jacob had done nothing either good or bad in this life.[6] But this is simply excluded. Likewise, before life in this world there was no other; otherwise the world would not have begun simply as the beginning of Genesis holds. In the same way, if there had been such a life, the merits of creatures there could not be the cause of predestination, which is an act of God's will, because the temporal cannot be the cause of the eternal. That error having been rejected, others have said that the foreknowledge of merits which is eternal is the cause of predestination by which God wants to give glory to someone, just as a king may give a horse to a soldier because he knows that he will use it well.[7] But this is not a helpful way by which foreknown merits are or-

---

5. This is an interesting critical comment as "twins" are mentioned in Gen 25:24.
6. See Thomas Aquinas, ST I.23.5.
7. ST I.23.5.

dained to glory as to an end. Moreover, willing rightly and ordinately in this way belongs to God, who is unable to choose something except rightly or ordinately, and who in no way wills an end on account of those things that lead to an end; on the contrary. Thus merits, as foreknown by God, or the foreknowledge of merits cannot be the cause of predestination but proceed only from the divine kindness by which someone is chosen for glory. Because of this, God provides grace through which one is able to merit. Neither is the example of the king and soldier useful because the usefulness of the horse is not due to the king, just as merit is principally from God.

God's Right to Choose

v. 14 What shall we say then? Having said these things here, he moves to the question, namely, whether on account of this, God could be called unjust because from two wholly equal brothers one is rejected and the other elected. And this is what he says, **What shall we say then? Is there injustice on God's part** in rejecting Esau and electing Jacob? **By no means!** Here he has resolved the question, and the resolution is divided into two parts. First he resolves the question. Second he notes an objection to the contrary where he says, **You will say to me then** (Rom 9:19). The first is divided into two parts according to the double method of a solution; the second at the place, **For the scripture says** (Rom 9:17). Concerning the first one should know that there is no injustice in giving something to someone out of sheer grace if it is not given to another because grace can be given to one and not to another without injustice. The Savior says this clearly concerning the laborers in the vineyard, "Friend, I am doing you no wrong. . . . Take what belongs to you and go" (Mt 20:13-14).[8] The Apostle declares the teaching by the authority of the Scripture, saying,

v. 15 For he says to Moses (Exod 33:19), **"I will have mercy"** by giving grace in time **"on whom I will have mercy"** in eternal predestination. **"And I will show compassion,"** by giving glory **"on whom I will have mercy,"** by granting to that one final grace.[9] In the effects of divine predestination, the later cause is earlier in terms of its disposition, and the earlier cause is later in terms of its end, just as the infusion of grace is due to merit as to an end.

8. See ST I.23.5.
9. See ST I.23.3.

Meritorious works are due to glory [as an end], and grace is the principle of meritorious works, and a meritorious work makes grace worthy;[10] nevertheless, the cause of all predestination is nothing other than the will of God.[11] Therefore the Apostle concludes,

v. 16 So it depends not on human will or exertion, as to the human situation, or to accomplish merits' good effect which exceeds human ability, **but upon God's mercy**. It is wholly by **goodness** that God elects to glory eternally and gives grace to the elect temporally.

v. 17 For the scripture says. Here the same case is made based on the punishment of the wicked. Concerning this one must know that condemnation is taken in a broad sense, and thus he calls it a simple denial of glory. Therefore, it is not an accidental cause nor in the foreknowledge of God, as neither election nor predestination is opposed to it. In another manner properly it is the ordaining of someone to punishment which is not unjust nor willed by God except for guilt. And therefore what he calls condemnation, in which God rejects, is prior in God because of the foreknowledge of sins. Therefore, those not elected by God fall into sin not because of a failing in God and a failure of the divine impulses to incite them to the good as noted above, but grace is justly denied them because they do not receive these impulses due to the defect in the freedom of the will.[12] Thus [the will] is hardened further by their own malice, but only accidentally by God, who removes the restraint on sin by withdrawing grace, which is designed by nature to soften the human heart. Nevertheless, he justly withdraws it [grace], as was said. And thus those hardened are ordained to punishment. And thus it is clear that in the punishment of the unjust and of the wicked there is no injustice in God. To this teaching he introduces the Scripture:

10. Thomas writes in ST I.23.5, "We must say, therefore, that the effect of predestination may be considered in a twofold light — in one way, in particular; and thus there is no reason why one effect of predestination should not be the reason or cause of another; a subsequent effect being the reason of a previous effect, as its final cause; and the previous effect being the reason of the subsequent as its meritorious cause, which is reduced to the disposition of the matter. Thus we might say that God pre-ordained to give glory on account of merit, and that He pre-ordained to give grace to merit glory."

11. Thomas continues in ST I.23.5, "In another way, the effect of predestination may be considered in general. Thus, it is impossible that the whole of the effect of predestination in general should have any cause as coming from us; because whatsoever is in man disposing him towards salvation, is all included under the effect of predestination. . . ."

12. ST I.23.5.

For the scripture says to Pharaoh, speaking in the person of the Lord, **"I have raised you up,"** by miraculously and severely punishing you and your people. **"I have raised you up"** because they were born to lead you to penance. Pharaoh abused them by hardening his heart; therefore, they were not able to prevail. Nevertheless, this was for the glory of God to be announced throughout the earth, and thus we see that this was fulfilled. Thus it is said, **"to show my power in you,"** through marvelous deeds. **"So that my name may be proclaimed."** Therefore he concludes,

v. 18 So then God has mercy upon whomever he wills, by giving that one final grace and glory, and this happens to one on its own. **God also hardens the heart of whomever he chooses.** Nevertheless, this happens to one merely accidentally and justly, as was said.

v. 19 You will say to me. Having resolved the question, he argues the contrary. First he establishes the argument. Second he solves it at the place, **But who indeed are you, a human being?** (Rom 9:20). Such is the argument. If the hardening of the heart of a sinner and the call of the righteous depend on the will of God, it would seem that neither sin nor justification is imputed to a person according to merit or lack of merit because one cannot resist the will of God. This is what is said, **You will say to me**, arguing against me with my own words, **"Why then does God still find fault?"** With regard to the reward of the just and the punishment of the unjust, **"Who can resist God's will?"** That is, no one. Thus it seems to be wholly imputed to God, and consequently the unrighteousness of sinners or their punishment seems unreasonable to them.

v. 20 O human. Here the argument is solved, and second its resolution is announced [in Rom 9:25] with words from Hosea (Hos 2:23). The argument is resolved with a twofold solution, the second of which begins with, **Has the potter no right?** (Rom 9:21). First, he resolves the issue by showing the unreasonableness of the human argument. For the one who argues a fact with another ought to understand when the other argues unreasonably. At a minimum a human is not able to understand the work of God fully, namely, concerning a leaf of a tree, as to why there are so many and of such a size and with other conditions. Much less is one able to understand God's greatest works, concerning those who are elected and rejected, etc. Thus the Apostle says, **But who indeed are you, a human?** to argue about God's works. **Will what is made say to the one who made it, "Why did you make me?"** The answer is, "No," because one understands neither the method nor the reason of the making, and such is the assertion.

v. 21 Has the potter no right? Here he places the second solution to show that the argument has no force because one does not infer that the will of God is either irrational or unjust. First, God wants to be glorified, and just as it is clear that the elect are called to glory by mercy, so also the condemned are reserved for punishment by justice. Similarly, the glory of an earthly king shines not only in the palace where soldiers are honored but also at the gibbet where criminals are punished. Therefore, the divine will reasonably chooses some to blessedness by which the divine mercy shines the most; others God dismisses by not electing, who by themselves fall into their sin and finally have their hearts hardened. Thus they are justly punished by God. Their punishment results in the glory of God and of the elect. And to this opinion the Apostle introduces the example of the potter, who out of the same lump reasonably forms one vessel for honorable use and another for contemptible use. **Has the potter no right over the clay?** This indicates how much stronger God is with respect to what possesses more from God in its creaturely status than the clay from the potter, since the clay was not actually created by the potter but was only made subject to the potter's work.

v. 22 What if God, desiring to show wrath, that is, the vengeance of God's justice, **and make known God's power**, namely, in the punishment of sinners, **has endured with much patience the objects of wrath?** Sinners are called the vessels of wrath because they contain offenses to God. Moreover, God endures them patiently, because God does not immediately inflict their punishment but expects their repentance, which expectation they finally abuse, and thus they are more justly punished. Therefore, the Apostle adds, **Fitted for destruction**, because this results in the glory of God and the elect. Therefore, the Apostle adds,

v. 23 To make known the riches of God's glory, that is, God's abundance **for the vessels of mercy**, namely, the elect.

v. 24 Whom he has called, first to faith and afterward to glory, **not from the Jews only but also from the gentiles**, because the faith of Christ was proclaimed to all nations.

v. 25 As indeed he says in Hosea. Here consequently he declares what was said last, namely, that the elect are called from the Jews and from the gentiles; nevertheless, more from the gentiles. He divides the call into two parts. First the Apostle declares the call. Second he assigns his reason at the place, **What then?** (Rom 9:30). First, moreover, he proclaims from the Scripture, **As indeed God says in Hosea** (Hos 2:23), **"I will call my people not my people"** (Rom 9:26), that is, the gentiles, who were at first not called God's people because, unlike the Jews, they did not have the Law and the Prophets. **My people**. Because of their conversion to the Catholic faith. **"And her who was not beloved,"** that is, the gentiles who were earlier given to idolatry, which God hated, **"I will call beloved,"** through the assumption of worship. **"And she who had not obtained mercy,"** at the time of the Old Testament, **"has obtained mercy,"** at the time of the New Testament.[13] Similarly the Apostle adds,

v. 26 "And in the very place" (Hos 1:10). It is clear from the text that the call of the gentiles is spoken about because many were called. Consequently he appeals to the authority of Isaiah (Isa 10:22)[14] in speaking of the call of the Jews, because few were called. Therefore the Apostle adds,

v. 27 "Though the number of the children of Israel were like the sand of the sea" (Isa 10:22), that is, an exceedingly great number, **"only a remnant of them will be saved."** Because of this, that is, comparatively few. This is clear as only the apostles and a few other Jews became believers. One must know, nevertheless, that Isaiah is speaking of the children of Israel who were fleeing from the hand of the king of Assyria. For at the time of Hosea the kingdom of Israel was in captivity. Afterward they came to the kingdom of Judah at the time of [Zedekiah]. They were truly turned back to God, having heard the miraculous sound of the army of Sennacherib.[15] Because only a few converted, this was a figure of the conversion of the apostles and a few other Jews at the coming of Christ. Therefore, the Apostle alleges this by itself just as earlier he noted the election of Jacob and the temporal rejection of Esau,

13. Here Lyra's text is different from the NRSV. After the words "her who was not beloved I will call 'beloved,'" his text and the Vulgate add, "Non misericordiam consecutam, misericordiam consecutam."

14. The NRSV notes the LXX (Septuagint) next to these verses as they are in Isaiah 10, 22, 23, albeit in a different form.

15. See 2 Kings 19:29-35 and Isaiah 36. Nicholas refers to Zedekiah, and it should be Hezekiah.

which was a sign of eternity.[16] And one must add the call of the gentiles and of the Jews to faith in Christ.

v. 28 "For he shall complete his word,"[17] that is, the gospel, which is the law of perfection, **"while abbreviating it out of equity"** because God rescinds the laws which are not kept in the new law. **"In righteousness,"** because God retains the moral precepts containing the equity of the natural law. The Jews and the gentiles were commonly called to the evangelical word, but because comparatively few of the Jews believed, he again appeals to the authority of Isaiah,

v. 29 "If the Lord of hosts," that is, of the armies through which the angels are indicated, **"had not left survivors to us,"** that is, some of the Jews who were called to faith, **"we would have fared like Sodom."** That is, totally perverted from the truth.

True Righteousness Is by Faith

v. 30 What then? Here the Apostle explains why so many are called from the gentiles, which nevertheless seems a marvel because they were idolaters. This is what he says: **What then are we to say?** At the wonder of this, **gentiles, who did not strive for righteousness** because they worshiped idols, **have attained it**, that is, have followed **righteousness** by a sudden conversion to faith in Christ. This is because they saw miracles done in his name through the apostles and the other disciples, as many places in the Acts of the Apostles make clear. **Righteousness through faith** makes one worthy of eternal life. What is said here is distinct from the righteousness which was through the works of the Law of Moses, which does not make one worthy of eternal life, as he notes above. For if Abraham was justified by works of the Law, he had glory but not according to God (Rom 4:4-5).

---

16. Note the use of the double literal sense here in the history of Israel as a figure. Isaiah's remnant prophecy addresses his own context and prefigures the few apostles and Jews who converted to Christianity. The election of Jacob and the rejection of Esau as a figure of eternity employ the anagogical sense of the traditional fourfold method.

17. NRSV has "for the Lord will execute his sentence." See the alternative reading in the RSV note for a reading similar to the Vulgate. The Vulgate has: "Verbum enim consummans, et abbrevians in aequitate."

v. 31 But Israel, who did strive for righteousness based on the law, through the worship of the one God, **did not succeed in fulfilling that law,** that is, the law of the Catholic faith, which justifies by infused righteousness, making one worthy of eternal life.

v. 32 Why not? This is connected to the above. **Because not on the basis of faith**; hence they were seeking to be justified apart from the faith of Christ, without which there can be no salvation. **But as if it were based on works.** Evidently they were seeking to be justified by the Law of Moses, which these works are not able to do. On the contrary, it is by faith, as the Apostle declared above in chapter three, and in this they rejected Christ. Therefore he adds, **They have stumbled.** They have accepted the cause of their downfall.

v. 33 "See, I have placed in Zion a stone" (Isa 28:16 LXX). Just as this was the proof, according to the letter this authority concerns Christ, on whom the leaders of the Jews stumbled. They did so first by blaspheming his humanity, saying, "Look, a man who is a glutton and a drunkard!" (Lk 7:34). This they said out of envy. Second, they did so by speaking blasphemies against his divinity. "Through Beelzebul, the ruler of the demons, he casts out demons" (Mt 12:24), and thus they attributed his works of divinity to demons. **"And whoever believes in him,"** that is, through faith formed by love, **"will not be put to shame"** (Isa 28:16 LXX), that is, finally, but will be honored more in glory. This the authorities and others like the Apostle allege, according to the translation of the Septuagint. In our translation of Isaiah it is rendered this way: "The one who trusts will not stumble" (Isa 28:16). This can be understood in two ways, as I said when I commented on that passage. In one way it refers to the time of Isaiah, so that the sense is: The one who believes my prophecy will not stumble but will trust that the Messiah will come forthwith because there was a long time between Isaiah and the first coming of Christ. In another way, it refers to the time of Christ and speaks of his coming to judge. This is the sense: The one who trusts Christ proclaimed will not stumble but will trust that he will come to judge quickly. Either way believing and not stumbling is not confusing. The Seventy translated in this way because they did not always translate word for word, but according to the sense of the words.[18]

---

18. *Sensum ex sensu.*

ROMANS 10

Nicholas of Lyra

Christ Is the End of the Law

v. 1 Brothers. Here the Apostle shows his love for the Jews by praying for their salvation. He divides his manner of loving them into two parts: first, he addresses the method of his prayer; second, the motive at the place, **I can testify** (Rom 10:2). Concerning the first he says, **Brothers, my heart's desire**. This means, I pray for them not only by mouth but also from the heart. **And prayer to God**, that is, his prayer for a holy thing. This method of prayer is all the more efficacious in accomplishing its object because it relies upon the merit of the sacred thing which he includes, just as when it is said, "Through your passion you deliver them."[1] In this way Paul prays for the Jews. Therefore he adds, **That they may be saved**, evidently by me, that is, to be converted and consequently saved.

v. 2 I can testify. Here he places the motive of his prayer, and he divides it into two parts. First, he describes the motive. Second, he declares what he says at the place, **For Christ is the end of the law** (Rom 10:4). The Apostle's motive was that the Jews, by persecuting the faith of Christ, had an indiscriminate zeal for God, and he understood such things. For the Apostle who first zealously persecuted the Church of God said this about himself: "I received mercy because I acted ignorantly" (1 Tim 1:13). Therefore he says,

---

1. Perhaps from the Litany of the Saints.

I can testify, because he was their companion in zeal for holiness. **That they have a zeal**, that is, zeal **indeed for God**, he declares, saying,

v. 3 For, being ignorant of the righteousness that comes from God, which makes one worthy of eternal life and which one holds by a faith formed in Christ. This ignorance does not excuse because it is under the Law. **And seeking to establish their own**. Some explain this with regard to the priests and lawyers who made the command of God useless through their traditions, but this does not seem true from what precedes, namely, that they were moved, although indiscriminately, by zeal for God. Indeed, their useless divine laws that came from the tradition were inspired not by a zeal for God but out of a selfish zeal for gain or glory. The Apostle makes this clear when he says, **And seeking to establish their own**. One should understand righteousness through the works of the Law as their own. Because that Law was given to them and was dead, it was no longer from God but from the Jews who defended the Law with stubbornness. **They have not submitted to God's righteousness**, that is, the righteousness held through faith in Christ which they rejected.

v. 4 The end. Here the Apostle declares that the righteousness that makes one worthy of eternal life does not come from the Law, but from faith in Jesus Christ. And he divides the intention into three parts. First, he shows the usefulness of this faith. Second, he shows its lack of difficulty at the place, **But what does it say?** (Rom 10:8). Third, he accuses them of infidelity who do not believe at the place, **But how are they to call on one?** (Rom 10:14). Concerning the first, one should know that the perfect does not consist in the condition of matter but in the introduction of the form to which the disposition is finally ordained, as is clear in natural and artificial things.[2] The old Law, moreover, was ordained to Christ, as the imperfect is to the perfect. Whence the Apostle, "The law was our disciplinarian until Christ came" (Gal 3:24). Rashi, that is, Solomon ben Isaac, the Hebrew, and many other Hebrew teachers say that all the prophets did not speak unless about the day of the Messiah, that is, the time of Christ at the end.[3] The cause of righteous-

2. Lyra is invoking the doctrine of hylomorphism here such that all finite beings are composed of matter and form and are subject to change. See Ilia Delio, *Simply Bonaventure: An Introduction to His Life, Thought, and Writings* (Hyde Park: New City Press, 2001), 57.

3. Rashi (1040-1105) was Lyra's favorite Jewish commentator, "Who among all the Jewish exegetes has put forward the most reasonable arguments, in order to illuminate the literal meaning of the text." Cited in A. J. Minnis and A. B. Scott, *Medieval Literary Theory and Criticism c. 1100–c. 1375: The Commentary Tradition* (Oxford: Clarendon, 1988), 270.

ness which makes one worthy of eternal life was not the Law, which was imperfect, but is our faith in Christ, for which perfection is owed. This is what the Apostle says, **The end of the law**, namely, of the Mosaic Law. He adds, **Christ**, because it is ordained to him, **that there may be righteousness**, infused righteousness. **For everyone who believes**. Hence the fathers of the Old Testament were not justified by works of the Law but by faith in Christ, as I said above. Acts says, "We believe that we are saved through our Lord Jesus Christ," just as those fathers of the Old Testament and the Scriptures lead to this teaching when they say:

v. 5 For Moses wrote, namely, in Leviticus, **concerning the righteousness that comes from the law**, because by the fulfillment of the works of the Law bodily death was avoided, which was brought on by transgression in many cases. But it did not make one alive spiritually, as noted above in chapter three.

v. 6 But the righteousness, that is, the righteousness held through faith in Christ, that comes from **faith, says, just as** Moses says in Deuteronomy (Deut 30:12-14), **"Do not say in your heart, 'Who?'"** This is taken negatively (**that is, to bring Christ down**). Evidently from the superior to the inferior, that is, to deny that Christ ascended to heaven.

v. 7 "'Or who will descend into the abyss?'" Similarly, **that is, to bring Christ up from the dead**. That is, do not deny that Christ descended to limbo to liberate the souls of the fathers from there. Thus the Gloss interprets this passage, and our other expositors commonly follow suit. However, this exposition does not seem to agree with the teaching of Deuteronomy (Deut 30:11-14) from which this passage is taken, nor with the following text, as is clear by looking at it. Therefore, one can interpret it without a preceding judgment in this way: **"Do not say in your heart, 'Who will ascend into heaven?'"** That is, to deny that Christ has come down. That is to say that he has not yet come to the earth in obedience to the Father. **"Or, 'who descended into the abyss?'"** Similarly, to deny that Christ was dead. In other words, he was not dead nor consequently resurrected from the dead to begin eternal life. The Jews denied both at the time of the apostles, and they still deny that Christ has come and was consequently raised from the dead. This exposition agrees with the following verse when it says, **If you confess with your lips that Jesus is Lord** (Rom 10:9), namely, that Christ came as was promised in the Law, **and believe in your heart that God raised him from the dead, you will be saved** (Rom 10:9). Similarly, this agrees with the teaching of Deuteronomy from whence this scripture was taken, **"Do not say in your heart,"** etc. What was said there is clear (Deut 30:11-14) to eliminate any excuse that one is able to keep the Law of Moses. As Deuteronomy states, it is not necessary to ascend to heaven or to cross the sea to bring it here and keep it, because it was already given to the people. Thus, having been written by the finger of God as far as the precepts of the Decalogue are concerned, and by Moses as far as the other things, Deuteronomy adds, "The word is near you; it is in your heart" (Deut 30:14). Deuteronomy was indeed a figure of the new law, as Jerome says in *To Paulinus*.[4] Thus the previous scripture here speaks figuratively about the new law which all are to observe, especially the Jews to whom Christ was especially promised and to whom he preached personally. Thus when Deuteronomy says here, **"Do not say in your heart,"** etc., it takes away the excuse not to observe the new law which was already given through Christ and delineated on the hearts of believers by the Holy Spirit. Therefore Deuteronomy says,

v. 8 "The word is near you," that is, the spiritual life and the beginning of immortality by Christ's rising from the grave, which the Law was not able to do. **But what does scripture say?** Here he shows that facility of righteousness that is by faith in Christ when he says, **But what does scripture say** concerning that righteousness? **"The word is near."** Here what is required is believing and confessing, namely, in the case of death when the ability to work is taken away. **That is, the word**, namely, Christ, **that we proclaim . . . that Jesus is Lord**, is our true savior.

vv. 9-10 And believe in your heart . . . raised him from the dead. To eternal life. **You will be saved**. For eternal salvation in faith. In believing these two articles of faith the testimony of Scripture is drawn upon where [Isaiah] says,

v. 11 "No one who believes in him will be put to shame." According to the letter, Christ is understood as I said at the end of the preceding chapter.

v. 12 For there is no distinction between Jew and Greek, in relation to righteousness through faith in Christ. **For the same Lord**, namely, of the Jews and of the Greeks, as Romans 2:10 says, [is Lord of all] **and is generous to all**, that is, all have the power to hear.

---

4. See Letter 53.8, CSEL 54:455.

v. 13 For this he appeals to the authority of Joel when he says, **"Everyone who calls upon the name of the Lord shall be saved"** (Joel 2:32).

Israel Responsible for Its Failure

v. 14 But how? Here he argues against the infidelity of unbelievers and first generally of all and secondly specifically of the Jews at the place, **But I ask** (Rom 10:18). First he shows the faithfulness of all as the catholic faith was made known throughout the world at the time of the apostles. The Apostle had just said, **"Everyone who calls on the name of the Lord shall be saved."** Now, continuing the teaching, he says, **How are they to call on one in whom they have not believed?** That is, they cannot because prayer presupposes the faith of praying. **How are they to believe in one of whom they have never heard?** Faith presupposes hearing from God through revelation or by humans through preaching. Therefore he adds, **And how are they to hear without someone preaching?** Indeed, the act of preaching presupposes the authority of the office. Therefore he adds,

v. 15 And how are they to proclaim him unless they are sent? By God, as the prophets, or by one holding God's place, as other preachers, and for this he appeals to the Scriptures (Isa 52:7): **"How beautiful are the feet of those who bring good news!"** This means the preachers of the gospel, as I said at that place. Therefore he adds,

v. 16 But not all received his preaching. For this he appeals to the authority of Isaiah (53:1), where, according to the letter, he speaks of Christ, as I wrote there. **"Lord, who has believed our message?"** By which Isaiah and the other prophets heard the mystery of Christ from God and which so few believed, especially of the Jews. Thus the Apostle concludes,

v. 17 So faith comes from what is heard. The meaning of this verse is clear.

v. 18 But I ask, Have they not heard, that is, do they have an excuse for their infidelity because of a defect in the proclamation? As he says, **Yes**, he appeals to the authority of the psalm. Indeed, **"To all the earth."** At the time of the apostles the gospel was announced through the whole world, as he demonstrates by citing Psalm 19.[5] Moreover, here it is possible to repeat briefly how

5. Psalm 18:5 in the Vulgate.

the apostles traveled throughout the world to proclaim the gospel from Jerusalem, which is in the middle of the inhabited world. While Saint Peter, the apostle, was living, the gospel was preached westward to the ocean where the inhabited world ends, according to the astrologers. For Saint Savinianus built a church in the city of Sens which at the time was a city of France for Saint Peter, who he heard had already suffered. Afterward, when he learned that he was still alive, he named the church Saint Pierre Vivant, in which I who have written these things have been many times.[6] Others who came to France with Saint Savinianus preached in other places in the west. In this same way, the gospel was proclaimed to the east and north of Jerusalem because Christ's disciples traveled all around to preach.

v. 19 Again I ask. Here he especially condemns the unbelief of the Jews because they had heard Christ preached and had seen his miracles. Thus Nicodemus said in the presence of the teachers of the Law, "Rabbi, we know that you are a teacher who has come from God; for no one can do these things that you do apart from the presence of God" (Jn 3:2). Then the Apostle said, **I ask, Did Israel not understand?** It did rather more than others, but among the teachers of the Law that understanding was blinded by envy against Christ, because he began to preach against their faults. Thus, insofar as they were able to turn the people from him, they blinded the people, and after the disciples left the Jews to cross over to the gentiles, the illumination of the gentiles began. To you it was appropriate to speak the word of God first, but because you reject it and are judged unworthy of eternal life, behold, we will turn to the gentiles, and Moses predicted this: **"I will make you jealous,"** that is, envious. **"I will make you,"** or I will permit you to be led against Christ by the deception of the devil. "[I will make you jealous of those] **who are not a nation"** by sending you away into infidelity in place of the gentiles, who were of no regard among you. For the Jews did not regard the gentiles as people, but they called them dogs, as Exodus states (22:31), by throwing them to the dogs. [I will make you] **"angry."** That is, in punishment for my vengeance, which the Romans accomplished by killing and capturing the people of Judea. Moreover, for this he appeals to the authority of Isaiah concerning the illumination of the gentiles when he says,

---

6. Nicholas frequently left traces of his biography in comments in the *Postill*. Biographers of Nicholas have used passages such as this one to confirm the records that he served as the Franciscan Provincial Minister in Burgundy from 1324.

v. 20 "I have been found" (Isa 65:1). That is, by the gentiles, who, having served idols, piously received the preaching of the apostles and were thus illumined. Concerning the blindness of the Jews he adds,

v. 21 But of Israel [the prophet Isaiah] says, in the person of the Lord, **"All day long I have held out my hands"** to you by conferring for the whole time all the benefits of the Mosaic Law. **"To an unbelieving people"** (Isa 65:2). First they did not believe the prophets, and then afterward Christ. **"But denying."** First by rejecting the words of my prophets and by killing them, and afterward myself in my own person.

ROMANS 11

Nicholas of Lyra

Israel's Rejection Not Final

v. 1 I ask, then. Here the apostle shows his affection for the Jews by restraining the gentiles in their arrogance. The gentiles caused this discord in that they reproved Jewish unbelief even among converts from Judaism, which the Apostle restrains. He does so first by taking up the reasons for the fall of the Jews; second, the conversion of the gentiles, at the place, **But if some of the branches**, etc. (Rom 11:17); third, out of consideration of the Jews belonging to God, at the place, **I do not want you to be ignorant** (Rom 11:25). For the fall of the Jews he proposed three reasons. The first is that the fall of the Jews is not universal. Second, it is not useless, at the place, **So I ask** (Rom 11:11). Third, it is not irredeemable, at the place, **Now I am speaking to you** (Rom 11:13). The first is in two parts. In the first he asserts the proposition. In the second he concludes the intent, at the place, **What then?** (Rom 11:7). Moreover, in the first he asserts by a twofold example, and the first is about himself. He says, therefore, **I ask, then, has God rejected**, generally, **his people**, the Jews, who are called God's peculiar people? **By no means! For I myself am an Israelite, a descendant of Abraham**, etc., who, nevertheless, am called not only to faith in Christ but also to be his apostle. Therefore he concludes,

v. 2 God has not rejected. God predestined the Jews, as is clear in Paul and the other apostles. The second example concerns Elijah, who believed that the whole people had turned to idolatry, and all the prophets had been killed. Nevertheless, it was not so, and the Apostle says, **Do you not know what the**

scripture says of Elijah? That is, you should know **how he pleads with God against Israel**, not with a zeal for vengeance, but with love for justice.

v. 3 "Lord, they have killed," that is, they have not remained worshipers of God. **"They have demolished your altars,"** so that one could not find a place to worship. **"And I alone am left."** Just as he believed because the spirit does not always touch the hearts of the prophets about everything. Thus Elisha says about the Shunammite, "For she is in bitter distress; the Lord has hidden it from me . . ." (2 Kings 4:27). **"And they are seeking my life."** So that nothing remains of divine worship.

v. 4 But what is the divine reply to him? To reject his saying. **"I have kept for myself,"** that is, preserved, **"seven thousand who have not bowed."** Therefore, he is not alone. This is the proposition.

v. 5 So too at the present time, namely, of the new law, **there is a remnant chosen by the grace of God**, etc., especially some of the Jews elected by the grace of God. They were saved through faith in Christ, as is clear from the apostles and others who first believed, who were all Jews.

v. 6 But if it is by grace that they were saved in this way of speaking, **it is no longer on the basis of works**. In other words, it was not of the Law, which is not able to do this, as was said above. **Otherwise grace would no longer be grace**, because what is returned due to works is owed and is not grace.

v. 7 What then? Here he concludes the intent, namely, that the fall of the Jews is not general. Therefore, he says, **What then?** He adds what follows from what is said. **What Israel**, that is, the major part of the people, **was seeking**, namely, the righteousness through faith in Christ whose advent the Jews expected, it did not attain. **But the elect**, the apostles and others elected to it **[attained it]**. **But the rest were hardened**, that is, they remained in their infidelity.

v. 8 As it is written, "God gave them a sluggish spirit." In other words, their hearts, pricked with jealousy by hatred for Christ and his followers, were filled with blindness and stubbornness. Therefore he adds, **"Eyes that would not see."**

v. 9 And David says the same, **"Let their table,"** that is, the sacred Scripture by which the Jews were nourished, **"become a snare,"** etc. (Ps 68:23/

69:22).[1] By their hatred for Christ the scribes were moved to pervert the Scriptures, which spoke about Christ, as many places of the Old Testament show more fully, and thus those following them were entangled in errors.

"**And a trap.**" Through Titus and Vespasian. "**And a stumbling block.**" The leaders of the Jews were tormented because they inflamed the people to rebellion and unfaithfulness toward the Romans. "**And a retribution for them.**" For these things happened to them as punishment for the death of Christ, according to Luke 19:42-44. Their blindness and hardness of heart follow from what has been said before; therefore, he adds,

v. 10 "Let their eyes be darkened" in relation to the blindness of their understanding. "**And keep their backs,**" that is, their will, "**forever bent**" by their stubbornness.

v. 11 So I ask. This shows that the fall of the Jews was not without its usefulness. Because of this the apostles left Judea and crossed over to convert the gentiles throughout the world, as I noted above, and so the Apostle asks, **Have they**, the Jews, **stumbled so as to fall?** That is, that no usefulness will follow. **By no means!** Thus Augustine says in the *Enchiridion,* "God who is omnipotent and good does not permit evil to occur except to draw out the greater good from it."[2] **But through their stumbling, [salvation came to the gentiles]**, as noted before, "**to make Israel jealous**" (Rom 11:17), that is, to imitate the gentiles. For at the end of the world those Jews who were converted and many more will discover the falseness of the antichrist. They will imitate the gentiles by converting to the faith of Christ.

v. 12 Now if their, that is, the Jews', **stumbling means riches for the world**, as the situation arose, as was said, **and if their defeat means riches for the gentiles**, that is, for the simple little ones, the unlearned, and those as it were of no repute such as the apostles, because they founded churches among the gentiles, **how much more will their inclusion mean?** Here one must add the great good at the end in their conversion.

v. 13 Now I am speaking to you. Here he restrains the arrogance of the gentiles in that the fall of the Jews is not irredeemable. Instead, the Apostle offers it as an example in two ways, namely, of the patriarchs and of the apos-

1. Psalm 68:23 in the Vulgate.
2. Augustine, *Enchiridion,* 3.11, CCSL 46:53.

tles, who were Jews. Thus the Apostle exerts himself for their conversion. **Now I am speaking to you**, lest you insult the Jews. **Inasmuch, then, as** I am believed to be the evangelist to the uncircumcised and Peter to the circumcised, **I glorify my ministry** by adding what is beyond what he [Paul] owes, namely, by exerting himself for the conversion of the Jews when the office he holds calls him solely to preach to the gentiles.

v. 14 [**I glorify my ministry**] **in order to make my own flesh**, that is, the Jews from whom he descended, as he said at the beginning of this chapter, **jealous**, that is, to imitate me, **and thus to save some of them**. For the Apostle knew that it was not yet the time for all of them to convert, and thus he shows their infidelity's usefulness for the good, saying,

v. 15 For if their rejection, through their unfaithfulness, **is the reconciliation of the world**, making this possible, as was said before, **what will their acceptance**, their faith, **be but life from the dead?** The Jews, who knew the Scriptures and converted to the faith, were able to progress more than the others, as is clear from Paul and Apollos and many others. And for this he provides an example from the apostles, saying,

v. 16 If part of the dough offered as firstfruits is holy, that is, so are the apostles, who were an extract from the Judaic lump, **and if the root is holy**, that is, the patriarchs who were as roots to the Jewish people, so are the branches. By this the Apostle intends to show that the future would turn out well for the Jews. And in relation to this he offers to show that their fall is not irredeemable.

The Metaphor of the Olive Tree

v. 17 But if some of the branches. Here the Apostle restrains the gentiles from insulting the Jews because they owe their conversion to them. First he makes a proposition. Second he removes an objection to the contrary at the place, **You will say** (Rom 11:19). The reason consists in this, that, although the multitude of the Jews fell through unbelief, nevertheless, though some remained in faith, namely, the apostles and the disciples, the gentiles were converted as grafted branches proceeding through faith in imitation of the patriarchs.

Some of the branches, that is, out of the Jews proceeding in the flesh from the patriarchs who were the root of the tree, **were broken off** by their unbelief. **And you, a wild olive shoot**, a new olive unfit to be good fruit since the gentiles did not have the Law and the Prophets nor even the worship of God but were dedicated to idolatry, **were grafted in their place**. The branches that remained are the apostles and the other faithful of Judea. [The gentiles **share in**] **the fellowship of the root**, that is, the faith of the patriarchs, **and the richness of the olive tree itself**, that is, of the teaching of Christ and of grace.

v. 18 Do not boast over the branches, that is, the Jews broken by their infidelity. **If you do boast**, you do so "vainly." **It is not you that support the root**, because the gentiles obtained the goodness of their conversion from the Jews and not the other way around.

v. 19 You will say. Here he counters an objection. Second, he inserts the conclusion at the proper place, **Note then** (Rom 11:22). Concerning the first he posits the objection, saying, **You will say**. That is, you gentiles grafted in this manner of speaking argue thus: "Branches were broken off," that is, "I am able to boast over and against the broken branches, although not against the root!" Then he counters the objection, saying,

v. 20 That is true. They were broken off on account of their unbelief. This is true if you say that they were broken due to their unbelief, not because you were grafted in, except that the breaking made this opportunity possible and not per se. **But you stand only through faith**, which is not from you but is a gift of God. Since you are not to be haughty, but to be more humble, therefore he adds, **So do not become proud, but stand in awe**, and he adds the reason:

v. 21 For if God did not spare the natural branches, that is, the Jews in their arrogance, that is, if God **did not spare** by punishing them severely, **perhaps God will not spare you** if you will be haughty. Nor does the Apostle say "perhaps" here as if he is uncertain with respect to God, but rather with respect to the freedom of choice.

v. 22 Note then the kindness and severity of God. Here he concludes from what he claims before regarding the material cause of the gentiles' conversion by the divine goodness itself. They coexist in faith by the grace of Christ and by the severity of his justice among the Jews, who departed from faith in Christ.

And this he indicates, **Note the kindness and severity of God.** The meaning of the text is clear to this point.

vv. 23-24 Even those, if they do not persist in unbelief, [shall be grafted in]. For other things being equal, a natural branch has a greater ability to be grafted in than one foreign to a particular root. The meaning of the text is clear.

All Israel Will Be Saved

v. 25 So that you may not claim. Here the Apostle restrains the gentiles from insulting the Jews considering the divine judgments. He divides the discussion into three parts. First, he shows the present blindness of the Jews and their future illumination. Second, he declares the cause of both at the place, **As regards the gospel** (Rom 11:28). Third, he concludes the depth of the divine wisdom at the place, **O the depth of the riches** (Rom 11:33). Concerning the first he says, **So that you may not claim to be wiser than you are,** that is, you gentiles converted to faith in Christ and thus through faith have been made my siblings. [**I do not want you to be unaware of**] **this mystery,** the divine mystery, **so that you are not wiser than you are,** that is, according to your estimation. The Apostle says this to restrain their presumption, which is the mystery that **a hardening has come upon Israel in part** but not entirely because the apostles and the first believers from the Jews were especially enlightened. [This will be the case] **until the full number of the gentiles has come in** by receiving faith in Christ. One must know, moreover, that this "until" here should not be taken causally but consecutively and without necessity because the apostles crossed over from the Jews who were blind to convert the gentiles.

v. 26 And so all Israel will be saved. At the end of the world, after the lie of the antichrist has been detected, the Jews who stand firm will rise from the dead in faith in Christ. **As it is written** in Isaiah (59:20-21), **"Out of Zion."** There in the past, the faith of Christ was first preached, and proclaimed to all, and must be distributed in the future, as Isaiah said more fully,

v. 27 "And this is my covenant with them," that is, the catholic faith proclaimed in the New Testament and to be completed among the Jews, **"when I take away their sins,"** through justifying faith.

v. 28 As regards the gospel. Here he demonstrates the cause of their blindness and jealousy. First of all, he establishes two reasons for their blindness. The first is the rejection of the teaching of Christ, which he treats when he says, **As regards the gospel they are enemies**. The other is the jealousy concerning the grace given to the gentiles, which he treats at the place, **For your sake**. Next he posits the cause of the enlightenment when he says, **As regards election, they are beloved for the sake of their ancestors**. On account of the merits of the ancestors some are now elected to faith, and many will be elected at the end of the world. He offers the reason for this, saying,

v. 29 Moreover, the gifts and calling, that is, the promises made to the ancestors about what their children would become and the promises fulfilled at this time, **are irrevocable**, that is, without change, because with God there is no change. And consequently he offers this parallel that, just as before the advent of Christ the gentiles were under the sin of idolatry, so also after the advent of Christ the Jews for the most part fell into the sin of unfaithfulness. Thus in both he shows human weakness in their sins and divine goodness in the kindness of the call. The Jews now fallen will be called. And this is what he declares:

vv. 30-32 For just as you did not believe. The meaning of this text is clear.

v. 33 O the depths of the riches. Here finally he draws two conclusions about the depth of divine wisdom and judgment in two ways. First he concludes this from divine eminence and secondly from human deficiency. Concerning the first he says, **O the depths of the riches of the wisdom and knowledge of God!** That is the depth of wisdom and knowledge, just as it is said in John (4:11), "the well is deep," that is, "profound." He speaks of wisdom in relation to the divine and of knowledge in relation to what will become of humans which we are not able to understand. Therefore he adds, **How unsearchable are God's judgments!** because they exceed our capacity of natural understanding.

vv. 34-35 For who has known the Lord's mind? Here he shows the same from the deficiency of our knowledge, when he says, **For who has known the Lord's mind**, etc.? That is, no one, because this is impossible. It is the Lord from whom we have all the power not only of doing but also of knowing and the very power to exist, which he declares, saying,

v. 36 For from him, that is, in relation to the power of creation, which is appropriate to the Father. **And through him**, in relation to exemplary wisdom, which is appropriate to the Son. **And to him**, as a goal to conserve that which is appropriate to the Holy Spirit. **To God be the glory forever. Amen.** Some books have inserted two words, namely, "honor" and "of ages," but these are neither in the text nor in the corrected books.

ROMANS 12

Thomas Aquinas

LECTURE 1

v. 1 Having shown the need for virtues and the origin of grace, the Apostle here teaches grace's use, which pertains to moral instruction. In this regard, he does two things. (1) He sets forth moral teaching in general. (2) He turns to something of particular concern to those to whom he writes, and this in Romans 15:14, "I am convinced," etc.

Concerning the first [moral teaching], he does two things. (1) He teaches the use of grace for a person to be perfect. (2) He teaches the use of grace for a perfect person to uphold an imperfect one, and this in Romans 14:1, "But the weak."

Concerning the first [the use of grace], he does three things. (1) He urges to perfection of life with regard to the holiness that one observes before God. (2) He urges to the righteousness that one shows a neighbor, and this in Romans 13:1, "Let every soul," etc. (3) He urges with regard to the purity that people maintain in themselves, and this in Romans 13:11, "And knowing this," etc.

Concerning the first [encouragement in perfection of life], he does two things. (1) He admonishes people to present themselves as holy before God. (2) He teaches how to use the gifts of God's grace by which one is sanctified, and this in Romans 12:3, "For I say, by the grace," etc.

Concerning, the first [the presentation of oneself before God], he does two things. (1) He teaches how people should conduct themselves before

God with regard to the body and (2) with regard to the soul in Romans 12:2, "Do not be conformed," etc.

Concerning the first [how to conduct oneself bodily before God], the Apostle does two things.

Our Bodily Sacrifice

First, he urges observation of what is taught, and this in two ways. First, on his behalf, **Therefore, I implore you**, as if to say, God's judgments have been called incomprehensible and God's ways inscrutable (cf. Rom 11:33); **therefore, I implore you** to observe what is said.

He uses the word "implore" for three reasons.

First, he does so to demonstrate his humility. Proverbs 18:23, "The poor speak by imploring." The poor in this case are those who do not trust in their wealth and therefore do not attempt to urge people to the good by their own means but by God's. For to implore [*obsecrare*] is to call on sacred things as witness [*ob sacra contestari*].

Second, he implores in order to stir more by love in inviting than by fear in ordering authoritatively. Philemon 8-9, therefore, says, "Though I have much confidence in Christ Jesus to order you to what is proper, instead, I implore you out of charity." Galatians 6:1, "You who are spiritual should correct in a spirit of gentleness."

Third, he implores out of respect for the Romans to whom he was writing. 1 Timothy 5:1, "Do not rebuke elders, but implore them as parents."

He urges [observation of what is taught] in another way, on God's behalf, when he says, **Through God's mercy**, through which you have been saved. Titus 3:5, "God saved us out of mercy." Therefore, out of consideration for divine mercy, we ought to do what we are taught. Matthew 18:33, "Should you not also have had mercy on your servant, as I had on you?" Or, **Through God's mercy** can mean the authority of apostleship committed mercifully to me. 1 Corinthians 7:25, "I am trustworthy by the Lord's mercy."

Second, he admonishes with the words, **That you may present your bodies**, etc.

It should be known that, as Augustine states, the visible sacrifice offered externally to God is a sign of the invisible sacrifice by which people present themselves and their belongings in obedience to God.[1]

---

1. Augustine, *City of God*, 10.5, CCSL 47:277.

People have a threefold goodness.

First, they have a goodness of the soul that they present to God through the humility of devotion and contrition, according to Psalm 50:19/ 51:17, "My sacrifice to God is a broken spirit."

Second, they have an exterior goodness that they present to God through the largess of alms. Therefore, Hebrews 13:16, "Do not neglect kindness and neighborliness since God is pleased by such sacrifices."

Third, they have the goodness of their own body, and so the Apostle writes, **That you might present your bodies** to God as a kind of spiritual sacrifice. An animal offered to God used to be called a sacrifice [*hostia*] either for the sake of victory over or security from enemies [*hostibus*] or because it was offered at the entrance [*ostium*] to the tabernacle.

People present their bodies to God as a sacrifice in three ways.

They do so in one way when they expose their bodies to suffering and death for God's sake, as is said of Christ in Ephesians 5:2, "He handed himself over as an offering and sacrifice to God." Speaking of himself, the Apostle states in Philippians 2:17, "If I am offered as a victim upon the sacrifice and service of your faith, I rejoice."

Second, they wear down their bodies in service to God through fasts and vigils, according to 1 Corinthians 9:27, "I chastise my body and bring it into subjection."

Third, they present their bodies to carry out works of righteousness and divine worship. Romans 6:19, "Present your members to serve righteousness unto sanctification."

One should consider that a sacrifice offered to God used to have four characteristics.

First, the offering itself needed to be whole and undamaged, as stated in Malachi 1:14, "Cursed are the deceitful who have a [healthy] male in their flock and, vowing it, instead offer a feeble one to the Lord." Therefore, the Apostle says, **Living** so that the sacrifice of our body that we offer to God is alive through faith formed in love. Galatians 2:20, "Insofar as I now live in the flesh, I live in the faith of the Son of God."

It is to be noted, however, that the natural sacrifice was first alive and then slain as an offering to show that death was still reigning in a person ruled by sin, as was noted above in Romans 5:12-21. Yet this spiritual sacrifice always lives and causes life, according to John 10:10, "I have come that they may have life, and have it more abundantly," because sin has now been removed by Christ. We might also say that the sacrifice of our body is alive to

God through the righteousness of faith but dead to the disordered desires of the flesh. Colossians 3:5, "Mortify your earthly members."

Second, the sacrifice offered to God was sanctified in the offering itself. Thus Leviticus 22:3, "Every one of your lineage in whom there is uncleanness and who approaches the sacred offerings that the children of Israel have consecrated to the Lord will perish before the Lord." Therefore, the Apostle adds, **Holy**, namely, through the devotion by which our body is given over in service to God. Leviticus 20:7, "Sanctify yourselves and be holy, for I the Lord your God am holy." Thus sanctity is properly spoken of in relation to God, inasmuch as humans do what is righteous before God.

Third, with regard to its consumption, the sacrifice was said to be sweet and acceptable to the Lord, according to Leviticus 1:9, "The priest will burn everything offered on the altar as a holocaust and a most sweet aroma for the Lord." Therefore, the Apostle here says, **Pleasing to God**, namely, through uprightness of intention. Psalm 55:13/56:13, "That I may be pleasing in God's sight, in the light of the living."

Fourth, in the preparation of the sacrifice, salt was added. Leviticus 2:13, "Whatever you offer in sacrifice, season it with salt." Mark 9:49, "Every sacrifice will be sprinkled with salt." Salt signifies the discretion of wisdom. Therefore, Colossians 4:5-6, "Conduct yourself wisely toward outsiders; let your speech always be gracious, seasoned with salt."

Therefore, the Apostle continues, **Your reasonable service**. That is, with discretion you should present your bodies as a sacrifice to God, whether through martyrdom, abstinence, or some work of righteousness. 1 Corinthians 14:40, "Let all things be done in you honorably and according to order." Psalm 98:4/99:4, "The honor of the king loves the administration of justice."

The righteous are related in one way to interior acts, by which they obey God, and in another way to exterior acts. For human goodness and righteousness consist principally in interior acts, by which people believe, hope, and love. Thus Luke 17:21, "The Reign of God is within you." It does not consist principally in exterior actions. See Romans 14:17, "The Reign of God is neither food nor drink." Therefore, interior acts are as an end sought in themselves. Exterior acts, by which bodies are presented to God, are a means to an end.

No limit is set to something sought as an end; the greater it is, the better it is. In that which is sought on account of an end, one measures the means in proportion to the end. For example, doctors heal as much as they can, but they do not give as much medicine as possible but only as much as seems to lead to health. Similarly, with regard to faith, hope, and love, no limit ought to be set; the more one believes, hopes, and loves, the better. Therefore, Deuteronomy 6:5, "Love the Lord your God," etc.

Yet, in exterior acts one should apply a discreet measure in comparison to charity. Thus, as Jerome states, "Do not rational people lose dignity who prefer fasting and vigils to bodily health so that in their singing of the Psalms and the offices they are marked by folly and gloom?"[2]

Conformity and Transformation

v. 2 Then when the Apostle says, **Do not be conformed**, etc., he shows how people should present themselves before God with regard to the soul.

First, he rejects conformity to the present age. **Do not be conformed to this age**, that is, to things that pass away in time.

The present age is a kind of measure of what slips away in time. A person is conformed to temporal things through affection, by adhering to them with love. Hosea 9:10, "They became abominable like the things they loved." James 1:27, "This is clean and undefiled religion before God, the Father: To visit the fatherless and widow in their tribulation and to keep oneself undefiled by this age." One is also conformed to this age [*saeculo*] by imitating the life of those living in a worldly way [*saeculariter*]. Ephesians 4:17, "I testify in the Lord that you should no longer walk as the gentiles walk."

Second, the Apostle calls for interior transformation of the mind [*mentis*]. **Be transformed in the renewal of your understanding**.

Reason is here called human understanding [*sensus*]; by means of it humans judge what should be done. They had this understanding, whole and flourishing, at their creation; thus Ecclesiasticus 17:6, "God filled their hearts with understanding, and showed them both good and evil." Yet this understanding is damaged by sin and has, so to speak, aged. Baruch 3:10, "You have grown old in an alien land." As a result, it has lost its elegance and beauty. Lamentations 1:6, "All her elegance has departed from the daughter of Zion."

The Apostle therefore admonishes us to be **transformed**, that is, to assume again the form and elegance of mind that it had through the grace of the Holy Spirit. People should be zealous to partake of this grace, so that those who have not yet recognized it may do so, and those who have recog-

2. Cf. Gratian, *Decrees*, 3.5.24.

nized it may make progress in it. Ephesians 4:23, "Be renewed in the spirit of your mind." Psalm 102:5/103:5, "Your youth will be renewed like the eagle's."

Or otherwise **Be renewed**, in exterior acts, **in the renewal of your understanding**, that is, through the renewal of grace that you perceived in your mind.

Third, he gives the reason for the admonition just mentioned: **So that you may prove what God's will is**.

In this regard, one ought to consider that people with a defective sense of taste lack right judgment about flavors so that they sometimes hate sweets and desire the repulsive. However, those with a healthy sense of taste have right judgment about flavors. Similarly, those with a damaged affection, as if conformed to things of this age, lack right judgment about the good. Those with an upright and healthy affection, with an understanding renewed by grace, have right judgment about the good.

Therefore, the Apostle has said, **Do not be conformed to this age, but be renewed in the renewal of your understanding, so that you may prove**, that is, know by experience — Psalm 33:9/34:8, "Taste and see that the Lord is sweet" — **what is God's will**, by which God wishes you to be saved — 1 Thessalonians 4:3, "This is God's will, your sanctification." [God's will is] **good**; that is, God wants us to desire the worthy good and urges us to it by divine precepts. Micah 6:8, "I will show you, O human, what is good and what God requires of you." [God's will is also] **pleasing** inasmuch as one is well disposed to what is delightful, which God wants us to desire. Psalm 18:9/19:8, "God's justice is right, gladdening hearts." [God's will] is not only useful for achieving the end, but also **perfect**, as if joining us to the end. Matthew 5:48, "Be perfect, as your heavenly Father is perfect." Genesis 17:1, "Walk before me and be perfect."

Therefore, they who are not conformed to this age but are transformed in renewal of their understanding experience God's will in these ways. However, they who remain in the old way, conformed to this age, consider God's will oppressive and useless, not good. Ecclesiasticus 6:21, "How harsh is your wisdom to the unlearned."

v. 3 Then when the Apostle says, "For I tell, by the grace," etc., he teaches how a person should use God's gifts.

(1) He teaches this with regard to the gifts that are not common to all, such as gratuitous grace,[3] and (2) with regard to the gift of charity that is

---

3. For a discussion of gratuitous grace, see ST I-II.111, in which Thomas distinguishes

common to all, and this where he says, "Let love be without falsehood," etc. (Rom 12:9).

Concerning the first, [the gifts not common to all,] he does two things. (1) He teaches in general how one should use gratuitous grace. (2) He identifies the elements of gratuitous grace, "Having different gifts" (Rom 12:6).

Concerning the first, [the teaching about the general use of gratuitous grace,] he does two things. (1) He sets forth his teaching. (2) Second, he offers the reason for it where he writes, "For just as in one body," etc. (Rom 12:4).

With regard to the first, [the teaching,] he does three things.

First, he excludes the unnecessary when he says, I have admonished you to be "transformed in the renewal of your understanding," which you ought to do in moderation. **For I say**, that is, I direct **by the grace** of the apostolic office and authority **given to me**. Galatians 2:9, "When they had recognized the grace given to me among the gentiles," etc. Ephesians 3:8, "This grace was given to me, the least of all the saints," etc. for **all who are among you** because this is useful for all. 1 Corinthians 7:7, "I want all people to be as I am."

I direct you **not to be wiser than you should be**. That is, none, trusting in their understanding or wisdom, should presume beyond their measure. Ecclesiastes 7:16, "Be no wiser than necessary." Psalm 130:1/131:1, "I have busied myself neither in great matters nor in wonderful things beyond me."

Second, he exhorts to moderation, **Be wise in sobriety**. That is, I direct you to be wise commensurate with the grace given to you. For sobriety implies measure. Although this term is properly used about drinking wine, it can nevertheless be used concerning any matter in which a person observes proper measure. Titus 2:12, "Let us live soberly, justly, and devoutly in this age."

Third, he teaches on what basis one should receive the measure of moderation. **And so, God has divided**, that is, distributed, **to each a measure of faith**, that is, a measure of God's gifts ordered to the building up of faith. 1 Corinthians 12:7, "To each a manifestation of the spirit is given for some benefit."

For God gives gifts of this sort, not the same to all, but God distributes different gifts to different people, according to 1 Corinthians 12:4, "There are varieties of graces." God does not give to all equally but to each on the basis of a certain measure. Ephesians 4:7, "Grace has been given to each of us according to the measure of Christ's giving." Therefore, the Apostle was so-

---

it from sanctifying grace. The latter, sanctifying grace, directly ordains the human to union with God. The former is the means — through prophecy, miracles, or other people — by which someone is united to God.

berly wise according to this measure when he stated in 2 Corinthians 10:13, "Let us not glory beyond measure, but according to the measure of the rule God has measured to us." To Christ alone is given the Spirit, without measure, as indicated in John 3:34.

God not only gives to others gratuitous grace but also gives in measure the faith that works through love. Thus the disciples told Christ in Luke 17:5, "O Lord, increase our faith!"

LECTURE 2

The Mystical Body

v. 4 Having admonished above about the use of grace, the Apostle here assigns the reason for this teaching, and it is based on the resemblance of the mystical body to the natural body. Concerning the natural body, he makes three points. He asserts, first, the unity of the body, **For just as in one body**, and, second, the plurality of its members, **we have many members**. For the living human body consists of a diversity of members. Third, he asserts the diversity of duties, **But all members do not perform the same function**. For the diversity of members would be meaningless unless they were appointed to diverse functions.

The Apostle then adapts these three points to the mystical body of Christ, the Church. Ephesians 1:22, "God made Christ head over the whole Church, which is his body."

v. 5 Here also he makes three points. First, he indicates the multitude of the faithful, like the multitude of a body's members, **Thus we many**. Luke 14:16, "A certain person made a great meal and invited many." Isaiah 54:1, "Many are the children of the deserted wife."

Although the faithful are relatively few in comparison to the fruitless multitude of the condemned according to Matthew 7:14, "Narrow is the way that leads to life, and few find it," nevertheless, absolutely speaking, they are many. Revelation 7:9, "After this I saw a great crowd that no one could count."

Second, he touches on the unity of the mystical body. **We are one body** (Rom 12:4). Ephesians 2:16, "So that he might reconcile both in one body," etc.

The unity of this mystical body, through which we are united together with God in faith and the fervor of charity, is spiritual. Ephesians 4:4, "One body and one spirit." Because the spirit of unity comes from Christ to us —

Romans 8:9, "If they do not have the Spirit of Christ, they are not his" — the Apostle adds **in Christ**, who by his Spirit, which he gives us, unites us together also in God. John 17:11, "That they may be one in us, as we are one."

Third, he touches on the diversity of duties, a diversity rooted in the general welfare, **individually members of one another**.

Each member has its own function and power. Insofar as one member profits another by its power and function, it is said to be a member of the other. For example, the foot is said to be a member of the eye inasmuch as it transports the eye, and the eye is said to be a member of the foot inasmuch as it directs the foot. 1 Corinthians 12:21, "The eye cannot say to the hand, 'I do not need your help.'"

So also in the mystical body, one who has received the grace of prophecy needs another with the grace of healing, and so it is for the rest. Therefore, when the faithful, according to the grace given to them, serve another, they are made members of the other. Galatians 6:2, "Bear one another's burdens." 1 Peter 4:10, "Each has received grace to assist another."

v. 6 Then when the Apostle says, **Having different gifts**, he develops in detail his admonition about the sober and moderate use of grace. First, he posits the diversity of graces. "We are," I say, "members one of another" (Rom 12:5), not due to the same grace but **having** a range of **different gifts**, not from a diversity of merits but **due to the grace** given to us. 1 Corinthians 7:7, "All have their particular gift from God, one in this way and another in that." Matthew 25:14-15, "He called his servants and handed over his goods to them; to one he gave five talents, to another two, and to another one."

Second, he teaches the use of diverse graces, and he does so first with regard to the knowledge of divine matters. **If we have prophecy**, we use it **according to the rule of faith**.

Yet it is said that prophecy is a kind of apparition from divine revelation of things that are remote. Thus 1 Samuel 9:9, "They who are called prophets today were once called seers." There are some things remote from our knowledge in themselves, such as future contingents, which are not knowable due to a lack in their being. However, divine matters are remote from our knowledge, not in themselves, since they are utterly knowable, as 1 John 1:5 indicates: "God is light; in God there is no darkness at all." They are remote because of a lack in our intellect, which relates to those things that in themselves are most manifest in the same way that an eye, accustomed to the dark, relates to the sun. Something is more properly said to be this or that because it is so on its own rather than it is so in relation to something else.

Thus it is that future contingents are more properly said to be remote from our knowledge. Therefore, prophecy is particularly of these things. Amos 3:7, "The Lord God will do nothing without revealing divine secrets [to the prophets]." Nevertheless, prophecy is also commonly said to be a revelation of any secrets.

This gift of prophecy was found not only in the Old Testament but also in the New. Joel 2:28, "I will pour out my spirit on all flesh; and your children will prophesy." Those who explain prophetic discourse are also called prophets in the New Testament because sacred scripture is interpreted in the same spirit in which it was produced. Ecclesiasticus 24:33, "I will still pour out doctrine as prophecy."

Yet, also like other gratuitous graces, the gift of prophecy is ordered to the building up of faith. 1 Corinthians 12:7, "To each a manifestation of the Spirit is given for some benefit." Hebrews 2:3-4, the teaching of faith "has been confirmed by God's testimony through signs, wonders, and various miracles, and by distributions of gifts of the Holy Spirit." Therefore, prophecy is to be used **according to the rule of faith**, that is, not in vain and not against faith but so that through it faith might be confirmed. Thus Deuteronomy 13:2-3, "If a prophet should arise in your midst and say to you, 'Let us go and follow alien gods,' do not listen to the words of this prophet" because they oppose the rule of faith.

v. 7 With regard to administering sacraments, he adds, **Or if ministry, in ministering**. That is, if any have received the grace or office of ministry, such as a bishop or priest who are called ministers of God — Isaiah 61:6, "You will be called priests of the Lord; to you it will be said, 'You ministers of our God'" — let them carry it out diligently **in ministering**. 2 Timothy 4:5, "Fulfill your ministry."

Second, he touches on what pertains to human affairs in which one person can assist another. First, he addresses knowledge, whether speculative or practical.

About speculative knowledge, he says, **Or if they teach** [*docet*], that is, have the duty or grace of teaching, let them use **doctrine** [*doctrina*], so that they teach eagerly and faithfully. Job 4:3, "Behold, you have taught many." Matthew 28:19, "Go forth and teach all nations."[4]

---

4. Thomas is playing on the Latin word *doceo* in this paragraph. The variations of "teach" all come from the Latin word *doceo,* from which the word "doctrine" *(doctrina)* also derives.

v. 8 Concerning practical knowledge, he adds, **They who exhort**, that is, who have the duty or grace of exhorting people to the good, let them use it **in exhorting**. 1 Thessalonians 2:3, "Our exhortation was not from error, impurity nor deceit." Titus 2:15, "Speak these things, and exhort."

Then he posits what pertains to exterior works in which at times one assists another by bestowing some gift. In this regard, he says, **They who give**, that is, who have the means and grace to give, should do so **in simplicity**. One, therefore, should not intend evil with this and, with gifts, entice people to evil, nor should one with a small gift intend to acquire something much greater. Ecclesiasticus 20:14-15/13-14, "Fools' gifts will do you no good, for their one gift in their eyes is equal to seven. They will give little and criticize much." Also, Proverbs 11:3, "The simplicity of the righteous guides them."

Sometimes one assists others by caring for them. In this regard, the Apostle says, **They who rule**, that is, those established in the office of prelate, should use that office **with care**. Hebrews 13:17, "Obey your leaders, and be subject to them. For they keep watch and will have to account for your souls." 2 Corinthians 11:28, "Apart from those things, there is the daily urgency of my concern for all the churches."

Sometimes one assists others by relieving their misery. In this regard, he says, **They who have mercy**, that is, who have the means and disposition to be merciful, should carry it out **in cheerfulness**, as if doing it freely. 2 Corinthians 9:7, "Not from sadness or from necessity. For God loves the cheerful giver." Ecclesiasticus 35:9, "In every gift, show a cheerful expression."

v. 9 Then when the Apostle says, "Love without deceit," etc., he teaches the use of the gratuitous gift that is common to all, namely, that of charity. He sets forth (1) what pertains to charity in general and (2) what pertains to love for certain people, "the needs of the saints," etc. (Rom 12:13).

Concerning the first, what pertains to charity in general, he does three things. (1) He shows how the love of charity should be in the one who loves.[5] (2) He shows how it should relate to one's neighbor, "With the charity of brothers and sisters," etc. (Rom 12:10). (3) He shows how it should relate to God, "With care, not sloth," etc. (Rom 12:11).

---

5. The "love of charity" *(dilectio caritatis)* is a particular kind of love for God. It considers God as the beatific goal and extends to other humans and even other creatures insofar as they are loved for God's sake. In contrast, the "natural love" *(dilectio naturalis)* of God flows from knowledge of God as the source and support for every natural good. See ST I.60.5 ad 4; II-II.25.

The Quality of Love

Regarding the quality of charity [i.e., how it is in the one who loves], the Apostle teaches three things.

First, love should be true. Therefore, he states, **Love without deceit** so that it exists not only in word and outward appearance but also in true affection of the heart and in effectiveness of deed. 1 John 3:18, "Let us love, not in word or speech, but in deed and truth." Ecclesiasticus 6:15, "Nothing compares to a faithful friend."

Second, he teaches that love should be pure when he states, **Hating evil**. Love is pure when people do not conspire with their friends for evil but so love people that they hate their vice. Therefore, he says in 1 Corinthians 13:6, "Charity does not rejoice in injustice, but rejoices with the truth." Psalm 118:113/119:113, "I hated the unjust."

Third, he teaches that love should be upright when he says, **Adhering to the good**, so that someone adheres to others because of their virtuous goodness. Galatians 4:18, "Always emulate the good in what is good." This is the noble love of which Ecclesiasticus 24:24 speaks, "I am the mother of noble love."

v. 10 Then with the words **fraternal charity**, the Apostle shows how charity should relate to a neighbor.

First, with regard to interior disposition, he says, **Loving one another with fraternal charity**. We love not only others in charity but also the charity itself by which we love them and are loved by them. For if we hold charity as precious, we will not allow it to be easily destroyed. Hebrews 13:1, "Let fraternal charity endure in you." Song of Songs 8:7, "If people give all their household's wealth for love, they will despise it as nothing."

Second, with regard to outward effect, he says, **Anticipating one another in honor**. He designates three things here.

First, people should hold their neighbors in reverence, which is the reason for honor. For people cannot truly love another whom they look down upon. Philippians 2:3, "In humility, let all esteem others above themselves." This occurs when people consider their own failings and their neighbors' goodness. Yet honor involves not only reverence but also assistance with necessities. Exodus 20:12, "Honor your father and your mother," commands assistance with necessities, as is clear when the Lord in Matthew 15:3-9 accused the Pharisees of hindering children from assisting their parents, contrary to this commandment.

Second, he designates that the effect of love should be shown mutually so that someone wishes not only to receive kindness but also to show it. Ecclesiasticus 4:31, "Do not let your hand be open to receiving and closed to giving," and Ecclesiasticus 14:15-16, "In dividing money, both give and receive." He indicates this when he says, **One another**.

Third, he designates that effects of love should be eagerness and speed. He does so with the word **anticipating** so that someone should anticipate a friend with kindness. Ecclesiasticus 37:1, "Every friend will say, 'I am also bound in friendship.'"

v. 11 Then when he says, **With care**, etc., he shows how the love of charity should relate to God.

First, he mentions the attentiveness of mind when he says, Serve God **with care** [*sollicitudine*], **not sloth**. Micah 6:8, "I will show you, O people, what is good, and what God requires of you." Later he adds, "Walk carefully [*sollicite*] with your God." 2 Timothy 2:15, "Take care to show yourself as acceptable to God."

Second, [he shows how love of charity relates to God] regarding its effect when he says, Be **fervent in spirit**, that is, in the love of God.

Yet fervor results from an abundance of heat, and so it is called fervor of spirit when, because of the abundance of divine love, the whole person burns with God. In Acts 18:25, it is said that Apollos was speaking, fervent in spirit. 1 Thessalonians 5:19, "Do not extinguish the spirit."

Third, [he shows how it relates to God] with regard to outward obedience when he says, **Serving the Lord** with the service of worship, which is owed to God alone.[6] Deuteronomy 6:13, "You will honor the Lord your God, and you will serve the Lord alone." Psalm 2:11, "Serve the Lord in fear."

Another text states, **Serving in time**, so that we might serve God at the right time. Ecclesiastes 8:6 states, "There is a time and opportunity for everything."

v. 12 Fourth, [he shows how it relates to God] with regard to the reward of service when he says, **Rejoicing in hope**, namely, of a reward, which is the enjoyment of God. Genesis 15:1, "I am the Lord, and your reward will be exceedingly great." Romans 5:2, "Let us glory in the hope of the glory of the children of God." Hope causes a person to rejoice because of certitude, yet it afflicts because of delay. Proverbs 13:12, "Hope deferred afflicts the soul."

---

6. Worship here translates *latreia*, which, along with *dylia*, distinguishes different kinds of honor or reverence. The former designates the reverence owed to God, while the latter points to the honor properly owed to particular creatures. See ST II-II.84.1 and 103.3.

Fifth, [he shows how it relates to God] with regard to the difficulty a person suffers in the service of God. Thus he adds, Be **patient in the tribulation** that you endure for God. Romans 5:3, "Tribulation produces patience."

Sixth, with regard to all that has preceded, the Apostle says, **Persevering in prayer**, by which he means constancy in prayer. Luke 18:1, "We should pray always and not grow weary." 1 Thessalonians 5:17, "Pray without ceasing."

Through prayer, care is stirred up in us; fervor is enkindled; we are urged to serve God; the joy of hope is strengthened in us; and we are promised help in our tribulation. Psalm 119:1/120:1, "I called to the Lord in my tribulation, and the Lord heard me."

Then, beginning with the words, "needs of the saints," etc. (Rom 12:13), the Apostle defines charity with regard to particular persons, that is, (1) the poor and (2) enemies: "Bless those who persecute you" (Rom 12:14).

Concerning the poor, he does two things.

v. 13 First, he presents the benefits of charity to the needy in general when he says, **Share in the needs of the saints**. Three things should be noted here. First, alms should be given out of charity to the poor or those suffering need. Ephesians 4:28, "Let them labor, working with their hands, at what is good so that they might have the means by which to give to those suffering need."

Next, it is preferable to assist the righteous and saints rather than others. Thus he speaks of the **needs of the saints**. Ecclesiasticus 12:5, "Give to the righteous, and refuse the sinner." One should understand that even sinners should be assisted with their needs but not so that they are assisted in the spark to sin. Nevertheless, it is more useful to assist the righteous because such alms are fruitful not only for the donor but also due to the prayer of the recipient. Luke 16:9, "Make friends for yourselves with dishonest wealth so that when it fails, they may receive you into eternal dwellings," namely, with their prayer.

Second, in particular, he encourages hospitality, **Pursuing hospitality**. In this work of mercy are included other works of mercy. For hosts not only offer their houses for shelter but also furnish other necessities. Hebrews 13:2, "Do not forget hospitality." 1 Peter 4:9, "Be hospitable toward one another without complaining."

LECTURE 3

v. 14 Above, the Apostle explains how charity ought to be shown to the needy, and here how it should be shown even to enemies.

(1) He sets forth an admonition. (2) He proves what he has said beginning with the words, "For it has been written," etc. (Rom 12:19).

Regarding the admonition, consider that three things pertain to charity. First, benevolence, which consists in desiring good and not evil for another; second, harmony, which consists in desiring good and not evil for friends; third, kindness [*beneficentia*], which consists in doing good and not harming those whom one loves.

(1) Therefore, he sets forth what pertains to benevolence; (2) to harmony where he says, "Rejoice with those who rejoice" (Rom 12:15); and (3) to kindness where he says, "To no one evil," etc. (Rom 12:17).

Benevolence

Concerning benevolence, the Apostle does two things.

First, he advises that it should be ample so that it extends even to enemies, **Bless those who persecute you.**

One should note that to bless [*benedicere*] means to assert the good [*bonum dicere*]. One comes to assert the good in three ways. First, one does so by revealing, such as when one praises the good points of another. Ecclesiasticus 31:23, "The lips of many will bless those who are generous with their bread and whose testimony of the truth is faithful."

In another way, [one asserts the good] by commanding. To bless by authority is proper to God by whose command the good is directed to creatures. Yet ministry extends to God's ministers who invoke the Lord's name upon the people. Numbers 6:23-26, "Thus you will bless the children of Israel, and you will say to them, 'May the Lord bless you and keep you. May the Lord's face shine on you, and be merciful to you. May the Lord's face turn to you, and give you peace.'" And later in Numbers 6:27, "They will invoke my name upon the children of Israel, and I will bless them."

Third, some bless by desiring. Psalm 128:8/129:8, "They who passed by did not say, 'The blessing of the Lord be upon you!'" According to this text, to bless is to wish good for someone, as if to beseech the good for another. Blessing is understood in this way here.

When the Apostle says, **Bless those who persecute you**, he means that we owe benevolence even to enemies and persecutors by desiring good things and praying for them. Matthew 5:44, "Love your enemies and pray for those who persecute you and accuse you falsely."

The text, **Bless those who persecute you**, is in one sense a commandment and in another a counsel.[7] If, in general, people direct the affect of love to enemies by not excluding them from the universal love of neighbor and from the universal prayer that they make for the faithful, this text concerns a commandment. Similarly, if people in a particular circumstance direct the affect of love to an enemy in a moment of need, this text concerns a commandment. Exodus 23:4, "If you meet your enemies' ox or ass going astray, return it to them."

Yet, if sometimes, beyond a situation of manifest need, people present the affect of love and the assent of prayer or the benefit of whatever kind of assistance to an enemy, this text concerns the perfection of the counsels. Through such an act is shown such perfect human charity toward God that it entirely surpasses every human hatred. Yet they who do penance and seek mercy are no longer counted among enemies and persecutors. Therefore, signs of charity should be shown to them without any difficulty. Ecclesiasticus 28:2, "Forgive your neighbors if they hurt you, and then your sins will be forgiven when you pray."

Second, the Apostle teaches that benevolence or blessing should be pure, that is, without anything contrary mixed in. Therefore, he says, **Bless, and do not curse**. That is, you should bless what you should in no way curse. This text opposes those who bless with their mouth but curse in their heart. Psalm 27:3/28:3, "They who speak words of peace to their neighbor, but have evil in their hearts." It also opposes those who sometimes bless and sometimes curse, or who bless some and curse others. James 3:10, "From the same mouth proceed both blessing and curse. This should not be so." 1 Peter 3:9, "Do not repay a curse with a curse."

On the other hand, sacred Scripture seems to contain many curses. For example, Deuteronomy 27:26, "Accursed is the one who does not abide by the words of this law nor carry them out in action."

In response, one ought to say that to curse [*maledicere*] is to assert evil [*malum dicere*]. As with blessing, this happens in three ways, by revealing, commanding, and desiring. Any of these three can be for good or evil.[8]

For if what is materially evil is called evil in any of these three ways and for a good purpose, this is not illicit. It is to bless instead of to curse. Each

---

7. On the distinction between a counsel and a commandment, see ST I-II.108.4. ". . . commandments of the New Law have been given about matters that are necessary to gain the end of eternal bliss. . . . [T]he counsels are about matters that render the gaining of this end more assured and expeditious."

8. Thomas devotes an entire question in the *Summa* to cursing, ST II-II.76.

thing is judged more according to its form than its matter. If indeed people speak for an evil purpose, they curse formally. This is entirely illicit.

In both of these, someone communicates evil by revealing it[; in one case, it is licit, while in the other it is not].

Sometimes one reveals evil about someone to make known a necessary truth and so speaks of evil out of real necessity. This is good and so licit. In this way, Job in Job 3:1 and following cursed the day he was born by revealing the wickedness of the present life. As the Apostle says in Ephesians 5:16, "Redeeming the time because the days are evil."

Yet sometimes one reveals evil about another for an evil purpose, with the intention of insulting. This is illicit. As 1 Corinthians 6:10 states, "Neither slanderers nor thieves will possess the kingdom of God."

Likewise, even when people speak evil by commanding, it can happen at times that they say what is materially evil for a good purpose, such as when the evil of punishment is justly meted out by someone's command; this is indeed licit. In this way, lawbreakers are cursed; that is, punishments are justly assigned.

Sometimes, indeed, someone unjustly speaks evil of another by commanding, such as on account of hate and revenge. Such cursing is illicit. Exodus 21:17, "They who curse mother or father should be put to death."

The same holds for someone who speaks evil by desiring it. If someone were to desire evil for a good purpose — so that, for example, through adversity someone may make spiritual progress — this is licit. Job 5:3, "I have seen a fool firmly rooted [like a stately tree] and immediately cursed his beauty."

If, indeed, a person did this for hate or revenge, it is entirely illicit. 1 Samuel 17:43, "The Philistine cursed David by his gods."

Harmony

v. 15 Then when the Apostle says, "Rejoice with those who rejoice," etc., he sets forth what pertains to harmony.

(1) He gives examples of harmony. (2) He removes obstacles to it where he says, "Not minding high things," etc. (Rom 12:16).

Harmony can be understood in two ways, first, with regard to its effect in good and bad situations. In good situations, one rejoices in others' goods. Thus the Apostle says, **Rejoice**, that is, you should rejoice **with those who rejoice**. Philippians 2:17, "I rejoice and congratulate all of you." This ought to be understood about someone who rejoices about the good. However, there are some who rejoice about evil, according to Proverbs 2:14, "They are glad when they have done evil, and they exult in the worst things." One should not rejoice with these. 1 Corinthians 13:6 speaks about charity: "It does not rejoice over iniquity, but with the truth."

In evil situations, one should be saddened about another's evils, and so the Apostle adds, **Weep**, that is, you should weep **with those who weep**. Job 30:25, "I wept for the afflicted." Ecclesiasticus 7:34, "Do not fail to console those who weep, and walk with those who mourn."

The compassion of an empathetic friend brings consolation in two ways. First, from this is deduced convincing proof of friendship. Ecclesiasticus 12:9, "Friends are known in their adversity," that is, in misfortune. It is indeed delightful to know that someone is a true friend. In another way, when friends empathize, they also seem to offer themselves to help carry the weight of adversity that causes sadness. Indeed, something is lighter if it is carried by many rather than by one alone.

v. 16 Second, harmony consists in unity of opinion [*sententiae*], and in this regard the Apostle states, **Be of one mind** [*sentientes*], that is, be the same **toward one another**, so that you unite around the same opinion. 1 Corinthians 1:10, "Be perfect with the same mind and with the same opinion." Philippians 2:2, "Complete my joy by having the same charity, being of one accord, and having the same opinions."

One should know that opinion is twofold. One is intellectual judgment concerning speculative things, such as geometrical or natural considerations. To dissent in such matters is not antithetical to friendship or charity because charity is in the will. Judgments of this sort proceed not from the will but from the necessity of reason.

Another kind pertains to the judgment of reason about action. In such matters, dissent is contrary to friendship because such dissent involves contrariety of will. Because faith is not only speculative but also practical, inasmuch as it works through love, as Galatians 5:6 states ["faith works by charity"], to dissent from right faith is contrary to charity.

Then when the Apostle says, **Do not be haughty**, etc., he excludes two obstacles to harmony.

The first is pride, by which people inordinately seek their own distinction and avoid subjection while wishing to subject others and obstruct their distinction. From this results discord. Proverbs 13:10, "There are always quarrels among the proud." Therefore, to remove this he exhorts not to **be haughty**, so that you do not inordinately desire your own distinction. See Romans 11:20, "Be not haughty, but fear." Ecclesiasticus 3:21, "Do not seek what is higher than you." Instead, **Associate with the humble** [*humilibus*], that is, with what is lowly [*humilia*]. That is, do not, as appropriate, reject what seems abandoned. Psalm 83:11/84:10, "I have chosen to be wretched in the house of my God." 1 Peter 5:6, "Be humbled under the mighty hand of God," etc.

The second obstacle to harmony is presumption of wisdom or also of prudence, by which someone doubts the opinion of others. To remove this obstacle, the Apostle states, **Do not be prudent in your own estimation**, so that you judge as prudent only what seems so to you. Isaiah 5:21, "Woe to you who are wise in your own eyes, and prudent in your own estimation." See above, Romans 11:25, "lest you be wise in your own estimation."

v. 17 Then when the Apostle says, "Do not repay anyone evil for evil," etc., he teaches what pertains to kindness by excluding the contrary. (1) He teaches that one should not do evil out of vengeance. (2) He teaches that one should not do evil to another for the sake of defense, "Do not defend yourselves" (Rom 12:19).

Love of Neighbor and Enemy

Concerning the first [vengeance], he does three things. First, he forbids it. You should **not repay anyone evil for evil**. Psalm 7:5-6/7:4-5, "If I have repaid those doing evil to me, let me fall before my enemies." 1 Peter 3:9, "Do not return evil for evil."

This should be understood formally as cursing was above. For we are forbidden from returning evil for evil out of hatred or envy so that we delight in another's misfortune. Yet if, for the evil of an offense that people commit, judges justly return the evil of punishment to compensate for the malice, they introduce evil materially. Yet formally and intrinsically they introduce a good. Thus, when judges hang a thief for murder, they do not return evil for evil but rather good for evil. In this way, the Apostle handed over someone for the sin of incest "to Satan for the destruction of the flesh so that his spirit may be saved," as 1 Corinthians 5:5 states.

Second, he teaches that goods should also be furnished to neighbors. You should **be concerned for what is good not only before God**, out of an interest to satisfy for your conscience before God, **but also before all people** to do what is pleasing to people. 1 Corinthians 10:32-33, "Be without offense to Jews, gentiles, and to the church of God, just as I also please all people in all things." 2 Corinthians 8:21, "Be concerned for what is good not only before God but also before all people."

This happens for both good and bad reasons. If this is done for human favor, it is done for the wrong reason. Matthew 6:1, "Take care lest you perform your righteous works before people for them to see you." But if it is done for the glory of God, it is done for the right reason, according to Matthew 5:16, "In the same way, let your light shine before people, that they may see your good works and glorify your Father in heaven."

v. 18 Third, the Apostle assigns the reason behind both sayings. We should refrain from doing evil and be concerned for what is good before people to be at peace with them. Therefore, he adds, **Be at peace with all people**. Hebrews 12:14, "Pursue peace with all."

Here he adds two reasons. The first is, **If possible**. For sometimes the malice of others prevents us from being at peace with them, for peace is impossible with them unless one consents to their malice, which is obviously an illicit peace. Therefore, the Lord says in Matthew 10:34, "I came not to bring peace but the sword."

He also adds, **As much as is in you**. That is, even if they act against peace, we should do what is in us to obtain their peace. Psalm 119:7/120:6-7, "I was peaceful with those who hated peace." And again Psalm 33:15/34:14, "Seek peace and pursue it."

v. 19 Then when the Apostle says, **Do not defend yourselves**, etc., he shows that evils are not to be inflicted on neighbors by way of defense.

First, he gives an example. You should **not defend yourselves**, O beloved, as Isaiah 50:6 states about Christ, "I gave my body to those who struck me, and my cheeks to those who plucked them." And Isaiah 53:7, "He was silent like a lamb before its shearer," etc. So also the Lord himself commanded in Matthew 5:39, "If any strike you on one cheek, offer them also the other."

Yet, as Augustine indicates in *On Lying*, those things done by saints in the New Testament serve as examples for understanding what in Scripture are given as precepts.[9] For when the Lord himself was struck with a blow, he did not say, "Behold the other cheek," but "If I have spoken evil, testify to the evil; however, if well, why do you strike me?" (Jn 18:23). Here he shows that one must prepare in the heart to offer the other cheek. For the sake of human

---

9. Augustine, *On Lying*, 15.26-27, CSEL 41:446-48.

salvation, the Lord was prepared not only to be struck on the other cheek but to be crucified in his entire body. As Augustine states in his letter to Marcellinus, the commandment works correctly when people believe it benefits those for whom it works to produce in them amendment and harmony, even if another result follows.[10] These precepts concerning patience should always be held in readiness in the heart, and that kindness which prevents returning evil for evil should always be fulfilled in the will. Yet, many things should also be done with the unwilling to correct them with a kind of benevolent severity.

Second, the Apostle assigns the reason for the admonition, "Do not defend yourselves," when he says, **but leave room for wrath**, that is, for divine judgment. It is as if he said, Commit yourselves to God, who can defend and avenge you with divine judgment. According to 1 Peter 5:7, "Cast your every concern upon God, who cares for you."

These words are to be understood about a situation in which we otherwise lack the ability to act justly. As Deuteronomy 1:17 states, "Judgment is the Lord's." When people by a judge's authority either seek vengeance to suppress wickedness — and not out of hatred — or obtain their defense by the authority of some superior, they are understood to **leave room for wrath**, that is, for divine judgment whose ministers are princes, as noted below in Romans 13:4. Even Paul obtained for himself armed men to defend against Jewish plots, as described in Acts 23:12-35.

v. 20 Then when the Apostle says, "As it is written," etc., he proves what he said. (1) He does so by means of scriptural authority and (2) by means of reason: "Do not be conquered by evil," etc. (Rom 12:21).

Concerning the first he does two things. First, he proves that vengeance is forbidden. It has been said, "Leave room for wrath," that is, for divine judgment. **For it is written**, in Deuteronomy 32:35, **"Vengeance is mine."** That is, reserve it for me, and **"I will repay, says the Lord."**

Our text has the following, **"Revenge is mine, and I will repay them in time."** Psalm 93:1/94:1, "The Lord, a God of revenge." Nahum 1:2, "The Lord is a jealous and avenging God."

Second, he proves by means of scriptural authority what has been said about showing kindness to enemies.

This authority first offers an example about enemies in their moment of need, and this carries the necessity of a precept, as noted above. Thus, **"if**

---

10. Augustine, Letter 138.2.11, 14, CSEL 44:136-41.

your enemies are hungry, feed them; if they thirst, give them drink." Matthew 5:44, "Do good to those who hate you."

Second, he assigns the reason, **"For in doing so, you will heap burning coals on their head."** In one way, this can be seen as evil. If you do good to them, they will turn your good to evil because they will incur the consuming eternal fire due to their ingratitude. Yet this sense is repugnant to charity. Indeed, one would oppose charity who assisted people in order that things turned out ill for them.

Therefore, let us interpret it as good so that this is the sense, **"For in doing so,"** that is, helping them in their need, **"burning coals"** — that is, the love of charity spoken of in Song of Songs 8:6, "Its lamps are fire and flames" — **"you will heap,"** that is, you will concentrate, **"on their heads,"** that is, on their minds. As Augustine states in *On the Catechizing of the Uninstructed,* "There is no greater spark to love than to anticipate in loving. For they have a hard heart indeed who not only refuse love but refuse to respond to it."[11]

v. 21 Then with the words, **Do not be conquered by evil**, etc., he proves, through reason, what he has asserted.

It is natural for a person to want to conquer and not be conquered by an adversary. Yet one thing is conquered by another when the former is drawn to the latter. For example, water is conquered by fire when it is drawn to the heat of the fire. If, therefore, good people, due to evil inflicted on them by others, are drawn to do evil, good is conquered by evil. On the contrary, if out of kindness the good show to persecutors good people draw them to their love, the good conquer evil.

The Apostle states, therefore, **Do not be conquered by [the] evil** of those who persecute you that you might in turn persecute them. Instead, **conquer** their **evil by** your **good** so that by doing good to them you draw them from evil. 1 John 5:4, "Our faith is the victory that conquers the world." Jeremiah 15:19, "They will be converted to you, and you will not be converted to them."

---

11. Augustine, *Instructing Beginners in the Faith,* 4.7, CCSL 46:127.

ROMANS 13

Nicholas of Lyra

The Christian and the State

v. 1 Let every person. After the apostle instructs the Romans about customs generally, here he does the same specifically. First, he instructs those who are inferior and, second, in the following chapter those who are superior. The first chapter he divides into three parts because, first, he notes that those who are inferior must be subject to those who are their superiors; second, they must render assistance, at the place, **Therefore one must be subject** (Rom 13:5); third, they must love, at the place, **Owe no one anything** (Rom 13:8). He proves the obedience of inferiors in two ways. He does so, first, based on the divine decree that holds that it is good to obey and evil to resist. This is indeed a divine decree because those who are superior rule the inferior, and those who are inferior obey them, as is evident in the natural body. The elements are governed by the influence of the celestial bodies, as the Philosopher says in *Meteorology,* so that the motion of the stars rules the elements and governs from there the lesser powers.[1] Similarly, this is evident in the spiritual world because the lower angels are ruled and illumined by the higher, and thus it ought to be among humans, as he says, **Let every person**. That is, every person must be wholly governed by the more worthy part. **[Let every person] be subject to the governing authorities**, to the prelates in spiritual affairs and the earthly princes in temporal affairs, and he pro-

---

1. Cf. Thomas Aquinas's *Commentary on Aristotle's Meteorology,* Book 1 Lecture 2.13.

vides the reason. **For there is no [other] authority** granted or ordained; the rest is clear from what has been said to this point.

v. 2 Therefore they who resist . . . will incur judgment, whence the Savior says, in Luke 10:16, "They who reject you reject me." The same applies in temporal affairs in which people are punished in body or in material possessions. Next he proves the proposition from the perspective of superiors through whom evils are repressed insofar as the evil are fearful of punishment, and thus evil is deterred. This is what is said:

v. 3 For rulers are not a terror to good conduct, that is, to good work, because just as by their offices they restrain the evil, they also promote the good. Their intention ought to be that their subjects do good, as is clear to this place.

v. 4 For they do not bear the sword in vain. For the temporal power carries the material sword of the Lord, the ecclesiastical power the spiritual. The Apostle supplies the reason: **They are the servants of God**, to punish the one who does evil.

v. 5 Therefore one must be subject. He shows that the inferior ought to be subject to their superiors according to the condition of their status because no soldiers pay their own wages (1 Cor 9:17), and this is what is said, **Therefore**, by attending to superiors, **one must be subject**, by paying what you owe, **not only to avoid God's wrath**, to avoid punishment, **but also for the sake of conscience**, because one remembers to pay what is owed. He explains this in more detail, saying,

v. 6 For the same reason you also pay taxes; for this they are instituted. **For the authorities are ministers of God** because they are administrators of justice. **They attend to this very thing**, to God and to all persons preserving the republic. Therefore he concludes,

v. 7 Pay to all, to the princes, **what is due them**. This is a tax which is paid for the whole country. **Pay revenue to whom revenue is due**. This payment is a kind of toll, and it is paid by an individual person because not everyone has to pay such things. They must be rendered to toll keepers who commonly accept them for such a purpose. **Pay respect**, namely, to the lord **to whom** [respect is due]. [Pay honor] to the virtuous and dignified who are the custodians of virtue [**to whom honor is due**].

Love Fulfills the Law

v. 8 Owe no one anything. Here he shows that the inferior should love those above them. First, he demonstrates the proposition; second, love should be shown especially at the time of the new law. **Besides, you know what hour it is** (Rom 13:11). Concerning the first he says, **Owe no one anything, except to love one another.** He holds this with respect to this special debt that, however much it has been paid in the past or present, it must still be paid in the future.

v. 9 For one who loves the neighbor has fulfilled the law. For all of the Ten Commandments are instituted for the act of loving. The precepts of the first table are instituted to love God, and the precepts of the second table for the love of neighbor, the first of which is "Honor your father," etc. (Exod 20:12). The precepts of the second table teach us to return what is owed to every neighbor, though the others mentioned are negative; they instruct by way of warning what to avoid.

v. 10 Love does no wrong to a neighbor, that is, the Apostle warns us to do no harm to the neighbor. **Therefore, the fulfilling of the law,** that is, its full observation, **is love,** because it is loving God above all things and loving the neighbor as oneself.

The Imminence of Christ's Second Coming

v. 11 And besides this, you know what hour it is. Here as a result he shows that this debt ought especially to be paid in the time of the new law, which is the law of love just as the old law was the law of fear. Therefore he says, **And besides this, you know what hour it is,** that is, the condition of the new law. **It is now the moment for you to wake from sleep,** that is, from ease to works of love, because, as Gregory says: "The proof of love is in the works. Where love exists, it works great things. But when it ceases to act, it ceases to exist."[2] **For now is salvation,** that is, the time of grace, **nearer to us,** because through Christ salvation begins and opens what was closed in the time of the Law. Moreover, he adds, [**Salvation is nearer to us now**] **than when we first believed,** and it was nearer at the time of the Apostle than before the coming

2. A saying attributed to Gregory the Great.

of Christ. For then the patriarchs knew that they would descend to limbo. Therefore, the patriarch Jacob says in Genesis 37:35, "I shall go down to Sheol to my son, mourning." And Saint Job in Job 17:16, "Will all my things descend to the depths of Sheol?"

v. 12 The night, that is, the obscurity of figures of the old law, **is far gone. The day**, that is, the clarity of the truth revealed in the new law, **is at hand. Let us then cast off the works of darkness**, that is, sins which are called works of darkness, because they are done in the darkness (Jn 3:20). "For everyone who does evil hates the light" because they obscure the spirit, according to which the Philosopher says in the *Ethics,* "All evil is ignorance because it leads to the utter darkness, namely, to Gehenna."[3] "And do not come to the light" (Jn 3:20), that is, the virtues which are called the armor of light because they war against the darkness of sin and are done in the light (Jn 3:20). "But the one who does what is true comes to the light" because it illumines the soul and finally leads to eternal light. Therefore he adds:

v. 13 As in the day, of judgment, **let us conduct ourselves becomingly**, that is, for glory. **Not in reveling and drunkenness**, but by avoiding sins of appetite; **not in debauchery and licentiousness**, but by avoiding the sins of lust; **not in quarreling and jealousy**, namely, not in the spiritual sins that are more seriously blameworthy.

v. 14 But put on the Lord Jesus Christ, and make no provisions for the flesh, to gratify its desires, that is, its excess. This does not exclude necessities but what is superfluous.

---

3. Cf. Aristotle, *Nicomachean Ethics,* 3.5.

ROMANS 14

Anonymous Commentator of Mont Saint-Michel

Refrain from Judging Others

v. 1 Welcome the weak in faith, but not to quarrel over opinions. Those who are **weak in faith**, the Apostle says, have doubt in some part of their faith.[1] Welcome them, and in your weakness support their weakness. Do not judge them as unfaithful according to your own opinions.

v. 2 For some believe they may eat anything, while others who are weak eat only vegetables. Since in the time of apostolic preaching, many were already strong in their faith and had knowledge from the Lord that things they put in their mouths do not defile (cf. Mt 15:11-18), they ate foods indifferently with a sound conscience. The weaker ones, however, abstained from meat and wine, lest unknowingly they obtain meat that had been sacrificed to idols. All sacrificed foods were sold in the market at a high price, and gentiles poured the first of their wine as an offering to their idols. The Apostle, therefore, ordered those who used such food and drink with a sound conscience not to scorn the weakness of those who abstained from them, and he commanded the weaker ones not to judge as defiled those who consumed them. This is as if to say that if some become weak of soul

---

1. As noted in the Introduction, the anonymous commentator of Mont Saint-Michel had very intricately interwoven his patristic sources into his own commentary, most often without explicitly identifying them. Throughout this chapter he is continuously drawing upon Augustine, Ambrosiaster, Pelagius, and Origen. We will cite his sources in the notes, however, only when he specifically mentions them by name in the text.

because of their horror that others of the same way of life eat meat, let them not judge another's will. If this practice is a stumbling block to them and they are unwilling to eat meat, they should assign the rule to themselves and eat only vegetables.

But some consider this statement contrary to the practices of those who believed in Christ and yet maintained Jewish customs. For the Apostle instructs gentile believers not to scandalize the others with their food since they were still weaker in faith. He also orders those weak in faith, who distinguished between clean and unclean meat, to eat vegetables, which are eaten indifferently by all. He, however, would permit those to eat meat legally who were stronger in the faith and believed nothing is to be abhorred that God created for humans to eat. This shows that he is not talking about Jews, but about those who abstain and do not eat meat that is clean according to the Law; instead they eat only vegetables.

We should not overlook Origen's statement that those who are called weak in faith are not perfected enough in their understanding of such things that they grasp the more hidden mysteries. These kinds of matters, which they cannot understand, should not provoke them to **quarrel over opinions**.[2] First, they should be shown what is ordinary and easy until their understanding becomes mature enough to approach stronger food. Elsewhere the Apostle says, "I gave you milk to drink, not solid food" (1 Cor 3:2). But those who believe that they **may eat anything** realize that it is through the ability to choose that "they have their perceptions trained to discern good and evil" (Heb 5:14).

v. 3 So that there should be no dissension among believers over food, the Apostle then adds, **Let those who eat everything not despise those who abstain, and let those who abstain not pass judgment on those who eat.** The strong were stubbornly ridiculing as fools the weaker and considering them overly scrupulous; and the weak were rashly judging the strong as carnal. The Apostle thereby admonishes those whose faith is so strong that they believe that they may or could eat anything not to disdain or to despise the weaker. In turn he orders those incapable of more mature teaching not to judge those of broader understanding and greater intellectual capability. The subsequent text shows why the weak should not be despised. It is because **God has welcomed them**, that is, because God has called them according to his grace; or because God has called them just as he also called you. For all

---

2. See Origen, *Commentary on the Epistle to the Romans*, PG 14:1235c.

are welcomed by God provided they are called according to his grace. The Apostle also explains why one should not rebuke and judge another.

v. 4 Who are you to judge someone else's bond servant? Servants stand or fall in relation to their own lord. And servants will stand, for God has the power to make his servants stand. Here the Apostle intends to repress the insolence of both groups. The first comprises those who, since they are ignorant and lazy, judge in a reversed order the knowledgeable and the zealous. The second includes those who, just advancing in knowledge, are exalted over others who seem to be less capable. So he rebuked them, **Who are you?** What authority do you have to judge your fellow servant? For with whatever conscience one may eat or not eat, God is the servant's judge. In fact, the Apostle does not forbid judging the obvious. For he taught that there should be judgment in the case of abominable sexual disgrace where a certain man took his own father's wife (cf. 1 Cor 5:1-5). He does, however, forbid judgment in uncertain matters. When things happen in such a fashion that the intention behind them remains uncertain, they should not be judged. Instead, they should be reserved for God's verdict. But it is not wrong to pass judgment in those matters that happen in such a fashion that it is obvious that they could not have been done with a good and pure intention. The ignorant judge the more profound to have fallen away from the state of faith, while those inflated with knowledge think similar things about the ignorant. Therefore, in accord with the thought of the one whom he is rebuking, the Apostle says, **Servants stand or fall in relation to their own lord**. In order to show the ineffable goodness of God, he says of those who seem to have fallen away, even if they have truly fallen away, **The servants will stand**, even if you yourself perhaps did not believe that this should be done. Although the Apostle might be speaking of all those regenerated and living piously when he asked, **Who are you?** he immediately had regard for the predestined and said, **and the servants will stand**. That they might not arrogate this to themselves, he says, **For God has the power to make** God's **servants stand**. It is God who gives perseverance and is able both to establish those who stand in order that they may stand with the greatest perseverance and to restore the fallen. "For the Lord lifts up all who have fallen" (Ps 145:8/ 146:8).

v. 5 For one person regards one day differently than another — or as an alternate translation has it — differently than **various days. Another person regards every day alike. Let both be fully convinced in their own think-**

ing. Since some people decide to abstain from eating flesh at certain times or days of the year, and others judge and thus determine in their own minds to end every day in abstinence, all are left to their own counsel. For they are not guilty if they eat with gratitude, nor are others culpable if they refrain, provided they do not spurn eating as unlawful. Each choice, therefore, was allowed, because the calling that is in Christ specifies no foods as common or unclean, but the regard for self-control urges one to abstain even from things that are lawful. For whoever has a mind to carry out what is not lawful ought to abstain from what is lawful (cf. 1 Cor 6:12). And because the lawful and the unlawful can both become acceptable before God, the Apostle states the following.

v. 6 Whoever observes the day does it for the Lord, and whoever eats meat does it for the Lord and gives thanks to God. And whoever abstains from eating does it for the Lord and gives thanks to God. To eat for the Lord and to abstain for the Lord are good. Both give thanks to God, the latter for the benefit of abstinence and the former for the freedom to eat. Observing the day for the Lord and abstaining for the Lord signify the same thing. Whoever observes the day for the Lord and does not eat for the Lord, therefore, abstains from lawful things in order to please God by abstinence. Whoever eats for the Lord gives thanks to God for the freedom to eat. This is true whether one perceives that every good thing created by God ought to be eaten indifferently, or whether by not pursuing one's own appetite, but providing for the salvation of another, one eats in order to have the strength to preach.

Just as illumination is taken as the day, so ignorance is taken as the mind's darkness. Therefore, the passage running from "one person judges between one day and another" to "and gives thanks to God" can be understood in different ways. For those who understand some things, having overlooked others, judge "between one day and another" (Rom 14:5). But others who understand that all things are possible if rightly understood, and ought to be seen as such, do not regard one day differently from another but each day the same. Since they observe every day and eat all things, that is, since they recognize and understand all things, they give thanks to God, whose favor has been granted in order to attain such gifts. Although the others may not eat all things and do not possess knowledge of all things, they are still said to give thanks to God for what they do receive.

With regard to these things, therefore, we should recall blessed Father Augustine's belief that these words ought not to be understood of two human beings, but rather of a human being and God. For he states that it is the human who judges between days. The human can judge something one way today and another way tomorrow. For example, today one may condemn someone else as evil but tomorrow, after self-correction, find that same person good, or vice versa. Today one may praise someone as righteous but tomorrow consider that person depraved. God, however, regards each day alike. This is because God knows not only what sort of person someone is at present, but also what that person will be like on every future day. Whence the Apostle provided the following good counsel, "Let both be fully convinced in their own thinking" (Rom 14:5), that is, let both dare to judge as much as is conceded to human understanding. And whoever judges well for the present day discerns the day for the Lord.[3] Which of these readings ought to be considered better, I leave to the reader to decide.

vv. 7-9 For none of us live for ourselves, and none die for ourselves. If we live, we live for the Lord; and if we die, we die for the Lord. Therefore, whether we live or we die, we are the Lord's. For this reason Christ died and rose again, in order to reign over both the dead and the living. According to Origen, this should not be understood as carnal life or death,[4] but rather as the dying away of vices and the newness of life that we live in Christ through faith in his resurrection. This living in Christ through faith, therefore, is attributed to the Lord since it receives its genesis from him and not from us. He, indeed, has left behind a model of obedience and a type of dying for those willing to die to sin and vices. He has left behind a model first of suffering and death and later of resurrection and newness of life. Although Christ holds power over all things by the force of his majesty, he does not want to compel rational spirits by violent means to obey his law. Instead, he waits for them to come voluntarily and would persuade them by teaching rather than commanding, and by inviting rather than forcing. For this reason the Apostle mentions that Christ died and was resurrected **in order to reign over both the living and the dead**. Christ reigns over the living who by the model of his resurrection lead a new and heavenly life on earth. He also reigns over the dead who put to death the parts of themselves that are earthly (Col 3:5) so that they may no longer live for themselves but for Christ (2 Cor 5:15). And in order to cut short the blame coming from both sides of those who judge each other, he renders them both subject to rebuke.

3. See Augustine, *Commentary on the Epistle to the Romans,* CCSL 84:49.
4. See Origen, *Commentary on the Epistle to the Romans,* PG 14:1239a.

v. 10 But you, why do you sit in judgment over your brothers or sisters? Or you, why do you look down on your brothers or sisters? The Apostle says that if the mortification of sins were in you, you would not have produced it; rather, it would be a gift from Christ's death. Or if the newness of life is yours, you would have obtained it from Christ's resurrection. Therefore, he asks, by what authority do you condemn your brothers or sisters as voracious? **Or why do you look down on your brothers or sisters** as if they were weak or their abstaining pointless? And in order to show that one person sins more gravely in judging a brother or sister than another does in looking down on them, the Apostle overlooks the blame due to such despisers and emphasizes the presumption of the brother or sister who renders judgment over others when he says, **For we shall all stand before the judgment seat of God.**

vv. 10-12 For we shall all stand before the judgment seat of God. For it is written, "As I live," says the Lord, "every knee will bend before me, and every tongue will confess to God." So then, we will all give an account of ourselves to God. If the text reads that we must **all stand before the judgment seat of Christ** and that **we will all give an account of ourselves to God,** then why by judging others do you commit a crime of such great arrogance that you appear to usurp God's judgment seat and forestall the judgment of the Only Begotten? In fact, Isaiah's testimony shows that all of us must give account of our actions to the Lord alone (cf. Isa 45:24).

Let us hearken back to what was stated earlier lest we seem to disregard a better and more distinguished exposition. "For none of us," the Apostle says, "live to ourselves alone," etc. (Rom 14:7). Those who live for God do not seek their own glory but God's, and those who die for God glorify him with their own death. So, then, Jesus "signifies by what death [Peter] should glorify God" (Jn 21:19). Accordingly, none of the faithful live or die for themselves because in living or dying they do not seek their own glory but that of the Lord. For when we do a good work in praise of the one whose grace is given that we may do it, then we do it rightly, then justly, and then devoutly. "For if we live, we live for the Lord. If we die, we die for the Lord" (Rom 14:8). Since the Apostle said that none of us faithful live or die for ourselves, he goes on to show for whom we should live or die. "Therefore, whether we live or we die, we are the Lord's" (Rom 14:8). Lest any of the faithful, much more those alive today, fear that they are the Lord's but that after dying they will be another's and not the Lord's, he gives them assurance that as they were placed in this flesh they have also been freed from it. They will be the Lord's, since those who believe in Christ, although they may die, will live.

For "God is not God of the dead but of the living" (Mt 22:32). In order to show the cost by which they came to be God's, the Apostle immediately added, "For this reason Christ died and rose, in order to reign over both the dead and the living" (Rom 14:9). Blessed Ambrose wants "the living" in this passage to be understood as those to whom Christ shows the way of salvation and "the dead" those whom he has freed from hell.[5] But Pelagius understood the "living" as those whom Christ, when he comes to pronounce judgment, will find alive; and the "dead" as those whom he will bring back to life first.[6]

I think there is no difference between what Paul specified as "the judgment seat of God" here and "the judgment seat of Christ" in his Letter to the Corinthians (cf. 2 Cor 5:10). They are the same according to what Christ himself says, "Father, everything I have is yours, and everything you have is mine" (Jn 17:10). Since the name Christ pertains to the special character of his designation as the Word manifested in flesh and is evidence of one "reconciling the world to himself" (2 Cor 5:19), therefore, it is possible to designate the judgment seat of God as that of Christ. Every creature will bend the knee and every tongue confess to God at the name of Jesus by whom they have been reconciled to God. It is thus stated elsewhere, "At the name of Jesus every knee will bend, in heaven and on earth and under the earth" (Phil 2:10). We must not take this statement in a carnal way. For we should not believe that angelic spirits worship with bodily knees bent or confess with tongues of flesh. Rather, it means that all are subject to bend the knee and submit in worship to God.

Do Not Cause Another to Stumble

v. 13 Therefore, let us no longer pass judgment on one another, but rather decide never to put a stumbling block or obstruction in the way of a brother or sister. Since, the Apostle says, so great is the truth of the judgment before God and so wide a net will the investigation cast, **let us no longer pass judgment on one another.** You have done enough. **But rather decide**, that is, resolve not to produce stumbling blocks or obstructions for

---

5. See Ambrosiaster, *Commentary on the Epistle to the Romans*, CSEL 81:439.
6. See Pelagius, *Commentary on the Epistle to the Romans*, Souter 2:108.

others by the observance of foods. For just as the feet of those climbing or walking might stumble against an object found on the road, so those who recently began the road of faith may trip on the contentions, negligence, contempt, and arrogance of those in front of them. They are repulsed by their example and are turned away from faith.

v. 14 I know and have confidence in the Lord Jesus that nothing is unclean in itself, but it is unclean to any who think it unclean. I know, he says, and am certain that **in the Lord Jesus nothing is unclean in itself,** that is, of its own nature. For nothing God has created is unclean of its own nature. Everything the good God creates is good and clean. **But it is unclean to any who think it unclean.** In other words, it is unclean to any who, as they understand it in their heart, consider something unclean and allow for observance of the distinction. To put it more clearly, it becomes unclean in the conscience of any who, after [receiving] faith in Christ, still in such cases, and by Jewish custom, reckon something unclean. For just as the mind's thinking makes food impure that is not impure by nature, so in contrast the simplicity of mind and the lack of scrupulous thinking, after every suspicion of contamination has been stricken, cleanse food made impure for any reason. Temple vessels assigned or consecrated for service were called the Lord's holy vessels, but other vessels were considered unclean. In this vein, therefore, foods assigned or consecrated for service were said to be clean and were to be eaten according to the Law, whereas others were deemed unclean.

v. 15 If your brother or sister is scandalized or is grieved by what you eat, you are no longer walking in love. Do not let your eating cause the ruin of those for whom Christ died. The Apostle had shown through the Lord Jesus that nothing should be considered unclean of its own nature, and he granted freedom to each of the faithful in the use of foods. Here, however, he limits freedom's license for the sake of building up love for one's brothers and sisters. He says that even if nothing is impure and the use of all foods freely permitted, if, because of the food you consider lawful to eat, you scandalize others who are unready for this knowledge, then you no longer walk according to love, nor do you exhibit a loving disposition toward them. For how would it harm you if, in order not to grieve another, you should abstain even from lawful things? It is no crime for you to abstain from lawful things, but to any who distinguish between these things and consider them unlawful, their use is defiling. "For those who distinguish are condemned if they eat" (Rom 14:23). But if this should happen because of what you do, certainly you bring about the ruin of your brother or sister for whom Christ died, and you will be the cause of their destruction.

vv. 16-17 Indeed, do not let your good be reviled. For the kingdom of God is not food and drink but righteousness and peace and joy in the Holy Spirit. What is the need, the Apostle asks, to disturb the peace of others so greatly because of the foods and the sorts of meat that we consume? The Kingdom of God, for which we labor, is established neither by food nor by drink, but consists in righteousness and in all other things that have been spiritually acquired. It is as if he said, "Since the sorts of food that cannot remain with us have been given up, let us train ourselves in the things that can cross over with us into the kingdom of heaven." Therefore, **the kingdom of God is not food and drink but righteousness**. For it is not established or obtained from food and drink, but from a **righteousness** in which we do not judge others but love them. It is from a **peace** in which quarreling is eliminated so that the relationship of brothers and sisters may be preserved. It proceeds from a spiritual **joy** in which the righteous delight in the benefits of others as well as of their own, and from such other things as are acquired from the Holy Spirit. Not physical foods but rather peace and righteousness and things of this sort from the Holy Spirit, if there are such, will be food and sustenance for us in the Kingdom of God. Since just as those having the Kingdom of God "will neither marry nor be given in marriage," so they will not consume food or drink but will be "like the angels of God" (Mt 22:30), which is to say that they will live by the word of God. Nevertheless, if they wanted to eat other foods, they could lawfully do so, according to what blessed Father Augustine refers to in *The City of God* when he mentions the angel who ate with Tobit (Tob 12:19).[7]

But in accord with the same doctor, you should understand that what **we consider good**, which the Apostle forbids to **be reviled**, is the faith by which we believe that all things are pure to the pure. This view is reviled as the cause of dissension in the dispute about the differences in foods. But blessed Ambrose wants this good of ours to be understood as Christ's teaching, which appears to be reviled when a believer is reprehended in anything.[8] Pelagius believed that this good of ours ought to be understood as the

7. See Augustine, *City of God*, 13.22, CCSL 48:405. According to Augustine, the angel Raphael explained to Tobit that angels do not eat only in appearance, but when they do eat, they do not have to take food, as humans do, to nourish the body.

8. See Ambrosiaster, *Commentary on the Epistle to the Romans*, CSEL 81:445.

liberty that we have in God so that all things are clean to us.[9] Origen also believed that the good of spiritual knowledge, which is liberty or knowledge, should not be reviled undeservedly.[10] If, therefore, permission in all things would serve our appetite more than our abstinence, I do not overlook Cassiodorus, who also wanted our good to be understood as abstinence. For this appears to be true from the words that the Apostle immediately adjoined, **the kingdom of God is not food and drink.**[11]

v. 18 For whoever serves Christ in this way pleases God and receives human approval. In other words, **whoever serves Christ** in these things that have been acquired through the Spirit is pleasing to God, who sent Christ to redeem the human race. If some take care not to create a scandal and seek what is profitable for others but not for themselves, they please God. If they serve Christ in the Holy Spirit, they also please God. No one, therefore, can doubt that such people are righteous. For those serve Christ in the Spirit who, after receiving the grace of the Holy Spirit, obey God's Word. They serve wisdom and at the same time all the virtues, which Christ is said to be. Therefore, those who fulfill God's will in these things are said to please God.

v. 19 So then let us pursue what makes for peace and for building up one another. Since they please God who have served Christ in matters of love, let us not judge each other in such things. Instead, let us painstakingly pursue what establishes peace, and edify one another whether by mutual devotion or by showing each other love. For people are edified who see you obtaining necessities not only for yourself but for others as well. But some have realized that this edification should be understood to include abstinence. This is because food, even though it fails to ruin anyone, spiritually edifies no one. Since the edifice of faith arises through the constructive work of love, the Apostle states the following.

v. 20 Do not destroy the work of God because of food. Do not let the indulgence of food cause you to set a stumbling block before your brothers and sisters or to destroy the edifice of love.

   Indeed, all things are clean, but it is wrong to cause offense to an-

9. See Pelagius, *Commentary on the Epistle to the Romans,* Souter 2:110.
10. See Origen, *Commentary on the Epistle to the Romans,* PG 14:1249c. In this case Origen is saying that we can cause the good to be reviled by insisting that we must consume all common foods in order to attain faith, grace, or salvation.
11. See Cassiodorus, *Commentary on the Epistle to the Romans,* PL 68:500d.

other by eating. The Apostle repeats what he said above lest he appear to condemn creation, since "nothing is unclean in itself, but it is unclean to any who think it unclean" (Rom 14:14). Therefore, even what is good of its own nature produces evil when it scandalizes. This happens either when a brother or sister is offended because the use of these foods creates a stumbling block for them, or when someone deems what is good to be impure and so comes to think of it that way.

v. 21 It is good not to eat meat or drink wine or do anything that offends your brothers and sisters, scandalizes them, or weakens them. This might perhaps appear contrary to the Apostle's statement above that **it is good not to eat meat or drink wine** had he not added, **or do anything that offends your brothers and sisters.** For it is good "never to put a stumbling block or obstruction in the way of a brother or sister" (Rom 14:13). Therefore, since everything ought to be done that God's work not be destroyed, Paul orders even those who judge that something is to be eaten to abstain for the sake of those who do not agree. Those who are offended in this should not be compelled to eat for the sake of those who judge that something is to be eaten, lest by chance, once the wall of continence has been broken down and license taken, those offended would be plunged into the storm of gluttony and the depths of excess.

v. 22 You who have faith should keep that to yourself before God. If, says the Apostle, you consider yourself faithful in this matter, since you know that "all things are clean to those who are clean" (Tit 1:15), then eat in such a way that no one is weakened by your example. On the other hand, he says that if you judge nothing in God's creation as unclean, it is enough for you to have such faith before God. Yet someone else who does not yet have the faith to believe that all things may be eaten should not, for that reason, be forced to eat all things. Therefore, to show that it is proper for us to act so that our faith is not slandered before humans but approved before God, he added, **Keep [your faith to yourself] before God.**

vv. 22-23 Blessed are those who do not convict themselves by what they approve. But those who have doubts are condemned if they eat, because this is not from faith. This, however, should be read with reference to the preceding statement, "You who have faith should keep that to yourself before God" (Rom 14:22). For this faith is good by which we believe that "all things are good to those who are good" (Tit 1:15), and in it we approve ourselves. Let us, therefore, use well this good that we have lest we sin against our brothers and sisters by creating a stumbling block for weaker ones. For when we scandalize the weak, we convict ourselves through the very good by which we approve ourselves when our faith seems agreeable to us. The statement can also be understood in the following way. Blessed are those who remain so constant and unwavering in what they approve and decide upon that they neither convict nor shame themselves in any way. They do this by avoiding everything that they know should not be done, whether in the observance of foods — about which Paul is speaking here — or in some other practice of what is good. **But those who discriminate**, that is, those who are unsure whether what they consume is truly pure or impure because of the uncertainty in their minds, they are condemned as their conscience accuses them. According to blessed Ambrose, those who judge that something should not be eaten, and yet eat it anyway, stand condemned since they are acting against what they think is beneficial for them.[12] For it is not **from faith**, but rather against faith, if you do the very thing that you believe should not be done. Although you know all food to be pure, you then — to the contrary — are uncertain whether or not it ought to be consumed.

For all that is not from faith is sin. Everything that is different from what conscience knows ought to be done is sin. But since the Apostle is speaking here to those who were offending others over the observance of food, this statement can be understood in the following way. Whatever destroys another is sin since it is not "from faith, which works through love" (Gal 5:6), nor is it to the glory of God. Elsewhere the Apostle says the same thing, "whether you eat or drink, or whatever else you do, do all to the glory of God" (1 Cor 10:31).

---

12. See Ambrosiaster on Romans 14:23, CSEL 81:451.

ROMANS 15

Nicholas of Lyra

The Strong Should Bear Burdens Patiently

v. 1 We who are strong. After showing how to behave toward the weaker in the avoidance of evil, the Apostle here shows how to promote the good. First, he offers his instruction, and second its implementation, at the place, **I myself am satisfied** (Rom 15:14). The first he divides into two parts because, first, he encourages the strong to sustain the weak and, second, he encourages them to do good, at the place, **Welcome one another, as Christ has welcomed you** (Rom 15:7). He divides the first yet again into two parts because, first, he sets out the instruction and, second, he adds the prayer at the place, **May the God of steadfastness** (Rom 15:5). He divides the first yet again into two parts because, first, he offers the instruction and, second, he draws a certain conclusion from what has been said, at the place, **For whatever was written** (Rom 15:4). First, moreover, he persuades twice and initially says, **We who are strong ought to bear with the failings of the weak**, just as in the natural body when the stronger muscles and bones sustain other parts that are weaker. [**We ought**] **not to please ourselves**, that is, we ought not to seek our own will but the common good; therefore he adds,

v. 2 Let each of us please our neighbors for their good and to edify them. Moreover, we ought not to seek to please our neighbors in evil things. Second, he introduces the example of the divine Christ.

v. 3 For Christ did not please himself, that is, he did not seek his own will (Jn 6:38), "For I have come down from heaven, not to do my own will. . . ." **But as it is written** (Ps 68:10/69:9), **"The insults of those,"** etc. The words of Christ speaking to the Father to do God's will sustain him from the reproach of the Jews who are speaking to him, "You are a Samaritan, and you have a demon" (Jn 8:48). The same when he was hanging on the cross, "You who would destroy the temple of God," etc. (Mt 27:40). And these reproaches of God the Father they turned on Christ. Therefore he says, **"The insults of those who insult you have fallen on me."** By these reproaches the Jews intended to confound Christ.

v. 4 For whatever. Here from what has been said he draws the conclusion, namely, that those things that are in the sacred Scriptures, chiefly concerning Christ, serve for our instruction. He demonstrates four uses provided for us from the Scriptures. First is clarity of understanding, which is noted with the words, **For whatever was written in former days was written for our instruction.** Second is forbearance, at the place, **so that through patience.** Third is the sweetness of internal happiness, at the place, **and by the encouragement of the scriptures.** Fourth is the security of obtaining glory, at the place, **we might have hope.** For hope is the certain expectation of future blessedness provided by grace and merits.[1]

v. 5 May the God. Here he adds his prayer to complete what was said before, and he says, **May the God of steadfastness and encouragement** give endurance in adversities and consolations after tribulation: "After tears and wailing you pour out joy and exaltation" (Tob 3:22).

[May God] **grant you to live in such harmony with one another**, that is, desiring mutual progress as I do also, **according to Christ Jesus**, that is, according to his teaching.

v. 6 So that together, in relation to the unity of faith, **you may with one voice**, in relation to the unity of confession because, as he said above in Romans 10:10, "For a person believes with the heart, and so is justified, and one confesses with one's lips," etc., **glorify God**, in relation to the unity of works, because faith without works is dead.

---

1. Luther will criticize this definition of hope in an early commentary on Psalm 5. See *Luther's Spirituality,* Classics of Western Spirituality, ed. and trans. Philip Krey and Peter Krey (New York: Paulist, 2007), 63.

v. 7 Therefore. Here he exhorts the stronger ones to move the weaker to the good. First he articulates his exhortation, and second he adds his prayer, at the place, **May the God of hope** (Rom 15:13). Concerning the first he says, **Welcome one another,** by lovingly attending to the good of the other, **just as Christ did,** by assuming the common humanity of all, namely, of Jews and gentiles. The members ought to conform to the head, and for that reason every Christian ought to attend to the good of their brothers and sisters. Moreover, he accepted a common humanity of both Jews and gentiles. Nevertheless, he procured the salvation of the Jews and the gentiles in different ways, because he preached to the Jews in his own person and by promise, and this is what he says:

v. 8 For I tell you that Christ has become a servant of the circumcised, by preaching to the Jews who were circumcised, not thus to the gentiles; for that reason Matthew says, "I was sent only to the lost sheep of Israel" (Mt 15:24). **He did so on behalf of the truth of God.** Although the salvation of the Jews and the gentiles is simply by means of grace, for the Jews the cause is the certain promise which, when fulfilled, is the truth of God, that is, the promises of the Jewish patriarchs proclaimed in the Law and the Prophets given only to the Jewish ancestors. Psalm 147:20, "He has not dealt thus with any other nation; they do not know his ordinances." Thus the salvation of the gentiles is by means of mercy, because, although the Law and the Prophets spoke concerning the same call to faith in Christ, nevertheless, as I have noted, neither the Law nor the Prophets were given to their fathers, on account of which he adds:

v. 9 [Christ became a servant of the circumcised] in order that the gentiles, as it was granted to them by God, **might glorify God,** namely, that they might serve in words and deeds. **As it is written** (Ps 17:50/18:49), **"Therefore I will confess you."** "That I may cause you to be praised by all believers" are the words of the Son to the Father concerning the worship of the gentiles. Nevertheless, although in my commentary on Psalm 17:50/18:49 I interpreted this text in the mystical sense as David's words, it was a figure of Christ, and it was more perfectly fulfilled in Christ than in David. Other authorities allege that the literal sense simply concerns the calling of the gentiles to faith in Christ.[2]

---

2. Note here the double literal sense.

v. 10 And again it is said, "Rejoice," where our translation has, "The desert rejoices and is glad" (Isa 35:1).[3]

v. 11 And again (Ps 116:1/117:1): **"Praise the Lord, all you gentiles,"** that is, by your worship.

v. 12 And again Isaiah says (Isa 11:10), **"The root of Jesse shall come,"** that is, Christ according to the flesh descending from Jesse, that is, **"the one who rises"** from the dead **"to rule."** For this he was given the power in heaven and on earth (Mt. 28:18).[4] **In him**, having been called to faith, they have the consequent hope through him of eternal life.

v. 13 May the God. Here the Apostle completes his prayer, saying, **May the God of hope**, that is, the Giver of hope, **fill you** spiritually **and [with] peace** by quieting the passions which trouble the soul and with **believing**. He says this because formed faith creates belief. **So that you may abound in hope**, through the increase of merits, **by the power of the Holy Spirit**, which is principally meritorious works, because one has freedom of choice like a rider on a horse.[5]

Personal Notes

v. 14 I myself feel confident. Here the apostle offers them a defense, and he does so first concerning what he writes to the Romans and second why he has not yet visited them (Rom 15:22), **This is the reason.** Concerning the first he excludes the falsehood that some consider his writings unlettered and simple and that they are by necessity poor. He rejects this, saying, **I myself feel confident about you, my brothers and sisters, that you yourselves are full of goodness**, and this he knew because they did good, which results from goodness. **[You are] filled with all knowledge**, pertaining to salvation, **and able to instruct one another**, that is, not only to rule your own life but also that of others.

v. 15 Boldly. Here he expresses the true reason of his writings, namely, the duty of his office because he was the Apostle of the gentiles, and this is di-

---

3. Like Thomas Aquinas, Nicholas is aware of the variety of biblical texts that have been available in the history of interpretation.
4. The text notes Matthew 6.
5. See Lyra's discussion of grace and free will in Romans 9.

vided in two parts. First he shows his office, and second its effect, at the place, **I have reason** (Rom 15:17). Concerning the first he says, **I have written to you rather boldly**, that is, briefly and succinctly **by way of reminder**, of the things you have a habit of understanding, and not to teach you something unknown. For this reason, he said in Romans 7:1 above, "For I am speaking to those who know the law," and I am doing so **because of the grace**, that is, the office of an apostle.

v. 16 [I have written to you because of the grace given me by God to be a minister] to the gentiles in the priestly service of the gospel, that is, to be a holy man disclosing and preaching. **I have done this in order that the offering of the gentiles may be acceptable**, that is, so that the offering which the gentiles make through faith in Christ might be accepted by God the Father [and sanctified] **by the Holy Spirit**, that is, sanctified through the grace of the Holy Spirit, and not through the observation of the Law.

v. 17 I have. Here he shows the effect of the office given to him. First, his preaching was by the authority of Christ. **In Christ Jesus, then, I have reason to boast**, that is, I have the authority of the office from Christ. **For God**, that is, ordained to the honor of God. Second, the execution of the Apostle's office was not only through words, like the preaching of the false apostles, but also through miracles by the power of Christ to confirm his apostolic preaching. Therefore he says,

v. 18 For I will not, as the false apostles did who were not sent by Christ [dare to speak of anything except what Christ has accomplished through me to lead the gentiles to obedience] **by word**, because from Christ I have proclaimed the word confirmed by miracles. Therefore he adds, **and**, as though, that is:

v. 19 By the power refers to the minor miracles, **and signs** refers to the major ones. Consequently, in effect he implies the efficaciousness of preaching. First, he expresses this extensively, saying, [I have preached] **from Jerusalem and as far around as Illyricum**, a place at the end of Greece, whence it is called the sea of Illyricum. Second, he expresses this intensively because he preached where others had not preached. Thus he worked more in distant places to proclaim the message, but they did not travel as far. This is what he says.

v. 20 Thus I make it my ambition to proclaim the good news. The text is clear, and he consequently calls upon the authority of Isaiah 52:15:

v. 21 "Those who have never been told," that is, the gentiles who through Paul's preaching were illumined in Christ by faith, because they had not heard about Christ through the prophets as the Jews did; nor through other apostles, as other gentiles to whom they preached. For Matthew preached to the Egyptians, and others to many other gentiles earlier.

v. 22 This is the reason. Here the Apostle excuses himself for not having visited Rome personally. First he announces his impending arrival; second, with the obstacle removed, he promises to come there.

v. 23 But now, with no further place. Third, to accomplish these things he seeks their prayers, at the place, **I appeal to you** (Rom 15:30). Concerning the first he says, this is the reason that I have so often been hindered. Many times the Apostle was occupied by preaching to the gentiles in the regions of Greece, who in large part had been seduced by profane philosophy and by false prophets before the Apostle's preaching, as I will make clear below, the Lord willing, in other epistles. **But now**. Here consequently he promises his arrival, saying, **But now with no** further **place for me in these regions**, that is, he had no need to remain there anymore, although not all were converted. Nevertheless, the Apostle had ordained bishops and presbyters in the cities and places to convert those remaining and in the absence of the Apostle to instruct those who had been converted. Thus the Apostle hurried to other places in which it was incumbent upon him to preach. **I desire [to come to you]** because the city of Rome was the capital of the whole world.

v. 24 But when, for as he preached in the east, so now he desires to do the same in the west, where Spain is. **I do hope [to see you in passing]**. By this he intimates that he does not intend to remain there very long, since the Apostle Peter was in Rome with his disciples. Thus Paul's preaching was not as necessary there as in Spain. **[I do hope to] be sent on by you**, because Spain was subject to the Romans, as is clear in 1 Maccabees 8. **Once I have enjoyed [being with you]** and delighted in your company and in your faith.

v. 25 At present, however, that is, before I go to Rome, **I am going** to those converted to the faith remaining in Jerusalem, who, to be an example of perfection to the rest, renounced ownership of all their earthly goods, as Acts 4:32 makes clear. They wanted to be more free for prayer and preaching on account of which they are called **"saints."** The apostles were eager that those who had converted and did not renounce their possessions would sustain them with their alms. Peter and John commended this appeal to Paul, as is clear in Galatians 2:[10]. He himself did this carefully, as the text indicates here.

v. 26 Macedonia and Achaia, that is, converts from these lands, and through this one understands converts from other places, **have decided**, that is, consented to a **certain collection**, that is, a donation from their possessions **to the poor**, that is, who are of the number of the saints.

v. 27 And indeed they owe it to them, evidently as they did this for them. **For if the gentiles have come to share in their spiritual blessings**, since the preaching of the gospel went out from Jerusalem, as I have already noted frequently. **So they ought to be of service to them in material things**, for just as they owe expenses to the priests out of necessity because they are preachers by right of office, so also those who do this by grace are owed what is proper.

v. 28 So when I have completed this, by giving them the alms sent through me, **I will set out**, for thus he was proposing to do.

v. 29 And I know, that is, in the abundance of spiritual goods, as in Genesis 30:30 Jacob says to Laban, "The Lord has blessed you with my coming," concerning the multiplication of temporal goods and more properly the multiplication of spiritual goods. Concerning the first part two things must be noted. First is the concern of the Apostle for the Church of God in that, having proclaimed the gospel in the east, he hurries to Jerusalem to provide the necessities of life for the saints, and then travels quickly to Rome to preach the Word of God in the west. In this our negligence is shown to be rather reprehensible. Second, from this it seems that Paul preached in Spain, which appears contrary to what is said in the *Decretum,* Distinction 11, chapter 11, which denies this, but that only the Apostle Peter taught in these provinces of Italy, Gaul, Spain, Africa, and Sicily. On account of this some say that Paul proposed to preach in Spain subject to the will of God, just as it is said here; on account of this he spoke the truth, although there had been no previous hindrance. Others hold that he did preach in Spain, for example, Isidore in the *Birth and Death of the Saints.* And Jerome seems to say the same in the *Lives of Illustrious Men* [Chapter 5], that at his first defense Paul, dismissed by Nero, preached in the western regions. Over against the *Decretum* some respond that it does not simply deny that Paul preached in Spain and in other such provinces, but that this cannot be read here. But against this it seems to be said in the last chapter of Acts that Paul was in Rome for two years, where he disputed and taught. Nevertheless, Rome is in Italy, about which the *Decretum* speaks just as about Spain. On account of this it is possible to say otherwise, that the intent of the *Decretum* is that no one preached or established churches in these provinces except Peter or others by his ordination or command. In this way Paul did not preach in Italy or in Spain.[6]

v. 30 I appeal to you. Here consequently the Apostle seeks the prayers of the believers to fulfill that which was predicted, since by going to Jerusalem he faced many dangers from the unbelieving Jews both on the way and at the end, as he knew through revelation and as became clear after the event in Acts 20:19-24. **I appeal to you, brothers, through our Lord**. The text is clear to this place.

v. 31 And that my ministry, that is, the alms given by the gentiles through my service, **may be acceptable**, namely, to the glory of God, **to the saints**, to relieve the poor of their poverty.

v. 32 So that I may come, accomplished by his office. **And be refreshed**, by receiving spiritual gifts after many tribulations borne by me.

v. 33 The God of peace. . . . Amen. This is the confirmation of what has been said.

---

6. D. 11, c. 11; *Corpus Iuris Canonici*, ed. Emil Friedberg, 2 vols. (Graz: Akademische Druk–Universität Verlagsanstalt, 1959), 1:26.

ROMANS 16

Nicholas of Lyra

Greetings

v. 1 I commend to you our sister Phoebe. After the Apostle instructed the Romans in customs by preaching (Rom 14), here he does the same by imitation, proposing to them certain exemplary persons. He divides this into two parts: in the first he proposes the examples that must be imitated; in the second he encourages them to persevere, at the place, **All the churches of Christ greet you** (Rom 16:16). The first is in two parts, because first he proposes those to be imitated and second those to be avoided, so that with the opposites juxtaposed they shine forth more, at the place, **I urge you** (Rom 16:17). The first is again in two parts, because first he names the persons familiar to him and then those who are common, at the place, **Greet Apelles** (Rom 16:10). The first is in three parts because first he names the persons familiar to him by reason of kindness and second by reason of merit, at the place, **Greet Epaenetus** (Rom 16:5). The third by reason of comfort, at the place, **Greet Ampliatus** (Rom 16:8). The first is again in two parts, because first he greets persons familiar to him by reason of kindness done to him and to others commonly; second, especially to him, at the place, **Greet Prisca** (Rom 16:3). Concerning the first he says, **I commend**, that is, worthy of praise by writing. I commend **Phoebe**, namely, in the Christian faith, not in a carnal relationship. **A deacon of the church at Cenchreae**. Cenchreae is the harbor of the sea near Corinth where this Phoebe established the church, and there she provided for the servants of God at her expense.

292

v. 2 So that you may welcome. For she came from Caesar's court and was involved with his business because this province was subject to the Romans. Through her the Apostle wrote this epistle, as the Gloss indicates. Jerome, however, says that the Apostle sent it through Timothy. To harmonize the two, one can say that Timothy went to the fellowship of this house. Both were in the embassy, or the letter was duplicated because of the danger of the sea, and one copy was sent through Phoebe and one through Timothy. **As is fitting for the saints**, that is, appropriate for saints. **And help her** because among the converts to the faith at Rome some were members of the emperor's household, hence the last chapter of Philippians says, "Those of the emperor's household greet you." **For she has been a benefactor**, by providing and ministering benefits to me and to others.

v. 3 Greet Prisca. Here he names the exemplary persons and those familiar to him who provided him with benefits, saying, **Greet Prisca and Aquila**. For Prisca was the wife of the Jew named Aquila, before whom the Apostle places her because she believed first and the order of grace must precede the order of nature, or because she was more well known. **Who work with me in Christ Jesus**. This is said in Acts 18, where this woman is called Priscilla, just as Joanna is called Joannita. For Acts 18 mentions that Paul stayed with them in Corinth since they had been expelled from Rome by the emperor Claudius, and they withdrew with Paul from there after the attack on Paul by the Jews.

v. 4 And who, to preserve my life, **risked their necks for me**, exposing themselves to mortal danger. They did this as if contrary to the order of charity, for they knew that Paul's life was more necessary for the Church, so they placed his before their own lives out of greater love. **To whom not only I give thanks**, for they were useful for the entire church community.

v. 5 Greet also the church in their house, that is, the congregation of the faithful in their home. **Greet my beloved Epaenetus**. Here he notes the persons familiar to him because of merit, and the first such person, because of his faith, was Epaenetus, concerning whom he adds, **Who was the first convert in Asia**, that is, the first to be renewed in Christ, and thus an example for others to follow. He was an educated man, and he went to Rome to instruct others. The second because of merit in works, at the place,

v. 6 Greet Mary. She was a citizen of Rome working for the communal peace of the converted for faith; therefore it is added, **Who has worked very hard**

among you. In the dissension rising among them because the Jews preferred themselves to the gentiles and the other way around (see above in Chapter 1), she reported to the Apostle as often as he wished and could do something about it. Third, because of their meritorious preaching, he says,

v. 7 Greet Andronicus and Junia. They were Jews and perchance from the Apostle's tribe, and they sustained many tribulations for Christ just as he did. **They are prominent among the apostles**, for they were among Christ's seventy disciples, and therefore he adds, **And they were in Christ before I was** because they were called earlier by him.

vv. 8-9 Greet Ampliatus. Here he notes the persons familiar to him by reason of encouragement, and he names three, but he does not say where they associated with him, as is clear from the text.

v. 10 Greet Apelles. Here he notes the persons less special to him and, first, as examples of faith. Second, in good works, at the place, "Greet Tryphaena" (Rom 16:12). Third, as an example of concord, at the place, "Greet Asyncritus" (Rom 16:14). Concerning the first he notes four examples of faith strong in the fight, when he says, **Greet Apelles**, proved in faith in Christ, enduring the tribulation. Second, the faithful who are united:

v. 11 Greet those who belong to the family of Aristobulus, for he gave his home to the faithful poor to assemble. In this greeting one should understand principally a home. Third is the professing of the faith, saying, **Greet my relative Herodian**, by tribe and religion. Fourth is the congregation made firm in faith, saying, **Greet those**. This Narcissus was a certain presbyter traveling through the cities and towns to confirm the faithful in faith and receiving the poor believers with hospitality. Thus he greets them with him, or, as it says in the Gloss here, he was absent for the confirmation of the faithful; therefore, the Apostle does not name him but those from his household.

v. 12 Greet Tryphaena. Here he notes the examples of good works and, first, in the administration of earthly goods. Here he cites three women who excel in such things, for it was then the custom for pious women to do this, as is clear in Acts and the other legends of many saints. Nevertheless, the third excelled the other two in this work, and therefore he says concerning her, **Greet the beloved Persis**, that is, in the love of the Lord.

v. 13 Greet Rufus. Here he notes the examples of good works and, first, in the administration of spiritual goods. He says, **Greet Rufus**, who was a priest ready to administer the things belonging to God, **and his mother** in the flesh, **and mine also**, spiritually.

v. 14 Greet Asyncritus. Here he notes examples of harmony and of the same mind in love, naming many who were there. Thus they were examples for others. In this manner he greets the following, saying,

v. 15 Greet Philologus. Here he shows how they ought to view the other faithful who are not named, saying,

v. 16 Greet one another. This was the manner of receiving the faithful in the first church as a sign of peace and love. Hence he says correctly, **With a holy kiss**, excluding the adulterous kiss by which Absalom kissed the people (2 Sam 15:5), the feigned kiss with which Joab kissed Amasa (2 Sam 20:9), the kiss of betrayal by which Judas kissed the Lord (Mt 26:49), and the shameless kiss of the adulterous woman seizing and kissing the young man (Prov 7:13).

v. 17 I urge you. After the Apostle proposes the things to imitate here, he then proposes the things to avoid. And the section is divided into two parts because first he makes an exhortation and second a prayer, at the place: **The God of peace**, etc. (Rom 16:20). The first part is also divided into two, because the first exhorts to understanding what to avoid and the second what to acquire, at the place, **For your obedience**, etc. (Rom 16:19). Concerning the first he says, **I urge you, brothers and sisters, to keep an eye on**, by diligently considering and avoiding **those who cause dissensions**, that is, deviating from the correct faith. They do so **in opposition to the teaching that you have learned**, providing the occasion for ruin. This the false apostles do, whom the Apostle warns believers to avoid. Consequently he shows how they are to be known, for evil cannot be avoided unless it is understood. He demonstrates this in three ways in conclusion, noting that they preach and teach for the good of their appetites. Therefore, he says,

v. 18 For such people do not serve our Lord Christ, but their own appetites. Second, in their manner of speaking they encourage the vices of many and flatter them. Therefore he says, **By smooth talk and flattery**. Third, they mislead in what they say to them. Therefore, the Apostle says, **They deceive the hearts of the simpleminded**, for the simpleminded are the first to be deceived by acquiescing to such things. They are called innocents here not because of purity of conscience but because of a lack of wisdom, just as Proverbs 14 says, "The simple believe everything" (Prov 14:15).

v. 19 For your obedience. Here the Apostle urges them to persevere in their readiness because the Romans dominated the whole world. Thus their good example had been carried to all parts of the world by messengers coming from Rome. The faithful remaining in Rome needed to turn away from the teaching and comforts of the wicked ones. Their good example must be spread to others throughout the world. Therefore he says, **For your obedience**, that is, faith in the gospel, **is known to all**, in a manner of speaking. **I rejoice over you** because your goodness spreads to other parts. **I want you to be wise**, namely, in knowing and doing. **And guileless in what is evil**, namely, in doing, not simply in knowing, because knowledge of evil to avoid it is not only good but necessary for salvation.

v. 20 The God of peace. Here he adds the aid of his prayer and, first, to avoid evil, saying, **The God of peace**, namely, the author and preserver, **will shortly crush Satan**, that is, the adversary of our salvation, and, second, for the good things that will follow. Therefore he adds, **The grace of our Lord**, etc.

v. 21 Timothy, my co-worker, greets you. Above, the Apostle noted examples to be imitated in doing good; here he notes examples of perseverance in goodness so that many rejoice in their excelling in good. Hence they must persevere all the more. Therefore he says, **Timothy**, the bishop of Ephesus, **my co-worker** in proclaiming the gospel, **greets you. So does Lucius**, who was the individual companion of the Apostle, as Jerome says and is clear in the Acts of the Apostles. **And** so do **Jason and Sosipater**, who were Jews, about whom we hear in Acts.[1]

v. 22 I Tertius, the writer of this letter, greet you. This Tertius is not a numeral but the name of the personal secretary of Paul, and thus he has the freedom to put his name in the greeting.

v. 23 Gaius greets you. Gaius was the bishop of Corinth, to whom John wrote the epistle; he received the preachers of the gospel. Therefore, Paul

---

1. For Jason, see Acts 17:5-9; Sosipater may be the same companion of Paul as Sopater, referenced in Acts 20:4.

turned aside to him when he went there. **And to the whole church**. In other words, those subject to the rule of Gaius. **Erastus, the city treasurer, greets you**. Erastus was its leader. Thus the title is said to come from "magistrate,"[2] which means "ruler."

Or, otherwise and much better, he says treasurer because he was the custodian of the public treasury, where the writings, acts, and tributes of the city were held. **And our brother Quartus**. Quartus was a brother not by blood but by faith, and this is a personal name.

v. 24 The grace of our Lord. This is said to confirm what has been said.[3]

The Benediction

v. 25 Now to God. This is the final part of the epistle, namely, his conclusion, which is set apart from the prologue and the narration by a beginning in which the Apostle concludes his epistle and his proclamation of divine grace. This conclusion is made up of two parts: the call to faith and its confirmation. This is because the mystery of Christ, longed for in ancient times and known only to God before time, was revealed in our time. Therefore he says, **Who is able to strengthen you**, namely, to the one, triune God be honor and glory, which is again noted in this part and again joined at the end of this part with others following. **According to my gospel**, that is, the proclamation of which Christ is the author. Therefore he adds, **and**, for it is **the proclamation of Jesus**, who I said is the author of the gospel. **According to the revelation**, that is, of the sacred secret of our redemption, which is reported in the gospel. Therefore, in the interpretation of the Septuagint in Isaiah 9:6 our translation has, "And his name will be called Wonderful, Counselor, Mighty God, Everlasting Father, Prince of Peace." Thus they translated, "his name will be called an angel of great council." **For long ages**, to humans, but nevertheless known to God. Moreover, he says "for long ages" because eternity, which is measured by divine knowledge, is not understood by us, except by comparison to infinite time.

v. 26 But is now disclosed, namely, the time of the new law. **And through the prophetic writings**, as delivered to the apostles in the last chapter of

---

2. Nicholas uses the word *archos*.
3. Note that verse 24 is not in the NRSV.

Luke (Lk 24:27): "He revealed the sense to them so that they might understand the scriptures." **According to the command**. According to his design
because he has eternally arranged for these things to be known in time. **The
obedience of faith**, that is, so that all the gentiles might be obedient in faith.

v. 27 To the only wise God. This refers to that which was proclaimed in the
times of eternal silence. **Through Jesus Christ**, who is our mediator to lead
us back into God. **To whom**, namely, Christ, **be the honor**, which is reverence exhibited in witness. For in the human Christ are all powers and gifts.
Be the glory, which is the honor exhibited to anyone before many. Honor,
moreover, is exhibited by the human Christ before saints and angels. **Forever and ever! Amen**. That is, eternally, of which eternal glory he makes
participants, who with the Father and the Holy Spirit lives and reigns forever
and ever. Amen.

Bibliography

Primary Texts

Ambrosiaster. *Ad Romanos,* ed. Henry Joseph Vogels. Vienna: Hoelder-Pichler-Tempsky, 1966. CSEL 81/1.

————. *Commentaries on Romans and 1-2 Corinthians,* trans. Gerald Bray. Downers Grove: InterVarsity Press, 2009.

Anonymous of St. Michel. *Expositiones Pauli Epistolarum ad Romanos, Galatas et Ephesios,* ed. Gérard de Martel. Turnhout: Brepols, 1995. CCCM 151.

Aristotle. *Aristoteles Latinus: Ethica Nicomachea,* ed. Renatus Antonius Gauthier. Leiden: Brill, 1972-73. AL 26.

————. *Aristoteles Latinus: Physica,* ed. Fernand Bossier and Jozef Brams. Leiden: Brill, 1990. AL 7.1.

Augustine. *Answer to Julian,* in *Answer to the Pelagians II,* trans. Roland J. Teske. The Works of Saint Augustine: A Translation for the Twenty-First Century 1.24. Hyde Park, NY: New City Press, 1998.

————. *Answer to Maximinus,* in *Arianism and Other Heresies,* trans. Roland J. Teske and Paulus Orosius. The Works of Saint Augustine: A Translation for the Twenty-First Century 1.18. Hyde Park, NY: New City Press, 1995.

————. *Answer to the Two Letters of the Pelagians,* in *Answer to the Pelagians II,* trans. Roland J. Teske. The Works of Saint Augustine: A Translation for the Twenty-First Century 1.24. Hyde Park, NY: New City Press, 1998.

————. *The Augustine Catechism: The Enchiridion on Faith, Hope, and Love,* trans. Bruce Harbert. The Works of Saint Augustine: A Translation for the Twenty-First Century 1. Hyde Park, NY: New City Press, 1999.

————. *Confessions,* trans. R. S. Pine-Coffin. New York: Penguin, 1961.

————. *Contra Julianum pelagianum.* PL 44:641-874.

———. *Contra Maximinum.* PL 42:743-814.

———. *De catechizandis rudibus,* ed. I. Bauer. Turnhout: Brepols, 1969. CCSL 46.

———. *De diversis quaestionibus LXXXIII,* ed. Almut Mutzenbecher. Turnhout: Brepols, 1970. CCSL 44A.

———. *De libero arbitrio,* ed. W. M. Green. Turnhout: Brepols, 1970. CCSL 29.

———. *De mendacio,* ed. Joseph Zycha. Vienna: F. Tempsky, 1900. CSEL 41.

———. *De nuptiis et concupiscentia,* ed. Joseph Zycha. Vienna: F. Tempsky, 1900. CSEL 42.

———. *De praedestinatione sanctorum.* PL 44:959-92.

———. *De spiritu et littera,* ed. Karl Franz Urba and Joseph Zycha. Vienna: F. Tempsky, 1913. CSEL 60.

———. *De Trinitate,* ed. W. J. Mountain and Fr. Glorie. Turnhout: Brepols, 1968. CCSL 50A.

———. *Enarrationes in Psalmos,* ed. D. Eligius Dekkers and J. Fraipont. Turnhout: Brepols, 1956. CCSL 38.

———. *Enchiridion,* ed. E. Evans. Turnhout: Brepols, 1969. CCSL 46.

———. *Epistulae,* ed. Alois Goldbacher. Vienna: F. Tempsky, 1895-1923. CSEL 44.

———. *Exposition on the Psalms 33–50,* trans. Maria Boulding and John E. Rotelle. The Works of Saint Augustine: A Translation for the Twenty-First Century 3.16. Hyde Park, NY: New City Press, 2000.

———. *The Free Choice of the Will,* in *The Teacher,* trans. Robert P. Russell. The Fathers of the Church 59. Washington, DC: Catholic University of America Press, 1968.

———. *In Iohannis Evangelium tractatus CXXIV,* ed. Radbodus Willems. Turnhout: Brepols, 1954. CCSL 36.

———. *Instructing Beginners in the Faith,* trans. Raymond Canning. The Works of Saint Augustine: A Translation for the Twenty-First Century 5. Hyde Park, NY: New City Press, 2006.

———. *Letters 1-99,* trans. Roland Teske. The Works of Saint Augustine: A Translation for the Twenty-First Century 2.1. Hyde Park, NY: New City Press, 2001.

———. *Letters 100-155,* trans. Roland Teske and Boniface Ramsey. The Works of Saint Augustine: A Translation for the Twenty-First Century 2.2. Hyde Park, NY: New City Press, 2003.

———. *Miscellany of Questions,* in *Responses to Miscellaneous Questions,* ed. Boniface Ramsey. The Works of Saint Augustine: A Translation for the Twenty-First Century 1.12. Hyde Park, NY: New City Press, 2008.

———. *On Marriage and Desire,* in *Answer to the Pelagians II,* trans. Roland J. Teske. The Works of Saint Augustine: A Translation for the Twenty-First Century 1.24. Hyde Park, NY: New City Press, 1998.

———. *On the Gift of Perseverance,* in *Answer to the Pelagians IV,* trans. Roland J. Teske. The Works of Saint Augustine: A Translation for the Twenty-First Century 1.26. Hyde Park, NY: New City Press, 1999.

Bibliography

———. *The Predestination of the Saints*, in *Answer to the Pelagians IV*, trans. Roland J. Teske. The Works of Saint Augustine: A Translation for the Twenty-First Century 1.26. Hyde Park, NY: New City Press, 1999.

———. *Sermons*, trans. Edmund Hill. The Works of Saint Augustine: A Translation for the Twenty-First Century 3.5. New Rochelle: New City Press, 1992.

———. *The Spirit and the Letter*, in *Answer to the Pelagians*, trans. Roland J. Teske and Edmund Hill. The Works of Saint Augustine: A Translation for the Twenty-First Century 1.23. Hyde Park, NY: New City Press, 1997.

———. *Tractates on the Gospel of John*, trans. John W. Rettig. The Fathers of the Church. Washington, DC: Catholic University of America Press, 1988-95.

———. *The Trinity*, trans. Edmund Hill. The Works of Saint Augustine: A Translation for the Twenty-First Century 1.5. Hyde Park, NY: New City Press, 1995.

Bede. *Ecclesiastical History of the English People*, ed. Bertram Colgrave and R. A. B. Mynors. Oxford: Clarendon, 1969.

Commentarius Cantabrigiensis in Epistolas Pauli e Schola Petri Abaelardi, 3 vols., ed. Artur Landgraf. Notre Dame, IN: University of Notre Dame Press, 1939.

Cooper, Stephen Andrew. *Marius Victorinus' Commentary on Galatians: Introduction, Translation and Notes*. New York: Oxford University Press, 2005.

de Bruyn, Theodore S. *Pelagius's Commentary on St. Paul's Epistle to the Romans*. Oxford: Clarendon, 1993.

Eusebius. *Historia Scholastica*, PG 20:45-910.

———. *The History of the Church from Christ to Constantine*, trans. G. A. Williamson. London: Penguin, 1989.

Frede, Hermann Josef. *Ein neuer Paulustext und Kommentar*. Freiburg: Herder, 1973-74.

Froehlich, Karlfried, and Margaret Gibson. *Biblia Latina cum Glossa Ordinaria*, Facsimile Reprint of the Editio Princeps Adolph Rusch of Strassburg 1480/81. Turnhout: Brepols, 1992.

Gratian. *Decretum*. In *Corpus iuris canonici*, vol. 1, ed. Emil Friedberg and Aemilius Ludwig Richter. Graz: Akademischer Druck, 1959.

Gregory the Great. *Moralia in Job*, ed. Marcus Adriaen. Turnhout: Brepols, 1977. CCSL 143-43A.

———. *Morals on the Book of Job*, trans. James Bliss. Oxford: J. H. Parker, 1844-50.

Haimo of Auxerre. *In Epistolam ad Romanos*. PL 117:361-508.

John Chrysostom. *Ad Demetrium de compunctione*. PG 47:393-410.

———. *Homilies on Romans*. NPNF 11.335-564.

Landes, Paula Fredriksen. *Augustine on Romans: Propositions from the Epistle to the Romans, Unfinished Commentary on the Epistle to the Romans*. Chico, CA: Scholars Press, 1982.

Luther, Martin. *Martin Luther: Selections from His Writings*, ed. John Dillenberger. New York: Anchor Books, 1961.

Nicholas of Lyra. *Biblia sacra cum glossa ordinaria et Postillae Nicolai Lirani necnon*

Additionibus Pauli Burgensis et Matthiae Thoringi Replicis, ed. Johannes Meursius. 6 vols. In fol. Antwerp, 1634.

———. *Postilla super totam bibliam.* Strassburg, 1492. Reprint, Frankfurt/Main, 1971.

Origen. *Commentaria in Epistolas B. Pauli ad Romanos.* PG 14:839-1292.

———. *Commentary on the Epistle to the Romans,* trans. Thomas Scheck. Washington, DC: Catholic University of America Press, 2001-2.

———. *On First Principles,* trans. G. W. Butterworth. New York: Harper and Row, 1966.

Pelagius. *Pelagius's Expositions of Thirteen Epistles of St Paul,* 2 vols., ed. Alexander Souter. Cambridge: Cambridge University Press, 1926.

Peter Abelard. *Commentaria in Epistolam Pauli ad Romanos,* ed. Eligius Buytaert. Turnhout: Brepols, 1969. CCCM 11.

———. *Commentary on the Epistle to the Romans,* ed. Steven R. Cartwright. The Fathers of the Church Mediaeval Continuation 12. Washington, DC: Catholic University of America Press, 2011.

———. "Prologue to the *Yes and No.*" In *Literary Theory and Criticism, c. 1100-1375: The Commentary Tradition, Revised Edition,* ed. A. J. Minnis and A. B. Scott, 87-100. Oxford: Clarendon, 1988.

Peter John Olivi. *Petri Iohannis Olivi Lecturae super Pauli Epistolas,* ed. Alain Boureau. Turnhout: Brepols, 2010. CCCM 233.

Peter Lombard. *Collectanea in Epistolam ad Romanos.* PL 191:1301-1534.

Pseudo-John Chrysostom. *Opus imperfectum in Matthaeum.* PG 56:611-948.

Tertullian. *De anima,* ed. J. Waszink. Turnhout: Brepols, 1954. CCSL 2.

———. *On the Soul,* in *Apologetical Works,* trans. Edwin A. Quian. The Fathers of the Church 10. New York: Fathers of the Church, 1950.

Thomas Aquinas. *Commentaire de l'Epître aux Romains,* ed. Jean-Eric Stroobant de Saint-Eloy and Jean Borella. Paris: Cerf, 1999.

———. *Kommentar zum Römerbrief,* ed. Helmut Fahsel. Freiburg: Herder, 1927.

———. *Summa theologiae,* ed. Pietro Caramello. Turin: Marietti, 1963.

———. *Summa theologica,* trans. Fathers of the English Dominican Province. Westminster, MD: Christian Classics, 1981.

———. *Super Epistolas S. Pauli Lectura,* ed. Raphael Cai. Turin: Marietti, 1953.

William of St. Thierry. *Expositio super Epistolam ad Romanos,* ed. Paul Werdeyen. Turnhout: Brepols, 1989. CCCM 86.

———. *Exposition on the Epistle to the Romans,* ed. and trans. by John Baptist Hasbrouk and John D. Anderson. Kalamazoo, MI: Cistercian Publications, 1980.

Bibliography

Secondary Sources

Affeldt, Werner. "Verzeichnis der Römerbriefkommentare der lateinischen Kirche bis zu Nikolaus von Lyra." *Traditio* 13 (1957): 369-406.

Babcock, William S. "Augustine's Interpretation of Romans (A.D. 394-396)." *Augustinian Studies* 10 (1979): 55-74.

Barney, Stephen A. "Ordo paginis: The Gloss on Genesis 38." *South Atlantic Quarterly* 91 (1992): 929-43.

Bauer, Walter. *Orthodoxy and Heresy in Earliest Christianity,* ed. Robert A. Kraft and Gerhard Krodel. Philadelphia: Fortress, 1971.

Bond, H. Lawrence. "Another Look at Abelard's Commentary on Romans 3:26." In *Medieval Readings of Romans,* ed. William S. Campbell, Peter S. Hawkins, and Brenda Deen Schildgen, 11-32. Romans through History and Culture Series 6. New York: T&T Clark, 2007.

Bray, Gerald. "Ambrosiaster." In *Reading Romans through the Centuries: From the Early Church to Karl Barth,* ed. Jeffery P. Greenman and Timothy Larsen, 21-38. Grand Rapids: Brazos, 2005.

Brown, George Hardin. *Bede the Venerable.* Boston: Twayne Publishers, 1987.

Brown, Peter. *Augustine of Hippo: A Biography.* Berkeley: University of California Press, 1967.

Burr, David. *Olivi and Franciscan Poverty.* Philadelphia: University of Pennsylvania Press, 1989.

————. *The Spiritual Franciscans.* University Park, PA: Penn State Press, 2001.

Carlson, Charles P. *Justification in Earlier Medieval Theology.* The Hague: Nijhoff, 1975.

Chazelle, Celia Martin, and Burton Van Name Edwards. "Introduction: The Study of the Bible and Carolingian Culture." In *The Study of the Bible in the Carolingian Era,* ed. Celia Martin Chazelle and Burton Van Name Edwards, 1-16. Turnhout: Brepols, 2003.

Clark, Elizabeth A. *The Cultural Construction of an Early Christian Debate.* Princeton: Princeton University Press, 1992.

Colish, Marcia. *Peter Lombard.* 2 vols. Leiden: Brill, 1994.

Contreni, John J. "Carolingian Biblical Culture." In *Iohannes Scottus Eriugena: The Bible and Hermeneutics,* ed. Gerd Riel and Carlos G. Steel, 1-23. Leuven: Leuven University Press, 1996.

Cranfield, C. E. B. *A Critical and Exegetical Commentary on the Epistle to the Romans.* International Critical Commentary. Edinburgh: T&T Clark, 1975.

de Bruyn, Theodore S. "Constantius the Tractator, Author of an Anonymous Commentary on the Pauline Epistles." *Journal of Theological Studies* 43 (1991): 38-54.

de Hamel, Christopher. *Glossed Books of the Bible and the Origins of the Paris Book Trade.* Suffolk, Eng.: D. S. Brewer, 1984.

del Punta, Francesco. "The Genre of Commentaries in the Middle Ages and Its Relation to the Nature and Originality of Medieval Thought." In *Miscellanea Mediaevalia* 26, ed. J. A. Aertsen and A. Speer, 139-51. Berlin: Walter de Gruyter, 1998.

Ferguson, John. *Pelagius: A Historical and Theological Study.* Cambridge: Heffer, 1956.

Fitzmyer, Joseph A. *Romans.* Anchor Bible. New York: Doubleday, 1993.

Froehlich, Karlfried. "Romans 8:1-11: Pauline Theology in Medieval Interpretation." In *Faith and History,* ed. John T. Carroll, Charles H. Cosgrove, and E. Elizabeth Johnson, 239-60. Atlanta: Scholars Press, 1990.

Gaca, Kathy L., and L. L. Welborn, eds. *Early Patristic Readings of Romans.* London: T&T Clark, 2005.

Geerlings, Wihelm. "Zur exegetischen Methode des Ambrosiasters." In *Stimuli: Exegese und ihre Hermeneutik in Antike und Christentum. Festschrift für Ernst Dassmann,* ed. Georg Schöllgen and Clemens Scholten. Münster: Aschendorff, 1996.

Gibson, Margaret. "The Place of the Glossa Ordinaria in Medieval Exegesis." In *Ad Litteram: Authoritative Texts and Their Medieval Readers,* ed. Mark D. Jordan and Kent Emery Jr., 5-27. Notre Dame: University of Notre Dame Press, 1992.

Gorday, Peter. "Jews and Gentiles, Galatians 2:11-14, and Reading Israel in Romans: The Patristic Debate." In *Engaging Augustine on Romans: Self, Context, and Theology in Interpretation,* ed. Daniel Patte and Eugene TeSelle, 199-236. Harrisburg, PA: Trinity Press International, 2002.

————. *Principles of Patristic Exegesis: Romans 9–11 in Origen, John Chrysostom, and Augustine.* New York: Edwin Mellen, 1983.

Hadot, Pierre. *Philosophy as a Way of Life,* trans. Michael Chase. Malden, MA: Blackwell, 1995.

Hagen, Kenneth. *A Theology of Testament in the Young Luther.* Leiden: Brill, 1974.

Hailperin, H. *Rashi and the Christian Scholars.* Pittsburgh: University of Pittsburgh Press, 1963.

Hood, John Y. B. *Aquinas and the Jews.* Philadelphia: University of Pennsylvania Press, 1995.

Hunter, David G. "Ambrosiaster." In *Dictionary of Major Biblical Interpreters,* ed. Donald K. McKim, 123-26. Downers Grove, IL: InterVarsity Press, 2007.

————. "On the Sin of Adam and Eve: A Little-Known Defense of Marriage and Childbearing by Ambrosiaster." *Harvard Theological Review* 82 (1989): 283-99.

————. "The Paradise of Patriarchy: Ambrosiaster on Women as (Not) God's Image." *Journal of Theological Studies* 43 (1992): 447-69.

Kannengiesser, Charles. *Handbook of Patristic Exegesis: The Bible in Ancient Christianity.* Leiden: Brill, 2006.

Bibliography

Kelly, J. N. D. *Jerome: His Life, Writings, and Controversies.* New York: Harper and Row, 1975.

Klepper, Deeana Copeland. *The Insight of Unbelievers: Nicholas of Lyra and Christian Readings of the Jewish Text in the Middle Ages.* Philadelphia: University of Pennsylvania Press, 2007.

Kraus, Christina Shuttlesworth. "Introduction: Reading Commentaries/Commentaries as Reading." In *The Classical Commentary: Histories, Practices, Theory,* ed. Roy K. Gibson and Christina Shuttlesworth Kraus, 1-27. Leiden: Brill, 2002.

Krey, Philip D. W. "Many Readers but Few Followers: The Fate of Nicholas of Lyra's *Apocalypse Commentary* in the Hands of His Late-Medieval Admirers." *Church History* 64 (1995): 185-201.

————. "The Old Law Prohibits the Hand and Not the Spirit: The Law and the Jews in Nicholas of Lyra's Romans Commentary of 1329." In *Nicholas of Lyra: The Senses of Scripture,* ed. Philip D. W. Krey and Lesley Smith, 251-66. Leiden: Brill, 2000.

Leclercq, Jean. *The Love of Learning and the Desire for God: A Study of Monastic Culture,* trans. Catherine Misrahi. New York: Fordham University Press, 1982.

Lohse, Bernhard. "Beobachtungen zum Paulus-Kommentar des Marius Victorinus und zur Wiederentdeckung des Paulus in der lateinischen Theologie des vierten Jahrhunderts." In *Kerygma und Logos: Beiträge zu den geistesgeschichtlichen Beziehungen zwischen Antike und Christentum,* ed. Adolf Martin Ritter, 351-66. Göttingen: Vandenhoeck & Ruprecht, 1979.

Lohse, Eduard. *Colossians and Philemon.* Hermeneia. Philadelphia: Fortress, 1971.

Lunn-Rockliffe, Sophie. *Ambrosiaster's Political Theology.* Oxford: Oxford University Press, 2007.

Madigan, Kevin. *Olivi and the Interpretation of Matthew in the High Middle Ages.* Notre Dame: University of Notre Dame Press, 2003.

Markus, Robert. *The End of Ancient Christianity.* Cambridge: Cambridge University Press, 1990.

Martin, Thomas F. "Vox Pauli: Augustine and the Claims to Speak for Paul, An Exploration of Rhetoric at the Service of Exegesis." *Journal of Early Christian Studies* 8 (2000): 237-72.

Matter, E. Ann. "The Bible in the Center: The Glossa Ordinaria." In *The Unbounded Community: Papers in Christian Ecumenism in Honor of Jaroslav Pelikan,* ed. William Caferro and Duncan G. Fisher, 33-42. New York: Garland, 1996.

Mews, Constant J. *Abelard and Heloise.* Oxford: Oxford University Press, 2005.

Miller, John W. *How the Bible Came to Be: Exploring the Narrative and Message.* New York: Paulist, 2004.

Nicholson, M. Forthomme. "Celtic Theology: Pelagius." In *Celtic Theology: An Introduction,* ed. James P. Mackey, 386-413. Edinburgh: T&T Clark, 1989.

Oberman, Heiko, *Forerunners of the Reformation: The Shape of Medieval Thought.* Philadelphia: Fortress, 1981.

Ocker, Christopher. *Biblical Poetics before Humanism and the Reformation.* Cambridge: Cambridge University Press, 2002.

Otey, W. Rush. "The New Pelagians." In *Persons in Community: Theological Voices from the Pastorate,* ed. W. H. Lazareth, 37-43. Grand Rapids: Eerdmans, 2004.

Patton, Corrine. "Lyra's Commentary on Genesis." In *Nicholas of Lyra: The Senses of Scripture,* ed. Philip D. W. Krey and Lesley Smith. Studies in the History of Christian Thought 90. Leiden and Boston: Brill, 2000.

Roest, Bert. *A History of Franciscan Education (ca. 1210–1517).* Leiden: Brill, 2000.

Rosemann, Philipp. *Peter Lombard.* Oxford: Oxford University Press, 2004.

Ryan, Thomas F. *Thomas Aquinas as Reader of the Psalms.* Notre Dame: University of Notre Dame Press, 2000.

Scheck, Thomas P. *Origen and the History of Justification: The Legacy of Origen's Commentary on Romans.* Notre Dame: University of Notre Dame Press, 2008.

Schild, Maurice. "Leading Motifs in Some Western Bible Prologues." *Journal of Religious History* 12 (1972): 91-109.

Sorabji, Richard. "The Ancient Commentators on Aristotle." In *The Ancient Commentators and Their Influence,* ed. Richard Sorabji, 1-30. Ithaca: Cornell University Press, 1990.

Souter, Alexander. "The Commentary of Pelagius on the Epistles of St. Paul: The Problem of Its Restoration." *The Proceedings of the British Academy* 2 (1905-6): 409-39.

———. *Earliest Latin Commentaries on the Epistles of St. Paul.* Oxford: Clarendon, 1927.

Stendahl, Krister. "A Last Word." In *Engaging Augustine on Romans: Self, Context, and Theology in Interpretation,* ed. Daniel Patte and Eugene TeSelle, 270-72. Harrisburg, PA: Trinity Press International, 2002.

Stuehrenberg, Paul Freder. *Cornelius and the Jews: A Study in the Interpretation of Acts before the Reformation.* Ann Arbor: UMI Dissertation Services, 1988.

TeSelle, Eugene. *Augustine the Theologian.* New York: Herder, 1970.

Torrell, Jean Pierre. *Saint Thomas Aquinas: The Person and His Work,* trans. Robert Royal. Washington, DC: Catholic University of America Press, 1996.

Wetzel, James. "Pelagius Anticipated: Grace and Election in Augustine's Ad Simplician." In *Augustine: From Rhetor to Theologian,* ed. J. McWilliam, 121-32. Waterloo, Ont.: Wilfrid Laurier University Press, 1992.

Wiles, Maurice. *The Divine Apostle: The Interpretation of St. Paul's Epistles in the Early Church.* Cambridge: Cambridge University Press, 1967.

Williams, Thomas. "Sin, Grace, and Redemption." In *The Cambridge Companion to Abelard,* ed. Jeffrey E. Brower and Kevin Guilfoy, 258-78. Cambridge: Cambridge University Press, 2004.

Index of Names

Abelard, Peter, 26, 29-33, 31n.112, 34, 38, 65n.1, 66n.2, 69, 69n.4, 71nn.7-8, 74n.12, 80n.18, 81n.20, 97-121, 114nn.18-19

Affeldt, Werner, 1n.1

Ambrosiaster, 9, 10-11, 10n.45, 11nn.53-54, 21, 23, 23nn.102-3, 25, 137, 272n.1, 278, 278n.5, 280, 280n.8, 283, 283n.12

Anselm of Canterbury, 79n.16, 144nn.18-19

Aquinas, Thomas, 4, 33, 40-45, 40nn.119-20, 46, 51, 53-54, 57, 91n.11, 151-219, 223nn.6-7, 224nn.8-9, 225nn.10-12, 246-67, 268, 268n.1

Aristotle, 4, 8, 30, 31, 40, 45, 68, 100nn.5-6, 177, 177n.3, 181, 181nn.6-7, 197, 197n.15, 271, 271n.3

Arius, 14

Augustine of Hippo, 1, 1n.2, 3, 9, 10n.45, 11, 11n.54, 13, 16-20, 17n.74, 17n.77, 18nn.78-81, 19nn.85-86, 19n.89, 21, 25, 27, 35, 49, 51, 52, 52n.133, 56, 58, 72, 72n.9, 85, 85nn.3-4, 89n.9, 92n.12, 102-3, 102n.7, 103nn.8-9, 110, 110n.15, 112n.17, 121, 121n.27, 130, 130n.9, 131, 131n.10, 132, 132n.11, 135-36, 136n.2, 136, 136n.4, 141, 146, 146n.3, 148, 148n.4,

149, 149n.5, 150, 150n.6, 153, 153n.1, 157, 157nn.4-5, 163, 163nn.6-7, 166, 166n.8, 168, 168n.9, 183, 183n.8, 197, 197n.15, 205, 205n.21, 206, 206n.24, 207, 215, 216n.25, 240, 240n.2, 247, 247n.1, 265, 265n.9, 266, 266n.10, 267n.11, 272n.1, 275-76, 276n.3, 280, 280n.7

Babcock, William S., 18, 18n.84

Barney, Stephen A., 22, 22n.101

Basilides, 7

Bauer, Walter, 3n.7

Bede, 20, 20n.91

Berengar of Tours, 21

Bernard of Clairvaux, 26, 32-33, 38

Boethius, 75, 75n.14, 81, 81n.19, 99, 99n.3

Bond, H. Lawrence, 31n.113, 117n.22

Bonner, Gerald, 17, 17n.73

Boureau, Alain, 46n.124

Bray, Gerald, 10, 10n.45, 11n.52

Bright, Pamela, 17n.75

Brown, George Hardin, 20n.92

Brown, Peter, 14n.63, 17, 17n.76, 19, 19n.87

307

Index of Names

Lunn-Rockliffe, Sophie, 10n.46
Luther, Martin, 1, 1-2n.3, 3, 16, 51,
   55n.139, 56-58, 285n.1

Macrobius, 80n.17
Madigan, Kevin, 46n.123
Marcion, 2-3, 6
Markus, Robert, 19n.88
Martin, Thomas F., 16n.72
Matter, E. Ann, 22n.101, 24n.105
Melanchthon, Philipp, 51
Mews, Constant J., 29, 29n.109, 118n.24
Miller, John W., 2n.6

Nicholas of Lyra, 24, 33, 50-56, 50n.126,
   55nn.137-38, 57, 220-45, 268-71, 284-98
Nicholson, M. Forthomme, 13n.62,
   14n.65

Origen, 2, 2n.4, 5-7, 7nn.24-29, 12-13,
   13nn.59-60, 23, 25, 27, 30, 56, 62, 62n.1,
   65, 65n.1, 66, 70, 70nn.5-6, 86n.5,
   87n.6, 88n.7, 106-7, 107n.12, 223,
   272n.1, 273, 273n.2, 276, 276n.4, 281,
   281n.10
Otey, W. Rush, 13n.61

Paul of Burgos, 51, 51n.129
Pelagius, 9, 11, 12, 13-16, 25, 34, 35n.117,
   48, 62, 62n.3, 272n.1, 278, 278n.6, 280-
   81, 281n.9
Peter of John Oliva, 33, 45-50, 122-50
Photinus, 14
Plato, 4, 30, 80, 80n.17, 103, 103n.10, 170
Porphry, 8
Primasius, 20
Pseudo-Ambrose. See Ambrosiaster
Pseudo-Chrysostom, 153-54, 154n.2
Pseudo-Dionysius, 40n.120, 47, 128,
   128n.7
Pseudo-Jerome, 12

Quintilian, 74, 74n.12

Rabanus Maurus, 21, 25
Rashi, 24, 232, 232n.3
Robert of Melun, 33, 33n.114, 34-35,
   35n.117, 74n.13, 81n.20
Rosemann, Philipp W., 37n.118, 50n.125
Rufinus of Aquileia, 6, 12-13, 13n.60,
   30, 65, 65n.1
Ryan, Thomas F., 41n.122

Scheck, Thomas P., 6nn.19-20
Schild, Maurice, 16n.67
Sedulius Scottus, 21
Sorabji, Richard, 5n.13
Souter, Alexander, 8nn.32-33, 9,
   9nn.38-39, 9n.42, 20, 20n.90
Southern, Richard W., 90n.10
Stendahl, Krister, 16, 16n.69
Stoelen, Anselme, 21-22n.98

Terence, 68
Tertullian, 170, 170n.10
TeSelle, Eugene, 10, 10n.48
Theodore of Mopsuestia, 5, 21
Torrell, Jean Pierre, 41n.121

Valentinus, 7
Victorinus, Marius, 8-10
Virgil, 4
von Harnack, Adolf, 9

Welborn, L. L., 5n.16
Wetzel, James, 18, 18n.83
Wiles, Maurice F., 6n.17
William of St. Thierry, 26-29, 32, 38,
   83-96, 116n.21
Williams, Thomas, 31n.113

Zier, Mark, 50n.127, 52n.132

Index of Subjects

Index of Scripture References